Concepts and Themes in the Regional Geography of Canada

Concepts and Themes in the Regional Geography of Canada

by J. Lewis Robinson

copyright © 1983 J. Lewis Robinson

published with assistance from the Canada Council and
financially assisted by the Government of British Columbia
through the British Columbia Cultural Fund and Lottery revenues

Talonbooks
201 1019 East Cordova
Vancouver
British Columbia V6A 1M8
Canada

This book was typeset by Baseline, designed by David Robinson
and printed in Canada by Hignell for Talonbooks.

The cover photograph was taken by Thomas Hayes.

Maps by Paul Jance.

Third printing: May 1985

Canadian Cataloguing in Publication Data

Robinson, J. Lewis (John Lewis), 1918-
    Concepts and themes in the regional
geography of Canada

    Bibliography
    ISBN 0-88922-204-5 (trade ed.). —
ISBN 0-88922-205-3 (textbook ed.)

    1. Canada — Description and travel — 1950- *
I. Title.
FC75.R62   917.1   C83-091236-3
F1016.R62

50,655

CONTENTS

LIST OF MAPS

PREFACE

This is a book *about* the regional geography of Canada; it is not meant to be a complete description of Canadian regions. The book discusses concepts and themes of geography as a discipline and uses Canadian examples to illustrate these concepts. Readers are asked to think about many geographical aspects of Canada's physical environments, natural resources and people, because the author believes that geographical concepts and principles can help in the consideration of many Canadian problems. Many questions are raised; some of them do not have easy answers, but they are meant to direct one's thinking about relationships. It has been said that geography can be defined by the type of questions it asks. It is hoped that readers will consider the questions important in thinking about the future of Canada; if so, they may gather factual information from other sources, consider the evidence and form opinions for discussion.

The organization of information and the selection of themes vary from chapter to chapter to illustrate that there need be no standard format for studying the geography of regions. Many topics are omitted because regional geography can *not* be a complete collection of information about a region. References are listed at the end of each chapter as a guide to the *type* of supporting information available. These references are not meant to be a full bibliography of regional information, nor should they replace standard bibliographic research. The references emphasize material published by geographers, and refer little to the enormous number of government reports, nor the literature about Canada written in other disciplines.

For a geography book, a heresy is committed of having no pictures. This decision was a difficult one for me, who lectures on the geography of Canada almost entirely with slides which I have taken in every region of Canada. A visual image of landscapes is undoubtedly important in understanding Canada's geographical patterns. But readers have ample access to a wide variety of pictures of Canada every day in newspapers, magazines and on TV; excellent films are available from the National Film Board and from TV documentaries. It is expected that readers of this type of book will look at pictures in the media and *see* them as illustrating similarities and differences from place to place in the rural and urban landscapes of Canada.

There is a minimum number of maps and they are deliberately simple, even though the distribution patterns of various phenomena are stressed in each chapter. Readers should USE alternate sources, such as the excellent maps which are available in the Atlas of Canada, provincial atlases, and other atlases prepared by Canadian publishers. Canadians have access to a wide range of maps of all types from the federal and provincial map distribution offices.

The book also has no index. It is not meant to be a reference volume in which information is presented about certain places which are then listed in

9

an index. This is a book of ideas and concepts about the regional geography of Canada and not a collection of factual information. Geography should not attempt to replace encyclopedias.

Because of the lack of pictures to "break" a page of reading, the book has been designed with numerous headings and subheadings to indicate the topics being discussed. The organization of topics within each chapter is shown at the beginning of each chapter, and the themes discussed are also stated.

This book is, therefore, *different* from other geography books. Some readers may like this approach, which tries to promote *thinking* about Canada from a geographic viewpoint rather than memorization of facts, but it may frustrate others because the book may seem to lack organized descriptive information and statistics to prove the generalizations. Readers are encouraged to read more about Canada's geography; each of the themes can be explored at greater length. The book should supplement other reading on Canada's history, economics, politics, etc., and the viewpoints of other disciplines.

This book is based upon more than forty years of reading, lecturing and travelling across Canada. I have done field work in every region of Canada and, in that time, have visited every city in Canada with more than 20,000 population, and most of the smaller places as well. These concepts about Canada have received feedback from several generations of students at the University of British Columbia, and elsewhere. The organization of the book is based on my geography course at U.B.C. and a set of study notes prepared for the British Columbia Open Learning Institute; the latter are available for students who wish to enroll there in a correspondence course called the Regional Geography of Canada.

J. Lewis Robinson,
Department of Geography,
University of British Columbia,
Vancouver, B.C.
May, 1983

CHAPTER 1

SOME CONCEPTS AND THEMES IN REGIONAL GEOGRAPHY

CHAPTER 1

SOME CONCEPTS AND THEMES IN REGIONAL GEOGRAPHY

INTRODUCTION

Canada is a large and complex country. A study of its geographical patterns shows similarities and differences in environments, peoples and economies from place to place. Canada's geography consists of several distribution patterns of physical, human and economic phenomena which are spread across the country in high, medium and low densities. These geographical patterns are probably too complex for one to comprehend the variety of landscapes within the large area. It is, therefore, one of the tasks of regional geography to divide the nation into smaller units within which there are certain degrees of similarity and some feeling of regional consciousness. Regions provide an organizational format by which selected themes may be discussed and analyzed in different parts of Canada.

One of the problems in regional geography is to decide how many regions can be identified. Each region should have some degree of internal similarity and should differ in certain characteristics from other nearby regions. But taken to the extreme, this concept could divide Canada into hundreds of small regions, each one different from another in some small way. We know that every valley and every village in Canada has its own "character." Regional geography must operate on a different scale and discuss similarities in environments, peoples and economies over large areas within the country. The selection of characteristic criteria to describe the distinguishing features of a region is subjective and difficult. One should "know" the region.

The concept of a hierarchy of regions is fundamental; it should be possible to combine smaller regions into larger regions, and large regions may be subdivided into smaller regions. Regions are building blocks. Sometimes the subjective decision about placing a small sub-region into a larger region is a difficult one. Which criteria should be used? Do the local people "feel" that they are part of a larger region?

DEFINITION OF REGIONS

Regions should have some degree of similarity in selected phenomena and are defined on the basis of certain criteria. Economists, and others, often use statistical units such as provinces, counties or census divisions — which have little or no internal similarities in landscapes or occupations — because the factual data which they need is supplied by such political units. Small political units such as counties may be a data source indicating statistical trends, but the figures in themselves will not tell about the differences in physical environments, natural resources, occupations and

13

peoples within the statistical unit. On a large scale, many of the general public, and politicians, think of Canada as groups of provinces, such as the Atlantic or Prairie Provinces. Such political groupings, in themselves, are not likely to remind one how different in appearance Prince Edward Island is from Newfoundland, or how different Alberta, in totality, is from Manitoba. Geographers may use these political or statistical units to help define regions, but also they use physical environmental characteristics as criteria. Landforms or vegetation lines may be very apparent on the landscape so as to make obvious regional boundaries, particularly if they separate or differentiate human activities.

Even though one accepts that regions *exist,* one should be aware that they are human, intellectual constructs. They exist only in the minds of the persons who define, and accept, the criteria and characteristics of the region. Despite this limitation, many people have a "regional consciousness" which intuitively tells them that their local area differs in certain distinctive characteristics from those of nearby or far-off regions. It is one of the tasks of regional geography to identify and define these characteristics more accurately. As people travel more throughout Canada, they begin to recognize the similarities that may be seen from place to place; thus, comparing similarities from region to region may be equally as important as defining differences. Each Canadian probably has a slightly different view of the "character" of his local region, and certainly each Canadian has a different view of the "totality" of Canada.

WHAT IS REGIONAL GEOGRAPHY?

Regional geography is *not* a collection of miscellaneous information about a region. Undoubtedly, some past geography texts and articles seem to contradict this negative definition. Older people who recall their high school geography may remember it as a dull collection of facts about almost anything in a region or country, or the memorization of places and products. Modern geography has recognized that the "knowledge explosion" of recent decades has provided simply too much information about any part of the world for the human brain to comprehend the totality of any region. Because of the vast amount of distributional information available, a regional geographer must develop the *art* of selecting information and the *skill* of describing themes which characterize developments and identify trends in certain regions. Regional geography is a description and interpretation of the distribution patterns of selected phenomena within a defined region.

Facts are necessary to describe a region accurately. However, facts are neutral; they must be selected and *used*; organized information in itself does not constitute a discipline. Geography is not defined by the type of phenomena it studies. The selection, arrangement and interpretation of certain types of information presents a viewpoint which can be called geographical. Other disciplines may look at the same data and give an economic, sociological, political, or other viewpoint. An historian, for example, selects certain evidence during a period of time to illustrate trends; similarly, geographers select facts which illustrate the character of areas or regions.

Relatively little statistical information is presented in the following chapters because it is *not* the purpose of this book to be a collection of data. Its purpose is to *interpret* facts, to present concepts and themes, and to encourage thinking *about* the geography of Canada. Some reference sources are listed at the end of each chapter in which statistics and other information may be checked or, if you wish, you may interpret these differently after reading other articles or studying maps. Federal and provincial government maps and provincial and regional atlases should be primary reference sources for further information.

Some readers may be less interested in the following section about themes. They are abstract; they do not deal directly with particular places in Canada. But the concepts are fundamental to understanding the philosophy and methodology of the rest of the book. There are other suitable ways to organize or discuss geography; the following pages present a philosophy about geography as a discipline. These views are not unique; the concepts and approaches are shared by most regional geographers. If one has trouble absorbing these concepts without specific examples now, please return to this section after reading the whole book.

THEMES IN REGIONAL GEOGRAPHY

By tradition, geography has studied and interpreted certain types of facts more than others. Geography is not a study of "everything" in a region. Four major themes run through much geographical work and writing.

1.) Man-Land Relationships

One of the centuries-old traditions of geography is the study of man-land relationships. A newer version of this old term is people-environment relationships. Many geographers tend to look first at the physical (or natural) environment of the earth—the rocks, landforms, drainage, soils, vegetation, climate. The terms "physical" or "natural" are usually used interchangeably in geography, meaning the elements in "Nature" (natural) or the physical elements of the earth independent of man. In some geographical writing the adjectives physical or natural may be omitted and the word environment alone is used to refer to the physical (natural) earth. Geographers recognize, of course, that there are other "environments"—urban, social, political, etc., and confusion may arise if these other environments are not defined. For example, what relationships do you think of when reading about peoples' urban environments?

Geography is concerned with how physical phenomena interact together; the word often used is "function." Geographers are concerned with how people use (or misuse) their physical environments and how their activities are influenced by them. Is there more than *one* physical environment? Can one perceive the totality of the natural environment that one sees or experiences? The following chapters have frequent references to the physical characteristics of Canada and to how people in certain regions relate to these features.

2.) Regional Landscapes

A result of the continuing process of peoples' adaptations and adjustments to their physical environments is the landscape in which they live. A landscape is made up both of the physical environment and the distribution patterns of man-made features. Geography is concerned with the spatial arrangements and areal relationships of natural and human phenomena in a region. Large areas of Canada have certain similar elements in their landscapes; by grouping these selected similarities into areal units, some of the "character" of a region may be defined and its differences from other regions clarified. There are obvious differences that can be discussed between a "natural" landscape (without settlement), an agricultural landscape and an urban landscape.

Identifying regional landscapes can be an interesting challenge as one looks at television or studies printed pictures. Try to identify in which parts of Canada such pictures are taken. Ask what distinguishing features in the scene suggest that it should be in some particular region of Canada.

3.) Distribution Patterns

Geography is concerned with distributions; geographers are interested in the arrangement or spacing of phenomena on the earth's surface. A word used frequently in this book is "areal," or areal distribution, meaning the spread of a certain element over an area, or over earth space. Some geographers use the word "spatial" rather than areal, but this word may be confusing to those who think of "space" as referring to outer space around the earth.

Few items are distributed evenly throughout the world or a country. Maps of distribution patterns record areas of high density, or concentration, and areas of low density, or dispersal, and wide ranges between these extremes. One of geography's tasks is to describe these distributions and the usual visual tool to represent them is a map. Distribution patterns can be described as "linear," "clustered," "circular," etc.; such words indicate a geometric arrangement within a defined area. The regularity of some distribution patterns suggests to geographers that there is *order* in the landscape. Geographers may compare regions to see if these regularities or patterns are repeated elsewhere. Does the real world actually have order to it, or is this something which is perceived by certain observers?

If the first step in geography is to describe a distribution, it should then be followed by explanation. Why is it there? Why do these distribution patterns occur or repeat themselves? This can be one of the interesting aspects of geography. Explanations may have varying depths. They may be generalizations of one sentence or may be many pages resulting from several years of research. Probably no explanation is ever complete. A question often asked in geography is: "*Why* is something located where it is and *how* is it areally associated with other phenomena?" Geography usually focuses on explanations which consider man-land relationships or the distributional aspects of phenomena. Explanations may also call on history, economics, politics, geology or other disciplines to give partial answers. In turn, certain geographical themes may be useful in helping other disciplines, such as history or economics, to explain their problems from another viewpoint.

4.) Changing Geographical Patterns

Distribution patterns are, of course, *not* permanent. Although the natural environment component in the landscape changes very little, man's adjustments to it change with the introduction of new tools and technology, or different needs. Geography is not static. It is changing all the time. The regional geographies of Canada in the last century, or even fifty years ago, are not the same as those of today. How much of the present can be explained by the establishment of distribution patterns in the past? How does one explain past distribution patterns if explanations are not recorded in historical accounts? Can one interpret the thoughts or motives of past decision-makers? One of the intriguing aspects of geography is to predict a regional geography of the near future. As one studies a region, it is challenging to predict that if certain areal trends continue (or change), the region's geography will be different in ten or twenty years.

REGIONS OF CANADA

Introduction

Into how many regions should Canada be divided in order to study it both in whole and in part? How many is a convenient but appropriate number between "too few" and "too many" to describe and explain the differences and similarities within Canada?

Canadians sometimes divide Canada into three vague regions known as "eastern," "western," and "northern," but these mean different things to

17

different people. Ontario is east to people in British Columbia and sometimes so is Manitoba, but both are west or central to people from Nova Scotia. The north is a vague area; because most Canadians live in the southern part of the country everything north of them is "north"—which is most of Canada. For example, Timmins is in the north to residents of southern Ontario, but it is about the same latitude as Vancouver, which considers itself to be in the south. The Prairie Provinces are "the west" to people in eastern Canada, but this definition may exclude British Columbia, which is even farther west.

Some geography texts have used landform (or physiographic) regions of Canada as a regional framework. These differing landform characteristics can be seen easily in the landscape; man's major uses of these landform regions have differed among regions; therefore, man-land relationships may be better understood using a landform organization. Some geographers have added other physical environmental lines in their regionalization, such as the northern treeline, which also separates climate areas called Arctic and Subarctic Canada.

Other geographers have divided Canada by human criteria:

1.) For example, settled or occupied Canada, with higher population densities, may be discussed separately from "northern" or less densely settled Canada.

2.) In most human regionalizations, French-speaking Canada is considered as different from other parts of Canada.

3.) In another regional concept, Canada may be described in a "heartland-hinterland" framework; southern Ontario and Quebec are the heartland of the nation and the rest of Canada is their hinterland. This geographical concept of Canada is discussed more fully in Chapters 4 and 9.

4.) As the nation becomes more urbanized and the economy is dominated by several large metropolitan cities, Canada can be studied as a set of urban-centred regions. This concept is useful across southern Canada, but it does not describe most of northern Canada. It is discussed in Chapter 8.

Most commonly in Canada, regional grouping is by provinces. For example, most of the public, and politicians, combine the three Prairie Provinces, even though there are major differences between and within them. In addition, the term "prairie" province is a poor one, and misleading environmentally, since these provinces are *not* completely covered with prairie grasslands.

Another source of regional confusion is the naming of the far eastern provinces near the Atlantic Ocean. The original term of "Maritime Provinces" included the three smallest provinces on the east coast. But what name could be given to these provinces when Newfoundland became part of the group after 1949? By history and tradition, Newfoundland was *not* one of the historical "Maritime Provinces." The term "Atlantic Provinces," used by the federal government for the four east coast provinces, may be confusing to some who still think of the area as "the Maritimes," but who are not specific as to whether this term includes three or four provinces.

In this book, Canada is divided into six major regions, and each has several sub-regions. The regions and their names are well known to Canadians and have the advantage of local familiarity and national recognition. No single criterion has been used for defining them. Regional boundaries are a mixture of landform and political criteria. A hierarchy of sub-regions, defined by various criteria, is used because each of the six large regions has internal diversity. Undoubtedly, one can organize the geography of Canada under other possible regional alternatives; a final decision becomes an arbitrary, subjective one based on a belief that the system selected is the "best" for the purpose. The purpose of this book is to interpret some (not all) of the geographic characteristics of parts of Canada.

The geographical *diversity* of Canada could probably be better illustrated by choosing ten to twenty regions, but, in doing so, there would be danger of losing sight of aspects of *similarity* and the "wholeness" of Canada. This regional geography of Canada is meant not only to characterize the landscapes and economies of particular parts of Canada, but also to see them as components of the whole country.

SIX REGIONS OF CANADA

Some of the distinguishing characteristics of the six major regions are noted briefly in the following sections and, at the same time, the criteria for, and problems of, selecting regional boundaries are discussed.

The Atlantic and Gulf Region

As defined on the accompanying map, this east coast region is something more and something less than the politically-defined Atlantic Provinces. The Labrador section of the province of Newfoundland, which is quite different in many ways from the island, is discussed in Chapter 7 as part of the Canadian Shield, an area with which it has similar environmental and resource use characteristics. Gaspé Peninsula of Quebec has been added to the Atlantic Provinces because of its similarity in people, economy and landforms to adjoining northern New Brunswick. This sub-region of Quebec seems to have more characteristics in common with the areas around the Gulf of St. Lawrence than with the agricultural and industrial area of the St. Lawrence Lowland of southwestern Quebec. Some geographers have placed the north shore of the Gulf of St. Lawrence of Quebec into this "Gulf region," but it may be preferable to think of this area as part of the Canadian Shield.

The political area of the Atlantic Provinces is probably known to many Canadians, in comparison with the rest of Canada, for the negative economic characteristics of relatively low incomes, high unemployment and dependence on federal financial aid. This part of Canada is relatively little known to people in western Canada. Many Canadians know of the region because of family roots of parents or grandparents; outmigration has been characteristic for many decades.

The region's economy is greatly dependent on its resource-based industries which have fragmented and dispersed distribution patterns. The region lacks a major, dominating urban centre which could be an important internal market. These themes are discussed in Chapter 3. Comparisons can be made between the geographical characteristics of this east coast region and the west coast of the Cordillera of British Columbia.

The Great Lakes-St. Lawrence Lowlands

This small region contains more than half of Canada's population and almost three-quarters of the value of its manufacturing. It is the "heartland" of Canada. Its geographical patterns emphasize high densities of rural population, large urban centres and industry.

Geology and landforms are the criteria for defining the region on its north side, where it is bounded by the Precambrian geological and landform escarpment of the Canadian Shield. This visible and distinct physical boundary separates the agricultural landscapes of the Lowlands from the forested, lake-dotted Shield.

Although these high density characteristics are different from those of other parts of Canada, they are not uniformly distributed across the Lowlands region. Because of the importance of this region to Canada, and despite its small size on a national scale, the area will be discussed under a hierarchy of three sub-regions:

1.) The rolling glacial deposits of the lowland between lakes Huron, Erie and Ontario contain most of the people, agriculture and industries of southern Ontario.

2.) The flat-lying marine deposition along the St. Lawrence River has similar physical and economic characteristics in southern Quebec, but was settled by people with a different language and culture from those who came later to southern Ontario. These two lowlands are physically separated by low, rocky hills of the Canadian Shield which occupy a small area east of Kingston.

3.) The linear hills of the low Appalachian mountains (excluding Gaspé Peninsula) are included in southern Quebec because they are occupied by French-speaking people, even

though this hilly area has different landscapes from those of
the adjoining St. Lawrence Lowland.

SIX REGIONS OF CANADA

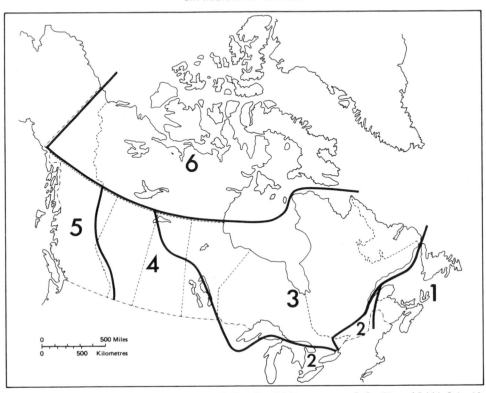

1 Atlantic and Gulf Region
2 Great Lakes – St. Lawrence Lowlands
3 Canadian Shield
4 Interior Plains
5 Cordillera of British Columbia
6 The North

The Canadian Shield

This largest region in Canada is another landform region, defined as the
area of exposed, old Precambrian rock. The Shield covers about half of the
area of mainland Canada. Its physical characteristics of rocky hills, forest
and lake cover are dominant criteria and are quite distinct from the Lowlands
to its south. Its natural resources of minerals, wood and water power help to
support the economy and people of the Lowlands. People occupy very small
sections of the rugged Shield.

Because the area is so large, one should expect internal variety in natural
environments and economic characteristics. It seems desirable, therefore, to
subdivide the Shield into at least three sub-regions:

21

1.) The large forested area across the southern Shield, extending from Labrador to northern Saskatchewan, is the developing "resources frontier" of eastern Canada. Most of the discussion in Chapter 7 will be concerned with this area, and it will be subdivided further into smaller regions to illustrate internal diversity.

2.) The treeless, Arctic section of the mainland Northwest Territories is so different from the rest of the Shield that it is discussed in Chapter 10 as part of the North.

3.) The flat, lake-covered, swampy lowland west of James Bay and south of Hudson Bay is underlain by rocks of Paleozoic age which are different from the Precambrian rock of the Canadian Shield. This lowland is little used and virtually unoccupied because of its unfavourable physical environments.

The Interior Plains

The Plains are defined by landforms and geology. The western boundary is marked by the magnificent wall of the Rocky Mountains, but the eastern boundary with the Canadian Shield is often hidden beneath former glacial lake deposition or by extensive coniferous forests. Many geographers, and others, prefer that this part of Canada be described as a political region consisting of the three Prairie Provinces. Within the Interior Plains landform region, a sub-region can be defined by the transitional parkland vegetation zone separating northern forests from southern grasslands. The characteristics of much of this former grassland area have been changed by settlement; it now has large rectangular grain farms and an interesting regularity of spacing of towns and cities.

The forested northern part of the Plains is similar to the forested Canadian Shield to the northeast. There is, therefore, some geographical logic in discussing this western interior part of Canada as a political region of three provinces, with an internal subdivision between the grassland and forested sections. On the other hand, the physical environments and resource use patterns of northern Saskatchewan and Manitoba are similar to the Shield sections of Ontario and Quebec. The choice is whether to consider the Shield parts of the Prairie Provinces as part of a larger region of Canada or as an internal division within a political region. These preceding comments illustrate some of the problems of geographical regionalization. Regions are mental constructs; they are not right or wrong.

The Cordillera of British Columbia

This distinct mountainous region is quite different in landscape characteristics from the Plains region to its east. The Cordillera is the name given to all of the mountains which extend through western North America from Central America to Alaska. The only other high mountains in Canada are in Baffin, Devon and Ellesmere islands in the northeastern Arctic. The British Columbia Cordillera is characterized by great contrasts within small areas in both the physical environment and in population densities. Similar to the hilly Atlantic and Gulf region, it is dependent upon a resource-based economy.

The plains of northeastern British Columbia are not part of the Cordillera and are discussed as part of the Interior Plains region. Northeastern B.C. is similar to adjoining Alberta in landscapes and economy.

It is debatable whether or not to consider Yukon Territory as a sub-region within the Cordillera. The landforms of the Territory are undoubtedly part of the Cordillera; the main population cluster in southern Yukon is connected with the Pacific Ocean. However, if combined with B.C., the Yukon could be overlooked within the Cordillera because of its small population and resource development. Therefore, it is discussed as part of the North region because of its many human, resource use and political similarities to the Mackenzie Valley, N.W.T.

The North

The term "North" means different things to different people in Canada. Because most Canadians live in a narrow strip across the southern part of the country, then everything north of them is "the North." The North is specifically defined here by political criteria as Yukon Territory and the Northwest Territories, north of 60 degrees north latitude. In this case, the political boundary can be considered just as "real" and influential upon people's activities as a landform or vegetation boundary.

The North has no landform or other environmental uniformity. Unlike the other major regions of Canada, the North has environmental diversity. It has landform variations in terms of mountains, hills and plains; some of these landform features are forested, others have tundra vegetation and some areas are bare rock. The North has both arctic and subarctic climates. It has a frozen ocean environment which is not found elsewhere in Canada.

There are some logical reasons for considering the northern mainland of Canada as northern extensions of three other regions to the south. As previously noted, Yukon Territory could be part of the Cordillera, linked with British Columbia and the Pacific. The Mackenzie River valley is a northern continuation of the Interior Plains landform region and has many similarities to northern Alberta. Keewatin District, west of Hudson Bay, is underlain with Precambrian rocks similar to the rest of the Canadian Shield; its mining potential could be considered along with mining developments in the Shield. If these three sub-regions were discussed as northern parts of other regions, only the Arctic Islands would be left as a separate

"Northern" region.

The North is divided into two large sub-regions in Chapter 10. The Northwest is forested in the valleys, has a subarctic climate, has most of the white (European) population and some resource potential. In contrast, the Arctic in the northeast is treeless, has an arctic climate, most of the Eskimo (Inuit) population and little resource potential.

SUMMARY

In traditional geographical methodology, a discussion of regionalization should come at the *end* of a book, not at the beginning. This introductory chapter has presented some of the problems of regionalization, with only a little discussion of reasons or solutions. Canada can be divided into its parts after one knows the whole of Canada and can then see the differences and similarities from place to place. One should know the total physical environment, people and resources of Canada; one should study areal patterns and regional differences; one should read in the geographic and allied literature; and, if possible, one should travel across much of Canada to see the landscapes personally.

These six regions of Canada are not fixed or permanent. They are academic devices or conceptual frameworks, and an organizational framework for studying Canada and its parts. Each large region is divided into sub-regions, and there are various ways of combining these sub-regions into sets of large regions. The boundaries for these regions are usually compromises; they have advantages and disadvantages and relate to the purposes and philosophies of the person organizing the material. By using large regions, some of the *national* characteristics of Canada may be brought out; one probably gets a feeling for the diversity within Canada by studying the sub-regions.

A warning may not be out of place here, in case the comments of this introduction are misinterpreted. It is *not* the purpose of this book to provoke an unproductive argument about the proper placing of regional and sub-regional boundaries. They are organizational devices. Our concern should be with the description, analysis, interpretation and understanding of the geographical patterns and their implications within parts of Canada, however defined. We should think about the distribution patterns of elements of the natural environment and how these vary from place to place; and we should be interested in how people have settled into these varying environments and created landscapes which illustrate similarities and differences from place to place and region to region across Canada. After reading the book, return to this section and think about it. If you understand the geographical patterns of Canada better than when you started the book, think how *you* would prefer to regionalize Canada.

This book does *not* put all of these regions and sub-regions together and then try to characterize Canada as a whole. Obviously, there is one Canada politically, but there is not one Canada geographically; this is a country of areal diversity. One of the purposes of regional geography is to illustrate and analyze the differences in the environments, peoples and resource patterns from place to place and region to region within Canada.

GEOGRAPHICAL TERMS

Geography has a number of words which have particular meaning within the discipline. Because these are used throughout this book, communication will be better if they are defined and explained briefly. These terms are *not* meant to be memorized—just understood.

1.) Physical or natural environment: the elements or components of the earth; such items as geology, landforms, climate, natural vegetation, soils, drainage. Although the term excludes people, it is recognized that they have affected most elements of the natural environment in some way.

2.) Areal distribution: the spread of phenomena over a defined area. Distribution connotes a geometric spacing of phenomena. Types of distributions may have descriptive words such as linear, dispersed, concentrated, even, etc. The word pattern is often added in a distributional sense; phenomena are observed, and usually mapped, to show regularity and order in their occupation of area. Some geographers prefer the word, spatial, rather than areal, referring to earth space; but some people confuse the word "spatial" on the earth with outer space off the earth.

3.) Areal association: a distributional relationship or coincidence between two (or more) sets of phenomena within a defined area. For example, the areal association one can observe between the distribution of tobacco and sandy soils, between types of geology and landforms, or between certain climates and vegetation. The degree or amount of this coincidence or association should be defined. An areal association should be observable and measurable; it suggests a need for explanation as to *why* the phenomena are associated in an area.

4.) Landscape: the totality of the physical environment and man-made features within an observable area or region. It is recognized that few people ever see, or record, the "totality." The use of this term recognizes the problem of *perception*—a person's mind absorbs or ignores certain elements in the landscape.

5.) Geographical features: this is a vague term; it should not be used. To some, it may mean only landforms; others may use the words to mean any feature (phenomenon) recorded on a map. In this latter sense, all place names are geographical features.

6.) Natural resource: something obtained from the natural environment and used by people. Sometimes geographers omit the adjective "natural" and this can cause confusion because the word "resource" alone has different meanings. (If you read about "human" resources, what do you think is meant?)

7.) Geography and geographical: it has been said, and perhaps not wholly in jest, that there are as many definitions of geography as there are geographers. Certainly the word, and the discipline, means different things to different people. The original Greek word meant "to write about the earth." This is somewhat inclusive! Some of the themes and traditions of geography are discussed briefly at the beginning of this chapter. To be "geographical," most geographers agree that one or more of these themes should be central, but not necessarily all of them. Because geography has different meanings and emphasis, the adjective "geographical" does not communicate well and probably should be avoided, even though the word was deliberately used as a heading for this section! You may have similar difficulty in defining the adjectives "historical" or "economic." For example, people have used the colourful statement, "Canada is a geographical impossibility." Exactly what does that mean to you, or to those who say it? Do they mean Canada is "impossible" (difficult?) because of its landforms, or because of great distances? Do they mean that we have large areas of unfavourable (for whom?) natural environment? Do they mean that Canada is divided into regions which do not function together? Do they mean *all* of these things or just some (or one) of them?

8.) Other words: proper communication is sometimes not clear because we use words which can be interpreted differently as a result of one's feelings and culture. For example, the bland word "development" may have an emotional meaning of "exploitation" to some. When one discusses how regions "function" (work, operate) together, one probably infers that this means functioning efficiently, unless stated to the contrary; however, phenomena in a region can also function poorly or lack integration. Do we, in fact, really mean that regions function together, or do we mean that the people and their activities in regions are interconnected in various ways?

REFERENCES

Books:

The following is a selection of books about the Geography of Canada, arranged in chronological order. They should not be looked at for their factual information, since it may no longer be correct, but study their organization and format. Most of the books use a regional approach to describe and discuss Canada, but the regional arrangements differ.

University Level:

1945   "Economic Geography of Canada" by A.W. Currie, Macmillan, Toronto. 455 pages.
         A regional geography organized around seven landform regions.
1947   "Canada: A Study of Cool Continental Environments" by Griffith Taylor, Methuen, Toronto. 526 pages.
         A regional and topical geography organized into 20 "natural regions" arranged in four zones south to north.
1952   "Canadian Regions" by Donald Putnam, B. Brouillette, Donald Kerr, J. Lewis Robinson, Dent, Toronto. 601 pages.
         The provinces are grouped together into seven political regions.
1964   "Economic Geography of Canada" by E.P. Weeks, Z.W. Sametz and Pierre Camu, Macmillan, Toronto. 393 pages.
         A topical organization of mainly economic information with a conclusion discussing 68 small regions which are groups of census divisions.
1967   "Canada: A Geographical Interpretation" edited by John Warkentin, Methuen, Toronto. 608 pages.
         Written by 22 Canadian geographers as a contribution to Canada's Centennial; 12 chapters deal with systematic topics and the latter part of the book discusses seven regions of Canada.
1968   "Canada: Its Problems and Prospects" by J. Wreford Watson, Longmans, Toronto. 320 pages.
         A reprinting and revision of the Canada section of his "North America" book; there are four regions across southern Canada and a fifth called the North.
1969   "Canada: A Geographical Perspective" by Louis Hamelin. Translated by Ian Jackson and M. Storrie, Wiley, Toronto. 234 pages.
         This has a systematic approach to the geography of Canada. Five main topics are discussed.
1970   "Canada: A Regional Analysis" by D.F. and R.G. Putnam, Dent, Toronto. 390 pages in 1979 revision.
         Two introductory chapters on physical and human patterns are followed by discussion of six political (provincial) regions.

1972   "Studies in Canadian Geography" edited by Louis Trotier and six other Canadian geographers, University of Toronto Press, Toronto. *Six volumes organized by political units (province or groups of provinces), prepared for the meeting of the International Geographical Union in Montreal. Within each volume the organization is topical, not regional.*

1972   "Regional Geography of Canada" by J. Lewis Robinson in Canada Yearbook, Statistics Canada, Ottawa. 26 pages. *A summary of the distinctive geographical characteristics of six regions using landform and political criteria.*

1979   "The Boundaries of Canadian Confederation" by Norman Nicholson, Macmillan, Toronto and the Carleton Library Series, No. 115. 252 pages. *A discussion of the evolution of provincial, and other, political boundaries.*

1982   "Heartland and Hinterland: Canadian Regions in Evolution" edited by Larry McCann, Prentice-Hall, Toronto. 500 pages. *Chapters by 15 Canadian geographers, developing a heartland-hinterland theme in a historical geography approach. Regions are mainly political.*

Secondary School Level:

1956   "A Regional Geography of Canada" by Donald Putnam and Donald Kerr, Dent, Toronto. 520 pages. *A simpler version of "Canadian Regions," (1952) (see above, under university texts).*

1962   "Canada: A Regional Geography" by George Tomkins and Theo Hills, Gage, Toronto. 387 pages. *Organized into six regions based mainly on landforms.*

1966   "Canada: A Geographic Study" by Donald Innis, McGraw-Hill, Toronto. 423 pages. *Mainly a topical treatment in 14 chapters, plus discussion of six regions defined by physical environment criteria.*

1968   "Canada: A New Geography" by Ralph Krueger and R. Corder, Holt Rinehart, Toronto. 469 pages; 502 pages in the 1974 revision. *A topical organization dealing with physical, economic and human patterns across Canada, with a regional summary in a final chapter.*

1970   "Canada: A Regional Geography" by George Tomkins, Theo Hills, Tom Weir, Gage, Toronto. 423 pages. *An expansion and rewriting of the 1962 edition above.*

1977   "Countdown Canada" by Ben Vass, R. Alderdice, G. Sled, Macmillan, Toronto. 227 pages. *A student activity book organized by six political regions after two introductory chapters. Selected topics for each region.*

1978   "Canada in View" by John Molyneux and M. Olsen, McGraw-Hill Ryerson, Toronto. 346 pages.

28

> *Organized both topically (8 chapters on physical environments, population and resources) and regionally (8 chapters on certain themes in regions which are mainly political).*

1978   "Focus on Canada" by John Washington, Andrew Burghardt, G. Hitchcox, P. Christian, McGraw-Hill Ryerson, Toronto. 314 pages. *Part two discusses six regions of Canada.*

Other References to Geographical Regions of Canada *(in chronological order):*

"The Problem of Geographical Regions in Canada" by J. Lewis Robinson, *The Canadian Geographer*, Vol. 7, 1956, pp. 46-49.

"Regions of Canada and the Regional Concept" by Norman Nicholson and Z.W. Sametz, *Resources for Tomorrow* Conference Papers, Vol. 1, 1961, pp. 367-383.

"Canada and Its Regions" by J. Wreford Watson, *Scottish Geographical Magazine*, Dec. 1962, pp. 137-149.

"Dimensions of Canadian Regionalism" by D. Michael Ray, Geog. Paper No. 49, Dept. of Energy, Mines and Resources, Ottawa, 1971, 59 pages, plus 65 maps and tables.

"Regional Patterns: Disparities and Development" by R. Krueger, R. Irving, C. Vincent, Dept. of Geog., Univ. of Waterloo, Waterloo, 1975. 87 pages.

"Living Together: A Study of Regional Disparities," Economic Council of Canada, No. 22-54, Ottawa, 1977.

Journal of Canadian Studies, Vol. 15, 1980. The whole issue deals with Canadian regionalism.

"National and Regional Economic Development Strategies" edited by Barry Wellar, Univ. of Ottawa Press, Ottawa, 1981. 180 pages.

"Regional Geography of Canada" by J. Lewis Robinson, *Canada Handbook*, Statistics Canada, Ottawa, 1981, pp. 1-17.

"Regional Geography of Canada in Canada" by J. Lewis Robinson, *Journal of Geography*, Dec. 1981, pp. 268-271.

"A Geographical Perspective" by Ralph Krueger, Ch. 1 in *Understanding Canada*, edited by Wm. Metcalfe, New York Univ. Press, New York, 1982.

Books of Collected Readings about the Geography of Canada:

1967   "Canada's Changing Geography" edited by R. Louis Gentilcore, Prentice-Hall, Toronto. 15 chapters, 224 pages.

1970   Regional and Resource Planning in Canada" edited by R.R. Krueger, Holt-Rinehart, Toronto. 27 chapters, 249 pages.

1971   "Geographical Approaches to Canadian Problems" edited by R. Louis Gentilcore, Prentice-Hall, Toronto. 17 chapters, 235 pages.

1969-71   "Process and Method in Canadian Geography" four volumes of readings edited by Gordon Nelson and M.J. Chambers. 1. Geomorphology. 2. Water. 3. Weather and Climate. 4. Vegetation, Soils and Wildlife, Methuen, Toronto.

1972   "Readings in Canadian Geography" edited by Robert Irving, Holt-Rinehart, Toronto. 35 chapters, 440 pages; 1978, revised third edition, 27 chapters, 357 pages.

1976   "Canada's Natural Environment: Essays in Applied Geography" edited by G.R. McBoyle and E. Sommerville, Methuen, Toronto. 10 chapters, 264 pages.

1977   "Managing Canada's Renewable Resources" edited by Ralph Krueger and Bruce Mitchell, Methuen, Toronto. 22 chapters, 333 pages.

1981   "Canadian Resource Policy: Problems and Prospects" edited by Bruce Mitchell and Derrick Sewell, Methuen, Toronto. 10 chapters, 294 pages.

Periodicals:

The Canadian Geographer, published by the Canadian Association of Geographers, Burnside Hall, McGill University, Vol. 1, 1951 to Vol. 27, 1983. For example, articles relevant to Chapter 1:

Vol. 23, No. 4, 1979. "The Geography of Canada and Its Regions in Canadian Universities" by Charles Forward, pp. 299-307.

Vol. 25, No. 4, 1981. "The Development of Canadian Geography: The First 25 Volumes of The Canadian Geographer" by J. Wreford Watson, pp. 391-398.

Canadian Geographic (formerly *Canadian Geographical Journal*), published by the Royal Canadian Geographical Society, Ottawa, continuous after 1935. Every issue has interesting articles and excellent pictures on some topic, or part, of Canada.

Atlases:

Atlas of Canada, 4th edition, published jointly by the Dept. of Energy, Mines and Resources, Ottawa and Macmillan, Toronto, 1974. 254 pages.
Canada Gazetteer Atlas, published jointly by the Dept. of Energy, Mines and Resources, Ottawa and Macmillan, Toronto, 1980. 98 pages and index.
Atlas of Canada, Reader's Digest Association, Montreal, 1981.
Canada's Special Resource Lands, Folio No. 4, Lands Directorate, Environment Canada, Ottawa, 1979. 232 pages, 88 maps.
Other commercial atlases with numerous maps of Canada have been published by Gage, Oxford University Press, T. Nelson and Sons, and others.

CHAPTER 2

THE PHYSICAL ENVIRONMENT AND THE EVOLUTION OF SETTLEMENT PATTERNS

CHAPTER 2

THE PHYSICAL ENVIRONMENT
AND THE EVOLUTION OF SETTLEMENT PATTERNS

FIRST SETTLERS

Canada could not be settled 15,000 years ago because most of the land was covered by a continental icecap several thousands of feet thick. As the front of the icecap slowly receded to the north, the ancestors of the people whom we now call Indians migrated northward from lands which they had occupied in the non-glaciated parts of North America. It is possible that some Indian ancestors arrived from East Asia prior to the last glaciation and other groups probably migrated southward from Alaska and northeastern Asia after the west coast and some interior valleys of the Cordillera became ice-free.

Archaeologists and anthropologists have much yet to learn about the origins and migration routes of our Indian ancestors, but they do agree that this continent was settled much later than the area around the Mediterranean Sea and nearby North Africa and southwestern Asia. If there were Indians inhabiting Canada prior to the last glaciation, all records of their occupance were, of course, removed by the icecap.

The ancestors of the Indians survived with what the physical environment had to offer. Eastern Canada became forested as the ice front retreated 6,000 to 10,000 years ago; Indians lived on the animals, fish and berries of this forest and some groups began to plant and harvest agricultural crops. Indians on both the east and west coasts seemed to thrive on ample fish resources. Life was undoubtedly hard and natural mortality high, but many thousands of Indians survived and multiplied in this natural environment.

The ancestors of the Eskimo (Inuit) people came to Canada later than the Indians. It was a few thousand years later before the icecap over northern Canada melted away. (Remnants of this icecap still remain on Baffin, Devon and Ellesmere islands of northeastern Canada.) It is believed that the forefathers of the modern Eskimo migrated from northeastern Asia along the northern Alaska coast and across the northern Canadian mainland and southern Arctic islands about 3,000 to 5,000 years ago. They may have reached the ice-free coast of southwestern Greenland about 1,000 years ago — just about the time the area was being "discovered" by the Norse from northern Europe. Eskimos probably numbered only a few thousand people and they lived near ice-covered seas in a treeless natural environment which was much different from the forested environment occupied by the Indians. The modern Inuit are discussed further in Chapter 10.

Essentially the same physical conditions known to Indians and Inuit were met by the first European settlers of the 16th and 17th centuries. However, these new immigrants came with new tools and technology and with a cultural background based on developed agriculture and an economy rooted in the exchange and manufacturing industries of towns and cities.

CANADA'S PHYSICAL ENVIRONMENT

Many aspects of the physical environment of what we now call Canada have not changed in the two to four centuries that the area has been occupied by Europeans. However, small areas of this original natural landscape have been greatly altered by rapidly-increasing thousands and then millions of people.

The following brief description of some elements of the physical environment emphasizes distribution patterns which show regional differences across Canada. The detailed description patterns should be studied on maps in the Atlas of Canada or in other commercial atlases. The purpose of this section is to present the physical environment as "the home of man" or "the stage upon which human drama is enacted." The information should be *used* to help explain similarities and differences in the regional landscapes across Canada. A discussion of the broad national patterns should stress that these physical conditions are *not* the same all over Canada. The specific ways in which people adapt to, and use, these varying environments are discussed in the regional chapters.

Landforms and Settlement

Some books and maps use the words "topography" or "physiographic" to refer to landforms. Because there are some definition problems with both of these words, it seems preferable to use the more descriptive word, landforms.

The shape of Canada's rock base may be compared to a huge saucer. The shallow centre of the saucer is occupied by Hudson Bay and the periphery of the country has upturned outer edges. In western Canada, the various high, linear ranges of the Cordilleran system extend from western continental United States to Alaska. In southeastern Canada, the lower mountains of the Appalachian system extend northeastward from United States through southeastern Quebec and the Maritime Provinces to Newfoundland Island. Along the northeastern edge of Canada, ice-capped mountains extend through Baffin, Devon, Axel Heiberg and Ellesmere islands. The outer edges of Canada presented rugged landforms to the first explorers and settlers from overseas.

Central Canada has lower landforms. The low hills of the Canadian Shield and the lowland across Manitoba slope toward Hudson Bay. This central lowland is flanked by two peripheral lowlands: in the southeast, the narrow and small lowland between the Great Lakes and along the St. Lawrence River holds more than half of the people of Canada, whereas the other lowland in the northwest along the Mackenzie River, sloping to the Arctic Ocean, has very few people. Only a few people live in the rocky, hilly parts of the Canadian Shield.

Most Canadians live in the narrow valleys, lowlands and plains across the southern part of the country. Very few people live on the hills, uplands or mountains. This areal association between certain landforms and population distribution is related to the original agricultural use of the lowlands and valleys by early settlers who came to Canada to establish farms and homes. These southern lowlands had (and have) the desired physical environmental properties of better soils and water supply for agriculture. Undoubtedly, some Canadians can, and do, live on hills, uplands and mountains — particularly for primary mining and forestry activities — but population densities are lower and dispersed in these rugged areas. Most Canadians are lowland and valley dwellers.

Geology and Minerals

The varying ages and types of rock beneath the landform regions not only cause differences in topography, but also result in different types of mineral resources. The young, flat-lying sedimentary rocks of Paleozoic age of the Great Lakes - St. Lawrence Lowlands were the first source in Canada of salt, petroleum and natural gas. Other sedimentary rocks of mainly Mesozoic geological age of the Interior Plains are now the main source of Canada's petroleum, natural gas, coal, salt and potash. The young, sedimentary rocks are not likely to contain metallic minerals. Do deposits of fuels and non-metallics lie within the sedimentary rocks beneath Hudson and James bays and in the northwestern Arctic Islands?

The Canadian Shield is composed of different types of volcanic rocks of ancient, Precambrian geological age. Some of these rocks are the sources of Canada's metallic mineral wealth, such as iron, copper, lead, zinc, nickel, gold, silver, etc. Because of the composition and age of the rocks, one should not expect to find fuels in the Canadian Shield. There is geographical (locational) separation of the distribution of types of mineralization related to geological characteristics.

The three other landform regions — Appalachians, Cordillera and Arctic Islands — have a mixture of rocks of several geological ages and composition. Not only do these landform regions have a mixture of landform types ranging through plains, lowlands, hills and mountains, but also they have a variety of mineralization including fuels, non-metallics and metals.

Climate and People

Winter:
Canada probably has a reputation among people in other nations as a

cold country; this is a correct description of most of the country during the winter. A distribution map of average monthly temperatures for January, illustrating average winter conditions, shows the coldest areas of Canada extending across the northern mainland and the adjoining Arctic Islands. These cold temperatures are caused by the lack of heat due to the low angle of the winter sun, the proximity of ice-covered seas and the frequency of vast, cold air masses from the Arctic Ocean, Alaska or northeastern Asia. These northern areas have no natural sources of warmth during the winter. Residences are expensive to heat and outside work is curtailed during periods of severe cold.

Cold conditions are carried south and southeastward by prevailing air mass movements during the winter, but monthly *average* temperatures are higher across southeastern Canada because these averages are raised by the occasional incursion of warm air from the United States or from the Pacific or Atlantic oceans. Whereas cold is continuous during the winter in northern Canada, it is broken by occasional warmer (or less cold) periods across southern Canada. Such warmer periods, due to more frequent warm air masses from the south, are more common in southern Ontario, which is the most southerly part of Canada. More than half of the people in Canada, living in the southeast, experience winters in which a few cold days are followed by a few warmer days.

Milder winters are experienced on both the east and west coasts where daily and monthly temperatures are moderated by air masses moving across the relatively warm water of the Atlantic and Pacific oceans. Unfortunately, for inland Canadians desiring mild winters, these moderate conditions are confined to narrow strips near the coasts. The relatively mild air moving eastward from the Pacific Ocean is partly blocked and modified by the mountain barrier of the Cordillera; on the east coast, warm air from the Atlantic seldom penetrates far inland because the prevailing movement of air masses is from west to east.

Most Canadians do, therefore, live in areas with cold winters. Our adaptations to cold conditions are different from people of southern United States. Canadians have higher costs than many Americans for heating homes, factories and offices, higher costs for snow removal from streets and highways, and also different winter recreational activities.

Summer:

There are fewer areal variations in summer conditions experienced across southern Canada. Summers there can be described (non-quantitatively) as warm to hot, as the result of frequent passage from west to east across the country of warm air masses from the Pacific Ocean, southwestern United States or the Gulf of Mexico. Short periods of high heat (above 30°C) can be experienced anywhere across southern Canada during summer. The coolest summers are recorded farthest away from these warm air sources; i.e., across northern Canada, and particularly in northeastern Canada adjoining the cold water in Hudson Bay and in the channels between the Arctic Islands. Summer conditions for most Canadians are similar to those across northern United States.

Frost-Free Conditions and Agriculture:
The length of summer can be measured by the length of the frost-free season. The period without frosts also influences the types of crops that can be grown in certain areas of "long" or "short" growing seasons. The longest average periods without frosts are recorded in southwestern British Columbia which is usually under mild Pacific air in the spring and fall when frosts are occurring elsewhere in Canada. This area is also protected by mountains from cold air masses which might flow westward from the interior valleys and plateaus of the Cordillera. Unfortunately for agricultural settlement, this coastal area with the longest frost-free season in Canada has a small and dispersed amount of level land.

The area with the second longest frost-free season extends across southern Ontario and into southwestern Quebec; it is south of the usual routes of cold air masses from the Arctic or Northwest during the critical (for agriculture) periods of spring and fall. The favourable climate of southern Ontario, combined with a large area of level to rolling land, was attractive to agricultural settlers in the last century.

Shorter frost-free seasons are a problem for farmers on the Interior Plains which are open to the north to the penetration of cold air masses from the Arctic and Northwest. The Atlantic Provinces have a wide range of frost-free periods in the valleys. Relatively long frost-free seasons are common near the moderating water of the coast, but much shorter periods are a problem inland and in the hills. The contrast between coastal and interior climatic elements influenced past patterns of agricultural settlement.

Annual Precipitation:
Canadians experience a wide range of average annual precipitation amounts. The wettest part of Canada is along the west coast where easterly-moving, moisture-laden air masses from the Pacific Ocean drop their frontal and orographic rainfall upon the mountain slopes and lowlands, particularly during the winter. These amounts decrease inland as precipitation is deposited upon successive mountain ranges across the Cordillera. Some of the sheltered interior valleys are, in fact, quite dry. Contrasts in vegetation, ranging from large, tall trees to scrubby sagebrush, are Nature's response to the variety of precipitation amounts within the Cordillera.

The next highest amounts of precipitation are recorded along the east coast where easterly or southerly moist winds blow in upon the low hills of the coast during the passage of frontal storms. This precipitation is spread evenly throughout the year, falling in both winter and summer. The tourist literature seldom tells visitors about the possibility of frequent rains near the east coast in summer.

Average annual precipitation amounts decrease inland from the east coast and progressively across central Canada. The driest area in southern Canada—farthest from any source of moisture supply—is along the southern Alberta-Saskatchewan border. Although precipitation amounts there, falling mainly as rain in summer, fluctuate greatly from year to year, the average is not enough to support forests. This grassland area has been a marginal environment for open-field farming without irrigation. The implications of precipitation upon agricultural settlement are discussed in Chapter 8.

North-central Canada receives the least amount of precipitation in the country. The cold or cool air masses contain very little moisture and there are few physical processes or barriers to cause this water vapour to condense and precipitate. Although the amount of snow recorded is minor, it does not melt during the continuously long winters and therefore remains on the ground for a long time; it can blow into drifts or hollows in sufficient depth for snowhouse building or can be packed around the walls of modern homes for insulation. The north is, of course, not always snow-covered, and in summer, when daily temperatures are above 0°C, small amounts of drizzle rain may fall.

Climate Variations:

The preceding descriptions of areal variations in the climatic elements have been stated in general terms, emphasizing differences from place to place. Canada has not one climate, but many. Canadians adapt to, and live with, various climates across the land. The preceding discussion described *averages* which can be shown on maps, and noted some of the mechanisms and controls—mainly air mass movements—which cause these conditions. One knows, however, from reading newspapers and watching TV that such conditions vary from day to day, month to month, and year to year. We should discriminate between daily *weather* and the long term averages which describe *climates.* These averages may actually seldom occur; they help to compare what can be expected in different regions of the country and they are a guide to general atmospheric conditions in a region.

The preceding paragraphs used vague words, such as cold, warm, wet, dry, in keeping with one of the purposes of this book which is to emphasize concepts rather than facts. They are subjective words which mean different things to different people. 0°C may be raw and miserable to residents of Vancouver and be brisk and exhilarating to residents of Quebec City. 625 mms. of annual precipitation would mean a wet year to farmers in southeastern Alberta and could be a dry year to people in Halifax. Readers are encouraged to study maps showing the actual distribution amounts of these various climatic elements. Maps should record exactly how much precipitation, for example, falls on the average in a "wet" part of Canada and how these average amounts compare with those received in a "dry" area. Study maps of areal variations in temperature conditions. If one needs to know, or to use, these figures for reference or comparative purposes, consult climate maps or statistical tables published by the federal Atmospheric Environment Service. Then, one can be accurate and factual when describing a day, month or year as "cold" or "hot."

NATURAL VEGETATION REGIONS

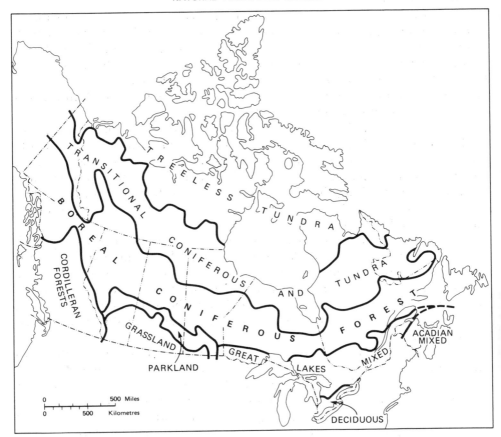

Vegetation

Average climate conditions across Canada are mirrored in vegetation patterns. For example, the dry area of southern Alberta and Saskatchewan corresponds areally with the grasslands, and most of the dry and cold parts of northern Canada are covered with tundra vegetation. The wet and cool slopes of the Cordillera are clothed with the tallest trees in Canada, mainly coniferous species. In eastern Canada, the areas of dominant deciduous forests

39

have relatively mild winters; many of these deciduous species are not able to survive northward in the colder winters of the Canadian Shield and northern Interior Plains.

Settlers arriving in eastern Canada in the 17th and 18th centuries met a forested landscape. Hunting, fishing, trapping and gathering were important uses of this forest by the early settlers, as they had been for the native Indians. Several generations of hard work were required to carve farmland out of the forests.

People probably think of Canada as a forested nation; the broad band of forest cover extends across the nation from the Atlantic Provinces to British Columbia and Yukon Territory. (Study the map on p. 39; colour in the Boreal Coniferous Forest and the two Mixed Forest areas to make them stand out.) But less than 40 percent of Canada is actually classified as forest area on the maps of vegetation regions, and within this forest are wide areal differences in tree sizes, densities and number of species.

It is possible that Canadians overemphasize the extent of prairie grassland across the southern Prairie Provinces. Such grasslands constituted only about one-third of the area of these provinces and much of that has been ploughed under to become grain farms. Grassland also seems to be a common sight to travellers along the interior valleys of southern British Columbia, but in fact, these grasslands are only narrow strips and the uplands above the valleys are forested.

On the other hand; the extent of tundra vegetation and barren rock north of the treeline in the Arctic region may be underestimated. This treeless area occupies about 2,400,000 square kilometres which is more than one-quarter of the area of Canada. In addition, within the Canadian Shield and across the northern Interior Plains, the aggregate area of lakes, swamps, muskegs and glaciated bare rock constitutes a sizeable non-forested environment.

Forests still remain a part of the economy and lifestyles of Canadians, as they were in the last century. The forest and lake environments of the Canadian Shield and the Appalachian hills are a nearby attraction for recreation for more than half of Canadians who live in the cleared lowlands of eastern Canada. The cutting, processing and management of forest products is a major component in the economy of both eastern and far-western Canadians.

Soils

All of southern Canada was covered with glacial deposition left behind following the melting of the continental icecap. This deposition, of different kinds, has been worked over by ice, water and wind and has had organic matter mixed into it from the decaying covering vegetation of deciduous and coniferous trees and various grasses and bushes. The types of sand, silt, gravel and clay deposition and the types of vegetative matter vary regionally across Canada. The soil-forming process, having a longer dormant period in northern Canada than in the south, has been going on for a few thousand years since the last glacial period.

Because of the complexity of glacial deposition, Canada's soils actually vary greatly in composition and fertility within relatively small areas. The large soil groups shown on a map of soil regions of Canada record only general characteristics and tell little about the specific soils on a particular farm. For example, all of eastern Canada is classified as having podzol soils; this name says little about the range of fertility which can be found in river valley floodplains, former glacial valley bottoms or on eroded hillsides.

Although natural fertility (however defined) may have been found by trial and error methods by agricultural settlers of the last century, these natural conditions are now of less significance to farmers who can change soil properties with the extensive use of organic and chemical fertilizers. Study of a map of major soil regions of Canada may add little to the understanding of the settlement patterns and rural landscapes of Canada. It is more significant to look at the influence and use of particular soils in particular regions.

Drainage and Water Bodies

Canada is reported to have a larger area of fresh water lakes than any other country. The largest of these lakes form a linear pattern along the southern and western edges of the Canadian Shield and include the Great Lakes lying between Ontario and the United States, the sometimes-called "Great Lakes" of Manitoba—Winnipeg, Manitoba and Winnipegosis—and the other "Great Lakes" of the northwest—Athabasca, Great Slave and Great Bear. Canadians were not shy—and probably accurate—in the use of the word "great"!

Two of these river and lake systems are still used for water transportation. A great volume of traffic moves along the St. Lawrence River and Great Lakes for about nine ice-free months of the year, serving the people and industries of Quebec and Ontario and the adjoining states of the United States. A much smaller volume of traffic uses the Mackenzie River system of the Northwest for about three months of the year. Recall the comparison and contrast in intensity of use and population densities between these two lowland regions noted in the section on landforms (pp. 34-35). If the physical characteristics of lowlands and water transportation have been important to the people and economy of the Great Lakes-St. Lawrence region, what influence might they have on the future of the Mackenzie River valley?

The drainage patterns of the Canadian Shield and Cordillera are discussed in the regional chapters. The lengths, volumes and directions of flow of these rivers have been important in the past development of log transport in one (which one?) of these regions, and these physical characteristics are significant now to hydro-electric power development in both.

Offshore Water:
Canada's national boundaries have been extended 370 kms. offshore for certain purposes, mainly control and management of fisheries. The physical characteristics of the areas beneath these offshore waters vary on our three coasts. A broad continental shelf slopes gently downward off the east coast; sunlight penetrates into this shallow water and produces plankton, the food for millions of fish. Canada's right to manage the fisheries above the continental shelf has been recognized internationally — even though the fish migrate into and out of the region to waters which Canada does not control. However, "ownership" of the resources within the continental shelf, both in Canada and elsewhere, such as petroleum and perhaps metallic minerals, is still in debate — not only among nations, but locally between the federal and provincial governments within Canada.

There is no broad, shallow continental shelf on the west coast. The submerged, fiorded coast of British Columbia has relatively deep water offshore and is lined with many hilly offshore islands — all of great appeal to tourists. There is a different type of fishery, and different species of fish in the contrasting physical environments of the west coast and ocean, compared with the east coast.

Another broad, shallow continental shelf extends northward into the Arctic Ocean. The numerous straits and channels between the Arctic islands are generally shallow, but they have sufficient depth for the passage of strengthened ocean vessels. The main physical hazard is not depth of water, but ice cover for nine to twelve months of the year. The political status of the ice-covered ocean north of Canada is not clear. Some federal government maps show a political boundary line extending north from the Yukon-Alaska boundary to the North Pole, and north of the channel between Greenland and Ellesmere Island, indicating that this wedge of the Arctic Ocean belongs to Canada. Other written statements say only that Canada claims any islands that may be found within this pie-shaped area. In either case, the use of the Arctic Ocean is minor.

Physical Environment Interrelationships

One of the methodologies of physical geography is to study the interrelationships among the various elements (or components) of the physical environment, both in process and in area. In this book, interest in the distribution patterns of the physical environments in regions of Canada encourages the study of associations in area rather than in processes. One should look at places where physical environment patterns are similar or related and, in particular, observe how people fit into this interrelated total natural envi ronment. This "man-land" theme will appear in every regional chapter.

Another reason for studying the physical environment is to see how people *use* it. Distribution variations in the types and qualities of the natural environment should result in distribution variations in the amounts and uses of our natural resources. The natural environment is the basis of our natural resources depending on the decisions which people make about the uses of these environments. For example, various rocks are the sources of different minerals; diverse soils, plus different climates, can produce a range of agricultural crops; grasslands are a basis for ranching and forests supply a variety of wood products. Water probably has the widest uses — and conflicts — in the process of turning an element of the natural environment into a natural resource: for example, water is used for fish (and fishermen), for hydro-electric power, for agricultural irrigation, for transportation, for domestic drinking water and for industrial processing. Which use should have the highest priority in particular areas? Who makes these decisions? The use of water is one of the major "man-land" relationship problems.

THE EVOLUTION OF RURAL AND URBAN SETTLEMENT PATTERNS

THEMES

1.) Some discussion, with examples, of the many relationships among people and their physical (natural) environments in the process of settling Canada. Two contrasting distributional patterns in Canada are balanced — large areas with few people versus small areas with many people.

2.) The distribution patterns and characteristics of the various elements in the natural environments have helped or hindered, encouraged or discouraged the settlement of rural Canada, mainly in the 19th century. How much of the outer limits of the effectively-occupied parts of southern Canada are controlled by physical environment conditions?

3.) The areal relationships between the distribution of present large cities and the past distribution of agricultural land is discussed. Most large cities of Canada have grown in the midst of surrounding agricultural lands and in areas of former high rural population densities. Urban population increase is parallelled by outward areal expansion onto some of the best agricultural land.

4.) The metropolitan cities and their supporting hinterlands are central nodes in an interlinking urban network within the Canadian economy. They have a hierarchy of size gradation and often a geometric pattern of even spacing.

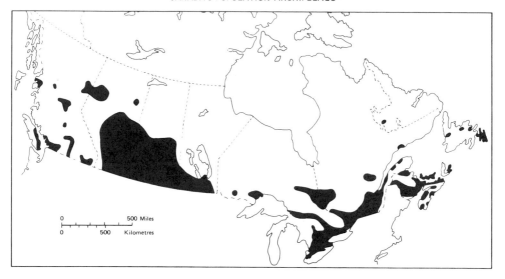

NATIONAL SETTLEMENT PATTERNS

The areal pattern of distribution of population in Canada has been compared to an archipelago of people amid a sea of rocks and forests (see map above). These islands of higher population density are strung across the southern part of the country. Each "island" has one or more large cities and is surrounded by various sized areas of agricultural land with lower population densities. One of the problems of Canada's economy, related to its geographical patterns, is the lack of coalescence of these dispersed areas of population; they may never come together.

The islands of population are separated from one another by physical environments which have not been attractive to settlement, particularly to agricultural settlement in the 19th century. The linear hills of the Appalachians separate the dispersed, small patches of population in the Maritimes from the large area of high density population in the St. Lawrence Lowlands. A southern extension of the Canadian Shield to the St. Lawrence River separates the population concentration of Quebec from that of south-western Ontario. The rocky Canadian Shield rims the north shore of Lake Superior and has been a century-old barrier between the high population concentrations of "eastern" Canada and the lower densities of "western" Canada. The largest continuous area of occupied land in Canada spreads across the southern Prairie Provinces in a wedge which broadens from east to west. It, in turn, is separated from the islands of settlement in British Columbia by the Rocky Mountains. The dispersed pattern of settlement clusters in the Cordillera is similar to the fragmented pattern of people in the Atlantic and Gulf region.

This areal pattern of settlement was established in eastern Canada by about 1900 and in western Canada by about 1940. The distribution pattern has not changed significantly since then; population numbers, and therefore densities, have increased, but not the distribution patterns. What is "wrong" with the rest of Canada if so much area is not fully occupied by people?

Population, like other phenomena, should be considered on at least three scales—national, regional and local. In the following sections, population distribution is discussed at both the national and regional 'scales, and as agricultural and urban populations. It is recognized that "population" is an inclusive term and there will be few specific references to such topics as national origins, religions, incomes and occupations which describe particular characteristics of this population. All of these are valid topics for specific classroom discussion and in-depth analysis of variations in Canada's population distribution.

AGRICULTURAL SETTLEMENT

Introduction

About 25 million Canadians occupy a narrow strip 150 to 300 kilometres wide across the southern part of the country. How and why did this pattern evolve? Is there something unattractive about the remainder of the country since it is sparsely occupied? In terms of agricultural settlement—the reason why most people came to Canada in the 19th century—there *is* something "wrong" with much of Canada; it does not have favourable combinations of environmental conditions for farming. About 90 percent of Canada is classified as having unfavourable soils, climate, landforms or drainage conditions which inhibit agricultural crops. Not all immigrants were farmers. Other people who migrated to Canada were concerned with fur, fish and forest resources in some particular areas, and many people came to the small towns and cities to perform trade, industrial and service occupations. However, physical environment conditions which encouraged or hindered the agricultural crops of that time were important influences on broad settlement patterns.

Agriculture is no longer the major occupation of Canadians; farm population decreased greatly as city populations increased. Although the area of farmland in Canada has not changed greatly in total in recent decades, this national figure masks the opposing internal trends of *decreasing* acreage in the east and *increasing* cultivation in the west. One needs to be careful, however, in interpreting trends which resulted from the several changes in the definition of a census farm. Although the *area* of cultivation did not decrease as farm mechanization increased, fewer people were needed on the farms to produce the crops. Was increased farm mechanization a reaction to decreased farm labour available or a cause of decreased numbers?

Most of Canada's present large cities arose in areas that are surrounded by, and supported by, agricultural land; some of these cities grew because they supplied and serviced this nearby agriculture. However, all cities have other industrial, commercial and service functions which may not be related to local agriculture. Nevertheless, the areal association between urban distribution and farmland area needs exploration and explanation.

Settlement of Eastern Canada

Atlantic Provinces:

The hilly landforms of the Atlantic and Gulf region offered few large blocks of level land attractive to large numbers of agricultural settlers. Whereas in the valleys and lowlands of the Maritime Provinces, the warmth of summer temperatures, ample precipitation and a sufficient frost-free season were permissible for agriculture, along coastal Newfoundland cool summers and a lack of soil were deterrent environmental conditions. In the Maritimes, small valleys with narrow strips of alluvial soil and patches of level land around the heads of bays and inlets supported the first settlers who often combined farming, fishing and logging activities. Agricultural settlement was therefore dispersed. The exception to this fragmented pattern was on the broad, rolling lowland of Prince Edward Island and along the long valleys of the St. John and Annapolis-Cornwallis rivers. Service-centre towns were established in these more favourable areas to serve agriculture, but most other settlements around the coasts were dependent on trade or some other resource base.

The distributional characteristics of dispersal and fragmentation were negative influences upon the prosperity of agriculture for several decades in parts of the Atlantic Provinces. The area of occupied and cultivated farmland decreased steadily in this century due more to economic and cultural influences rather than any change in environmental conditions. Large local markets of prosperous urban people never developed.

Farms which had been cleared in the forests during the 19th century could not survive in their marginal locations and under marginal economic conditions after about 1960. Farm abandonment was common. Rural poverty was one of the notorious characteristics of the Atlantic Provinces in the middle of this century, but it was concentrated in particular places. A significant change occurred in the rural landscapes and farm economy in these poverty areas; between the census years of 1961 and 1976, almost 50 percent of the farmland was abandoned in south and southwestern Nova Scotia, Cape Breton Island, north and eastern New Brunswick, and the east and south sides of Gaspé Peninsula. Although some of this abandoned land had marginal physical environmental qualities for farming, abandonment also took place on some good quality land—for social and economic reasons and due to the decrease in local infrastructures to supply agricultural needs.

Quebec:
French-speaking settlers occupied the plains along the St. Lawrence River in southern Quebec. Physical environmental conditions were generally favourable:

1.) although soils were not fertile everywhere on this lowland and poor drainage was sometimes a problem, much of the land was usable;
2.) the average frost-free season was longer and the number of growing days above 5°C much greater than in most of the lowlands of the Atlantic and Gulf region;
3.) although annual precipitation was slightly less than on the east coast, it was still ample for crops.

Agriculture was established over large areas on the Quebec Lowland, characterized by the distinct narrow, long-lot subdivisions of the French-Canadian habitants (discussed in Chapter 5). The cities which grew on the Lowland (for a variety of reasons) received much of their food, particularly dairy and livestock products and vegetables, from surrounding farms. These large local urban markets permitted Quebec lowland farmers to maintain a relative prosperity. The feeding of almost three million people in Montreal alone required large areas of Quebec farmland.

Agriculture was more difficult to establish in Quebec in the more restrictive natural environments of the Canadian Shield to the north and the hilly Appalachians to the south. Agriculture developed in dispersed patterns in these two latter landform regions. The negative characteristics of the Shield's physical environment (for agriculture) were obvious. Agricultural settlement across central and northern Quebec is improbable in the harsher environments north of the Lac St. Jean Lowland and the Clay Belt; large areas of level land are lacking, soils are mainly sand and gravel, drainage is poor, summer temperatures can be cool and the frost-free season is short. Much of the farmland cleared by generations of hard labour in the Appalachians and Shield was marginal, both in location and economy; abandonment began early in this century and accelerated after 1950. Rural poverty in Quebec was consistently associated areally with regions of limited physical environments for agriculture. A rural way of life and its associated cultural and social conditions changed rapidly after 1960. About 80 percent of the people of Quebec now live in urban places. The survival of the small settlements established across the southern Shield, north of the level land of the Lowland, depends on some other element in the natural environment, usually mineral or forest resources.

Ontario:
The lowland across southern Ontario has more favourable natural environmental conditions for farming than does southern Quebec:

1.) the area of contiguous level land south of the Canadian Shield in Ontario is larger than that in the Quebec lowland;
2.) the average frost-free season is longer—in fact, the longest in eastern Canada is in the peninsula of southwestern Ontario;
3.) precipitation decreases from east to west across Ontario becoming an occasional problem in the southwest where insufficient amounts of rainfall are received in some summers;
4.) the Ontario lowland has more fertile soils and fewer drainage problems than does southern Quebec.

Both regions were originally covered with continuous stands of deciduous or mixed forest which required several decades of hard work to clear. By the end of the 19th century, most of the land across southern Ontario physically suitable for farming was occupied.

Many villages and towns arose in southern Ontario as processing centres for nearby agricultural products; they also supplied services to the farmers living nearby. This areal, functioning relationship between agriculture and small towns was established from the beginning of settlement; it is an important part of the social and cultural history of Ontario at the beginning of this century. Certain of these towns grew into cities, usually because of better transportation, which brought a variety of resources from a wider hinterland to be processed in the town and then redistributed. This theme is discussed in Chapters 6 and 8. The geographical patterns of southern Ontario are dominated by the greatest concentration of urban people in Canada and supporting these cities is the best combination of environmental conditions for agriculture in eastern Canada. Is this agriculture so prosperous because of the market or because of the environment—or part of both?

Conflicts between urban and rural land uses have become critical in some parts of southern Ontario. The decrease in farmland and cultivation in eastern Canada has been of two types:

1.) the abandonment of land of marginal physical environments, chiefly in parts of Quebec and the Maritime Provinces;
2.) the conversion of good quality farmland to urban uses around the large cities of the lowlands of southern Ontario and southern Quebec.

Statements about the "loss" of agricultural land may be controversial and relate to the viewpoints of local groups. A loss of farmland may be considered as a gain by urban residents and businessmen. Measurement of the scale of this conversion, or change, of land use may have two stages and is sometimes difficult to record; farms are sold near large cities and the land may cease to produce and lie idle for a few years before being put into urban uses. One should also remember an opposing trend; decreased farm acreage near large cities is balanced by increased yields per acre on other farms because the availability of large nearby urban markets permits greater use of fertilizers and other intensive production methods (discussed in Chapter 6).

The rocky hills of the Shield of central and northern Ontario are not suitable for agricultural settlement, with the exception of small areas of level land which are the bottoms of former glacial lakes. Most landform, climate, soil, drainage and vegetation conditions in the Shield are unattractive and usually repelling to persons seeking agricultural land. Similar to that in Quebec, agricultural settlement on the Ontario Shield occupied strips and pockets of land. As in the marginal lands across most of eastern Canada, farm population and the area of cultivated land decreased noticeably after about 1950. Sufficient food for Ontario cities can be produced in the fertile Great Lakes Lowland (or imported from even more favourable environments in the United States) so little profit can be made by farmers on the poorer lands of the Shield. Settlements in the Ontario Shield are based on the mineral, water and forest elements in the natural environment rather than on the landform, climate and soil elements there. The Shield environment offers resources to people, but this environment does not favour agriculture. These themes are discussed in Chapter 7.

Summary:

A theme in the preceding pages was regional differences in the combinations of environments available to agricultural settlers in eastern Canada. These differences influenced the distribution patterns and densities of people who made decisions about the use of these environments for farming.

What do you think about the concepts of "environmental determinism"[1]

---

[1]"Environmental Determinism" is a controversial philosophy in geography which was debated in the early part of this century. It stated that the physical environment *determined* what people could do. Some geographers were not so "deterministic" and said that the physical environment gave strong *suggestions* to those in agriculture who cared to look. Cultural geographers, and others, objected to determinism saying that people were offered choices by the environment and could make good, or bad, decisions about the ways they used their environment. One of the advocates of modified determinism was the late Canadian geographer, Griffith Taylor. His beliefs were stated in his text whose title indicated his theme, "Canada, A Study of Cool, Continental Environments." The word "determinism" is seldom used now, being replaced by the words "influences of."

The debate in geographical philosophy continues in another form as to how much (and how measured?) people are *influenced* by (or ignore) their natural environment in their activities. In addition, many people now look at the other side of the question—how much do people influence or affect their environment?

in the man-land theme? For example, did the less favourable environmental conditions for agricultural settlement in the Canadian Shield direct the flow of British settlement through southwestern Ontario into the more attractive agricultural lands of central United States? Can we determine how many ancestors of present-day Americans were *attracted* from Canada by good farmland in the mid-west of the United States or *repelled* by their perceived knowledge of the harsh environments of Ontario's Shield? Was the influence of the physical environment a push or a pull?

Regional changes in the amount of cultivated land in Canada over the past 20 years are recorded in the following table. The notable decrease in cultivation in eastern Canada appears to have levelled off in the Atlantic Provinces and Ontario, suggesting that most of the marginal farms have now been abandoned. Increased cultivation acreages are still being added across western Canada. For example, the *increase* in improved land across the Interior Plains in the 20 years is greater than the *total* cultivated area of Ontario.

Table 1

Regional Changes in Improved (Cultivated) Acreages,
1961-81 (in Thousands of Acres)

	1961	1971	1981	CHANGE 1961-81
Eastern Canada				
Atlantic Provinces	1,800	1,400	1,440	−360
Quebec	7,800	6,500	5,800	−2,000
Ontario	12,000	10,900	11,100	−900
Total	21,600	18,800	18,340	−3,260
Western Canada				
Prairie Provinces	80,000	88,000	93,000	+13,000
British Columbia	1,300	1,700	2,300	+1,000
Total	81,300	89,700	95,300	+14,000

Settlement of Western Canada

The Interior Plains:

The largest area of level land in Canada stretches across the Interior Plains part of the Prairie Provinces. Because of their interior location, these lands had to await transportation improvements which made them accessible in this century to land seekers from Ontario and Quebec and to immigrants from crowded Europe. The favourable physical environments of level land and lack of forests were balanced by negative conditions such as a short frost-free season and low annual precipitation. A different type of agricultural economy evolved in these environments which differed from those of the

Great Lakes-St. Lawrence Lowlands and Western Europe. Many of these resulting adaptations were achieved by trial and error methods.

Between about 1890 to 1940, most of the land suitable for grain and pasture was occupied across the grasslands and settlers had moved north into the adjoining area of parkland vegetation. Refer back to the map on p. 39. The northward penetration of farmers slowed as they entered a forest environment which had poorer soils, still shorter frost-free seasons, and they were faced with increased costs of cutting trees. The agricultural frontier ceased to advance after 1950, but *within* the occupied agricultural area both farm abandonment and consolidation became common. New areas of cultivation are still being opened up as a result of irrigation (in the dry areas), more efficient, mechanical bush clearing (in the forested areas), and new crops and farm consolidation throughout the region. One of the major differences between eastern and western Canada in geographical patterns of agriculture is the decline of acreages in the east and the increase in the west. What are some of the reasons for these contrasting areal patterns and trends?

Increased urban population in the Plains cities has had little impact upon the general patterns of agriculture because most crops and livestock produced in the region are for export. With the exception of some mining towns, most of the population of the Prairie Provinces lives within the area of agricultural settlement. Although farm population has declined in the region, as elsewhere across Canada, farming remains relatively more important on the Interior Plains than in other Canadian regions (discussed in Chapter 8).

The Cordillera:

The Cordillera of British Columbia is not a major agricultural region and its settlement history is different from that of other parts of Canada. Level land in the mountainous Cordillera is quite limited in amount and dispersed, similar to the lack of level land in the Atlantic Provinces. Because people came to British Columbia mainly for fur, forest, fish and mineral resources, the settlement process was different. The Cordillera was settled mainly by "urban" people—that is, people who lived in small communities to utilize a local natural resource. Most farms were established to feed people working in these other economic activities, rather than as "pioneer" agricultural settlement in itself. Despite the small amount of arable land in British Columbia, cultivated acreage and the number of farms are still increasing because of the market in the rapidly growing urban population (discussed in Chapter 9).

Physical environmental conditions influence patterns and types of agriculture in British Columbia, as elsewhere in Canada. The small coastal lowlands and valleys have favourable conditions, including the longest frost-free season in Canada. Although annual precipitation is too abundant in some areas, fortunately, lesser amounts fall during the summer growing season. However, these same favourable environments for crops also promote luxuriant forest growth; therefore, most of the lowlands and lower mountain slopes distant from the big market of Vancouver remain in forest cover or are being logged over. Relatively small areas are cleared for farming.

Agriculture in the southern interior valleys, hindered by lack of precipitation, requires costly irrigation; farther north, the narrow strips of level land in the valleys have sufficient precipitation, but a shorter frost-free season. The northern part of the Cordillera is virtually empty. Is the lack of agricultural settlement there due to the unfavourable combination of environments or to a lack of transportation and accessibility?

The direction of flow of settlement in the Cordillera was different from that east of the Rocky Mountains. Settlement penetrated inland and eastward from the southwest corner of the province, unlike the westward waves that peopled the Prairies. Also, British Columbia was partially settled by people from different source areas. Whereas areas east of the mountains were occupied by Europeans, British Columbia received a sprinkling of immigrants with different cultures from East and South Asia. However, very few of these Asians looked for agricultural land; they became urban dwellers.

The North:

Northern Canada has virtually no agriculture and very few people. Undoubtedly, the strips of level land along the Yukon and Mackenzie river valleys have environmental limitations; the frost-free season is short, precipitation is scanty, soils are poor. However, vegetables grow well and some hardy grain and pasture crops did mature in the past, when there was a local market in Dawson City at the beginning of this century. Most present "agriculture" is only gardening. The North does not produce enough food to feed people in the small towns which are based on other resource developments.

Summary:

The main concept of the preceding section is the coincidence between areas of favourable natural environmental conditions for agriculture and most of the present population of Canada. In the 19th century, while most of the good land suitable for agricultural settlement was being occupied, this areal association was direct and probably the result of cause and effect relationships. Agriculture has been, and is, influenced directly by the distribution and character of elements of the physical environment. Geographers are interested in the influences of the natural environment upon peoples' activities — in this chapter, on one particular activity, agriculture. In this approach, there always is danger that too much explanatory power will be given to physical environmental influences; cultural, transportation and market influences may be neglected. The environment does not *determine* how people use it; it only presents choices. People, in their wisdom or folly, make these choices and the natural environment is only *one* of the factors considered.

URBAN POPULATION

Introduction

Whereas agriculture covers a large *area* across southern Canada, the land supports relatively few people compared with the high density of people in the small areas of cities. Almost 80 percent of Canadians live in urban places (defined by the census as a place with more than 1,000 inhabitants). Therefore, further discussion of population distribution must focus on the distribution and density of cities. Cities are not evenly distributed across Canada; some regions have many cities, others have few. What are some of the reasons for these distribution patterns?

Cities are the centres of regions or hinterlands. Some of the occupations of people in cities are dependent on the resources of nearby areas. An understanding of the functional interactions between cities and their surrounding regions helps to explain some of the similarities and differences in the regional geography of each part of Canada.

CANADA'S 25 LARGEST METROPOLITAN CITIES, 1976

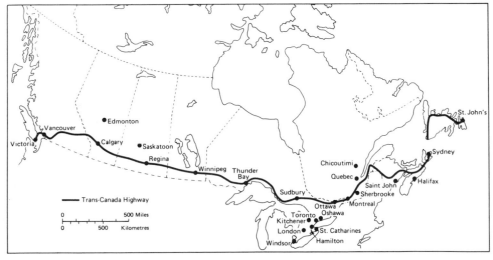

It is difficult to define a "large" city in Canada, since large (in *population* rather than area) means different things to different people. The Canadian census defines metropolitan cities as those with more than 100,000 people, but the census also compiles population totals for metropolitan areas with smaller populations. These metropolitan areas usually include more than one political city and are often a cluster of adjoining towns or cities with separate political administrations. The name given to the metropolitan area is usually that of the largest political city. As large cities expand outward areally, former rural villages or small towns may be included into a new definition of a metropolitan area. Thus, the *areas* and populations of metropolitan cities may not be comparable from one census to another. In addition, there are many examples of *declines* in populations of the original political cities while the figures for the metropolitan areas show *increases*. This latter trend was particularly noticeable in 1981 in several metropolitan cities.

Similarities of Canadian Cities

Canadian cities have a great deal of internal similarity in their forms and functions—as, indeed, do most Anglo-American cities. For example, the downtown cores of tall office towers and nearby high-rise apartments look about the same in Halifax, Toronto, Edmonton or Vancouver. There may be internal differences in the number of buildings and their height, but their physical appearance and urban functions are similar. The industrial and manufacturing plants look very much the same in most Canadian cities and they have comparable locations within them: older industrial buildings, often made of brick, are on railway lines or harbours and are close to the city's commercial core; new industries, often low and spreading, are located on the edges of the city and near highways. These commercial and industrial areas are obvious and mapable in every city, but the amounts of each and their significance vary from city to city.

What gives a city its "character"? Is one city different from another because of its physical setting—is distinctiveness due to the rivers, beaches, hills, mountains or the "natural" setting of its parks? Are certain architectural styles or building materials more dominant in certain cities or regions? Although each house may look different from its neighbour, are the combinations of house styles nearly the same in most Canadian cities? If one travels across Canada or looks at Canadian cities in pictures, is there anything in residential architecture that a non-professional would recognize as being typical of eastern or western Canada?

This book discusses only a few large cities, and mainly to observe them as part of larger regions or to compare them. It would be too lengthy to describe or explain *why* each large city has grown or to discuss the hundreds of smaller Canadian cities. A few cities are discussed briefly as examples in the regional chapters, suggesting that similar methodology be used to study other cities of interest to readers. Each city has specific and different reasons for its establishment and for its increase in population and areal growth.

Hierarchy of City Size

The distribution of cities by population falls into a size hierarchy, as is common in other countries. The following table lists the 27 largest metropolitan cities of Canada in order of population size, leaving breaks between the cities of over 1,000,000; over 500,000; and over 200,000 (refer to Table 2, below). In line with the concepts of scale, how does one define Canadian cities as national, regional or local?

Table 2

Population of Metropolitan Cities of Canada, 1981, and
Numerical Increase in Population, 1971-81.

CITY	POPULATION 1976	INCREASE 1971-76	POPULATION 1981	INCREASE 1976-81
Toronto	2,804,000	200,000	3,000,000	196,000
Montreal	2,803,000	72,000	2,830,000	28,000
Vancouver	1,167,000	84,000	1,270,000	103,000
Ottawa-Hull	694,000	73,000	718,000	24,000
Edmonton	555,000	60,000	657,000	102,000
Calgary	470,000	67,000	593,000	123,000
Winnipeg	580,000	28,000	585,000	5,000
Quebec	543,000	41,000	576,000	33,000
Hamilton	530,000	27,000	542,000	12,000
St. Catharines-Niagara	302,000	16,000	305,000	3,000
Kitchener-Waterloo	273,000	24,000	288,000	15,000
London	270,000	17,000	284,000	14,000
Halifax	268,000	18,000	278,000	10,000
Windsor	248,000	-1,000	246,000	-2,000
Victoria	220,000	24,000	234,000	14,000
Regina	151,000	11,000	165,000	14,000
St. John's	145,000	13,000	155,000	10,000
Saskatoon	135,000	7,000	155,000	20,000
Oshawa	135,000	15,000	155,000	20,000
Sudbury	157,000	-700	150,000	-7,000
Chicoutimi-Jonquière	129,000	-2,000	135,000	6,000
Sydney - Glace Bay	124,000	-1,000	122,000	-2,000
Thunder Bay	120,000	7,000	122,000	2,000
Sherbrooke	110,000	12,000	117,000	7,000
Saint John	113,000	6,000	114,000	1,000
Kingston	91,000	5,000	114,000	23,000
Trois Rivières	98,000	1,000	112,000	14,000

The above 27 metropolitan areas have a total population of 14,022,000 which is 55 percent of Canada's population.

Canada has only two major, dominating metropolitan centres—Toronto and Montreal. These cities, each with about three million inhabitants, dominate the economies of their large nearby regions in Ontario and Quebec and their influences spread over much of Canada. They are *national* cities. The next largest city, Vancouver, is less than half the population of the two largest cities. It dominates the economies of a region which has fewer people than in the Heartland of Canada. Is Vancouver a *regional* city rather than a national city because of its smaller population or because of its peripheral location? Is there a relationship between a city's large population and the large area and population of its hinterland?

The next group of six cities are about half the population of Vancouver, each having more than 500,000 people. These latter cities are centres of sub-regions and are of great importance to local areas. These are *regional* cities rather than national cities. They are not clustered, but are spread across the Great Lakes-St. Lawrence Lowlands—Quebec City, Ottawa and Hamilton—and on the Interior Plains—Edmonton, Calgary and Winnipeg. The significance of these cities within their regions is discussed in the regional chapters.

A geometric progression of decreasing city population size is further illustrated in the preceding table. Six cities, having about 200,000 to 300,000 people each, are also about half the population of cities in the preceding group. Twelve cities with about 100,000 to 150,000 population are about half the size of the preceding group. Why is there an apparent regular, geometric ordering of city size across Canada, with each group of cities being double (or half) the population of the next group? Is there a relationship between numerical size of cities and areal population distribution? This geographical concept is discussed further in Chapters 6 and 8.

Table 3

Metropolitan cities of between 50,000 - 100,000 population, 1981
(Excluding Cities Considered as Part of Larger Metropolitan Areas)

Moncton	98,000	Shawinigan	63,000
Brantford	88,000	Barrie	61,000
Sault St. Marie	87,000	St. Jean	61,000
Peterborough	86,000	Nanaimo	58,000
Sarnia	84,000	North Bay	57,000
Guelph	78,000	Drummondville	55,000
Kelowna	78,000	Lethbridge	54,000
Prince George	68,000	Cornwall	53,000
Kamloops	65,000	Medicine Hat	50,000
Fredericton	65,000		

The largest cities increased in population at a very high rate after the 1950s, but the *rate* of increase levelled off in the 1970s. Compare columns 2 and 4 in the preceding table for exceptions to this generalization. Some of the central cities which give their names to the metropolitan areas are no longer increasing in population. (See population tables in the regional chapters.) The conversion of residential land to commercial and industrial uses in the original city required that residences expand in the suburbs; thus, central city population decreased. Some people think that our big cities are becoming *too* big. What will be the trends in urban population increases in the 1980s?

The 1981 census recorded 19 metropolitan areas with urban populations between 50,000 and 100,000 persons. These populations are all larger than those listed for the political cities, but are more meaningful in describing where relatively large groups of people are concentrated. About half (9) of these "medium-size" cities are located in the Great Lakes-St. Lawrence Lowlands; the significance of these smaller metropolitan areas there is discussed in Chapters 4-6. Four of the medium-size cities in British Columbia appeared on the list for the first time indicating a changing pattern of urban distribution there.

Regional Distribution of Cities

The regional distribution of Canada's 27 metropolitan cities is recorded in the following table, with their population increase noted over the 1961-1981 period. An enlarged Kingston and Trois Rivières joined this list in 1981. The map of 1976 cities (p. 53) shows their locations with reference to the Trans-Canada Highway. Each region has a different number of large cities. There are none in the North. When comparing population increases, recall that the census definition of the area of these cities can change in each census.

Add a fifth column to the right of Table 4 recording the population increase of each of the metropolitan cities in 1976-1981 as listed in column 4, Table 2. Note that some cities increased very little. Convert these figures to an annual average for 1976-1981 and compare this derived figure with the annual average for each city during the 1961-1976 period. Are trends changing?

The largest western cities were still growing rapidly in the 1976-1981 period. Vancouver, Edmonton and Calgary each added 100,000 people to their populations in the five-year period—an average of 20,000 persons per year. In eastern Canada, metropolitan Toronto continued to be Canada's fastest growing city, increasing by 200,000 people between 1976-1981—an average of 40,000 people per year. Other large cities in southern Ontario and Quebec increased by about 15,000-20,000 people—an average of less than 4,000 people per year.

Table 4

Distribution of Metropolitan Cities of Canada by Region, 1981

CITY	1961	1976	NUMERICAL INCREASE 1961-76	1981
1.) Atlantic and Gulf Region				
Halifax-Dartmouth	194,000	268,000	74,000	278,000
St. John's	91,000	144,000	53,000	155,000
Sydney-Glace Bay	107,000	125,000	18,000	122,000
Saint John	96,000	113,000	17,000	114,000
2.) Great Lakes-St. Lawrence Lowlands				
Toronto	1,825,000	2,803,000	978,000	3,000,000
Montreal	2,110,000	2,802,000	692,000	2,829,000
Ottawa-Hull	430,000	694,000	264,000	718,000
Quebec City	358,000	542,000	184,000	576,000
Hamilton	396,000.	530,000	134,000	542,000
St. Catharines-Niagara	155,000	302,000	147,000	305,000
Kitchener-Waterloo	155,000	272,000	117,000	288,000
London	181,000	271,000	90,000	284,000
Windsor	194,000	248,000	54,000	246,000
Oshawa	81,000	135,000	54,000	155,000
Sherbrooke	67,000	105,000	38,000	117,000
Kingston ·	53,000	56,000	3,000	115,000
Trois-Rivières	53,000	98,000	45,000	112,000
3.) Canadian Shield				
Sudbury	110,000	157,000	47,000	150,000
Chicoutimi-Jonquière	105,000	129,000	24,000	135,000
Thunder Bay	94,000	120,000	26,000	122,000
4.) Interior Plains				
Edmonton	338,000	555,000	217,000	657,000
Calgary	280,000	470,000	190,000	593,000
Winnipeg	476,000	579,000	103,000	585,000
Regina	112,000	152,000	40,000	165,000
Saskatoon	96,000	134,000	38,000	155,000
5.) Cordillera				
Vancouver	790,000	1,167,000	377,000	1,270,000
Victoria	154,000	219,000	65,000	234,000

REGIONAL GROWTH AND SIGNIFICANCE OF CITIES

Numerous population figures and percentages are stated in the following section. They cannot be remembered and are for reference purposes. The census figures are presented to illustrate urban population trends and to compare urban growth in different parts of Canada. In themselves, these figures tell one nothing about the geographic characteristics of Canadian cities.

The Atlantic and Gulf Region

Only four of the metropolitan cities of Canada are in the Atlantic and Gulf region. They are dispersed among three of the four provinces; there is no very large concentration of urban people in one place. Each of the metropolitan cities dominates its local region, but none is of *national* significance. Within the region, however, the four cities are now large enough to be markets for the *regional* economy. Can one speculate what the consumer goods manufacturing industries of the Maritimes would be like if there was a consuming and service population of one million people in Halifax — similar to the population and function of Vancouver in British Columbia?

Comments about the distribution of population in Chapter 3 must consider the significance of many "small" towns and cities, some of which are single-industry resource-based towns. These latter towns are dispersed along the coasts and are *not* a large market for either local agricultural products or for local consumer goods manufacturing.

The population increase in the four metropolitan cities in the 20 years, 1961-1981, was 181,000 people—a larger urban increase than the present *total* population of all of Prince Edward Island. In the period of urban growth between 1941 and 1976, Halifax and Fredericton had a high *percentage* of population increase (more than 100 percent) among the six largest cities, and Sydney had the least increase. Although this urbanizing trend indicates changes in the population patterns in the region, these metropolitan cities still held only 30 percent of the Atlantic Provinces population in 1981—a notably lower figure than the percentage of urban concentration in other parts of Canada. This relative lack of urban population concentration is one of the distinguishing characteristics which helps to define the region as being different from other parts of Canada.

The Great Lakes-St. Lawrence Lowlands

The Great Lakes-St. Lawrence Lowlands has the greatest concentration of large cities in Canada. However, the 13 metropolitan centres are less than half of the 27 large cities of Canada, whereas the region is the home of more than half of the total Canadian population. This apparent anomaly is explained by the presence there of the largest number of "medium-size" cities (30,000-100,000 population) in Canada. Together, the medium and large cities form an efficient network which constitutes an "urban system." Movements of people, products and ideas among the interlinked cities of the Lowlands are carried by an elaborate transportation and communications system (discussed in Chapter 6).

The main concentration of urban people in Canada stretches around the western end of Lake Ontario, from Oshawa to St. Catharines-Niagara Falls, in an area sometimes called the "Golden Horseshoe." This densely populated area holds more than four million people, a population about equal to the *total* population of the Prairie Provinces. The second greatest population concentration, almost three million people in Greater Montreal, is larger than the population of the four Atlantic Provinces. These high density population patterns result in other geographical patterns which distinguish the Lowlands region from other parts of Canada. Supporting these many large cities is an intensively-used agricultural lowland with numerous specialty crops. No matter how measured, the high densities of this Heartland of Canada make it the most fully used and occupied part of Canada.

The rapid population increase and allied areal expansion of the Lowlands cities have caused distinctive changes in the internal geographical patterns in the region. The scale of population increase is different from that of other parts of Canada. In the twenty-year period of 1961-1981, for example, population *increase* in the five boroughs of metropolitan Toronto was more than the present *total* population of Manitoba. Another way to state the enormous increase in Montreal comparatively is to note that New Brunswick required almost 200 years to attain a population which Montreal added in the 20 years between 1961-1981. The main purpose of noting these figures is to indicate the great scale of metropolitan city population increase. The total twenty-year population increase in Canada's 10 largest cities is greater than the total present population of British Columbia. During the period of urban expansion, 1941-1976, most of the metropolitan cities increased in population by more than 100 percent, with Toronto having an increase of almost 200 percent. The area of nearby farmland which this increasing urban population is eating up annually is discussed in Chapter 6; several hundred acres of agricultural land were converted to urban uses for every 1,000 increase in city population.

Population increase in Canada, or any region, is made up of three parts:

1.) natural increase—the number of births less deaths;
2.) the number of immigrants less emigration;
3.) internal migration—which consists of the well-known rural to urban movements, and also city to city and region to region movements for employment (or retirement) purposes.

The Heartland of southern Ontario and southern Quebec has been the receiver of most immigrants coming to Canada after 1945, whereas western Canada has been the new home for many migrating eastern Canadians. Migration from the Atlantic Provinces "to the west" was an internal flow for most of this century and, in the 1970s, the westward flow also took people from Quebec and Ontario.

The scale of urban population increase may be difficult to comprehend for people living outside of this heartland of Canada. But, within the region, population growth is obvious in the landscape because of the outward areal expansion of cities. For many miles around each of the large cities, land use has changed from farm and village patterns to urban and potential urban land uses. Will these numerical trends and areal patterns continue in the 1980s? Since most urban planning is geared toward controlling or directing growth, do we know how to plan for decline? Whether or not these changing areal patterns and their social and economic implications should be controlled by governments or the forces of the "open market" is controversial. The changing geographical patterns, however, require political decisions.

The Canadian Shield

Population in the Canadian Shield lives mainly in urban centres; the region has very little occupied farmland. Most of the cities are small and are often single-industry resource-based towns (discussed in Chapter 7). The similar functions and visual appearance of these towns may be compared with the resource-based communities in the Atlantic and Gulf region and in the Cordillera. The only three metropolitan cities in the Shield are dispersed across the south-central part; each is a regional centre which supplies commercial and service functions to nearby small clusters of people. Their population growth has partially been due to amalgamation with nearby smaller cities rather than a large influx of population. The industrial characteristics of Shield metropolitan cities are quite similar to those of nearby Lowland cities.

The Interior Plains

Despite its popular image as the largest agricultural area of Canada, the Interior Plains holds five of the large cities of Canada. There are far more urban dwellers than farm people in the region. Each city is a *regional* centre for a large surrounding agricultural area. These large cities are farther south than some Canadians visualize; Winnipeg, Regina and Calgary are only 100 to 225 kilometres from the United States border. Manitoba's economy is dominated by metropolitan Winnipeg, which has half of the provincial population. This fact of concentration should indicate something about the low density population distribution in the rest of the province.

Similarly, a popular image of the vast ranchland area of southern Alberta should be tempered by the fact that almost 60 percent of the provincial population lives in the two cities of Edmonton and Calgary. The urban population corridor from Lethbridge to Edmonton is becoming a major population concentration in western Canada. More than 80 percent of the population increase in Alberta, 1941-1981, concentrated into Edmonton and Calgary.

The population increase of the five Interior Plains cities has changed the internal economy of the region. In the 1961-1981 period, their population increased by about 850,000 people—a figure equal to the *total* present population of Nova Scotia. Stated in another comparative way, the population which occupied Nova Scotia after 250 years of settlement was equalled by 20 years of influx to the five metropolitan Plains cities. Local urban consuming markets are now important. In the period 1941-1976, Edmonton and Calgary increased in population by a very large 300 percent—the highest among all metropolitan cities in the 35 years. Winnipeg was already a large city in 1941 and as a result its *percentage* growth rates were notably less than the other Plains cities. The increasing significance of the large Plains cities in the local regional economy and also the parallel decline of small towns and villages is discussed in Chapter 8.

The Cordillera

The Cordillera of British Columbia has only two of the large cities of Canada. Eighty percent of the provincial population is classified as urban and about half is concentrated in metropolitan Vancouver. Southwestern British Columbia, including the other large urban concentration, metropolitan Victoria, holds about 70 percent of the provincial population. The negative side of this figure indicates the lack of population in the rest of the Cordillera. Within metropolitan Vancouver, only one-third of the people live in the political city of Vancouver; surburban population has spread northward onto the mountain slopes and southward onto the agricultural land of the Fraser Valley delta. The land use conflict between priority of urban and agricultural uses of the limited amount of level land in southwestern British Columbia is similar to that in the Heartland of eastern Canada.

As an east-west comparison, the rapid population increase in metropolitan Vancouver in 1961-1981 was about equal to the *total* present population of Windsor and London, Ontario. Expressed in another way, four times the population of Prince Edward Island was added to Greater Vancouver in this twenty-year period. Between 1941-1976, Vancouver and Victoria increased in population by about 175 percent. Urban growth is much greater on the west coast than on the east coast.

Population began to increase in the smaller cities of the interior of the

Cordillera after about 1950 when interior transportation networks improved. Many of these settlements are supported by resource-based activities and are similar in function to those of the Canadian Shield. Chapter 9 discusses whether recent population trends have changed the areal patterns of human geography in the region.

The North

Northern Canada has no large cities. Most of the population lives in small settlements of less than 1,000 people, which are not officially classified as urban in the census. There is a myth among some Canadians that we are migrating north in great numbers to exploit the "unlimited" resources of the region, but this is not so. The total non-native population of the two territories, about 45,000 people, only equals that of one small southern Canadian city. Most of these northern residents migrated there after 1945.

Whitehorse holds about 65 percent of the population of Yukon Territory. This urban concentration is therefore similar to British Columbia, Manitoba and Quebec, where about half of the provincial population lives in the largest city; but the numerical *scale* of concentration in the Yukon is much smaller. Urban concentration is not so notable in the Northwest Territories; if one excludes the dispersed native populations, only about one-third of the white population lives in Yellowknife. The native population is relatively more significant in the North region; their changing distribution and their changing social and economic conditions are discussed in Chapter 10.

SUMMARY

Canada's urban population grew rapidly between 1941 and 1981. Population increase was parallelled by outward areal expansion of urban functions which changed local geographical patterns in every region of Canada. The percentages of urban population increase are greater in western Canada than in the east. One should use percentage figures carefully however, noting the actual numerical population of the base figure before growth is measured.

The metropolitan cities are *regional* centres which interact with surrounding agricultural areas. In the following regional chapters, one must look at the functional connections and areal associations between cities and their hinterlands. The internal physical characteristics of cities will seldom be discussed because these are not criteria for the "regional character" of parts of Canada. Canadian cities have a great deal of internal similarity and perform the same urban functions.

Agricultural use of the land was different when Canada was being settled by a dominantly rural population; now agricultural land use is more concerned with supplying food to increasing urban populations, particularly in eastern Canada. This is being done on decreasing areas of farmland and by a decreasing farm population. The physical conditions for, and functions of, agriculture are different in western Canada. Crops are grown mainly for export markets and areas of new cultivation are still increasing.

A theme of this chapter has been the relationships between elements of the physical environment and agricultural settlement, and the relationships between increasing urban population and nearby agriculture. The distribution patterns of both rural and urban people were discussed at the *national* scale. The following chapters comment on how people use these environments on regional and local scales.

REFERENCES

Physical Geography of Canada:

"The Natural Landscapes of Canada" by J. Brian Bird, Wiley, Toronto, 2nd edit., 1980. 260 pages.
"The Canadian Landscape: Map and Air Photo Interpretation" by C.L. Blair and R.I. Simpson, Copp Clark, Toronto, 1967. 172 pages.
"A Provisional Physiographic Map of Canada" by H.S. Bostock, Geological Survey of Canada, Paper 64-35, Ottawa, 1964. 24 pages and map.
Canada Handbook, Statistics Canada, Ottawa.
　1975 edition: "The Impact of Canada's Climates on Agriculture and Forestry," pp. 15-27.
　1976 edition: "Recreation and Tourist Seasons and Canada's Climate," pp. 15-29.
　1979 edition: "The Land (Landform Regions)" by O. Slaymaker, pp. 4-17.
　1981 edition: "Regional Geography of Canada" by J.L. Robinson, pp. 1-17.
"Topographic Map and Air Photo Interpretation" by E.D. Chevier and D.F.W. Aitkens, Macmillan, Toronto, 1970. 184 pages.
"Natural Resources and Regional Disparities," by L. Copithorne, Economic Council of Canada, No. 22-68, Ottawa, 1980.
"Harmony and Discord in the Canadian Environment" by Pierre Dansereau, Environmental Advisory Council, Environment Canada, Ottawa, 1975. 146 pages.
"Physical Geography: the Canadian context" edited by A. Falconer, B. Fahey and R. Thompson, McGraw-Hill Ryerson, Toronto, 1974. 307 pages.
"Climate Canada" by F.K. Hare and M. Thomas, Wiley, Toronto. 2nd edit., 1979. 230 pages.
"Environment: A Geographic Perspective" by F.K. Hare and C.I. Jackson, Geographical Paper No. 52, Environment Canada, Ottawa, 1972.
"Process and Method in Canadian Geography," four volumes of readings edited by J.G. Nelson and M. Chambers, Methuen, Toronto, 1969-70. Vol. 1, Geomorphology. Vol. 2, Water. Vol. 3, Vegetation, Soils and Wildlife. Vol. 4, Weather and Climate.
"Forest Regions of Canada" by J.S. Rowe, Forestry Branch Bulletin 123, Ottawa, Revised 1972. 172 pages and map.
"Wetlands of Canada," Lands Directorate, Environment Canada, Ecological Land Classification Series, No. 14, Ottawa, 1981.

Agricultural Geography of Canada:

Lands Directorate, Environment Canada, Ottawa.
　Land Use in Canada Series.
　　No. 17, The Changing Value of Canada's Farmland, 1961-76. 1979.

No. 20, Urbanization of Rural Lands of Canada, 1966-76. 1981.
No. 21, Agricultural Land Use Change in Canada, 1982.
Working Paper Series.
No. 3, The Influence of Exurbanite Settlement on Rural Areas: A Review of Canadian Literature. 1980.
No. 13, The Agricultural Use of Marginal Lands: A Review and Bibliography. 1981.
No. 22, The Impact of Exurbanite Settlement in Rural Areas. 1982.
"Canada's Special Resource Lands," 1979. 232 pages, 88 maps.
Land Use Programs in Canada Series.
Reports on land use issues and policies in each province, 1974-79.
"For Land's Sake" by David Welch, 1981. 46 pages.
"Agriculture Graphic Presentation (Farming Atlas of Canada)," Statistics Canada, Ottawa, 1980. 135 pages.
"Selected Thematic Maps of Man's Activities in Canada's Watersheds," Statistics Canada, Ottawa, 1980.
"People and Agricultural Land" by C. Beaubien and R. Tabacnik, Science Council of Canada, Ottawa, 1976. 137 pages.
"Soils of Canada" by J.S. Clayton et al, Soil Research Institute, Dept. of Agric., Ottawa, 2 vols. 1977.
"Canada's Farm Population: An Analysis of Income and Related Characteristics" by Paul Shaw, Statistics Canada, Ottawa, 1979. 284 pages.

Urban Geography of Canada:

Isodemographic Map of Canada, Geog. Paper No. 50, Lands Directorate, Environment Canada, Ottawa, 1971. Large map published separately.
"The Correspondence between the Urban System and the Economic Base of Canada's Regions" by Michel Boisvert, Economic Council of Canada, No. 22-60, Ottawa, 1978.
"Urban Systems Development in Central Canada: Selected Papers" edited by Larry Bourne, Univ. of Toronto Press, Toronto, 1972. 243 pages.
"The Urban-Rural Fringe: Canadian Perspectives" edited by Ken Beesley and Lorne Russwurm, Geog. Monographs, Dept. of Geog., Atkinson College, York Univ., Downsview, 1982.
"Changing Canadian Cities: The Next 25 Years" by L.O. Gertler and R.W. Crowley, McClelland and Stewart, Toronto, 1977. 474 pages.
"The Canadian City" by John Jackson, McGraw-Hill Ryerson, Toronto, 1973. 237 pages.
"Canada's Changing Landscape: Air Photos Past and Present" by John Koegler, Air Photo Supplies, Toronto, 1977. 88 pages.
"Urban Problems: A Canadian Reader" edited by R. Krueger, Holt Rinehart, Toronto, 1971. 408 pages.
"Cities of Canada" by George Nader, Macmillan, Toronto, Vol. 1, 1975.

404 pages. Vol. 2, 1976. 460 pages.

"Canadian Urban Trends, National Perspective," Vol. 1, edited by Michael Ray, Ministry of Supply and Services, Ottawa, 1976. 322 pages.

"Canadian Urban Growth Trends: Implications for a National Settlement Policy" by Ira Robinson, Univ. of B.C. Press, Vancouver, 1981. 154 pages.

"Essays on Canadian Urban Process and Form" edited by L. Russwurm and R. Preston, Dept. of Geography Series, No. 10, Vol. 1, 1977; No. 15, Vol. 2, 1980. Univ. of Waterloo, Waterloo.

"The Surroundings of Our Cities: Problems and Planning Implications of Urban Fringe Landscapes" by Lorne Russwurm, Community Planning Press, Ottawa, 1977. 112 pages.

"Perspectives Canada III," Statistics Canada, Ottawa, 1981.

"Urban Canada" by James and Robert Simmons, Copp Clark, Toronto, 2nd edition, 1974. 188 pages.

"Land and Urban Development" by Peter Spurr, James Lorimer, Publishers, Toronto, 1981. 160 pages.

"The Canadian City: Essays in Urban History" edited by G.A. Stetler and Alan Artibise, Oxford Univ. Press, Toronto, 1977. 464 pages.

"Canada's Industrial Space-Economy" by David Walker, Wiley, Toronto, 1980. 261 pages.

"Urban Landscapes" by Eric Winter, Bellhaven House, Toronto, 1969. 148 pages.

"Urban Prospects" by John Wolforth and Roger Leigh, McClelland and Stewart, Toronto, revised 1978. 176 pages.

Some relevant articles by Canadian geographers published between 1970-82 in *The Canadian Geographer*, Canadian Association of Geographers, Burnside Hall, McGill University, Montreal:

Vol. 25, No. 4, 1981.	"Industrial Diversification in the Canadian Urban System" by John Marshall, pp. 316-332.
Vol. 25, No. 1, 1981.	"Metropolitan Dominance and Foreign Ownership in the Canadian Urban System" by Keith Semple and Randy Smith, pp. 4-26.
Vol. 24, No. 3, 1980.	"Some Implications of Recent Trends in the Provincial Distribution of Income and Industrial Product in Canada" by Tait Davis, pp. 221-236.
Vol. 23, No. 2, 1979.	"On Continentalism, Distinctiveness, and Comparative Urban Geography: Canadian and American Cities" by John Mercer, pp. 119-139.
Vol. 23, No. 1, 1979.	"Regional Employment Changes in Canadian Agriculture" by Barry Smit, pp. 1-17.
Vol. 21, No. 2, 1977.	"A Nodal Structure for Canadian Cities" by H.G. Kariel and S.L. Welling, pp. 148-163.

Vol. 20, No. 4, 1976. "Short-Term Income Growth in the Canadian Urban System" by Jim Simmons, pp. 419-431.

Vol. 20, No. 1, 1976. "Natural Resource Developments in Canada, 1970-75" by John Chapman, pp. 15-40.

"La Géographie Sociale du Canada Urbain" by Paul Villeneuve, M. Polèse et S. Carlos, pp. 72-110.

Vol. 16, No. 2, 1972. "The Spatial Structure of Agriculture in Canada—A Review" by Wm. Found and G.T. McDonald, pp. 165-180.

CHAPTER 3

THE ATLANTIC AND GULF REGION

CHAPTER 3

THE ATLANTIC AND GULF REGION

INTRODUCTION

The Atlantic and Gulf region may be characterized geographically by internal dispersal and fragmentation—in its physical environmental conditions, in its resource utilization and in its settlement patterns. Although one of the first parts of Canada (and Anglo-America) to be settled, and with a relatively prosperous economy 100 to 150 years ago, the region has fallen behind other parts of Canada as measured by several national economic indicators. How much of this slower economic and population growth is due to the characteristics of fragmentation and dispersal? How much is due to its geographical position on the eastern flank of the country, separated from the central Heartland and often bypassed by traffic to and from that Heartland?

Two fundamental geographical characteristics of the region are the diversity of physical environments and the lack of large uniform areas. As a result, population is distributed in strips and small clusters and separated by unoccupied areas. There is no single very large urban centre to act as a market, service and supply focus. Many towns are dependent on the development of a single resource and are not able to combine two or more functions to diversify their economy and increase their work force.

The region often ranks at or near the bottom of economic and statistical measurements of development and prosperity in Canada. It has been called "underdeveloped," a region of "poverty," and it certainly has had high rates of unemployment. For many decades, young people migrated out of the region to find jobs elsewhere in Canada or in the United States. According to many local residents, it is a "neglected" part of Canada. This latter view is balanced by contrary evidence of the large amounts of federal funds for economic aid which have been granted to the region. However, the supplying of these funds in themselves indicates the region's needs and deficiencies compared with other parts of Canada.

If the region is characterized by slow economic development, then why do many people stay there? Why do Maritimers and "Newfies" love their region and defend it as an attractive part of Canada? The concept of "regional consciousness" is certainly strongly illustrated by the people in the Atlantic and Gulf region. They *are* different; they *know* they are different and they are proud of it! There are history, tradition and culture in the region which people in a "new" and "young" western Canada may not understand or appreciate.

Many of these economic indicators describe the region as a whole, whereas geographers should study the *internal* areal patterns of these statistics looking for sub-regional differences. Such regional analysis reveals that some centres and areas are as prosperous as other parts of Canada, whereas low incomes and economic problems have been concentrated in other parts. It is possible, therefore, to speak of a "geography of low incomes" in the region, just as there are geographical distribution patterns of other economic activities.

THEMES

1.) To illustrate the distributional concepts of fragmentation and dispersal in the natural environment and in natural resources and their implications for the regional economy.

2.) To illustrate the interrelationships among elements in the physical environment and the direct relationships between the natural environment and its use as a natural resource.

3.) To discuss some characteristics of single-industry resource-based towns and their significance in the regional economy.

4.) To describe the changing geographical patterns of settlement and resource use and to assess the factors influencing change.

DEFINITION OF THE REGION

The Atlantic and Gulf region was defined in Chapter 1 as including the original three Maritime Provinces, plus Newfoundland Island and Gaspé Peninsula. This region is something more and something less than the politically defined four Atlantic Provinces. Labrador is considered as part of the Canadian Shield landform region and is therefore discussed in Chapter 7 because its physical landscapes and resource-based economy are similar to other parts of the Shield and different from Newfoundland Island. It can be argued, on the other hand, that the sparse, dispersed population of coastal Labrador — and its fishing economy — are functionally linked to northeastern Newfoundland Island. Throughout this chapter, the word "Newfoundland" will refer only to the island. Gaspé Peninsula differs in economy, prosperity and landscapes from the heart of Quebec along the upper St. Lawrence River, and is similar in many ways to the landscapes, economies and French-speaking population of northern New Brunswick. The region is therefore also politically fragmented, consisting of three provinces and parts of two others. Various discussions have taken place over many decades about the political union of three, or four, of the small provinces into one, but agreement has never been reached. What are some of the advantages and disadvantages of political union?

POPULATION DISTRIBUTION

The region's population distribution differs from that of some other parts of Canada. It is mainly peripheral. People are distributed in uneven densities around or near the coasts and along the St. John River—the latter can be considered as the western, peripheral edge of New Brunswick. Despite the general coastal distribution, some coasts have only few settlements, such as around the Bay of Fundy (except Saint John), and along the southwest coast of Newfoundland Island. Higher population densities in the Annapolis Valley, for example, are *near* the coast, but not on it. At one time, fishing was a major occupation of these coastal people, but this is no longer so. Most of the interiors of Newfoundland Island, Nova Scotia, New Brunswick and Gaspé Peninsula are sparsely populated or almost empty. Local movement by roads is mainly coastal and peripheral and only a few main routes cross the interiors of each province.

This peripheral population became increasingly urban after 1961 when farm population decreased markedly. Most of the main cities and major towns are on or near the coasts or in the St. John River valley. A linear pattern of large cities curves from Halifax, through Truro, Moncton, Saint John and Fredericton. Many of these urban centres probably have more interaction with foreign places around the North Atlantic Ocean than they do with people in central Canada. On the regional scale, interaction is minor, for example, between Saint John and St. John's, or between Moncton and Sydney. Each large city functions as a sub-regional service and supply centre and the pattern of economic activities remains fragmented.

What have been the influences of the physical environment upon this peripheral settlement? Why have people chosen to live on, or near, the coasts rather than in the interiors? Have the characteristics of the coasts been attractive or have the interiors been repelling? The following sections discuss how people settled the region and supported themselves by using local natural resources and by trading and commerce. The theme is relationships between people and their natural environments.

RELATIONSHIPS IN THE PHYSICAL ENVIRONMENT

Introduction

One of the repeated themes in this book is the interrelationships among elements of the physical environment in particular regions. These links are present in every region and the discussion will not be repeated each time. This methodology is sometimes known as the "ecological" approach. Relationships between the natural environment and natural resources are discussed more specifically in Chapter 7. This can be interesting and exciting for those aware of an "ecological crisis" in society. Geographers are concerned with how people *use* the elements of the natural environment within a region. This book will focus more on the areal variations in these elements than on the explanatory processes. Understanding the close relationships between people and their natural environments may be shallow, if one does not understand the processes that operate within and between the separate elements of the environment. These processes, their relationships and their implications, are not simple. They are discussed in most physical geography texts.

On a regional scale, the general physical landscapes of the Atlantic and Gulf region are different from those of some other parts of Canada, but internally, on the local scale, there are wide variations from place to place. The environment illustrates diversity. The low linear mountains and rugged indented coasts are different landform types than those of the level St. Lawrence Lowlands. The numerous long inlets and bays of eastern Nova Scotia are similar to the fiords of British Columbia on a horizontal scale, but not on a vertical scale. The east coast maritime climate is not the same as that of the rest of eastern Canada and it differs from the maritime climate of the west coast. Trees are similar to those growing elsewhere in eastern Canada, but the way in which they are distributed results in classification as a separate vegetation region. These similarities and differences, compared with other regions of Canada, are apparent to visitors and known by local residents. Are you interested in analyzing them?

Landforms and Geology Relationships

It is not the purpose of the following comments to encourage learning the names of the geological ages of rocks, but to indicate that some knowledge of geology is helpful to understand *why* there are areal variations in the type and distribution of landforms. A distributional association between landforms and population will also be noted. Most people live in lowlands or valleys; the uplands and hills are relatively empty. Why is this so? Is there a causal linking of valleys, alluvial soils, agriculture and population? One of the methodologies of geography is to study areal association as a vehicle of explanation.

The folded, linear geological structures of the Atlantic and Gulf region are part of the Appalachian Mountain system—a series of folded mountains, ridges and linear valleys which occupy eastern North America. In Canada, the mountain part of this system extends through the Eastern Townships of southern Quebec, across northern New Brunswick and Gaspé Peninsula, and appears again in the Long Ranges of western Newfoundland Island. Few people live in these rugged areas because they did not attract agricultural settlers. In contrast to these folded mountains, horizontal strata of Carboniferous geological age underly the flat lowlands of eastern New Brunswick, all of Prince Edward Island and northern Nova Scotia. Farmland was cleared on these lowlands.

Central New Brunswick is another rugged, hilly area—also with few settlements—which is underlain by hard, ancient volcanic rocks of Devonian and Ordovician ages. The low plateau of central Newfoundland, composed of flat-lying rocks of Ordovician geological age, is similar in geology and landforms to the plateau of northwestern New Brunswick. The former is unpopulated, but the latter is well used for agriculture and forestry. These latter land use differences suggest that additional regional differences in climate may be important influences.

As an example of landforms-geology relationships on a still smaller scale, the linear Annapolis-Cornwallis Valley in western Nova Scotia has been eroded out of softer rocks of Triassic age. This narrow, fertile valley contrasts in physical appearance and in human use with the low, rough, forested, unpopulated hills of the uplands of central Nova Scotia, which consist of hard rocks of the Devonian and Precambrian geological periods.

Glaciation has had an important influence upon soils and drainage—or the lack of them—in this region, as in other parts of Canada. However, the effects of glaciation upon agricultural settlement, in particular, are discussed more specifically in other regions. Do you accept the concept that patterns of geology, landforms and agricultural settlement are related?

Climate Contrasts and Controls

Parts of at least two climate regions can be discerned in the Atlantic and Gulf region. Near the coasts, typical maritime characteristics of heavy precipitation and moderate temperatures are found, but inland the climate is continental, with less precipitation, warm summers and cold winters. In addition, at the local scale, diversity is illustrated by micro-climates associated with local landforms; for example, hills are cooler in summer, colder in winter, and receive more precipitation than nearby lowlands. These contrasting coastal and interior climates are similar to those of British Columbia; in the latter region, the vertical contrasts in climate caused by landforms are even more apparent. To *explain* these areal differences, how far does one penetrate into principles of air physics, air mass movements and influences of ocean currents?

A comparative study of maps shows areal relationships between cool summers along the coast and the southward-moving cold Labrador ocean current, which flows close to shore along eastern Newfoundland and Nova Scotia. Winds from the southeast, from air masses passing over this water, are cooled, but these air masses do not usually penetrate far inland because the prevailing movement is from west to east. Inland areas experience cold winter temperatures or warm summer temperatures similar to those in areas farther westward because they are more frequently affected by air masses moving eastward from central Canada or the United States. Differences in inland and coastal winter temperatures are further illustrated by the increasing amount of snow inland, and upward in the hills, compared with rain on the coasts. Have these climatic differences had any past influence upon agricultural settlement?

The longest frost-free periods are recorded near the coasts; these are longer in the Maritime Provinces than in more northerly Newfoundland. The average period without frosts in southern Nova Scotia is as long as that recorded in the agricultural lands of southeastern Ontario. However, this climate advantage is offset by cooler summer temperatures, lack of level land and lack of large markets in coastal Nova Scotia.

Climate influences even extend offshore where sea ice hampers transport off northeastern Newfoundland throughout the winter, whereas the harbours in southern Nova Scotia are ice-free. Will regional differences in offshore climates and ice conditions affect the costs and risks of placing oil rigs on the adjoining continental shelf?

This brief section introduced the topic of air mass movements; one will need to know more about this to understand the climates and their influences in other parts of eastern Canada.

Vegetation and Soil Relationships

Vegetation patterns are partly controlled by climate; and soils are related to geology, landforms and glacial history. These areal relationships, on a broad scale, are more apparent on the Interior Plains and will be discussed more specifically in Chapter 8. Deciduous trees, with their beautiful colours in the autumn, are common in the warmer lowlands and valleys of New Brunswick. Coniferous trees, in varying shades of dark green across the landscape, are the basis of the pulpwood industry; they grow throughout the region, but the number of species is greater in the southwest than in the northeast. Climate and glaciation effects are illustrated by the fact that about 80 percent of New Brunswick and Nova Scotia is forested, but only 35 percent of Newfoundland Island is covered with trees. Cooler summers in Newfoundland, plus more intense and recent erosion by glaciation, reduced the amount of forest cover there. This forest environment has been the basis of differing woodcutting and processing activities throughout the region for about two centuries.

Soils reflect the wide range of variations in the physical environments. They are the end result of complex process interactions between different kinds of bedrock, glacial deposition, vegetation decay and climate—all of which proceed at different speeds within the region. For example, the alluvial soils deposited on the floodplains and river terraces of the St. John River or in the Annapolis-Cornwallis Valley differ from the soils derived from glacial or marine deposition over the lowland of eastern New Brunswick. Visitors to Prince Edward Island recall the photogenic red soils which come from ingredients in the Carboniferous rocks. Although the quality of soils, and associated drainage, varies from place to place in the region, the total soil resource is not being fully used—more for economic reasons than because of physical properties.

A few people came in the 17th and 18th centuries into these interrelated physical conditions of geology, landforms, drainage, climate, vegetation and soils and attempted to make a living from the resources of the land and sea.

DISTRIBUTION PATTERNS OF HUMAN ACTIVITIES

Introduction

During the 19th century, people made a multitude of decisions concerning the ways that they would use the various physical environments of the Atlantic and Gulf region. The present distribution pattern of human activities is the result of these many man-land decisions. Interrelated patterns of roads, houses, fence lines, factories, office towers, parks, etc., were placed upon the natural environment.

These relationships and links to the natural environment are more obvious to rural dwellers and those working in primary industries than they are to city residents and office workers. The largest occupation groups in Canada are the urban dwellers in service and commercial activities and they may see little connection between what they do and their surrounding natural environment, except for recreation. However, some of the distinguishing characteristics of this region are the relatively fewer urban tertiary occupations and the significance of primary industries and their processing, particularly in comparison with the St. Lawrence Lowlands.

The human use geographical patterns which evolved in this region are the results of complex internal and external influences and decisions. Although the physical environment which supports resource-based activities changes very little, the weight and value people place on the external influences are continually changing. The distribution patterns of economic activity are not stable; geographical change is characteristic of all regions.

Forestry

The distribution of forest processing in the region is related to accessibility to the forest base and is influenced by human decisions about processing and marketing. Because most of New Brunswick and Nova Scotia are well forested, the natural resource base is widespread. However, on Prince Edward Island, which is more than half under cultivation, and on Newfoundland, where forest cover is limited, the natural resource is marginal and sawmills are few.

Some principles behind the location of economic activity can be illustrated by the forestry industry. These locative principles are introduced here and should be applied to other industries elsewhere in Canada.

New Brunswick and Nova Scotia:

In the 19th century, most sawmills were built on rivers because water was the cheapest and most convenient means of transporting logs. Because most lumber products, including wooden ships, were for export, the larger sawmills were located at river mouths, or other nearby harbours, where water was deep enough for ocean shipping. As road and rail transport became increasingly available, the need for river location decreased. As elsewhere in Canada, small portable sawmills, dispersed throughout the forest area and operated by a few individuals, gradually disappeared in this century; they were replaced by larger mills, located in towns, usually on the coast, and run by companies. The dispersed distribution pattern, once related more directly to the local availability of the natural resource, changed to a more centralized pattern where the raw material was transported to larger processing facilities. Here, workers could have the amenities of village or town life and the manufactured product could be transported directly to local or international markets.

Early in this century, as market demands changed, the forestry companies found another use for the natural resource in the production of pulp and paper. The distribution pattern of these mills is mainly peripheral because the product was meant to be exported. By this time, also, access to the forest resource was more specifically defined by government concessions and cutting rights, which assigned forest areas tributary to certain mills. However, the ownership of forest land remains fragmented, unlike the large cutting concessions in the Canadian Shield, because much of the Maritimes was settled for agricultural purposes and the land and its forests were already owned by individuals.

The pulp and paper mills of New Brunswick were built on water because it was used not only for log transport, but also water is a raw material in the pulping process. The mills were placed at certain river mouths because the pulp, newsprint or paper products were for export, mainly to the large market in nearby United States. The mills of northeastern New Brunswick do *not* use the rivers for hydro-electric power, as is done in the Canadian Shield. Power in the Maritimes comes mainly from thermal sources. Although land transport of pulpwood is now used as much as water transport, the original river mouth pattern of mills did not need to change. An apparent exception—the mill at Edmundston in northwestern New Brunswick—is not coastal, but it has the same peripheral location and export function; the pulp is exported across (under) the water (river) to the paper mill in the adjoining town of Madawaska in the United States. The only interior pulp mill, a more recent one, at Nackawic in the central St. John River valley, was located there primarily for accessibility to unused forest reserves and because of good land transportation (map on p. 79).

The distribution of pulp and/or paper mill towns in Nova Scotia is also coastal and peripheral. In many of these settlements in both provinces, the mill is the chief source of employment of local residents, and commercial and service occupations are dependent on the prosperity of the mill. Note how much the locative principles related to raw material cutting rights, transportation, power supplies and external markets, discussed for New Brunswick, also apply to Nova Scotia. This same coastal pattern is present in Gaspé Peninsula of Quebec. One element in explaining the peripheral distribution of settlements in the Atlantic and Gulf region is the coastal location of people in the wood processing industries.

PULP AND PAPER MILLS IN THE ATLANTIC AND GULF REGION

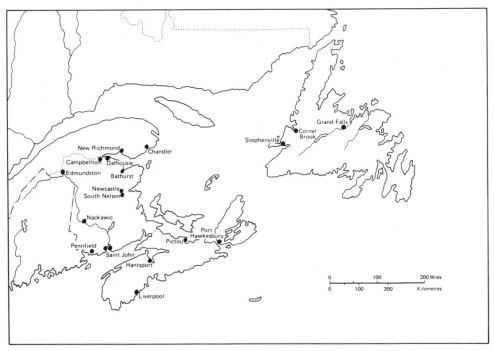

Newfoundland:
   The two older pulp and paper mills in Newfoundland can be considered as specific examples of locative factors in a resource-based industry. The mills at Grand Falls and Corner Brook began production in 1909 and 1925 respectively, and the residences of the workers were built nearby in what could be called "company" towns. The producing companies were given concessions in various areas, not all in one block, to almost 90 percent of the forest land of Newfoundland, mainly in the better-forested western and northern sections of the island. Each company built an adjoining hydro-electric power plant to produce the large amount of power required by a

79

pulp and paper mill. Power transmission technology of that time dictated that the power plant must be near a mill.

Logging camps were dispersed throughout the drainage basins of the Exploits and Humber rivers and these rivers were used for log transport in summer. Logs were also transported along the coasts in certain areas. Logging tended to be a winter activity because of the difficulty of moving on the poorly-drained land in summer. Methods of transportation gradually changed after approximately 1960 when the number of logging roads and use of truck transport increased. Logging was not an important supplementary activity to the dominant fishing industry of the 1930s and 1940s because these industries did not operate in the same places. Logging was an inland activity and fishing was coastal.

At one time, newsprint was exported directly from Corner Brook and Botwood (from Grand Falls) during the summer season and was moved by rail to St. John's or Port aux Basques during the winter. However, new technology and government assistance changed this seasonal pattern of movement by introducing federal government ice-breakers to keep the harbours open throughout the winter.

Single-Industry Resource-Based Towns

The preceding discussion of forestry noted that certain towns are dependent on the processing of forest products. Such towns (also common in mining) are known across Canada as single-industry resource-based towns. Early in the century, they may have been called "company" towns and sometimes a more colourful term, "instant" towns, is now used. They are planned communities and they are established to process the products of one resource. These single-industry towns depend on, and are vulnerable to, world demands for their products. In the Atlantic and Gulf region, these towns are generally older than those in British Columbia and they are not as isolated as those in the Canadian Shield. Compare and contrast the geographical patterns and functions of such towns in various regions of Canada as they are discussed later in the book.

Most of the pulp and paper mills in the Atlantic and Gulf region are the main source of industrial employment in such towns. Commercial and service people are also present, primarily to supply and serve the workers in the mills. Whereas many of the resource-based towns of the Shield and Cordillera lack adjoining agricultural land and other occupations, each of the Atlantic mills has agricultural land nearby to help feed the worker population.

Forestry-based activities are located in two types of towns. Examples of mainly single-industry towns are Campbellton, Dalhousie, Newcastle and Edmundston in northern New Brunswick; Chandler and New Richmond on the south side of Gaspé Peninsula; Liverpool in Nova Scotia; Grand Falls-Windsor in Newfoundland (Table 5, p. 98 for populations). However, not all pulp and/or paper mills are located in single-industry resource-based towns. Corner Brook has grown out of this category as it became a government and educational centre and a supply and wholesale hub for western Newfoundland. Grand Falls is also developing central place supply and service functions for the coastal settlements of northeastern Newfoundland. Similarly, Bathurst was mainly a pulp and paper mill town prior to 1950, but it has since taken on service-centre, supply and administrative functions for northeastern New Brunswick. The mills at Port Hawkesbury and near Pictou in Nova Scotia integrate into larger settlement clusters which include other types of industry. The two mills at Saint John are, of course, part of the broad industrial base of that large city.

Single-industry resource-based towns illustrate two aspects of the regional economy—and geography—the dependence on primary processing and peripheral, dispersed location. When external markets are good, these forestry towns are generally prosperous, producing relatively high incomes for the mill workers. In prosperous times, these towns do *not* illustrate the "poverty" characteristics for which the region may be known across Canada. Can some settlements where fish processing is the main economic activity also be classified as resource-based towns? Further discussion of the character and functions of single-industry resource-based towns is presented in Chapter 7.

Agriculture

The areal patterns of agriculture have changed over time. More farmland was occupied at the beginning of this century than now. Many of these farms were classified as subsistence or part-time farms (rather than commercial farms) and they have since been abandoned; they were located on poorer soils, steeper slopes, or distant from transportation. Many farms were cleared on small parcels of suitable soil and terrain and now cannot be consolidated into large, economic units. In economic terms, such farms are called "marginal," but the word can also be used geographically to refer to their marginal (less accessible) location or their marginal physical environment (less favourable for crops). These farm areas never obtained the agricultural infrastructure of southern Ontario; they lacked services and advice and had poor marketing arrangements; capital investment was low. Rural agricultural poverty was common in many parts of the Atlantic region; the low incomes in these dispersed, marginal farming areas lowered the averages of the whole region. But much of this has changed. Concentration patterns are becoming apparent. Although the changing geography of agriculture has helped to improve the regional economy, in some places rural poverty is being replaced by urban underemployment.

Most of the farms in the rural landscapes of the Maritime Provinces are similar in land use appearance and in farm buildings to those in other parts of eastern Canada. Although the region has a few specialty production areas, much of the land is used for pasture and feed grains for the feeding of livestock, similar to the farms of southern Quebec and Ontario. The regional character of agriculture in the Maritimes does not stem from its type of farm or land use, but is distinguished by the shape of its farmland strips and their areal dispersal. The pattern is fragmented. Except for the landscape of central Prince Edward Island, there are few large areas of continuous farmland and open rural landscapes, as in southern Quebec and Ontario or on the Interior Plains.

In the Maritime Provinces, relative location is significant. The prosperous farms have good transportation and are near the few large cities; the marginal farms lack nearby markets and accessibility. The prosperous areas include large blocks of cleared land — large enough to be called agricultural regions — whereas in the poverty areas the farms are narrow, separate strips, often along secondary roads. Relative location is a factor in rural poverty.

In the decade, 1961-1971, the farm population of the Atlantic Provinces declined by about 50 percent, a greater percentage decline than in any other region of Canada. Similar trends were recorded in Gaspé Peninsula. In 1976, the region had 126,000 fewer people listed in the census as farmers than in 1961 (see Table 1). What happened to these people? Did they move to jobs in cities? Were they older people who retired from farming? Did they leave the region for economic opportunities elsewhere in North America? There is no statistical evidence to fully answer these questions, but most farm abandonment occurred in the areas of former rural poverty, farthest from local markets. Decreasing farm population also affects some towns and villages. Schools and churches may close and businesses are abandoned. The process can accelerate; young people may leave when there are no local facilities for their children. This rural depopulation process is discussed more fully in Chapter 8.

Table 1

Decreased Farm Population in the Atlantic Provinces, 1961-81

PROVINCE	1961	1976	NUMERICAL DECREASE	1981*
Newfoundland	9,000	1,000	8,000	2,500
Nova Scotia	57,000	12,000	45,000	18,000
New Brunswick	62,000	11,500	50,500	15,500
Prince Edward Island	34,500	12,000	22,500	12,000
Regional Total	162,500	36,500	126,000	48,000

* A change in the definition of a census farm in 1981 resulted in an increase in the population on farms. Many of these newly-counted farmers are part-time operators.

Newfoundland:

Farming is a minor occupation in Newfoundland and it differs from that of the Maritime Provinces. Coastal Newfoundland has less favourable physical environment conditions for the production of crops compared with the Maritimes. Level land is scarce in Newfoundland, soils are thin and poor, and summer temperatures are seldom hot. Coastal Newfoundland was settled for its fishing sites; not by people looking for good agricultural land.

There were only 680 farms reported in all of Newfoundland in 1981 and they had only 26,000 acres in crops. Much "farming" really consists of gardening in the many small outport settlements around the coast, particularly along the northeast coast and around Avalon Peninsula. Because the definition of farming in the census requires a minimum size of land to constitute a "farm," it can be misleading in recording the amount of food production in Newfoundland. The many gardens which provide important supplemental local food for people in low income fishing villages are not included in the census.

Nova Scotia:

Small, fragmented patches of agriculture are located near most of the coastal settlements of Nova Scotia. In the 19th century, some farms were cleared in the forested, hilly upland of central Nova Scotia, but most of these are now abandoned. As in Newfoundland, but to a lesser degree, level land is scarce around the coast, soils are stony and poor, except in the alluvial strips of river valleys. However, summer temperatures are warmer in Nova Scotia than in coastal Newfoundland and the frost-free season is sufficient for pasture and grain crops. The more prosperous of this type of dispersed agriculture has survived near the urban markets of Sydney-Glace Bay and near Truro which has access to the large Halifax market. The large livestock barns and well-kept farmhouses near Truro, for example, are similar to those in southern Ontario, except for the lack of silos in Nova Scotia. Halifax, unlike Vancouver on the west coast, does not have a large adjoining lowland to feed this large urban population.

Table 2

Distribution of Improved (Cultivated) Land in Nova Scotia, 1981

REGION	ACRES	PERCENT
Northumberland coast-Chignecto	193,000	44
Annapolis-Cornwallis	165,000	38
Southwest counties	34,000	7
Cape Breton Island	25,000	6
East coast	23,000	5
Total	440,000	

The distribution of cultivated farmland is shown in the preceding table. Almost half of the land is spread along the coast of Northumberland Strait and along nearby inland roads. There are no large areas of cleared land; most farms report low incomes.

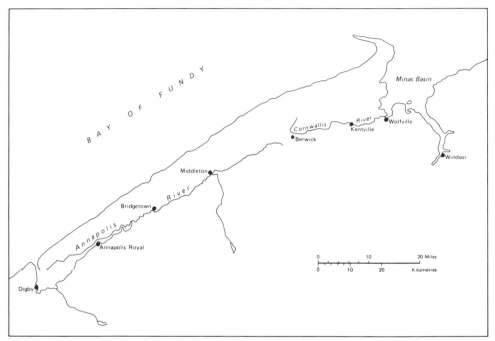

The well-developed agriculture along the Annapolis and Cornwallis rivers in western Nova Scotia is an exception to the pattern of dispersal. Although known locally and nationally as the Annapolis Valley, the largest area of cultivation and the larger towns are in the eastern end of the valley, through which the short Cornwallis River flows; the Annapolis River flows westerly in the narrow part of the valley. The Annapolis-Cornwallis Valley is an example of changing patterns of agriculture in a sub-region of the Maritimes (see map above).

Farming was developed by the French-Acadians in the 18th century. By the 1930s, the Annapolis Valley had become one of the three major apple producing regions of Canada and a major exporter, chiefly to Britain. During 1940-1950, when this export market was lost, economic conditions in the valley became severely depressed. The economic problem of depending on one main crop and one market became very apparent. Federal and provincial aid had to be given to the farmers, resulting in some changes noted below.

1.) Farmers were paid to reduce the number of trees on their farms in order to decrease production; more than one million apple trees were removed. However, most of the trees removed were old ones and they were gradually replaced by new trees with better yields and more popular varieties. Many marginal apple farms which had only a few trees ceased production altogether and the industry concentrated into fewer and larger farms with greater yields per acre (see Table 3). The total amount of cultivation decreased, but more food was produced. Much of the Annapolis Valley remains in forest cover, particularly in the central and western sections, indicating that the relatively small Nova Scotia market does not require the use of all physically suitable land in the valley. The Annapolis Valley has a different rural landscape from that of the other fruit regions of Canada—the Niagara Peninsula and the Okanagan Valley. Read case studies as to *how* these regions differ.

2.) The fruit industry turned to processing and began to produce more apple products, such as apple juice and apple sauce, for the eastern Canadian market. These processing plants were located in several small towns in the valley, giving new employment opportunities, and resulting in population increase and the areal growth of these towns. Some of these towns which had been mainly supply-service centres for nearby farms also became small industrial towns. On a small scale, this was the same rural-urban process and relationship that had developed in southern Ontario early in this century. For example, almost continuous commercial settlement, and highway-oriented establishments, line the old highway between Wolfville and Kentville. Note the population of "metropolitan" Kentville in Table 5, p. 98. The expansion of urban land uses has raised problems of how to protect agricultural land— problems which are better known, on a larger scale, in the Niagara Peninsula of Ontario and in southwestern British Columbia. The controversy over the location of a new multi-lane highway across agricultural land, which can also serve the urban settlements, was similar to the debate a few decades earlier about the Queen Elizabeth highway through the Niagara fruit lands.

3.) Farms broadened their crop base to supply the food needs (dairy, poultry, vegetables) of nearby Halifax. The eastern part of the valley is the largest area of level land with good soils near the region's largest urban market in Halifax-Dartmouth; it became the agricultural hinterland of that urban area. Thus, the Annapolis-Cornwallis Valley reduced its dependence on one-crop exports and diversified its economy. A drive through the picturesque valley, with its interesting historical sites, prosperous-looking farmhouses and variety of land uses, illustrates that this region is not a "poverty area" of the Maritimes.

The following table illustrates these trends and changes. Kings county is a statistical unit representing the eastern part of the valley; and Annapolis county occupies the western part. Study the interrelated rural and urban trends in the two parts of the valley. The change in the definition of a census farm in 1981 resulted in an increased number of farms and cultivated acreage.

In the eastern part, Windsor is not included in the sub-region, but could be considered as the "gateway" to the valley. Windsor is a service centre for the dairy farms along the highway to Halifax and also a transit centre for traffic between Halifax and the Annapolis Valley. The concept of gateway settlements is discussed in Chapters 7 and 8.

Table 3
Internal Changes in the Annapolis-Cornwallis Valley

	KINGS COUNTY			ANNAPOLIS COUNTY			
1951	1971	1976	1981	1951	1971	1976	1981
Total population							
33,000	45,000	48,000	49,700	21,800	22,000	23,200	22,500
Urban population							
9,300	20,700	21,000	20,900	2,500	4,400	5,000	3,800
Farm population							
10,600	4,100	2,300	2,800	7,700	2,200	940	1,300
Rural non-farm population							
13,300	20,500	24,300	26,000	11,400	15,300	17,300	17,400
No. of census farms							
2,100	900	600	800	1,800	515	275	375
Improved acreage							
95,500	78,000	76,000	86,000	48,300	31,500	30,500	34,200
Apple acreage							
15,500	9,500	9,400	9,400	2,900	900	950	780
No. of tree-fruit farms							
900	415	275	350	400	115	70	70

POPULATION GROWTH OF TOWNS

Eastern Part	1921	1941	1961	1971	1976	1981
Metro Kentville					19,200	21,000
Kentville	2,700	4,000	4,600	5,200	5,100	5,000
Wolfville	1,750	1,950	2,450	2,900	3,100	3,240
Berwick	—	960	1,300	1,420	1,700	1,700
Western Part						
Middleton	875	1,200	1,925	1,870	1,820	1,830
Bridgetown	1,090	1,020	1,050	1,040	1,040	1,050
Annapolis Royal	830	780	800	760	740	630
Digby	1,230	1,660	2,300	2,360	2,540	2,560

New Brunswick:
The distribution patterns of agriculture in New Brunswick have also been changing from dispersal to concentration. Total cultivated acreage and farm population decreased greatly between 1961-1976, as elsewhere throughout the region. About two-thirds of the farm acreage is now in the St. John River valley (see Table 4). The more prosperous farms are in the Moncton-Sussex-Saint John-Fredericton strip—along the main highway and near the largest local markets for dairy and livestock products. Many of the low income farms in the eastern, northeastern and southwestern parts of the province have been abandoned. East coast and Gaspé Peninsula farmers often tried to combine three occupations: they fished during part of the summer and logged in winter, in addition to working a small farm. They often had little economic success in any of these occupations. Abandoned farmhouses and scrub trees growing in former pastures are now typical of the rural landscapes along secondary roads.

Table 4

Distribution of Improved (Cultivated) Land in New Brunswick, 1981

REGION	ACRES	PERCENT
Central and Upper St. John River Valley	230,000	49
Southeast	101,000	21
Southwest and Lower St. John River Valley	96,000	20
Northeast	46,000	10
Total	475,000	

Most of the commercial farms are in the St. John Valley. In the south, dairying is the main farm type, supplying fresh milk to the urban centres of Saint John and Fredericton. In the north, mixed farming is common with potatoes as the main cash crop. Although the growing of potatoes was once dispersed throughout the province, most of the production is now in north-western New Brunswick; this concentration has been aided by the building of local processing plants. In turn, the establishment of these plants has encouraged farmers to grow other vegetables under contract to the processing companies. Such products are now sold all across Canada and abroad. Thus, similar to changes in the Annapolis Valley, the expansion of agricultural processing added employment to certain small towns, such as Grand Falls, and accelerated the rural to urban migration. This process is going on in many parts of southern Canada and can be studied in depth in many local areas.

Gaspé Peninsula:

Mountainous Gaspé Peninsula is similar to Newfoundland Island in that most of its land is mapped by the Canada Land Inventory as Class 7, not suitable for agriculture. Agricultural settlement around the edges of the peninsula, like that of northeastern New Brunswick, is in small patches where the forest has been cleared, on dispersed bits of level land near river mouths, or around sheltered bays.

In the past, farming survived because off-farm income could be obtained from nearby winter logging and summer fishing. As in the former farm-lands of northeastern New Brunswick, people are moving out of these economically marginal part-time occupations in the Gaspé; as a result, in both sub-regions, about 50 percent of the cultivated acreage was abandoned in the 15 year period from 1961-1976. The largest areas of cropland are along the south side of the peninsula, near Chaleur Bay, where the land is lower, and in the transverse valleys of the Matapedia and Temiscouta rivers which are the routes of the only main roads across the peninsula.

Agriculture in Gaspé Peninsula is marginal, both in location and econo-mically. There are no large urban markets in the sub-region, and competing agricultural lands nearby in the St. Lawrence Valley and the St. John Valley are better endowed environmentally and have local markets. Many people of Gaspé obtain more summer income from the tourist industry than from agriculture.

Prince Edward Island:

Prince Edward Island has been called the "garden province" because it is small and much of its area is used for agriculture. More than half of the province has been cleared of the original heavy forest. The agricultural economy is mainly concerned with livestock and livestock products, but the chief cash crop is potatoes for export off the island. The picturesque rural landscape of central Prince Edward Island is well known to tourists; the red soils, blue waters, green fields of hay, pasture and feed grains, and white farmhouses and churches are most photogenic! But there are regional differences in agriculture even on this small island; in the western and eastern parts, soils and drainage arc poorer, forest cover increases, and farms are more dispersed and less prosperous. Diversity of geographical patterns is apparent even in the small area of Prince Edward Island.

Summary:

The theme of man-land relationships should be dominant in a study of the geography of agriculture. The influences of, and areal differences in, landforms, drainage, vegetation, soils and climate have effects on agriculture. These are negative influences in some places, such as Newfoundland, and positive attractions in other places, such as the St. John Valley. Despite the permissive physical environment in many parts of the Maritimes for agriculture, and the large amount of land now unused for crops, why does the region still import part of its food from central Canada or from the United States? Individuals make the decisions as to how to use this varying physical environment; sometimes these are good decisions, sometimes they are not. Therefore, man-land relationships are continually changing and the geographical patterns which depict these relationships on the earth's surface are also changing.

Location concepts were stressed in the preceding comments on forestry and agriculture. Although the physical environment may favour, or handicap, agriculture, it is the *location* of farms with relation to markets in towns and large cities which is often decisively important. Could you predict the geography of agriculture in the Maritimes if Halifax held half of the population in the region?

Fisheries

Offshore of eastern Canada, the broad, shallow continental shelf, above which warm ocean currents from the south mix with cold ocean currents from the north, presents an excellent physical environment for the production of plankton and fish. Europeans have come to these waters as a source of food since the early days of discovery, exploration and settlement of Canada. They first established temporary settlements for the drying and salting of fish; many of these evolved into permanent villages. Most of the fish caught were taken back to the crowded, food-deficient countries of western Europe, and later, also, to people in the Caribbean area.

The distribution pattern of fishing settlements has been changing, particularly in Newfoundland. Throughout the region, the number of full-time fishermen has declined steadily, a trend similar to the decreasing number of farmers across Canada. Whereas fishermen were reported to constitute almost half of the working force in Newfoundland in the 1920s and 1930s, they were less than five percent of the work force in the 1970s. (Note, however, that there are problems in the census in defining full-time and part-time fishermen, similar to the problems of defining full-time and part-time farmers.)

Newfoundland:
About 90 percent of the people of Newfoundland Island live on or very near the coast. The island was settled by British fishermen who came mainly to the east and northeast coasts, closest to England. French fishermen had rights to dry their fish at shore stations on the south and west coasts at various early times and, therefore, British fishermen did not settle along these coasts. As a result, about two-thirds of Newfoundland's population is dispersed along the northeast and east coasts; 40 percent is concentrated around Avalon Peninsula. This general distribution has changed little

since 1951, except for minor percentage increases in west coast and western (interior) Labrador settlements. Within the coastal distribution pattern, however, changes are occurring as some places are abandoned and others increase in population.

FISHING BANKS AND SOME FISH PROCESSING CENTRES

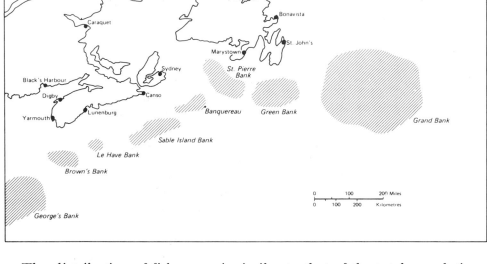

The distribution of fishermen is similar to that of the total population; about two-thirds are dispersed in small villages along the east and northeast coasts. They do *not* live beside the famous Grand Banks, contrary to the belief of many Canadians; the Grand Banks, and other adjoining fishing banks, are south and southeast of Newfoundland, whereas the fishing population lives mainly on the northeast (study the map above). For the past two centuries and more, most Newfoundland fishermen were "inshore" fishermen who fished close to shore; only a few used the Grand Banks, and some went to the coast of Labrador. Schooners from St. John's and from Burin Peninsula did go out to the Grand Banks to compete there with the international fishing fleets from Europe, but most inshore fishermen were too poor to own schooners and other large boats that were needed to fish in the offshore banks.

There are regional differences in the Newfoundland fishery. The southeast coasts have a longer ice-free season and more offshore vessels; herring supplement the catches of west coast fishermen; seal catching is important to some Northern Peninsula settlements; the Labrador fishery is pursued from many northeast settlements.

The typical small "outport" settlements of a few hundred people were dispersed unevenly along the numerous bays, headlands and islands. Small, square, two-storey frame houses were scattered near the shore so each family had access to its small docks, drying flakes and nearby fishing sites. The tiny settlements had no rectangular street pattern so well known in other Canadian villages. There were no sewers, few roads, many small elementary schools, but few secondary schools and almost no health or medical facilities. Rural poverty was characteristic of these small, dispersed fishing settlements and educational and health standards were low. These economic and social conditions of outport people lowered the *average* incomes of the population of the Atlantic Provinces. It seems likely that the dispersed patterns helped to perpetuate social and economic problems. Therefore, if social and economic conditions in these settlements were to be improved, it seemed wise to try to change the geographical patterns.

Several concurrent changes have been taking place in the Newfoundland fishery, and in fishing settlements, aided by federal and provincial financial assistance.

1.) Loans and other financial aid were given to fishermen and fishing companies to obtain larger boats and more efficient nets and gear to permit fishing farther offshore. As a result, Canadians increased their percentage of the international catch on the Grand Banks, and nearby banks to the south, and also on newly-discovered banks northward off Labrador. Offshore, or "banks" fishermen average much higher incomes than do inshore fishermen. This trend towards increased offshore fishing was accelerated when Canada claimed the right to manage the fisheries within a 200 mile (370 km.) zone off the east coast. The impact of increased offshore fishing is greatest in the settlements on Burin and Avalon peninsulas in the southeast; but increased offshore catches may have caused decreased inshore catches.

2.) Centralization is occurring in the areal pattern of fishing settlements. Several hundred small outports were abandoned after 1951; the residents moved, with government financial assistance, to larger settlements where new fish processing plants were built. Whereas the industry once produced mainly low priced salt or dried cod, it now sells higher value, fresh, frozen or processed fish products. Their market is mainly in the United States, which has higher average incomes than the former Caribbean and Mediterranean markets. The fish processing plants had to be located in settlements large enough to have a labour supply and in sections of the coast with enough fishermen to keep the plant operating for much of the year. Thus, certain settlements grew in population and others declined or were abandoned as a result of the change to centralized fish processing. The primary fishing population declined as many former fishermen became industrial workers in the fish plants. But, unfortunately, both fishing and fish processing remain seasonal occupations which give low annual incomes.

This change in geographical patterns and occupations is controversial in Newfoundland. The social and family disruptions in the moves were not always balanced by increased incomes in larger towns. Rural poverty has often been replaced by urban unemployment. However, the physical appearance of the new settlements is much more attractive than the old outports. New, low, ranch-style houses — similar to those in the rest of urban Canada — have replaced the distinctive old outport house; medical facilities and secondary schools have been placed in the larger towns. Most of the towns in the northeast now have access by road to the interior Trans-Canada Highway. Isolation has gone.

The similarities in areal trends and processes in both agriculture and fishing in the Atlantic Provinces should be apparent. In both industries, more processing is being done in local towns, which become places of employment and residence for formerly dispersed primary workers. Geographical patterns have changed. Will these trends continue?

The Maritime Provinces:

The Maritimes have a geographical location advantage in an international context because the processing plants in southern Nova Scotia and southern New Brunswick are closer to the large United States market than those of Newfoundland. However, fishing is *relatively* less important in Nova Scotia compared with Newfoundland, because the former has a greater variety of other resources and occupations. Almost half of the fishing population of Nova Scotia is distributed around the south (or southwest) coast, in Shelburne, Yarmouth and Digby counties, where they are near the offshore Georges, Browns and Sable Island banks to the south and east (see map, p. 90). Canada shares offshore fishing with New England fishermen in the United States and political discussions were lengthy as to which country had prime rights to the scallop, and other, fishery over the Georges Bank.

Nova Scotia fishermen live in small towns unlike the tiny villages of Newfoundland. Most settlements are at the heads of bays and inlets where there is shelter for the boats. The fishing towns in Nova Scotia have different landscape characteristics than those of Newfoundland: agricultural clearings and farms are nearby; forests cover the hills; streets are laid out in rectangular patterns; there is a central commercial core. Most houses have a garden nearby, and the pile of firewood in the yard is a reminder of the value of wood as a rural fuel in a region of high-cost energy.

Nova Scotian fishing boats were modernized some years ago to take advantage of the offshore banks fishery; large processing and freezing plants, producing mainly for the nearby United States markets, were built in several towns. These fish processing towns, such as Lunenburg, Yarmouth and Digby, are primarily supported by the catching and processing of fish, and are similar in function to single-industry resource-based forestry towns. The centralization of the fishing industry, which is still going on in Newfoundland, is almost complete in Nova Scotia.

Fishing is of less significance as a primary industry in New Brunswick, Prince Edward Island and Gaspé Peninsula. A well-developed herring (sardine) fishery supports a few towns around the Bay of Fundy, but in contrast, on the east coast of New Brunswick and around Gaspé Peninsula, the dispersed fishery has been of marginal economic value. These are the poverty areas of the region. Despite being surrounded by water, most of the primary workers on Prince Edward Island are engaged in agriculture. Lobster catches are significant to the fishermen of all three provinces fronting on Northumberland Strait, but otherwise the fish resources of the Gulf of St. Lawrence are less plentiful than those of the shallow waters of the Atlantic Ocean.

Some of the notorious economic characteristics of low incomes and seasonal unemployment of the Atlantic and Gulf region are in the fishing industry, but these characteristics vary internally within the region and changes in geographic patterns are occurring. Compare the geography of the Atlantic fishery with that of British Columbia in Chapter 9. The two coastal regions have different physical environments, different types of fish and different distribution patterns of fish processing plants.

Mining

Mining is less important in the primary economy of the Atlantic and Gulf region than in some of the other regions of Canada. Most of the mines are on or near the coast, thus fitting into the general geographical pattern of coastal or peripheral resources and settlement. Much of mineral production is for export out of the region, hence a reason for coastal location. Mining can be difficult to discuss in geographical terms; mineral development is often controlled directly by geology and economics. These principles are discussed more fully in Chapter 7.

Because the Appalachians are composed of rocks of a variety of geological ages and types, there is a wide range of mineralization—metallics, non-metallics and fuels. However, except for coal, few large deposits have yet been found.

The Sydney-Glace Bay bituminous coal fields of Cape Breton Island have been in production for most of this century. Their geographical location on the eastern flank of Canada is an economic problem; they are far from the industrial markets of the St. Lawrence Lowlands. However, the coal has had local value as a raw material and a power source in the economically marginal iron and steel industry at Sydney. Because of high world oil prices for imported petroleum, the Cape Breton coal fields, and other small coal deposits in Nova Scotia and New Brunswick, may have increasing regional importance in the near future as sources of local energy. Time will tell whether or not the critical energy deficiency of the Atlantic and Gulf region will be alleviated by the use of petroleum and/or natural gas from the east coast continental shelf, or by pipelines from Montreal and the faraway Interior Plains.

Like the mining industry elsewhere in Canada, only first stage processing of mineral resources is done within the region, and the products are exported elsewhere to manufacturing markets. For example, the lead-zinc deposits of northeastern New Brunswick are smelted near Bathurst and then exported; crude gypsum is exported from Nova Scotia and potash from southern New Brunswick. Most mines do not support single-industry resource-based towns similar to those discussed in the Canadian Shield in Chapter 7. Most of the few mines in the region are located near previously occupied settlements and have supplied alternate occupations to some residents. In summary, except for the Cape Breton coal fields, mining has had little direct impact upon regional settlement patterns.

Manufacturing

One of the major economic problems of the region is the lack of manufacturing industries producing for the national market. A regional population of about three million people is not a large consuming market compared with the population concentrations in the Great Lakes-St. Lawrence Lowlands. In addition, the east coast population is dispersed along thousands of miles of coasts and a few interior valleys. Because many of this population had low incomes in the past, they were not big markets for consumer goods manufacturing.

Manufacturing in the region can be classified into three types:

1.) The dispersed processing of natural resources discussed earlier in the chapter. Much of this processing is done in single-industry small towns having a coastal or peripheral distribution pattern. One of the themes of this chapter was the areal relationships between the location and extent of the natural resource and the location of processing centres. These industries include pulp and paper, lumber, fish products, processed apple and potato products, partly processed minerals and steel products. The most successful of these industries have been able to find and maintain international markets, thus taking advantage of their east coast location.

2.) Industries based on imported raw materials. These industries include such plants as oil refineries, sugar refineries, chocolates, automobile assembly and tires. Some of these industries take advantage of their coastal location to assemble raw materials and then send the processed goods inland. Tax reductions, and other incentives from governments, attracted some industries to the region. Most manufacturing is located in the large port cities, but some special industries have been established in small towns such as Port Hawkesbury and Bridgewater. One may include in this type of industry the employment in the container transfer activity in the ports of Halifax and Saint John. Manufacturing based on imports must compete, of course, with Montreal, whose industries can also import the same types of raw materials and are closer to the consuming markets in central North America. The lengthening of the navigation season through the Gulf of St. Lawrence and along the St. Lawrence River by the use of federal government ice-breakers decreased the advantages of coastal location for east coast ports and cities.

3.) Consumer goods for the local markets, such as food products, publishing, home furnishings and appliances, etc. Most of this manufacturing employs residents in the region's six largest cities: Halifax-Dartmouth, Saint John, St. John's, Sydney-Glace Bay, Moncton and Fredericton. The cities themselves are major consumers of such products, and each city also has surrounding sub-regional retail and wholesale hinterlands. This type of local manufacturing competes rather poorly with the greater volume and variety of goods which come into the region from the larger industries in the cities of central Canada. Sales within the Atlantic region are influenced by management decisions of manufacturers in the Heartland and by freight rates between the regions.

Successful manufacturing depends on several related ingredients: raw materials, power, labour, transportation, markets and good management. These are discussed more specifically in Chapter 6. The Atlantic and Gulf region lacks ample and cheap power.

The few large rivers in the region are already used fully for hydro-electric power and little future expansion seems possible. Utility companies within the region turned to thermal power based on imported petroleum during the 1950s when the latter seemed to be abundant and cheap, but this situation has changed. Alternate power sources are now being considered and these choices will probably be political decisions:

    1.) nuclear power is controversial;
    2.) greater use can be made of local coal resources;
    3.) perhaps the enormous power that can be obtained from
the high tides in the Bay of Fundy will be harnessed for use in
the future.

How many of the "depressed" economic characteristics of the Atlantic and

Gulf region are due to its hinterland position and function with regard to the Heartland of Canada in the Great Lakes-St. Lawrence Lowlands? Manufactures from the Lowlands' industrial cities can apparently be produced and delivered more cheaply to east coast consumers than they can be produced locally. Many management decisions of national corporations are made in Lowlands' head offices rather than in regional branch offices. Would higher freight rates on transportation from the Lowlands decrease the flow of manufactured goods or simply increase local costs of living to consumers? Although control and domination of the Heartland may sometimes be resented, it is also recognized that federal financial support from the Heartland has greatly aided many aspects of the regional economy. How much inter-city and inter-provincial rivalry, rather than cooperation, is due to the dispersal of people and activities in the Atlantic and Gulf region?

CITIES

Regional Character

The internal areal patterns of the major cities in the Atlantic and Gulf region will not be discussed here. Canadian geographers have written few descriptions of these cities and there are only a few comparative studies which analyze the regional urban system and its urban functions. Each city, like other cities across Canada, supplies services and consumer goods to nearby sub-regional hinterlands.

The large cities of the Atlantic and Gulf region are not much different from those elsewhere in Canada and they do not constitute a main element in the "regional character" of the area. It is true that the closely-packed streets of gaily-painted frame houses in old St. John's are unique in Canada, but the new bungalows on the western edge of the city near Memorial University look the same as in suburbs all across Canada. The age and architecture of some of the old brick commercial buildings in downtown Halifax are not duplicated elsewhere in Canada, but stores along the commercial streets and in the suburban shopping centres are repeated in most Canadian cities. The small frame homes of industrial workers in Sydney look about the same as those in closely-packed rows in Hamilton or Sault Ste. Marie. The stately elms along the riverfront streets of Fredericton are memorable landscape features, but most of the houses, stores, industries and government buildings there are no different in appearance or areal pattern from those across Canada. The landscaped grounds and attractive low buildings of the new industrial parks on the west sides of Moncton and Dartmouth produce the same types of consumer goods and secondary industrial products as similar industrial parks in other Canadian cities.

Halifax-Dartmouth has more than twice the population of any of the next group of sub-regional cities (see Table 5). It is undoubtedly the prime city of the region, having the largest concentration of manufacturing, port activity and volume, commercial retailing and wholesaling, and government and educational institutions. In addition, the presence of the federal government is very significant in the economy of the urban area. Many of the economic and cultural activities of Nova Scotia focus on Halifax; there are no major competing centres as there are in New Brunswick.

Comparison of Halifax, Montreal, Vancouver — Port Cities

Areal patterns of urban land use in metropolitan Halifax are similar to those of Montreal and Vancouver, its competing large ports. Industrial buildings and facilities, served by both water and rail transport, line the outer harbour of Halifax and extend along the eastern part of Dartmouth on the north side of the harbour. Similarly, an industrial zone adjoins the harbour of Montreal Island and expands to the east side of the St. Lawrence in Longueil and St. Lambert; and the industrial strip along Vancouver's harbour is duplicated on the north side of Burrard Inlet in North Vancouver.

In all three cities, the original commercial cores adjoined the harbour industrial area and, as newer commercial areas expanded inland, these old "city centres" have been restored and are promoted as historic tourist attractions. Modern high-rise office towers look the same in each city — the differences are in the number of them and their height.

All three cities have central landform features from which a visitor may see much of the urban land-use patterns from one place. The Citadel is a historic fort and museum crowning a low drumlin hill south of Halifax's city centre; from it one has a panoramic view of the harbour facilities and Dartmouth to the north, and the varied residential areas of Halifax to the south, east (to the universities) and west. In Montreal, Mount Royal is an old volcanic plug which rises a few hundred feet to the west of the downtown core; its grassy slopes and walks lead to a spectacular lookout over the universities and the commercial office towers, and beyond to industries along the St. Lawrence River and former Lachine Canal. In the centre of Vancouver, another ancient volcanic plug, now called Queen Elizabeth Park, juts up 300 feet; the former quarry there is now a colourful, year-round flower garden from which visitors can look north over the city centre to the scenic backdrop of the North Shore mountains.

As one travels about Canada and visits other cities, look for similarities in urban land use patterns. Although each city has a different physical site, they have many internal similarities in the ways that their industrial, commercial and residential land uses are distributed and related areally to each other.

Table 5

Main Urban Centres in the Atlantic and Gulf Region, 1981

NOVA SCOTIA	POPULATION 1976	1981	NEW BRUNSWICK	POPULATION 1976	1981
Total	830,000	848,000	Total	678,000	697,000
Metro Halifax	268,000	278,000	Metro Saint John	113,000	114,000
Halifax	117,000	115,000	Saint John	86,000	80,500
Dartmouth	66,000	62,000	Metro Moncton	95,000	98,000
Metro Sydney	124,000	122,000	Moncton	56,000	55,000
Sydney	31,000	30,000	Riverview	14,000	15,000
Glace Bay	22,000	21,000	Dieppe	7,500	8,500
New Waterford	9,300	8,800	Metro Frederiction	61,500	65,000
Sydney Mines	9,000	8,500	Fredericton	45,000	44,000
North Sydney	8,400	7,800	Metro Bathurst	23,000	24,000
New Glasgow cluster	38,000	40,000	Bathurst	16,300	16,000
New Glasgow	10,700	10,500	Metro Edmundston	21,000	22,000
Stellarton	5,400	5,400	Edmundston	12,700	12,000
Pictou	4,600	4,600	Campbellton	9,300	9,800
Metro Truro	38,000	40,000	Oromocto	10,300	9,000
Truro	13,000	12,500	Chatham	7,600	6,800
Metro Kentville	19,200	21,000	Newcastle	6,400	6,300
Kentville	5,000	5,000	Grand Falls	6,300	6,200
Amherst	10,300	9,700	Sackville	5,700	5,700
Yarmouth	7,800	7,500	St. Stephen	5,200	5,100
Bridgewater	6,000	6,700	Dalhousie	5,600	5,000
Antigonish	5,500	5,200	Woodstock	5,000	4,700
Springhill	5,200	4,900			

PRINCE EDWARD ISLAND	POPULATION	
Total	119,000	122,500
Metro Charlottetown	26,000	24,700
Charlottetown	17,000	15,300
Metro Summerside	15,300	15,000
Summerside	8,600	8,000
Sherwood	5,600	5,700

NEWFOUNDLAND	POPULATION	
Total	558,000	568,000
Metro St. John's	144,000	155,000
St. John's	87,000	84,000
Mt. Pearl	10,000	11,500
Metro Corner Brook	32,300	32,000
Corner Brook	25,200	24,200
Grand Falls-Windsor	15,200	14,500
Metro Carbonear	12,500	13,000
Carbonear	5,000	5,400
Gander	9,300	10,400
Stephenville	10,300	9,000
Marystown	6,000	6,300
Port aux Basques	6,200	6,000

GASPÉ PENINSULA, QUEBEC	POPULATION	
Rimouski	28,000	29,000
Matane	12,700	13,600
Mt. Joli	6,500	6,400
Ste. Anne des Monts	6,000	6,000
Percé	5,200	4,900
Grande Rivière	4,400	4,400
New Richmond	4,200	4,200

Other Atlantic Region Cities

The group of separate political units that make up the Sydney-Glace Bay urban area has an industrial emphasis which is different from the other large Atlantic cities. The metropolitan area has similar functions to those of the smaller single-industry resource-based towns of the region and like those of the Canadian Shield. The marginal economic viability of both the coal mining and steel making industries has given high unemployment rates to the area for several decades.

Smaller versions of the Sydney industrial area are located in the cluster of towns near the Canso Causeway and in Stellarton-New Glasgow. Neither of these small industrial clusters seems to have much growth potential.

Three major cities divide up the industrial, commercial and institutional functions in New Brunswick, and therefore none is as large as Halifax. Saint John is the gateway to the prosperous St. John River valley and the transfer port for products coming into and going out of the province. But the market for its retail and wholesale commercial activities is limited by the proximity of Moncton and Fredericton in its immediate hinterland. Saint John lost some of its transportation significance as eastern Canada's main winter port when it became possible to keep the St. Lawrence River open to winter traffic. Both Saint John and Halifax have tried to counter this loss of winter rail traffic by improving container facilities, thus taking advantage of their coastal locations.

Moncton has a crossroads or "hub" position in the Maritimes. Because of its location near the narrow isthmus connecting New Brunswick and Nova Scotia, railroads and roads converge there. The city attracted a diversified range of plants producing consumer goods for the region. Moncton has the central geographical position to develop retail and commercial functions, but its nearby hinterlands in eastern New Brunswick and northwestern Nova Scotia are not heavily populated and many people there have low average incomes.

Fredericton was a small quiet, picturesque government and university town which grew into a small city as it added retail and other commercial functions to serve the people of the central St. John River valley. Its institutional functions are still important, but they are partly shared with Saint John. Fredericton has not dominated the service and commercial activity of the central and upper St. John River valley because of the competing functions of the small service centre towns northward, such as Woodstock, Grand Falls and Edmundston.

The commercial and service employees of Charlottetown serve a relatively small population on Prince Edward Island. Although government workers help to increase the small urban population, the city lacks industrial and consumer goods manufacturing like that in other larger Maritimes cities.

St. John's has most of the commercial and institutional employees in

Newfoundland, plus the transportation functions related to the port and the rail and road terminal. It has been the major and only big city of the island and it has dominated the economic life of the province. In population size, however, it is one of the few capitals which holds a relatively small percentage of the provincial population. The city, together with its immediate hinterland on Avalon Peninsula and around Conception Bay, holds almost half of the population of the island. Corner Brook is beginning to duplicate some of St. John's functions, on a smaller scale for a smaller hinterland, on the west coast.

OTHER TOPICS

Regional geography must not be a compilation of facts about everything in the region. In this book, certain themes are developed and selected items discussed which are believed to make the region different or distinct from other parts of Canada. Therefore, certain topics have been omitted and they may be investigated by interested readers at some other time.

The cultural, ethnic and language mosaic of the Atlantic Provinces can be compared with that of the Interior Plains—both had separated mixtures of British and European peoples. For example, the interesting cultural geography of New Brunswick can be illustrated by the distribution of French-speaking people. French-Canadians are concentrated in the northern parts of New Brunswick and English-speaking people live mainly in the southwest. Compare these English-French distribution patterns with the results of federal and provincial elections. Is there an areal association to be investigated? Has the increase in French-Canadians levelled off? How many people of French ethnic background no longer speak French at home? What are the differences between the Acadians, who trace their ancestry back to French persons who settled in the area in the 18th century, and the Quebecois who have migrated into the region from Quebec in this century? These two French groups generally live in different parts of the province. Why are there few French-speaking people in the other Atlantic Provinces? What and where is the "French shore" of Nova Scotia? Some aspects of this topic are discussed in Chapter 5 as part of the areal expansion of French-Canadians in eastern Canada.

What is the distribution of people of Scottish background? Are there places where the Gaelic language or the swirl of bagpipes at ceremonies tell you something of the cultural characteristics of those regions?

Do Black people live in separated geographical areas in Halifax and other parts of Nova Scotia as they do in many American cities?

Are you interested in the geographical aspects of recreation and tourism? What elements of the natural environments and landscapes of the region attract visitors from other regions? How close (or far away) are the empty parts of this region to high density urban people? Can you interpret the tourist literature which may tell about the beautiful ocean beaches, but say nothing about the cold water? Do you know enough about the natural environment, settlements and people to know what to expect in a drive along one of the prettiest parts of Canada, the St. John River valley?

SUMMARY

There are many questions which help to focus one's thinking upon themes and concepts. Can you now define the "regional character" of the Atlantic and Gulf region? Is it possible to visualize and understand how the region is different from some parts of Canada, but similar to other parts? This may be difficult now because you may not have studied the "other parts" of Canada.

How do the distribution patterns and areal associations of many of the activities in the region operate together? What are the functional links (or lack of them) between this region and the St. Lawrence Lowlands or the Canadian Shield? How are the advantages and disadvantages of east coast location on the edge of Canada illustrated in levels of the economy and in distributional patterns of activity? How much do varying regional physical environments affect the lives of local residents?

One of the themes expressed throughout the chapter has been that of distributions. Three questions should always be asked: what, where, why? "What" defines exactly what we are talking about. "Where" locates it locally, regionally and nationally. "Why" asks for some explanation of its location and some evaluation of the significance of location with relation to other phenomena. Throughout this chapter, the words "dispersed" and "concentrated" appear often; they are reminders of sub-regional differences in distribution patterns. This chapter emphasized areal patterns in the Atlantic and Gulf region, particularly those which make it different from other parts of Canada.

REFERENCES

Atlases:

"Resource Atlas, Island of Newfoundland," Nfld. Dept. of Forestry and Agriculture, St. John's, 1974. 14 maps.
"Census Atlas of Newfoundland 1971" by Mark Shrimpton, Institute of Social and Economic Research, Memorial Univ., St. John's, 1977. 79 maps.
"Atlas of the Gulf of St. Lawrence Region" edited by Wendy Simpson, Geographical Paper No. 53, Lands Directorate, Environment Canada, 1973. 20 maps.

Periodicals:

Acadiensis: Journal of the History of the Atlantic Region, published by Dept. of History, Univ. of New Brunswick, Fredericton, N.B. *Most articles are concerned with aspects of history of the region, but some issues have articles on historical geography.* For example:
Vol. 8, No. 2, 1979, "Late 18th Century Agriculture on the Bay of Fundy Marshlands" by Graeme Wynn, pp. 80-89.
Vol. 10, No. 2, 1981, "The Mercantile-Industrial Transition in the Metal Towns of Pictou County, 1857-1931" by Larry McCann, pp. 29-64.
Atlantic Region Geographical Series, Dept. of Geog., Saint Mary's Univ., Halifax, No. 2, "The Role of Physical Factors in the Process of Farm Abandonment in Nova Scotia, 1953-74" by R. Crickmer, 1981. 162 pages.
Atlantic Insight, published in Halifax, N.S.
A monthly newsmagazine discussing events and developments in the region.
Studies in Marine and Coastal Geography, Dept. of Geog., Saint Mary's Univ., Halifax. Vol. 1, 1982.

Books:

"Sydney, N.S. — An Urban Study" by Roy Harvey, Clarke, Irwin, Toronto, 1971. 94 pages.
"Coastal Zone: Framework for Management in Atlantic Canada" by Douglas Johnson et al, Institute of Public Affairs, Dalhousie Univ., Halifax, 1975. 249 pages.
Lands Directorate, Environment Canada, "The Impact of Federal Activities on Fruitland Use: Annapolis Valley, N.S.," Working Paper, No. 21, Ottawa, 1982.
"The Natural Environment of Newfoundland, Past and Present" edited by Alan and Joyce Macpherson, Dept. of Geography, Memorial Univ., St. John's, 1981. 265 pages.
"The Peopling of Newfoundland: Essays in Historical Geography" edited

by John Mannion, Social and Economic Papers, No. 8, Institute of Social and Economic Research, Memorial Univ., St. John's, 1977. 289 pages.
"Point Lance in Transition: The Transformation of a Newfoundland Outport" by John Mannion, McClelland and Stewart, Toronto, 1976. 63 pages.
"Regional Patterns of Ethnicity in Nova Scotia" by H.A. Millward, St. Mary's Univ., Halifax, Ethnic Heritage Series, No. 6, 1981. 58 pages.

Some relevant articles in *The Canadian Geographer* between 1970-82, Can. Assoc. of Geog., Burnside Hall, McGill Univ., Montreal:

Vol. 20, No. 4, 1976.   "Post-Glacial Emergence of the Fundy Coast" by John Welsted, pp. 367-383.

Vol. 19, No. 2, 1975.   "Changes in the Political Geography of New Brunswick" by Ralph Krueger, pp. 121-134.

CHAPTER 4

THE GREAT LAKES-ST. LAWRENCE LOWLANDS

CHAPTER 4

THE GREAT LAKES-ST. LAWRENCE LOWLANDS

INTRODUCTION

This small region is the population and industrial Heartland of Canada. It holds almost 60 percent of Canada's population, produces about 70 percent of the value of manufactured goods, has more than 65 percent of the labour force engaged in manufacturing, and has many of Canada's large and medium cities. It is characterized by the highest densities of people, agriculture and economic activities in Canada, but these high densities are not uniform throughout the region. As the Heartland of Canada, the people and businesses of the region have tended to dominate economic and political activity in much of the rest of Canada. If this dominance decreases in the 1980s, is it the result of changing geographical patterns in other parts of Canada?

The region can be divided into two sub-regions, called southern Quebec and southern Ontario, each of which is centred by one of Canada's two largest cities, Montreal and Toronto. This short chapter is an introduction to the whole region, and Chapters 5 and 6 further discuss the two sub-regions.

THEMES

1.) Southern Ontario and southern Quebec together constitute the Heartland of Canada. The small region has the highest densities of people and economic activities in Canada, but these densities are not evenly distributed throughout the region.

2.) Some of the similarities and differences between southern Ontario and southern Quebec are discussed.

DEFINITION OF THE REGION

The Great Lakes-St. Lawrence Lowlands are defined as the areas of Quebec and Ontario south of the Canadian Shield. This latter landform and geological boundary is a sharp, low escarpment close to the north bank of the St. Lawrence and Ottawa rivers in Quebec, but the landform difference is less distinct along the hilly edge of the Frontenac Axis in Ontario (map on p. 109). This latter south-extending arm of the Canadian Shield is crossed by the St. Lawrence River east of Lake Ontario and it divides the Lowlands into two parts. Most of the level to slightly rolling lowlands has been cleared of its original forest cover and the neat, cultivated landscapes contrast sharply with the lake-dotted, forested landscapes of the Shield to the north.

107

The Appalachian Mountains are not part of the Great Lakes-St. Lawrence Lowlands. They have been included in a southern Quebec sub-region because of their French-speaking population, rather than separated because of their different landform characteristics. This is one of these regionalization decisions which is open to debate. An alternative would have been to call the small region simply "Southern Ontario and Southern Quebec," defined as all the area south of the Canadian Shield. In this book, the physiographic lowland along the St. Lawrence River, *including* the plain of eastern Ontario, is called the Quebec Lowland, but another regional term, "Southern Quebec" is used to include both the lowland in Quebec and also the hills and valleys of the Appalachians, excluding Gaspé Peninsula. As was noted in Chapter 3, Gaspé Peninsula is indeed a problem in being fitted into a regional organization; as a geographical "fringe" area in Quebec, the people of Gaspé sometimes claim that they are forgotten by the provincial government located at the edge of the heartland of southwestern Quebec. Such a political statement may have some geographical basis.

REGIONAL VARIATIONS

Landforms, Soils and Drainage

What should one know about the landform variety in this region, or in others? The gently rolling lowland in Ontario, southwest of the Canadian Shield, is covered with a variety of deposition left during the Glacial Age. The minor features of the landforms affected the variety of soils there, but otherwise they had little influence upon the broad pattern of agricultural settlement. Some agricultural crops, however, are directly related to particular physical conditions. One of the noticeable landform features is the Niagara Escarpment which curves from Niagara Falls through Hamilton and northward to the Bruce Peninsula (map, p. 159). The highest altitudes in southwestern Ontario are south and west of Georgian Bay where glacial deposition was left on top of the bedrock of the escarpment. These altitudes are reflected in different micro-climate conditions. In contrast, the lower, very flat plain between lakes St. Clair and Erie is the former bottom of a larger glacial lake and has still other soil and drainage characteristics.

East of the Frontenac Axis, the lowland of eastern Ontario is flatter than southwestern Ontario and is similar to the level plain of southwestern Quebec. Toward the end of the Glacial Age, this area was covered by an extension inland of the Gulf of St. Lawrence; the marine deposition there is of different origin than that laid down along the ice front in southern Ontario, but there is a similar variety in micro-landforms and drainage conditions in both regions. The narrow lowland along the north side of the St. Lawrence River is bounded by the sharp Shield escarpment which rises a few hundred metres above the plain. The wider, flat lowland south of the river merges gently into the higher, linear hills of the Appalachians. Soil capabilities for agriculture decrease in quality in the latter region.

SUB-REGIONS OF THE GREAT LAKES - ST. LAWRENCE LOWLANDS

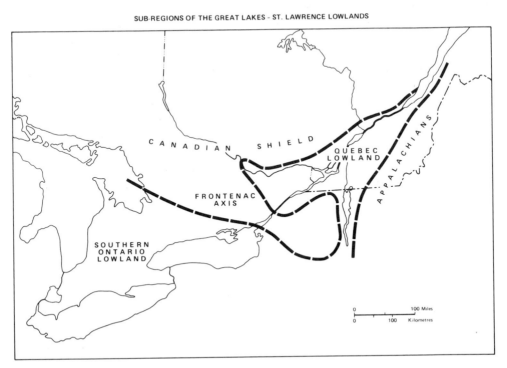

Will understanding and appreciation of Canada's geographical landscapes be increased by knowing that there are several different types of landforms across southern Ontario and southern Quebec? Should one know *more* about the glacial history of the Lowlands region because so many of the present activities of people can be attributed to the variety of lacustrine, marine and glacial deposition left at the retreating front of the icecap? Do readers appreciate that, on the scale of geological time, these glaciation events were recent—10,000 to 15,000 years ago—when other parts of the world had already been occupied by people for several thousand years?

The large areas of level land within the Lowlands have generally been permissive to human activities: they offered only a few hazards to agricultural settlement; barriers to railroads and roads were few; people could spread out and intermix. Does the study of man-land relationships become less obvious in a favourable, permissive physical environment? Are the relationships more apparent as restrictions for people in negative environments?

Vegetation

Southwestern Ontario was covered with deciduous trees and the rest of the Lowland was forested with mixed deciduous and coniferous trees when Indians occupied the region after the icecap receded northward. The present variations in the amount of forest cover are mainly the results of clearing for agriculture. Toward the end of the 19th century, much of the forest of southern Ontario had been cut and now more than 90 percent of the land is in agricultural use.

Although most of the plain near Montreal has been cleared, the amount of forest cover increases elsewhere in the Quebec Lowland, even though some areas have been occupied by farming people for two centuries. This forest cover indicates local areas of poor soils or poor drainage which have not been suitable for cultivation. Forests are more common than agricultural land in the Appalachians. Across southern Quebec, outside the Montreal Plain, the farm woodlot, sometimes used for maple syrup production or pulpwood, is more obvious in the rural landscape than it is in southern Ontario.

Climate

Southwestern Ontario, the most southerly part of Canada, is in the same latitude as northern California and Spain. Because the lowlands extend to the northeast into Quebec, climate differs notably between the southwestern and northeastern parts. These differences are most obvious in winter when warm air masses move periodically northward from the Gulf of Mexico over southwestern Ontario and raise average winter temperatures there to the mildest in eastern Canada (equal to southern Nova Scotia). In contrast, cold air masses from the Canadian Shield and northern Interior Plains pass over central and southern Quebec more frequently in winter. The famous "Winter Carnival" of Quebec City is more fitting there than it would be in the so called "banana belt" of southwestern Ontario. The frequency of these warm or cold air masses in spring and autumn affects the length of the average frost-free season, which is one month longer in southwestern Ontario. This longer frost-free period permits a greater variety of crops in the southwest than can be produced in the climate of southern Quebec.

There are few sub-regional differences in summer temperatures except for the greater number of growing degree days above 5°C in the southwest. Summers can be hot and sometimes very humid in both parts of the lowlands.

Average annual precipitation decreases from east to west across eastern Canada; lesser amounts are therefore recorded in southwestern Ontario. The combination of high summer temperatures and resulting higher evaporation rates also means less effective precipitation in the southwest for agriculture.

Agricultural Land Use

Partly as a result of these variations in the physical environment, agricultural land use differs between southern Quebec and southern Ontario. In both areas, the dominant use of the land is in hay, pasture and feed grains which support a dairying and livestock industry. Because about 90 percent of the land use is in these crops, the cultivated landscape of the Quebec lowland looks much the same throughout the area. Visual differences result from landform and vegetation variations. In southern Ontario, about 70 percent of land use is in hay, pasture and feed grains; large areas of farmland therefore have the same green colours in summer in both Ontario and Quebec. Southern Ontario differs, however, by having larger acreages of special crops, such as fruit, grapes, tobacco, corn, soybeans and vegetables. These are concentrated into particular small areas; some of these agricultural sub-regions are discussed in Chapter 6.

Agricultural Land Subdivision

Although farms across southern Quebec and southern Ontario grow similar crops, the landscape differs because of the historical land subdivision systems. In southern Quebec, one of the characteristics of the seigneurial system of land holding and tenant arrangements established during and after the French regime was a long-lot subdivision system. Some farms were laid out in this form and others were later sub-divided into long, narrow lots over many generations. As a result, farmhouses were close together along the rivers or along roads which parallelled the rivers. These parallel roads, with their lines of houses, were known as "rangs." This subdivision system had many variations; sometimes there were two or three, or up to seven or eight rangs; the houses were on one side of the road or on both sides. Driving along these rural roads now—even though many of the farmhouses have been abandoned or removed—gives the impression of continuous "village" settlement. This unique rural landscape is one of the distinguishing features of the regional character of southern Quebec.

In contrast, the farms in the Eastern Townships of southern Quebec near the United States border, and in Ontario, were subdivided for British settlers in the characteristic rectangular blocks which are common in the rest of Anglo-America. Even though French-speaking farmers took over most of the farms in the Eastern Townships, they did not change the English land subdivision system there. This part of Quebec, therefore, has a different rural settlement pattern from the lowlands, owing to the original land subdivision system as well as landform and vegetation differences.

Farmhouses in Ontario are farther apart than those in the rangs of Quebec, and usually a short distance back from the roads. Brick was more common as a building material in Ontario than in Quebec; Quebec farmhouses often had "tin" or tile roofs. Fields within the farms are usually divided into squares or rectangles in Ontario in contrast to the long lots of Quebec.

Rural Villages

As a result of these land subdivision differences, the small rural villages have a different form. In lowland Quebec, the village is often linear, as are the lines of rural farmhouses. Sometimes the village, with a limited range of commercial activities, grew at a crossroads in an "X" or "T" form; residential and commercial buildings are intermixed along the village "main" street. In contrast, a small Ontario village consists of a few rectangular blocks; stores usually occupy one block, often on both sides of the street, and residences are on other streets. If a village grows, the commercial core of the small town remains separated from the residential section and may occupy two or more rectangular blocks. The areal separation of farm, commercial and residential uses is usually clearer in southern Ontario than in Quebec.

Language and "Cultural" Differences

Behind all of these visible, landscape contrasts is the fundamental difference that the sub-regions were settled by people of different origins. French and English settlers came from different cultures and different environments in France and Britain. The French-speaking civilization that evolved in southern Quebec had different laws, customs and religion from those that became dominant among English-speaking people of southern Ontario. French-Canadians had few external additions to their racial stocks in the next 200 years; an inward-looking society evolved within a region which had a great deal of internal similarity and uniformity.

Across southern Ontario, in contrast, people came from a variety of environments from the British Isles, with a wider variety of occupations — both rural and urban. In this century, these English-speaking settlers were joined by a mixture of people from Europe who brought different cultures but who adopted, by the second generation, the English language and many local customs. These vague, intangible characteristics which make up a culture *are* different in the two sub-regions of southern Quebec and southern Ontario. They may be as much "felt" as seen in the landscapes.

The preceding sections noted some of the similarities and differences *within* the region. On the national scale, the region has several characteristics which are different from the rest of Canada.

THE HEARTLAND CONCEPT

This geographical concept states that the central lowland between the

Great Lakes and along the St. Lawrence River is the "heart" of Canada—in the centre of the body and its most vital organ. It dominates and controls the rest of the country. This concept has implications in political or economic terms and it also applies in geographical terms. The region has the highest densities of a number of phenomena in Canada. On a national scale, the term "Main Street, Canada" is appropriate. The region is the "downtown" core for many of the people in the rest of Canada. Within the Heartland, there is areal and functional integration. People in the Lowlands region have a great deal in common, despite the differences in language.

Population

The Great Lakes-St. Lawrence region holds more than half the people of Canada. The region had. 11 of the 25 large metropolitan cities in 1976, and also 17 of the 30 medium-size cities with 30,000 to 100,000 population (excluding those cities which are part of larger metropolitan cities). Few people live more than 100 kilometres from a medium to large city. These cities interact together in a functioning urban system having complex internal and inter-city movements of people, products and ideas.

The region also has the highest densities of rural population in Canada. Much of the original forest cover has been removed and the land is now almost fully utilized for farming. Farmhouses are reasonably close together along every mile of rural road; there are no large areas without people as in other regions of Canada.

However, population densities are not uniform throughout the region. The highest densities are concentrated around the western part of Lake Ontario and westward to London. Notably lower rural densities and fewer cities are seen southwest of Georgian Bay. In Quebec, the highest population densities are spread across the lowland; the western part, around Montreal, has higher densities of people than the eastern part, around Quebec City. Lower densities and dispersal characterize the population pattern of the Appalachians.

Manufacturing

The Lowlands region has the greatest concentration of industrial activity in Canada, whether measured by number of factories, number of manufacturing employees, or value of manufactured goods. About half the value of manufacturing in the region comes from the more numerous cities in the Ontario part. The manufacturing plants in the Golden Horseshoe around the western end of Lake Ontario produce almost as much value of goods as is manufactured in all four western provinces; similarly, the industries of metropolitan Montreal produce more than is manufactured in the four eastern provinces.

In many of the cities of the Heartland, more than half their labour force is engaged in manufacturing occupations. Some of almost every type of secondary manufacturing listed in the Canadian census is produced somewhere in the Great Lakes-St. Lawrence region. There seems, therefore, little point in listing the leading manufactures of the region except as a memorization exercise. Within the region, the manufactures of Quebec are more oriented to local raw materials and are more labour intensive than are those of Ontario.

In addition to high densities of urban manufacturing, this region differs from other parts of Canada in that much of its manufacturing activity has been American-owned or controlled. This industrial Heartland of Canada adjoins a similar dominant American manufacturing concentration south of the Great Lakes; as a result, many Heartland manufacturing operations are branch plants or subsidiaries of American firms. The number of such foreign-owned plants may decline in the 1980s. Why? Some of the geographical aspects of this international link are discussed in Chapter 6.

Financial Control

People in the many high-rise office towers of the large cities of the Heartland control much of the business and the financial institutions across Canada. Most of the headquarters of banks and financial institutions are in this region; company head offices are in cities of the Heartland, whereas branch offices are in hinterland regions across Canada. It is probable that most corporate decisions about the Canadian economy are made in this region, although financial activity is increasing in western Canada. Much of this financial control was concentrated in Montreal in the last century and the early part of this century, but the main centre is now in or near Toronto. Part of the migration of financial activity to Toronto in the 1970s was due to perceived political differences in Quebec, but also to the attractions of Toronto. The geography of this topic is not always obvious to Canadians, but the results of these financial decisions are apparent in the urban landscapes of Canada.

Consumers

The concentration of people with high incomes obtained from commercial and industrial activities makes the Heartland region the main concentration of consumers in Canada. These producers of manufacturing and agricultural wealth are also consumers. It has been estimated that almost one-third of the retail sales in Canada are made in, or within 150 kilometres of, metropolitan Toronto. For example, a retail firm can expect to have more consumers with higher incomes in a few square kilometres of Montreal than in the whole of the Atlantic Provinces; similarly, the concentration of consumers on the

114

west side of Toronto equals a market that might be found in all of British Columbia.

High incomes, as a measure of consumption, are not evenly distributed throughout the region. Average annual incomes are higher in southern Ontario than in southern Quebec. Incomes are lower in eastern Ontario than in the southwest. Some parts of rural Quebec, particularly in the Appalachians, have incomes well below average. These "poverty" areas are comparable to similar patches of low incomes in the Atlantic and Gulf region.

High concentrations of consumption also mean high concentration of wastes, disposal problems and pollution. Many Lowland rivers are now polluted and Lake Erie has been called an "open sewer." "Acid rain" from industries is polluting the air and probably damaging marine life in recreational lakes. Many of these negative characteristics of population concentration are being looked at more carefully by people from outside the Heartland who might have been attracted to the region for its economic advantages.

Agriculture

The cities, commerce and industries of the Heartland are supported by the most prosperous agriculture in Canada. Although the *area* of agriculture is larger across the southern Interior Plains, the *value* of agricultural production is greatest in the Lowlands. The average value of farmland is the highest in Canada, as is the value of farmhouses. Undoubtedly, the success of Lowlands agriculture is directly related to the large local urban markets which it supplies, as well as the favourable physical environmental conditions. Most of the food is consumed within the area, but canned and processed food products are also sent to the rest of Canada.

The value of farm production varies internally within the region. High-value crops are produced in the specialty agricultural regions of southern Ontario (discussed in Chapter 6); in contrast, rural farming poverty is common in the Appalachian hills of southeastern Quebec.

Other than agriculture, the natural resource base of the Heartland is not great. It produces no metallic minerals, and its non-metallics and fuel resources are minor, except for salt. Its forest cover has been largely removed. Its rivers are not major sources of electric power or fish, except for the Great Lakes system.

THE HEARTLAND-HINTERLAND CONCEPT

Smaller areas of high population density and economic activity are dispersed across Canada. These spots of concentration are poorly linked together; each is mainly concerned with serving the needs of its local region and there is limited interaction between them. But each of these outlying, dispersed sub-regional centres usually has direct connections with people and activities in the Heartland. Many activities within the sub-regional centres are controlled or directed by people in the Heartland. These outer areas are the hinterland which supports the Heartland.

Some of the evidence for the heartland-hinterland concept is based on the measurement of flows of people, products and ideas between the heartland core and the dispersed centres of the hinterland. This interaction may be recorded by airline passenger volumes, truck and rail freight, wholesale centres, telephone calls, newspaper circulation, etc. More movement and interaction takes place between any one hinterland centre and the core cities than between hinterland centres. For example, it is believed that there are more connections between Vancouver and Toronto than there are between Vancouver and Edmonton or Winnipeg. Similarly, more interaction occurs between Montreal and Halifax than between Halifax and St. John's.

The heartland-hinterland concept is a way of looking at the geographical patterns of Canada as a whole. In the concept, one can visualize Canada as being dominated by the people and activities in the Heartland; the rest of Canada is a hinterland serving that core. This concept is less tasteful to people in the "outer fringes" of Canada who sometimes resent the control and decisions from the Heartland (which includes Ottawa, the national capital). Readers may wish to discuss some of the political implications of this geographical concept.

The immediate hinterland of the Great Lakes-St. Lawrence Lowlands is the adjoining Canadian Shield with its wealth of natural resources. Interaction and movement between these two regions developed strong north-south flows, whereas movement of products from one centre to another *within* the Shield have been minor, except for direct transport to resource processing centres. A geographical concept of "gateways," funnelling and directing the flows between the Shield and Lowlands regions, is discussed in Chapter 7. Many of the industries of the Lowlands are supplied by raw materials from the Shield; much of the electrical power for Lowlands homes and industries comes from the Shield; the lakes, forests and "empty" places of the Shield are the recreational hinterland of high-density Lowlands residents.

Is the heartland-hinterland concept being modified by the increased natural resource base of Western Canada? As the consuming population increases in the West, and their incomes rise, will that region produce more of its own manufactured goods instead of importing them from the Heartland? Will the millions of external consumers around the Asiatic rim of the Pacific Ocean be a more attractive market to Western resource-based industries than those in the Lowlands? Or will the heartland-hinterland concept be strengthened as the raw materials of the Interior Plains move increasingly to the Lowlands, as the Shield resources have done in the past? Will the Edmonton-Calgary corridor become a rival to the Quebec City-Windsor "Main Street"? How much of Western prosperity is based on a depleting resource item, petroleum? These topics are discussed in Chapters 8 and 9.

The heartland-hinterland concept includes a hierarchical principle. The same core-periphery relationships, on a smaller scale, apply to Vancouver as a heartland controlling and directing the hinterland of British Columbia. Similarly, the concept fitted the geography and economy of the Prairie Provinces in the 1920s; Winnipeg, as a heartland, had a tributary hinterland all across the Interior Plains. What caused this pattern to change in the Prairie Provinces? Why did no secondary heartland develop in the Atlantic Provinces?

REFERENCES

Books:

"The Form of Cities in Central Canada" edited by L. Bourne et al., Dept. of Geography Research Publication No. 11, Univ. of Toronto, 1973. 246 pages.
Ontario Ministry of Agriculture and Food, Economics Branch, Toronto. "The Physical Base for Agriculture in Central Canada," 1978. 58 pages.
"An Overview of Land Use in Central Canada," 1979. 52 pages.
"Climate of the Great Lakes Basin" by D.W. Phillips and J. McCulloch, Atmospheric Environment Service, No. 20, Toronto, 1972. 40 pages.
"Main Street: Windsor to Quebec City" by Maurice Yeates, Macmillan, Toronto, 1975. 431 pages.

Periodicals:

"City Size, Economic Diversity and Functional Type: The Canadian Case" by John U. Marshall, *Econ. Geog.*, No. 51, 1975, pp. 37-39.

Special Maps:

"Great Lakes Water Use" from Map Distribution Office, Dept. of Energy, Mines and Resources, Ottawa, revised 1980.
"Windsor-Quebec Axis" prepared by Lands Directorate, Environment Canada, Ottawa, 1974.

Some relevant articles in *The Canadian Geographer* between 1970-82, Can. Assoc. of Geog., Burnside Hall, McGill Univ., Montreal:

Vol. 23, No. 3, 1979.	"Structural Divergence (in Industries) in Quebec and Ontario, 1961-1969" by G.B. Norcliffe and J.H. Stevens, pp. 239-254.
Vol. 20, No. 1, 1976.	"The Geography of Income and Its Correlates" by Michael Ray and Thomas Brewis, pp. 41-71.
Vol. 17, No. 1, 1973.	"Structural Divergence in Canada's Manufacturing Belt" by James Gilmour and Ken Murricane, pp. 1-18.
Vol. 16, No. 4, 1972.	"Locational Change in the Canadian Leather Footwear Industry" by Neil Seigfried, pp. 309-322.

CHAPTER 5

SOUTHERN QUEBEC

CHAPTER 5

SOUTHERN QUEBEC

INTRODUCTION

A cultural core of French-speaking people evolved in the Quebec Lowland. Mainly agricultural settlers came to the colony of New France during the 17th and early 18th centuries; they slowly cut back the forest along the St. Lawrence River and tributary rivers. They created a society which was closely tied to the land; the cleared land produced grain and vegetable crops and the surrounding forest produced game and berries. Their long, narrow farms spread back from the rivers and main roads in an unique settlement pattern based on parallel rangs. Their social and economic lives revolved around a land-holding system centred on the seigneuries. A society and a culture with relatively high rural densities evolved in the St. Lawrence Lowland, partially separated from the flow of life and economy which developed elsewhere in English-speaking Anglo-America. When most of the suitable land in the Lowland was occupied, the rapidly increasing surplus farm population migrated outwards into adjoining regions with different social and physical environments.

A closely related town and village urban system evolved along with the expanding agricultural patterns. The linear local villages were scarcely discernible from the linear rangs of farmhouses, but they supplied the basic goods and services needed by the agricultural population. Simple, basic manufactures and processed food products were produced in the towns. The towns that grew larger had better transportation to serve a wider hinterland and the main cities arose on the "highway" of the St. Lawrence River.

On top of this local and sub-regional hierarchy of urban places, Montreal had different functions and characteristics. It was mainly an English-speaking city in the early 19th century and a commercial and financial city for all of eastern Canada. Throughout the late 19th century, Montreal was a *national* city rather than a regional city. The economy and land uses around Montreal in southwestern Quebec were more intensive than in other parts of the province.

As defined in Chapter 4, Southern Quebec includes the St. Lawrence Lowland and the western part of the Appalachians; it is the area of Quebec south of the Canadian Shield, but excludes Gaspé Peninsula. Southeastern Ontario is considered here as part of the Quebec Lowland region because rural land use is similar and many of its people are French-speaking. Although the Canadian Shield of Quebec has different physical features, economies, population densities and landscapes, throughout this chapter the functional links between the Shield and

Lowland regions will be brought out.

THEMES

1.) The characteristics and evolution of a cultural core of people is discussed, including its concentration characteristics and the process of areal expansion of French-Canadians outwards from that core. The chapter illustrates a historical geography approach with a man-land theme.

2.) Southern Quebec has similarities in culture and language, but regional diversity in landscapes. The Quebec Lowland, Appalachians and Shield are sub-regions with different environments which have been used differently by people with a common culture.

3.) Montreal is one of Canada's two largest cities and its main industrial, commercial and financial centre prior to 1960. Montreal's industrial land-use patterns are observed as an example of principles of location of industrial activity within a large city.

THE OCCUPATION OF THE LOWLAND

Settlement During the French Regime

It has been estimated that only about 10,000 settlers came to France's colony of Quebec in about 150 years and they multiplied within the small area to about 70,000 persons by the time of the British conquest in 1763. Much of the land was granted to a few people in large seigneuries within which there evolved a distinct type of "feudal" land holding and tenant system. After several generations of land subdivision, the unique long-lot farms, rangs and linear streets of farmhouses formed a distinctive settlement pattern back from the St. Lawrence, Ottawa, Richelieu and Chaudière rivers. A dominantly rural, agricultural, almost self-sufficient economy was established. Settlement also concentrated into the three main forts and administrative centres of Quebec City, Trois Rivières and Montreal. One of the purposes of agriculture was to supply food to these urban residents.

Areal and Numerical Changes After the British Conquest

With almost no further immigration from France, the French-speaking settlers multiplied on their farms and their children established new farms across the Quebec Lowland. The rangs marched inland in parallel rows of farmhouses, here and there leaving a section in forest where there was poor drainage or poor soils. By approximately 1830, the original 70,000 inhabitants of 1763 had become about 600,000 mainly agricultural settlers; they occupied most of the good land of the Lowland. Although the St. Lawrence and other rivers carried freight and heavy traffic, the settlements were tied together by a close, rectangular network of narrow, local roads. However, movement from one town to another was not common for most "habitants." The landscapes of this French-speaking group were characterized by their imposing churches and manor houses, their linear rural villages and the rangs; these told of a closely-knit, almost self-sufficient society in which life centred on the farm, village and church. A people and their land were in close geographical relationship. Life was not easy and food was not plentiful, particularly in winter, but the environment offered a reasonably comfortable living for farming people.

As this cultural core was being established with its distinctive people and landscape, British settlers were also entering Canada and they surrounded the French-speaking society. During and after the 1790s, United Empire Loyalists fled from the United States and entered southern Quebec; they laid out the usual rectangular farm and road system in the Appalachian hills of the Eastern Townships near the U.S. border. Other British immigrants came southward to the Townships from the St. Lawrence after landing at Quebec City or Montreal. By the middle of the 19th century, this part of southern Quebec, near the U.S. border, was occupied by an English-speaking society; their numerous villages, usually with a rectangular block of commercial buildings, and often with a central "common" near a small church, were similar to New England villages. A grid pattern of roads, fields and villages gradually spread along the valleys and northward and westward onto the Lowland. Sawmills and wood working industries were started in some of the towns to supplement the dispersed agriculture; textile mills, using local water power, were also common, as they were in the New England towns nearby to the south. Towns in the Appalachians had different forms and structure from those on the Lowland. (Although the regional term "Eastern Townships" is still used, the local political units are now called counties, as they are elsewhere in eastern Canada. The regional grouping of political units in the Eastern Townships has changed from time to time, consisting of from 9 to 11 counties across southern Quebec between the Richelieu River and the Maine border.)

To the north of the Lowland, along the edge of the Canadian Shield, Irish immigrants settled in the narrow river valleys and in small pockets of level land. Their property was laid out in the rectangular subdivision system which, therefore, gave these Shield farms a different appearance than Lowland farms. Irish occupation of marginal farmland in the Shield edge delayed the northward expansion of French-Canadians for several decades in the early 19th century.

To the westward, in the political area then called Upper Canada, British immigrants and United Empire Loyalists settled on the level plain north of the St. Lawrence River and west of the Ottawa River during the first decade of the 19th century.

The original French-Canadian core was therefore surrounded on all sides by newly-arrived English-speaking immigrants. French-Canadians looked inward and strengthened their ties to the local land and forests. Within the core of rural French-Canadians, the two main cities, Montreal and Quebec, grew with the arrival of British immigrants. The residents of Montreal were 60 percent English-speaking in 1830, and these people controlled the commerce and finance of the city. Even in Quebec City, the cultural "heart" of the French-Canadian core, about 40 percent of the population was English-speaking in 1861. These latter British-origin people owned and controlled the lumber trade which used trees felled in the forests of the Canadian Shield and assembled the logs at Quebec for overseas export.

By the middle of the 19th century, cultural and economic differences were becoming apparent between the people of the two big cities and the rural population; the cities were establishing a *national* position in eastern Canada, whereas the countryside was inward-looking and *regional* in function. By around 1850, the Quebec Lowland was almost fully occupied by the simple agricultural economy of the French-Canadians; commerce and the beginnings of industry were controlled by English-speaking people in the two largest cities.

The small area of land in the Lowland and its physical environment could not support the agricultural economy of the rapidly increasing French-Canadian population. Birth rates were high in this rural society. Some of the land had been subdivided into such very narrow strips that large families had no nearby good land available for the sons. The surplus or overflow population began to migrate out of the core region in search of farm land, or they went to jobs in the forest industry of the Shield and Appalachians which surrounded Lowland agriculture. They also moved to the cities. Outward migration moved in four directions (see map on p. 125).

OUTWARD AREAL EXPANSION

Southward in the Eastern Townships:
By the middle of the 19th century, French-Canadians were migrating southward into the Eastern Townships. This movement and numerical increase was recorded in each census. First the northern counties on the Lowland edge changed in language character from dominantly English to French. By 1871, French-Canadians made up 50 percent of the total regional population in the Eastern Townships. Often the English names of the villages were changed to French names. By 1901, the northwestern counties, Drummond and Arthabaska, were 90 percent French-speaking and the adjoining counties—Shefford, Wolfe, Richmond, Megantic—were 75 percent French. In that year, only Brome and Stanstead counties in the south had an English-speaking majority. By 1921, the five northern counties were 90 percent French-Canadian and only one county, Brome, had less than 50 percent French-speaking people. Most of the English-speaking people on

the south side of the original French cultural core in the Lowland had gone. For almost a century, waves of French-Canadians had migrated out of their cultural core into another physical environment in the Appalachians. This areal migration took at least three forms:

1.) the sons of farmers on the Lowland moved into poorer and unoccupied land in the Appalachian valleys and cleared land for their subsistence farms;
2.) other French-Canadians found work in the forests or became labour in the lumber mills and textile mills in the Eastern Townships towns;
3.) settlers bought or took over abandoned farms of the original English-speaking settlers, many of whom moved west to other provinces or states.

AREAL EXPANSION OF FRENCH-CANADIANS

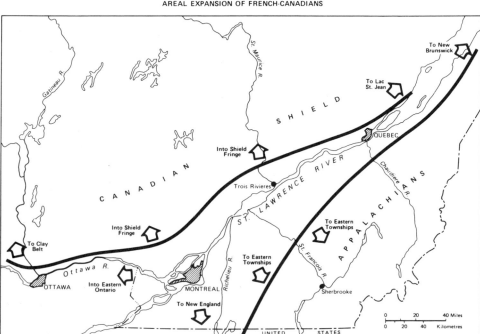

Although French language, religion and cultural characteristics became dominant in the Eastern Townships, the landscape remained different from that in the cultural core on the Lowland: the natural environment of the hills and forests presented a different physical setting; the textile industry and other small manufacturing towns formed a different economic base than the agricultural Lowland; the roads, farms and fields maintained their original rectangular patterns.

In addition to the "occupation" of the Eastern Townships, many thousands of French-Canadians continued southward into the New England states; perhaps as many as 700,000 French-Canadians became a notable minority in Vermont, New Hampshire and other New England states. They became labour in the textile mills there or settled on marginal lands for farming. In northeastern United States, they were a numerical and cultural minority; within a few generations, many lost their French language—as did other immigrants who came to the United States from Europe. Because of this national and cultural loss, the French-Canadian clergy, in particular, made a strong effort to encourage movement northward into the Shield to keep their people in Quebec.

Areal Expansion Westward into Ontario:

The characteristic large farm families of the Lowland had to find other nearby areas to support their rural lifestyle. By the early part of the 19th century, a few French settlers had crossed Upper Canada and settled on the British side of the Detroit River. Their long, narrow farm lines are still apparent in the landscape along the river southwest of Windsor, and French surnames are common in that city.

Continued outward migration from the cultural core in southern Quebec brought the overflow population into southeastern Ontario, which had been occupied by British settlers, particularly Scottish, in the first half of the 19th century. Some of the poorer soils of southeastern Ontario were abandoned within a few decades and French-Canadians from the Quebec Lowland began to occupy these marginal lands in the latter part of the 19th century. They multiplied in eastern Ontario and took over more and more of the farms, and also came to the small towns as workers. In 1981, the counties of Prescott and Russell, along the Ottawa River, were 75 to 80 percent of French ethnic origin. The same areal expansion penetrated westward along the north side of the St. Lawrence River; in 1961, the population of Glengarry county was 57 percent of French origin, and many French-Canadians worked in the industrial plants of cities such as Cornwall. In 1981, however, the percentage of those reporting French as their mother tongue had declined to 38. Because the dairy farm agriculture of southeastern Ontario is part of the hinterland of Montreal and much of the population is of French-Canadian origin, this sub-region can be considered geographically as similar to the Quebec Lowland.

Areal Expansion Eastward into New Brunswick:

The narrow lowland strip extending eastward along the south shore of the St. Lawrence River directed people towards Gaspé Peninsula. French-speaking farmers occupied this linear plain east of Lévis-Lauzon throughout the 19th century and made some attempts to settle the poorer lands on the uplands of the Appalachians. They brought with them their linear villages, long-lot farms and large churches; the dominant landscape characteristics of the French cultural core came with the people wherever an agricultural economy was established. But the narrow extent of the plain decreased and was broken by coastal hills in Gaspé Peninsula; they had to seek other means of making a living there. Many supplemented their subsistence farming by fishing during the summers and by working in logging camps during the winters. These fishing and/or forestry activities of Gaspé villages made them different from the occupations in the simple service centres of the St. Lawrence Lowland. Gaspé settlements are therefore more like those around Chaleur Bay and along the east coast of New Brunswick.

The eastward expansion of French-Canadians penetrated through the landform barrier of the Notre Dame and Shickshock Mountains of Gaspé Peninsula by way of the Temiscouata Valley. This valley route still connects the narrow lowland along the St. Lawrence to the upper St. John River valley. Another topographic break through the Appalachian hills farther east along the Matapedia River also brought French-speaking people to Campbellton, Dalhousie and other northeastern New Brunswick cities. Settlers and roads crossed through these valleys leading to farmland in the upper St. John Valley and to work in the sawmills and pulp mills of northern New Brunswick. (The Temiscouata Valley route is still important, being used by the Trans-Canada Highway and railways—the main land connection within Canada between Quebec and New Brunswick.) These "Quebecois" settlers had a different history than the French-speaking Acadians of eastern New Brunswick.

By 1921, Gloucester and Madawaska counties of northern New Brunswick were more than 80 percent French-speaking and Restigouche and Kent counties were more than 60 percent French. Often French-speaking settlers replaced English-speaking people on the farms as the latter moved west to other parts of Canada or to the United States. This replacement process was therefore similar to that earlier in the Eastern Townships. The French-speaking population continued to increase across northern New Brunswick and they mixed with the earlier Acadian French; but, by 1981, this increase had levelled off. The outward flow of French out of Quebec into New Brunswick had declined and as the population urbanized in the resource towns, birth rates decreased. Madawaska county around Edmundston in northwestern New Brunswick, with 94 percent of its population having French as their mother tongue in 1981, remains the cultural core of French people in that province. But this is *not* the French-Canadian rural society of 19th century lowland Quebec; people in northern New Brunswick are now mainly urban dwellers; others are successful commercial farmers. French-Canadian culture and economy are different from those of the Quebec Lowland in the different environments of northern New Brunswick.

Northward into the Canadian Shield:
Two aspects of the northern areal expansion of French-Canadians were different from that previously discussed:

1.) settlers penetrated into a different physical environment in which land was suitable in only a few places for their agricultural economy;
2.) they moved into areas which were generally unoccupied, rather than replacing English-speaking people as they did to the south, west and east.

Agricultural settlers found strips of suitable soils in the narrow river valleys along the southern edge of the Canadian Shield and they occupied small pockets of level land within the Shield fringe. In some places, they replaced earlier Irish settlers, but often they cleared virgin land. Usually the trees were sold and the men worked in lumber camps in the winter as a means of earning money to establish a farm and raise a family.

The largest areas of level land with suitable soils and climate in the Shield were in the Lac St. Jean Lowland-Saguenay River valley and in the Clay Belt of northwestern Quebec-northeastern Ontario. Lumbermen and farmers entered the former region before the middle of the 19th century via the broad Saguenay River estuary leading to the Lac St. Jean Lowland. The trickles of settlers became a flood after 1890 when a railway connected the Lowland to Quebec City. For the first 30 years of this century, the Lac St. Jean Lowland was an active agricultural frontier; rural settlement spread around both sides of the lake. The main purpose of agriculture was to support the growing industrial cities there. Once more, the culture, language and landscapes of the Quebec Lowland were transferred to another region — an agricultural lowland within the Canadian Shield. This sub-region will be discussed further in Chapter 7.

A similar pattern of occupation evolved on the level land of the former glacial lake bottom north and east of Lake Temiscaming. After about 1880, both lumbermen and agricultural settlers followed the Ottawa River to unoccupied lands around Lake Temiscaming. As elsewhere in the Canadian Shield, lumbermen and farmers complemented one another; first the trees were cut for lumber and floated down the Ottawa River, and then settlers moved in to farm the cleared land. After 1920, agricultural settlement expanded greatly following the laying of a railway to the Prairie Provinces across the northern Clay Belt. Although much agriculture was mainly subsistence, particularly during the 1930s, the farms had a local market in the mining and forestry towns of the sub-region. Areal relationships between Shield and Lowland activities were being established prior to 1940; the Shield absorbed some of the surplus rural population of the Lowland and at the same time supplied raw materials for manufacturing in the Lowland cities.

The rural landscapes in the Lac St. Jean Lowland are similar to those on the Quebec Lowland, whereas those in the Quebec Clay Belt are slightly different. Although farm houses form a linear pattern along Clay Belt roads, the houses are farther apart; rural densities were never as great as in the southern cultural core. Although some farms are long and narrow, they are not as narrow as in southern Quebec, and some fields have been subdivided into rectangles. Some of the linear villages are replicas of those of southern Quebec, whereas others look like those of Ontario. The landscape created by French-Canadians in the Quebec Clay Belt is a modified version of that of the cultural core in the Lowland, probably because it was settled at a much later time.

French-Canadians spread into the Ontario part of the Clay Belt after 1930. Many became workers in the mining and pulp and paper towns there. These new generations were urban dwellers and industrial workers; they were not the rural "habitants" of the 19th century. As Ontario Clay Belt farms were abandoned by English-speaking settlers after 1950, many were taken over by French-Canadians. By 1981, the population of the four large counties of northeastern Ontario was 26 to 48 percent of French ethnic origin (see Table 3, p. 132).

Beyond and to the West:

The wider movement of French-Canadians, and others, into the Prairie Provinces is not discussed here. Throughout the early part of the 20th century, French-Canadians, along with immigrant groups from Europe, established farming communities across the Interior Plains and also concentrated into certain cities. The largest French-Canadian community was (and is) in St. Boniface, a suburb of Winnipeg. The extent of this outward migration of French-Canadians across Canada is illustrated by the establishment in 1909 of a French-speaking community of lumber mill workers in Maillardville, a suburb of Vancouver.

A renewed westward migration of French-Canadians to greater economic opportunities in western Canada became apparent again during the 1970s. This new movement was no longer a "push" from crowded farmlands, but was a "pull" of more employment possibilities in the West. The 1981 census reported 183,000 persons with French as a mother tongue in the four western provinces, about 40 percent in Alberta. In the 1971-1981 decade, French-speaking persons increased notably in Alberta and B.C., but declined in Manitoba and Saskatchewan.

Into the Cities of the Great Lakes-St. Lawrence Lowlands:

The outward areal expansion of farming settlers and other primary industry workers was parallelled by a movement of French-Canadians to the cities of Quebec and, to a lesser extent, to the cities of Ontario. This rural-urban migration was, of course, occurring all over North America. Much of this movement in Quebec was to Montreal, which became a bilingual city. Thus, two geographical patterns were occurring together—outward areal expansion and dispersion and internal concentration in the cities.

Summary:
The areal concept developed in the preceding pages is that of a cultural, linguistic group occupying a geographical area. It is a particular variation of the man-land theme over a period of time. People with a common language and similar laws, customs and religion developed a unique landscape in a particular environment in the Quebec Lowland. As numbers increased rapidly among these farming people, pressure developed from within to expand outwards to other lands and to concentrate in the cities. As people moved into new environments, they tried to bring with them the characteristics of the culture that they knew in the core. From a small and densely-occupied core along the St. Lawrence River between Montreal and Quebec City, French-Canadians expanded outward over all of southern Quebec and into the edges of the adjoining provinces, Ontario and New Brunswick.

RETREAT AND CONCENTRATION

The century of areal expansion is over. French-Canadians are no longer increasing significantly outside of the borders of Quebec and their numerical increase within Quebec has slowed down. A number of interrelated factors are involved in these further changes in the geography of French-Canadians in Canada.

Decreased Farm Population and Decreased Birth Rate:
The French-Canadian society and culture which evolved in the 19th century was dominantly rural and agricultural and it was characterized by large families and high birth rates.

The agricultural population of Quebec has decreased greatly, even more than in some other parts of Canada, and the amount of cultivated land has also decreased. Farm acreage and cultivation reached a peak in Quebec in 1941. By 1981, about 80 percent of Quebec's population lived in urban places and only about 3 percent lived on farms. The decrease in farm population and acreage is recorded in the following table.

About a half-million less people were on Quebec farms after the 30-year period 1941-1971, and there was a spectacular decrease of about 200,000 persons in the 5-year period 1966-1971. This same trend, but on a smaller numerical scale, was apparent in the Atlantic Provinces (see p. 82). This decrease in cultivation and in occupied farmland was a result of the facts noted in the preceding pages—that many of the farms outside of the Quebec

Lowland were established on poor or marginal land which became uneconomic or undesirable in the present agriculture economy. Rural poverty was no longer accepted passively in Quebec; opportunities for improved education and a wider choice of employment were sought in the cities.

Table 1

YEAR	FARM POPULATION	NUMERICAL DECLINE	FARM ACREAGE	CULTIVATED ACREAGE
1941	840,000		18,000,000	9,000,000
1951	790,000	50,000	17,000,000	8,800,000
1966	500,000	290,000	13,000,000	7,600,000
1971	300,000	200,000	11,000,000	6,400,000
1976	200,000	100,000	10,000,000	5,900,000
1981			9,300,000	5,800,000

The change from a rural to an urban society was parallelled by rapidly decreasing birth rates, typical of urban societies elsewhere. From being the province with the highest birth rates early in this century, Quebec had one of the lowest birth rates in Canada in the 1970s. The internal pressure of an increasing population looking for land no longer applies.

In the past, Quebec's high birth rates increased its population at about the same rate as immigration, plus natural birth rates, increased the population in the rest of Canada. French-speaking Canadians made up a constant 30-33 percent of Canada's population through the first half of this century. Even though immigration to Canada decreased from the great waves of the early part of this century, the French-Canadian natural increase has decreased even more. By 1971, French-Canadians had declined to 27 percent of Canada's population and, in 1981, only 25 percent of Canadians reported French as their mother tongue. (The term "French" should be used carefully. It can be defined on an ethnic basis as those who trace their male ancestry back to France, or on a language basis as those who report that French is the dominant language spoken at home. Note that ethnic origin was not recorded in the 1976 census. A minor problem is the inclusion of a few recent immigrants from France who are not "French-Canadians" in a historical sense.)

Relative Decreases outside of Quebec:
The number of French-speaking persons is declining relatively outside of Quebec. In three provinces (New Brunswick, Alberta, British Columbia) the *number* of French-speaking persons increased between 1971-1981, but in all provinces the *percentage* of French-Canadians declined. This decrease outside of Quebec is recorded in the following table. Although numbers may *increase,* the percent could *decrease* if other ethnic or language groups increased at a faster rate.

131

Table 2

Number and Percent of French-Speakers Outside of Quebec, 1971-81

	−1971−		−1981−		NUMERICAL INCREASE/
PROVINCE	NUMBER	PERCENT	NUMBER	PERCENT	DECREASE
New Brunswick	215,700	34.0	234,000	33.6	+18,300
Nova Scotia	39,400	5.0	36,000	4.2	−3,400
Ontario	482,000	6.2	475,600	5.5	−6,400
Manitoba	60,500	6.1	52,600	5.1	−7,900
British Columbia	38,000	1.7	45,600	1.6	+7,600

The percentage decrease was particularly noticeable in certain small areas outside of Quebec in which French-Canadians made up a sizeable minority of the residents. The exception around Cochrane in northeastern Ontario is recorded in the following table. These trends in the concentration of ethnic and mother tongue French are noted in Table 3. Note the difference in the numbers of ethnic French recorded in each county compared with those who stated that French was their mother tongue. Will these trends continue in the 1980s?

Table 3

French Population, by Counties, in Parts of New Brunswick and Ontario

	ETHNIC FRENCH, 1961-71				MOTHER TONGUE FRENCH, 1961-81			
	−1961−		−1971−		−1961−		−1981−	
COUNTY	NUMBER	PERCENT	NUMBER	PERCENT	NUMBER	PERCENT	NUMBER	PERCENT
New Brunswick								
Madawaska	36,500	94	32,500	92	37,000	95	34,000	94
Gloucester	56,500	85	62,400	82	57,000	85	70,500	81
Kent	22,000	82	20,400	81	22,000	82	24,000	80
Restigouche	28,000	68	26,700	65	25,000	61	24,400	60
Southeast Ontario								
Prescott	23,000	83	23,000	81	23,000	85	23,300	80
Russell	16,000	73	14,000	84	16,000	76	16,700	75
Glengarry	11,000	57	10,000	52	9,000	47	7,800	38
Stormont	28,000	48	27,000	44	21,000	36	18,600	30
Northeast Ontario								
Cochrane	48,000	50	50,000	52	44,000	46	46,400	48
Nipissing	31,000	43	32,000	40	26,000	36	23,200	30
Sudbury	65,000	40	76,000	38	55,000	33	57,000	30
Temiskaming	16,000	30	16,000	33	14,000	27	10,900	26

Many French-Canadians living outside of Quebec, particularly second or third generation migrants from Quebec, no longer use French in their homes; they have adapted to, and been absorbed into, the dominant English-speaking society and business of the rest of Canada. Thus, the expansion of French as a first language, as a measure of French-Canadian culture, has virtually ceased outside of Quebec. Similarly, French as a first language in the home is minor across Canada outside of the core areas. The edges of the French-Canadian core are being nibbled away outside of Quebec and retraction and retreat into the core are taking place. Is a philosophy of political separatism within Quebec a reaction to, and defence against, the erosion of the French-Canadian cultural core from without? Are political developments in Quebec related to changing geographical patterns?

English-Speaking People within Quebec:
There has always been an English-speaking minority in Quebec since the early 18th century; they lived mainly in particular geographical areas such as Montreal and the Eastern Townships. For about a century, 1881-1976, French-Canadians consistently made up 79-81 percent of Quebec's population, but this figure increased slightly to 82 percent in 1981. In numbers, the other 18 percent constituted more than one million persons who spoke a language other than French in 1981. Most of these people live in metropolitan Montreal where 18 percent of the people there reported English as their mother tongue in 1981 and 4½ percent spoke Italian. Stated in another way statistically, 73 percent of the persons in Quebec who reported English as their mother tongue (520,000 out of 706,000) lived in metropolitan Montreal, mainly in the western sections of that city. The "outflow" (so called) of English-speaking persons from Montreal during the late 1970s—an average of 17,000 annually—had reduced this percentage. Since most of the other "minority" language and ethnic groups also live in Montreal, it is apparent that the rest of Quebec has a *high* percentage of French-speaking persons.

Summary and Questions:
The areal *expansion* of French-Canadians was a historical, geographical process of a people occupying an area. There were political, social and economic implications in this man-land relationship theme. If areal *contraction* is now going on, can one predict political, social and economic reactions? Is a separate political Quebec a means of saving and protecting a separate language and cultural group? Can such a group survive the language and cultural bombardment of newspapers, books, radio and television of more than 200 million English-speaking people who surround them? Economically, does Quebec have a sufficient natural resource base to support a separate economy? Are other Canadians concerned enough about this minority group to work together with Quebec residents to maintain their language and culture?

MONTREAL

Introduction

Montreal became Canada's first large city. Almost half the people of Quebec have concentrated into the expanding metropolitan city and its suburbs. Its population increase was the result of the interaction of several site and locational factors. The following comments about geographical patterns of land use that evolved in Montreal can be considered as an example of how people in large cities have arranged their urban activities and movements into spatial patterns to achieve an interacting political, social and economic unit. But this geographical entity, Montreal, with its internal patterns does not stand alone; it has external local, regional and national links. It is part of a hierarchy of larger and smaller regions, some of which it dominates and others with which it has a variety of spatial interactions. The significance of its geographical location, along with other political and economic decisions and influences, should be part of any explanation of Montreal's rise to become the leading industrial and financial city in Canada in the first half of the 20th century.

Site and Relative Location

The original settlement was established on the east side of Montreal Island and the city spread over the eastern and southern parts of the island. Originally the physical advantage of being on an island was important for defence against the Indians. Montreal became an ocean port and the western terminal of transport on the St. Lawrence River because of the barrier of the Lachine Rapids on the south side of the island; the rapids prevented further direct inland water transport.

Montreal was (and is) a "coastal" city because of its accessibility from the sea during the summer; it was a gateway into the heart of North America, the farthest inland that ocean ships could penetrate into the eastern part of the continent. After the late 18th century, Montreal had a central position in the developing economy of eastern North America and, for a short time, it competed with New York City. In those days, when water transportation was vital for commerce, Montreal was at the junction of four routes:

1.) From the east, the broad opening of the gulf and estuary of the St. Lawrence narrowed west of Quebec City, but was navigable for the ships of that time all the way to Montreal, except when the river was frozen three or four months of the winter. Quebec City was the prime port of entry into Canada until dredging of the shifting river channels east of Montreal early in the 19th century gave better ship access. As a result,

Montreal's trade and commercial functions increased and, by 1830, its population exceeded that of Quebec.

2.) To the south, a landform gap in the Appalachians was occupied by the Hudson River, Lake Champlain and Richelieu River. This water route could be used by only small vessels, but the interconnected valleys later became a major north-south land transport route. This landform pass connected Canada's largest city directly with the United States' largest city, New York. Undoubtedly, the interaction of people, ideas, products and finance between New York and Montreal aided the growth of the latter.

3.) To the west, several rapids in the St. Lawrence River between Montreal and Lake Ontario delayed and limited water transport. In the early days, canoes could be portaged around these rapids and the route led fur traders and explorers to the heart of north-central United States, south of Lakes Ontario and Erie. However, the significant use of the St. Lawrence west of Montreal came after the construction of shallow, bypass canals in the second quarter of the 19th century. Southern Ontario then came into the hinterland of Montreal; products moving between Ontario and Britain had to be transferred from one carrier to another in Montreal.

4.) To the northwest, the Ottawa River was one end of a water route for canoes to Georgian Bay, Lake Superior and western Canada. But the river had numerous rapids and never became important for water transport after the canoe-travel period. Towards the end of the 19th century, however, the Ottawa Valley became a strategic land route for the railroads leading to northern Ontario. This part of the Canadian Shield, and the Interior Plains beyond, were then brought into the hinterland of Montreal; raw materials from the north and west flowed to the increasing industries of the Heartland's largest city.

Although these water routes were important to Montreal early in the 19th century, their significance became greater near the end of the century when the valleys were used for rail transportation. The natural resources of four parts of North America could be transported into Montreal and the city could supply services and send out some manufactured products to an ever-broadening hinterland. From the earliest days, business and financial institutions in Montreal could control and direct the flow of trade out of and into eastern Canada. As a break-in-transport point between ocean and land transport, industries were established along and near the harbour in Montreal to handle and process the products moving through the city.

Montreal's steady population increase in the 19th century was mainly the result of its port activities and its financial and commercial institutions. Its site determined the exact location of the city and its geographical position influenced its growth.

What are some of the site and position features of the place in which you live? Adapt the preceding comments to other Canadian cities.

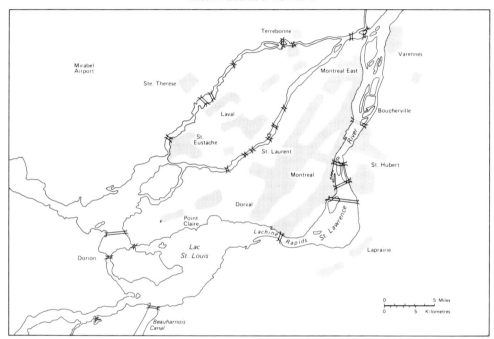

Location and Types of Industries

Montreal became an industrial city in this century. Industry developed in northwestern Europe in the late 19th century on or near coal fields, but the Quebec Lowland had no coal to supply power. However, as population and consumers increased in the Great Lakes-St. Lawrence Lowlands, industries in Montreal could use electric power derived from nearby rivers dropping over the edge of the Canadian Shield, and also from the rapids in the St. Lawrence River north of Montreal Island.

The main industrial areas were established at the port where the two types of transport—rail and water—came together. This industrial zone spread north along the waterfront on the east side of Montreal Island and to the west along the Lachine Canal (see map above). Industrial workers crowded into rather poor houses near these areas. Most of these people were French-Canadians who came to jobs in the city from the farms of the Quebec Lowland. After 1950, industrial land use spread inland in strips along highways served by truck transport; numerous new industrial parks dispersed over Montreal Island, particularly in St. Laurent. In addition, new industries occupied former farmland off the island to the north and east of the St. Lawrence River. Industrial land use also spread along the river as far east as Sorel.

Prior to 1970, the annual value of manufactured goods produced in metropolitan Montreal was greater than that of any other city in Canada. These products were consumed in every part of Canada. Heartland industries supplied hinterland consumers. The visual local response to this national importance appeared in specific areal patterns of industrial land use in Montreal.

Related to the geographical position of Montreal, the city had three types of industry:

1.) those dependent on imported raw materials and therefore located near the port;
2.) those dependent on Canadian resources and located on rail or road transport;
3.) those supplying the large local consumer market and which could be located anywhere within the metropolitan city.

The first two types of manufacturing usually consist of primary processing of raw materials transported into the metropolitan areas; the third type is mainly secondary manufacturing in which components are collected and assembled from various other plants and perhaps further processed at one main factory. The largest number of industries are in the latter category and they have many internal linkages within the city.

Does this simple classification of industry fit the type of industries of the city in which you live or a city near you? Adapt this format to factual information about other cities if you wish to probe into their industrial base.

Examples of Industries:
Some examples of industries in Montreal dependent on imported raw materials are: oil refineries, sugar refineries and the textile industry. However, the significance and relative importance of this external dependence are declining. The huge oil refineries which supplied consumers in the St. Lawrence and Ottawa valleys prior to 1970 were fed by petroleum coming in by pipeline from Portland, Maine, or by tankers in summer from Venezuela or the Middle East. This dependence on external petroleum—still

137

so vulnerable to the economy of the Atlantic Provinces—was reduced in the 1970s when the pipeline carrying Interior Plains oil to Toronto was extended to Montreal. Although Montreal has a major oil refining concentration in Canada, the area did not develop an allied petrochemical industry, as in Ontario.

The textile industry, for example, depended on imported cotton and wool until the middle of this century. The primary textile industry, producing cloth and yarn and similar items, was dispersed in towns and cities throughout the Eastern Townships where relatively cheap labour and power were available or in cities in the Lowland such as Cornwall, Trois Rivières and Quebec. However, the secondary textile industry, particularly clothing manufacturing, was concentrated in Montreal near the large local market, the design offices, and near transport to the rest of Canada. The dependence on external sources of textile fibres lessened as more and more of the industry used synthetic fibres which could be produced in Canada from petroleum by-products. The textile industry remains vulnerable, however, to lower cost producers in other countries. Part of the industry gradually moved westward to southern Ontario to be near the larger local market there.

Montreal's industries also process the natural resources of its nearby and distant hinterlands. For example, agricultural products of the surrounding Montreal Plain, such as dairy and meat products and vegetables, are collected, processed and distributed to about three million local consumers. Metal fabricating and furniture manufacture, further examples, depend on the mineral and forest resources of the Canadian Shield.

Wheat from the Interior Plains is brought to local flour mills and bakeries to help feed this large city. Prior to 1960, Montreal was the main transshipment point for wheat from the eastern Interior Plains en route to overseas markets in Europe. This transfer function decreased after the St. Lawrence Seaway was completed. Although the large grain elevators are usually fully used in Montreal, wheat and other grains carried in the long, narrow lake freighters from Thunder Bay may pass the city and be stored in elevators at such places along the St. Lawrence as Sorel, Quebec City and Baie Comeau.

The opening of the St. Lawrence Seaway west of Montreal had another effect on Montreal's harbour; some ocean vessels could bypass Montreal and carry their cargoes directly inland to Toronto or other lake ports. The significance of the Seaway has been much greater to American cities on the south side of the Great Lakes than to Canadian interior cities. Changes in water transport had only minor effects upon Montreal's industries because so many of the raw materials and semi-processed goods, produced locally, moved by road and rail. Many of the manufactured goods produced in Montreal do not move out of the city, but are consumed internally. However, land use changes are taking place in the old port of Montreal following the closing of the Lachine Canal; new facilities are expanding along the river in northeastern Montreal.

Despite the significance of industry in Montreal and its importance to Canada, only about 25 percent of Montreal's work force is employed in industrial occupations, whereas about 50 percent of the working population is in service occupations. In other words, half of the people in Montreal work for one another.

Summary:

Because this book does not discuss industrial patterns in every major city in Canada, the preceding comments about industry in Montreal were presented as a possible methodology for the consideration of geographical aspects of industry in other cities. The first geographical question is *where* are the industrial areas? Have these zones changed in location over time? *Why* are the industries where they are and *how* do they fit areally into other activities within the city? Where do the raw materials used in industries come from and how do they get there? What is the purpose of manufacturing — are the products consumed locally or are they distributed to other parts of Canada? ∠

Expansion of the Urban Area

When Montreal became the first city in Canada to have one million population in 1941, most of the urban land uses were confined to the south and east parts of Montreal Island. Even by 1951, less than 20 percent of western Montreal Island was occupied by urban uses and much of the land was still in agricultural production. With the addition of about two million people from 1941-1981, urban land uses expanded over most of Montreal Island, adjoining Isle Jesus, and on to the "mainland" across the rivers. Much of the direction of areal expansion off the islands was controlled by the many bridges which funnel the traffic of people and products to and from Montreal Island; these bridges link the "core" of Montreal with its immediate hinterland (see map p. 136). In addition to evolving patterns of outward areal expansion, Montreal is going through a process of internal replacement of past urban land uses. For example, old houses near the city centre have been replaced by apartments and expanding commercial areas. These changing geographical patterns of outward areal expansion and internal replacement are taking place in all large Canadian cities. They should be considered specifically when the urban geography of particular cities is discussed.

An Example of Scale

Montreal, like other cities in Canada, can be studied on several scales. One of the purposes of regional geography is to analyze the significance of location on various scales. Nationally, Montreal serves Canada through its industries and commerce; decisions made in tall office towers in Montreal influence the locations and function of many industrial and commercial activities in other parts of Canada. Regionally, Montreal dominates the eastern part of the Great Lakes-St. Lawrence Lowlands and the economy of the province of Quebec; it competes with Toronto in many activities. At another regional scale, Montreal competes with Quebec City, where political decisions are made.

On the local scale, Montreal is the only major city in the Montreal Plain of southwestern Quebec. Because so many supply and service functions are available in Montreal, no other medium-size city has arisen within 50 kilometres of it. The metropolitan city can be studied on the local scale, analyzing the internal areal patterns of land use within the city. Like other cities, the industrial zones, commercial strips and residential neighbourhoods are located in particular places and patterns—not only because of national and regional influences, but also because of local decisions and regulations. (Vancouver is discussed as an example of such historical urban geography methodology in Chapter 9.)

Other Topics

Many other topics within Montreal could be discussed, but it is not the purpose of this book to present a complete urban, historical or regional geography of Canadian cities. Montreal was discussed here mainly as an example of an industrial city.

Montreal could also have been studied in terms of its geographical patterns of ethnic and linguistic groups. Throughout the early part of the 19th century, Montreal was a mainly English-speaking city and the main "national" city in the colonial area which was then eastern Canada. Then the surplus farm population from the Quebec Lowland began to flow into the city by the middle of the century. When Montreal reached a population of 100,000 people in 1871, 55 percent of its residents were French-speaking. Although the linguistic character of the city had changed, the general distribution patterns of the main language groups had been established by then.

French and English-speaking residents have tended to occupy different geographical areas of Montreal. Irish immigrants settled near the east end of the Lachine Canal in an area known as Griffintown; Irish-Catholic churches and schools became the social centres there. Other English-speaking people lived on the west side of the old city at the base of Mount Royal and in what became the city of Westmount; they were engaged mainly in commercial and management occupations. French-speaking people occupied rows of brick tenements without front yards along the Lachine Canal and small houses northward near the harbour; they constituted most of the labour force in transport and industry occupations. Although the census reports the geographical pattern of the first language(s) spoken at home, do we know the areal distribution of the language(s) of business, industry and finance in Montreal during the day? Is the daytime linguistic pattern different from the residence (night) pattern?

By the mid-20th century, a wedge of "other" people extended northwest of the city core between the French and English areas. They came mainly from the Mediterranean countries such as Italy, Greece and Portugal; they were often labourers in the construction trades. In Montreal, about 200,000 people recorded these three languages as their mother tongue compared with more than 325,000 in Toronto. Compare this mixed ethnic area with that northwest of the central city core of Toronto.

Is there a geography of architecture? Early in this century, much of the residential area of Montreal was made up of two and three storey multiple dwellings, often with curving, iron stairsteps in front. In contrast, most Ontario cities consisted of single-family, detached homes.

Early in this century, high income people lived on the west side of Montreal and low income workers lived on the east side. This east-west geographical distribution pattern will be noted later in other cities. Why is this so?

MAJOR CITIES OF THE ST. LAWRENCE LOWLAND

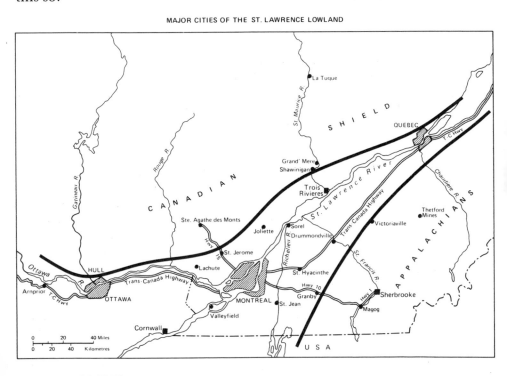

OTHER CITIES

One of the regional differences between southern Quebec and southern

Ontario in their urban systems is the number and distribution of medium-size cities. In southern Quebec, because of the domination of Montreal, there are only six such cities—Sorel, Drummondville, St. Hyacinthe, Victoriaville, Granby and St. Jean—compared with ten in southern Ontario (excluding those cities which are parts of larger metropolitan cities). Refer to Table 4. Study the distribution and spacing of these cities on the south side of the St. Lawrence River (see map p. 141). They are regional cities and service centres for nearby agricultural hinterlands. Note that they grew very little in population between 1976-1981. Fit this regional example into the national discussion of the distribution and hierarchy of cities in Chapter 2.

QUEBEC CITY

This city is properly named as only Quebec, but the term, "City" is often added to differentiate the city from the province. With a population of more than a half million in the metropolitan area, it is one of Canada's ten largest cities. Its site and relative location provide some explanations for the city's establishment and growth.

Site and Functions

From its beginnings, Quebec occupied a strategic site where the estuary of the St. Lawrence River was constricted and the channel was further narrowed by the Isle of Orleans filling much of the mid-section of the river. On the north side of the river, a steep escarpment of sedimentary rock rose directly above the river—an excellent site for military defence. Originally the main commercial and residential buildings were located on a narrow lowland at the base of the cliff. This section, now called Lower Town, with its narrow, "European" streets and old stone buildings, has been revived and restored as a tourist attraction.

On the north side of the city, the low area around the mouth of the St. Charles River was occupied by industries, including a pulp and paper mill and some of the port activities. Industrial workers are closely packed into this section; their houses are often two or three storey multiple dwellings or duplexes, fronting directly on the streets with no front yards or open space. The formerly unattractive river has been "cleaned up" and is now lined with broad walks.

The military fort and adjoining government, religious and educational buildings were located on top of the escarpment. This part of Quebec City became one of the attractive tourist sites of North America, featuring the restored fort, specialty shops along winding commercial streets, and the movement of photogenic horses and carriages. A first class residential area developed just west of the city centre on view sites near or overlooking the river. Why were the homes of wealthier people often built on the west sides

142

of cities?

The preceding comments indicate some relationships between the physical characteristics of the site and urban functions. City dwellers sometimes forget physical environment influences in an urban area.

Relative Location and Areal Growth

Quebec's population increased relatively slowly throughout the 19th century. Its main functions then—that of government, church and education —were significant, both locally and regionally. Its waterfront was more important as a port of entry for people than for products. Montreal had a more central location in eastern Canada and competed successfully with Quebec for industrial and commercial functions. Whereas Montreal's growth was aided by its focal position as a railway centre, Quebec had the dis-advantage of not being connected by rail to the western part of the Quebec Lowland until the 1880s. Quebec's location on the eastern fringe of the St. Lawrence Lowland did not encourage control of regional development within the Lowland, but the city did become a gateway to resource development and settlement in the Saguenay-Lac St. Jean Lowland in its hinterland to the northeast.

Quebec's areal expansion of residential and commercial land uses in recent decades has been mainly to the west, perhaps drawn by the activities related to the bridge to the south side of the river. The industrial area expanded eastward of the St. Charles River, aided by reclaimed land along the base of the Beaufort cliffs and oriented to ship and rail transport. Industrialization within the metropolitan area increased on the south side of the river in Lauzon and Lévis with ship-building specialization. Compare the similarities of east and west land-use expansion and differentiation with those in Vancouver (Chapter 9).

Although Quebec may be remembered only for its unique escarpment site and its attractions to tourists, it really is a diverse city, similar to others in Canada. Montreal is more cosmopolitan and influenced by English-speaking business and culture, whereas Quebec remains the political and cultural capital of French-speaking society.

Parallels with Victoria

There are many parallels between the history and geography of Quebec City and Victoria, B.C., although in different time periods and scales. Both were ports of entry during the beginnings of regional development; both were bypassed later when larger industrial and commercial cities developed inland; i.e., Montreal and Vancouver. Each of these latter cities now holds almost half of the population of its province and each is the major port on the east and west coasts respectively. Both Quebec and Victoria continued to grow, however, as government and cultural centres (Victoria held the remnants of British colonial society and culture). Both have promoted their tourist image—a "European" city in Quebec and "a little bit of olde England" in Victoria. Both have added industrial activities and are wholesale and distribution centres for their local regions. How much of this similar development is related to the similar geographical positions of these cities as gateways to developing regions inland and north of them? Think of these comparisons again when reading about Victoria and Vancouver in Chapter 9.

Table 4

Population of the Largest Cities of Southern Quebec and Southeastern Ontario, 1981

METROPOLITAN CITIES	1976	1981	METROPOLITAN CITIES	1976	1981
Metro Montreal	2,803,000	2,829,000	Metro Ottawa-Hull	694,000	718,000
Montreal	1,080,000	980,000	Metro Hull	172,000	171,000
Laval	247,000	269,000	Hull	61,000	56,000
Longueuil	123,000	124,000	Gatineau	74,000	75,000
Montréal Nord	97,000	95,000	Aylmer	26,000	26,700
St. Léonard	79,000	79,500	Metro Ottawa	522,000	547,000
Lasalle	77,000	76,000	Ottawa	304,000	295,000
St. Laurent	65,000	66,000	Nepean	77,000	73,000
Verdun	68,000	61,300	Gloucester	57,000	68,000
St. Hubert	50,000	61,000	Vanier	20,000	19,000
Brossard	40,000	52,000	Metro Trois Rivières	98,000	111,500
Dollard Ormeaux	37,000	40,000	Trois Rivières	53,000	50,500
Pierrefonds	35,400	38,400	Cap de Madeleine	32,000	32,600
Lachine	41,000	38,000	Trois Rivières Ouest	11,000	13,000
Anjou	36,600	37,400	Metro Sherbrooke	105,000	117,400
Chateauguay	36,000	37,000	Sherbrooke	77,000	74,000
Pointe Trembles	36,000	36,000			
Repentigny	27,000	34,500	OTHER CITIES		
Boucherville	26,000	30,000	St. Jean (metro)	56,000	60,700
St. Eustache	21,000	30,000	Sorel (metro)	44,000	47,000
Valleyfield	30,000	29,600	St. Jérôme (metro)	41,000	43,800
Côte St. Luc	26,000	27,500	Drummondville	40,000	39,200
Pointe Claire	26,000	24,500	St. Hyacinthe	38,000	38,300
Outremont	27,000	24,000	Granby	37,000	38,000
St. Bruno	21,000	23,000	Victoriaville (metro)	32,700	36,000
St. Lambert	21,000	20,500	Joliette (metro)	33,200	34,500
Westmount	22,000	20,500	Rimouski	28,000	30,000
Mt. Royal	21,000	19,200	Thetford Mines	21,000	20,000
Metro Quebec	543,000	576,000			
Quebec	177,000	166,000	SOUTHEASTERN ONTARIO		
Ste. Foy	72,000	69,000	Cornwall (metro)	53,000	53,400
Charlesbourg	63,000	68,400	Brockville (metro)	35,000	35,700
Beauport	55,000	60,500			
Lévis-Lauzon	30,000	31,000			

REGIONAL DIFFERENCES IN SOUTHERN QUEBEC

On one scale, Southern Quebec is a region with similarities in culture and language, but internally there are sub-regional differences in landforms, landscapes and economies. The Lowland displays much internal similarity in its agricultural landscapes and village forms; its level land, hay-pasture-dairying economy, long-lot farms and linear settlement patterns are not duplicated in totality elsewhere in Canada. Because the Quebec Lowland has no outstanding natural resource base, except its soil and agriculture, the industries of the cities depend greatly upon resources from outside of the region. The Lowland is dominated by one very large city, Montreal, with two secondary large cities—Quebec and Ottawa-Hull—serving the edges of the region. In this geometric spacing of cities (discussed nationally in Chapter 2), the third level of size is represented by Trois Rivières, halfway between Montreal and Quebec, and Sherbrooke, halfway between Montreal and the U.S. border.

The Appalachian hills and mountains of southern Quebec are different from the Lowland in several characteristics. The differences in landforms and vegetation cover are obvious in the landscape. The amount of cultivation and resulting farm population is much less in the Appalachians than in the Lowland. In the Eastern Townships, the cultural remnants of the English-speaking settlers are apparent in the farm and field subdivision system and in the forms of the villages and towns. Mining and forestry activities, and their primary industry settlements, add variety to the Appalachian economy. The pulp and paper mill towns and textile-based towns along the rivers flowing northward out of the Appalachians, plus mining communities such as Thetford and Asbestos, are similar to the resource-based towns in the Atlantic and Gulf region.

The southwestern Appalachians are a more fully occupied region than is the eastern part consisting of the Notre Dame and Shickshock mountains which extend to Gaspé Peninsula. The western sub-region is dominated by one large city, Sherbrooke, which performs many central place functions for its surrounding area. The Eastern Townships, known as Estrie, are increasingly a tourist and resort area for the people of Montreal—not only as a ski area which competes with the Laurentians (a similar hilly environment), but also for summer cottages and as a centre for numerous cultural and entertainment events during the summer. It is part of the recreation hinterland of Montreal.

The Canadian Shield lies north of the Quebec Lowland. Although the Shield is vastly different from the Lowland in landforms, vegetation, soils, population density and economy, there are numerous connections and interactions between the Shield and the Lowland. Shield rivers supply the hydro-electric power which runs the industrial plants of the Lowland cities; metallic minerals and forest products of the Shield move in semi-processed form to Lowland cities for further processing or for trans-shipment abroad; the narrow valleys within the Shield edge absorbed some of the past surplus farm population of the Lowland; the cool lakes, forests, animals and snow-covered ski hills supply recreation to the present dwellers in the crowded Lowland cities. The Canadian Shield is discussed in Chapter 7 and it is recognized that one cannot fully understand the geographical patterns and activities of the Quebec Lowland region without considering the influences and contributions of the Shield.

REFERENCES

Atlases:

L'Atlas Régional du Saguenay-Lac Saint-Jean, prepared by Dept. de Géographie, Université du Québec à Chicoutimi, Chicoutimi, 1981.
"Le Développement Inégal dans la Région de Québec" edited by R. Koninck, R. Lavertue, J. Raveneau, Les Presses de l'Université Laval, Québec, 1982.

Periodicals:

Le Bulletin de Recherche, Dept. de Géographie de l'Université de Sherbrooke No. 1, 1972 to No. 60, 1981.
Revue Canadienne de Géographie, Dept. de Geog., Univ. de Montréal, Vol. 1, 1947 to Vol. 30, 1976 (ceased).
Cahiers de Géographie de Québec, Institut de Géographie, Université Laval, Québec, Vol. 1, 1956 to Vol. 26, 1982.
These periodicals are the best sources of information and current geographical research in Quebec. The articles and reviews are written mainly by French-Canadian geographers. Special theme issues are common, such as in the *Cahiers de Géographie*. For example:
Vol. 25, No. 64, April, 1981. *Whole issue on Quebec City.*
Vol. 26, No. 67, April, 1982. *Whole issue on St. Maurice Region.*
Most articles are written in French, but in 1981-82, for example, there were two articles in English in the *Cahiers*:
"A Study of Changes in the Distribution and Mobility of Armenians in Montreal" by G. Chickekian, Vol. 25, No. 65, Sept. 1981, pp. 169-195.
"Port Service Industries: The Case of Montreal" by Brian Slack, Vol. 26, No. 68, Sept. 1982, pp. 235-240.

Journal of Canadian Studies, Trent Univ. Peterborough.
"Watching the Frontier Disappear: English-Speaking Reaction to French-Canadian Colonization in the Eastern Townships, 1844-90" by J.I. Little, Vol. 15, No. 4, 1980-81, pp. 90-111.

Books:

"Montreal Field Guide" edited by L. Beauregard for the Can. Assoc. of Geographers, Univ. of Montreal Press, Montreal, 1972. 197 pages.
"Language Zones in Canada" by Don G. Cartwright, Dept. of Secretary of State, Bilingual Districts Advisory Board, Ottawa, 1976. 115 pages.
"Montreal Geographical Essays" edited by D.B. Frost, Dept. of Geog., Concordia Univ., Montreal, Occasional Papers, No. 1, 1981. 197 pages.
"Two Societies: Life in Mid-Nineteenth Century Quebec" by R. Cole Harris,

McClelland and Stewart, Toronto, 1976. 62 pages.

"Les ports québécois" by J.C. Lasserre, Dept. de Géog., Univ. de Montréal, No. 80-07, 1980. 84 pages.

"The Climate of Quebec — Part 1, Climatic Atlas" by C.V. Wilson, Canadian Meteorological Service, Dept. of Transport, Toronto, 1971. 9 pages, 44 maps.

Some relevant articles in *The Canadian Geographer* between 1970-82, Can. Assoc. of Geog., Burnside Hall, McGill Univ., Montreal:

Vol. 25, No. 3, 1981.	"Language Policy and the Political Organization of Territory: A Canadian Dilemma" by Don Cartwright, pp. 205-224.
Vol. 24, No. 4, 1980.	"L'Exode Urbain des Cantons de l'Est" by Y. Brunet, pp. 385-405.
Vol. 21, No. 1, 1977.	"French-Canadian Settlement in Eastern Ontario in the 19th Century" by Don Cartwright, pp. 1-21. "Ecologie Factorielle Comparée Edmonton-Quebec" by A. Bailly and M. Polèse, pp. 59-80.
Vol. 20, No. 3, 1976.	"Montreal and Toronto Clothing Industries" by Guy Steed, pp. 298-309.
Vol. 18, No. 3, 1974.	"The Geographic Basis for the Viability of an Independent State of Quebec" by Jean Cermakian, pp. 288-294.
Vol. 18, No. 1, 1974.	A special issue on Quebec containing seven articles on topics such as population, agriculture, manufacturing, boundaries, geomorphology, cartography and northern Quebec. *All articles are written in French.*
Vol. 16, No. 3, 1972.	"Fleuve-Frontière: Deux Rives des Saint-Laurent Supérieur" by J.C. Lasserre, pp. 199-210.

CHAPTER 6

SOUTHERN ONTARIO

CHAPTER 6

SOUTHERN ONTARIO

INTRODUCTION

The greatest concentration of people and activities within the heartland of the Great Lakes-St. Lawrence Lowlands is in southern Ontario. The small region is the home of about one-third of Canada's population and it produces almost half of the value of Canadian manufacturing. Southern Ontario, south of the Canadian Shield, occupies less than 10 percent of the provincial area, but holds almost 90 percent of its population. The region has the largest number of medium-size and large cities in Canada; the thousands of industrial, commercial and service workers in these cities are fed by the country's best agricultural lands nearby. Although southern Ontario has high densities and obvious material prosperity, within it these characteristics show sub-regional differences and variations. Some of the features of southern Ontario as the Heartland of Canada are discussed in Chapter 4. This chapter will comment mainly on south-central and south-western Ontario, because eastern Ontario—east of the Frontenac Axis of the Canadian Shield—is considered in Chapter 5 as part of the hinterland of Montreal in southern Quebec.

This chapter emphasizes two main topics—agriculture and cities—following the themes which were discussed on a national scale in Chapter 2. The natural resource base of southern Ontario, like that of southern Quebec, is not extensive, except for two elements—the good soils and favourable climate which support agriculture. Man's use and adaptation to these elements of the natural environment are woven into the following discussion of agriculture, rather than described separately. The other outstanding characteristic in which this region differs from others in Canada is its concentration and interlinking network of cities and their manufacturing.

THEMES

1.) To illustrate some of the regional differences in the agricultural landscapes of southern Ontario and to relate these differences to local physical environments and regional markets.

2.) To discuss some aspects of industrialization in southern Ontario, particularly in the context of raw materials and the heartland-hinterland concept.

3.) To note the significance of relative locations of cities and the areal patterns of spatial interaction within the region's urban network.

4.) To comment on the relationships between city population increase and outward areal expansion of urban land uses; these principles also apply to other Canadian cities. Toronto is used as an example of this process.

AGRICULTURE

Environments and Land Use

Southern Ontario has a most favourable combination of excellent physical environmental conditions for crop production and the market advantages of a large nearby consuming population. Most of the gently rolling to level land left behind from deposition at the end of the Glacial Age has excellent to good soils; this land is favoured by warm to hot summer temperatures with the longest average frost-free season in eastern Canada. The environmental element causing occasional concern is the lack of sufficient summer precipitation in the southwestern peninsula. The original deciduous forest indicated this relatively mild climate, and the original Indian inhabitants already had established an agricultural economy before Europeans arrived there. Much of that forest was cut down for lumber or cleared for farmland during the 19th century.

Most crops are market-oriented and are consumed within the region. The dominant land uses of hay-pasture, corn and feed grains cover much of southern Ontario with different shades of green in summer. The main purpose of these crops is to support a livestock industry; its dairy, poultry and meat products help to feed the city dwellers. The rural landscape is dominated by large livestock barns, tall cylindrical feed silos, well-kept farmhouses, and neat, rectangular, small fields producing a variety of crops on any one farm. Rural population densities are much higher than in the other large area of agricultural land use in Canada—the southern Interior Plains.

Most of the rural countryside looks quite similar, except for the small areas where specialty crops are grown. The following comments are examples of three agricultural sub-regions:

1.) the Essex-Kent vegetable area;
2.) the Norfolk tobacco belt;
3.) the Niagara fruit area.

These examples are meant to illustrate a possible format and geographical methodology for studying man-land relationships in small areas where agriculture is a major occupation and land use. Readers may do the same for an agricultural area near where they live. Compare these areas in Ontario with the Annapolis Valley example in Chapter 3.

Essex-Kent Vegetable Area:
Prior to 1940, these two southwestern counties were known as the "Corn

Belt" of Canada (adjoining the better-known Corn Belt of central United States) because they were the only part of eastern Canada where the mild climate permitted the maturing of corn. It was also the only area where winter wheat was grown in any significant amount in Canada — the result of another climatic advantage. The introduction of hybrid corns, which could mature in a shorter growing season, permitted corn to be produced across all of southern Ontario. After 1950, a political decision to allow the production of margarine in Canada (in competition with the butter industry which was concentrated in the Great Lakes-St. Lawrence Lowlands), expanded the production of a new crop, soybeans. Most of Canada's soybean acreage is now grown in the southwestern peninsula. About 80 percent of the cultivated land in the two southwestern counties is occupied by these three crops: corn, wheat and soybeans. In contrast to this general land use, the sub-region has smaller acreages of high value crops — vegetables and fruit — in particular areas.

Two types of local soils have been excellent for vegetable production — the black, organic, muck soils of Point Pelee peninsula and the sandy soils around Leamington. Miles of intensive, commercial vegetable production stretch to the horizon in the Point Pelee horticultural area. Although the areal association of vegetables with suitable soils and climate indicates that the physical environment is favourable for the concentration of vegetables there, labour and farm ownership are also important. Labour was supplied several decades ago by immigrants from Europe who were willing to do the hard work of caring for the vegetable crops. In addition, investment capital came to the region and built vegetable processing plants. The Essex-Kent area had about one-quarter of the vegetable processing plants in Ontario in the late 1970s, emphasizing the relationships between the food-processing industries in several small towns and their supporting agricultural hinterlands. (Recall a similar relationship between vegetable and fruit production and small towns in the Annapolis-Cornwallis Valley of Nova Scotia, pp. 84-85, and the impact of the introduction of vegetable processing plants in northwestern New Brunswick, p. 87. Geographical patterns can be repetitive!)

Even though this sub-region has a climatic advantage permitting the production of early vegetable crops in the longest frost-free season in eastern Canada, the growing season has been extended by the use of greenhouses. Inside these glass-covered (and increasingly plastic-covered) "hot houses" either winter vegetables are produced or plants are started early in spring under protection. Although the area around Leamington has the greatest number of square feet of greenhouses in Canada, this concentration is the result of human decisions and initiative, rather than natural environmental conditions. It is quite possible, therefore, for this concentration to shift in future years to areas closer to the big Toronto market, if farmers there decide to make this capital investment.

The Essex-Kent area formerly produced two other specialty crops — sugar beets and tobacco. Sugar beet acreage declined during the 1960s owing to competition from imported cane sugar processed elsewhere in eastern Canada and the greater incomes available to commercial farmers from other specialty crops. The first tobacco-specialty area of Ontario developed prior to 1920 on the sandy soils of southern Essex county. Small tobacco factories were started there, protected by political tariff decisions, to produce for the new (then) cultural demand for cigarettes. As market demands for tobacco increased in the 1920s, new areas with suitable soils were opened eastward in Norfolk county.

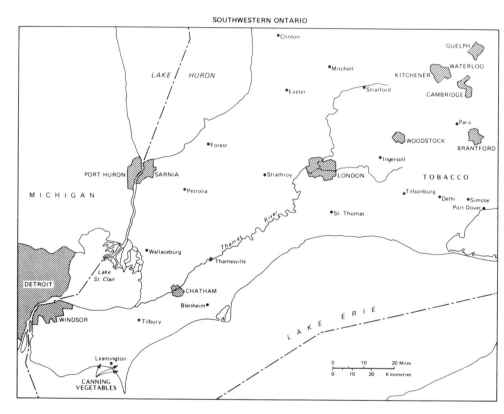

SOUTHWESTERN ONTARIO

The climatic advantages for tree fruits have been known for a long time in southwestern Ontario, but there have been few local growers interested. As tree fruit acreage, particularly of peaches, decreases in the Niagara Peninsula, the Essex-Kent area offers a suitably attractive physical environment alternative.

Despite the cash-crop significance of these specialty crops within the Essex-Kent agricultural region, the flat rural landscape also has hay, pasture and feed grains, similar to the other farmlands of southern Ontario and southern Quebec. Much of the rural landscape of the Great Lakes-St.

Lawrence Lowlands has the same general characteristics because of markets in the large local cities.

Windsor is the largest city in the Essex-Kent region. Its growth as an industrial city is due mainly to its international position on the Detroit River (see p. 163); the city has few direct links with its agricultural hinterland, except to supply services. Chatham, the next largest city, has a variety of industries, but also provides central place service and supply functions to its surrounding agricultural area. The outward areal expansion of these two cities resulted in only minor decreases in adjoining farm acreage—a trend which is balanced by the advantages of larger urban food-consuming markets available to nearby farmers.

Summary:

The preceding section discussed the location and concentration of certain agricultural crops and some of the relationships between human and natural factors. Although soils and climate are significant considerations, so too are human and political decisions.

The Norfolk Tobacco Belt:

Toward the end of the Glacial Age, a relatively large river flowed southward out of the hills of south-central Ontario and deposited a broad, sandy delta into the edge of a larger glacial Lake Erie. Lake Erie became smaller and shallower as the land uplifted after the Glacial Age and these deltaic (and other lacustrine) soils were exposed in what is now Norfolk county. (Although the many counties in Ontario and in eastern Canada no longer have important political and administrative functions, they are still used by geographers, and others, as locative units. Look up their locations in an atlas.) The sandy soils were not as fertile as other local soils, as indicated by the coniferous forests that originally grew there, in contrast to the deciduous trees which covered the better soils elsewhere across southern Ontario.

When this part of southern Ontario was occupied in the late 19th century, many farmers were not successful. Farm abandonment was common. The relatively poor soils of the physical environment of Norfolk county were less suitable for the agriculture of that time. If this conclusion is correct, then why does the area have such a prosperous agriculture now? Obviously physical environmental conditions did not change.

The answer was the introduction of a new crop, tobacco, which produced well on the poor sandy soils, plus greater use of fertilizers. Because growers were protected by Canadian tariffs from imported American tobacco, production expanded to supply the Canadian market; there was even a surplus for export to some British Commonwealth countries. Tobacco's value per acre became among the highest of the crops grown in Ontario.

Tobacco is grown on most farms in Norfolk and adjoining counties, but this cash crop constitutes only a small part of the total farm acreage because of production quotas. Because overproduction for the small Canadian market became a sales problem, tobacco growers formed an association to limit production and to set quotas for farms and regions. Thus, production areas are now fixed by what could be called "political determinism," rather than "environmental determinism" (refer back to p. 49 in Chapter 2).

About 80 percent of the rural landscape in the tobacco belt is made up of four main crops: corn, wheat, hay and oats—similar to that of the rest of southern Ontario. There are also increasing amounts of vegetables and strawberries grown for the urban market to the northeast. Despite the visual similarity to other parts of southern Ontario, the cultural landscape of the tobacco belt is recognized even in winter because of the distinct tobacco-curing barns. Many farms have these small barns with flue openings where the first stage of tobacco drying and curing is done.

Tobacco can be grown in other places in southern Ontario and eastern Canada which have permissible soils and climate, if there were no grower or market controls. For example, the introduction of tobacco into Prince Edward Island and New Brunswick in the 1970s was possible because these eastern farmers can export directly to foreign markets without reference to controls in Ontario. What would happen to Norfolk county tobacco producers if tariff protection were removed and cheaper American tobacco and cigarettes were permitted to enter Canada freely?

This region is unique in southern Ontario in being a valuable agricultural region without a major city as a service centre. Its geographical pattern can be explained by knowing its settlement history. Because it was an area of relatively poor agriculture early in this century, with low rural population densities, no big town arose there to supply central place services and functions to the surrounding farms. Some of the present small towns in the sub-region, however, do have small tobacco-processing plants and they supply low-order consumer goods. Most high-order goods and services are obtained in Brantford on the northern edge of the tobacco belt. (Central Place Theory, the relationships between agricultural towns and their hinterlands and the supplying of high and low-order goods and services is discussed further on p. 169 and in Chapter 8).

Summary:
The concentration of most of Canada's tobacco growing into a relatively small area is another example of the interaction of physical, human and political factors which influence agricultural specialty crop production.

The Niagara Fruit Belt:
Three relatively small areas produce much of Canada's fruit and each has a surplus; they are the Annapolis-Cornwallis Valley, the Niagara Peninsula and the Okanagan Valley. Each is a long, narrow agricultural strip with a

number of common characteristics, but also with some differences. Whereas the two valleys in the eastern and western parts of Canada are major apple producers, apples are a minor crop in the Niagara Peninsula. Although the name "Niagara Peninsula" is used to describe the fruit region, fruit and vineyard production are actually concentrated in only *part* of the region — mainly on the Lake Ontario plain on the north side of the Niagara escarpment (see map on p. 159).

The rural landscape of the fruit and vineyard area on the lake plain contrasts with the hay-pasture-dairy economy of the "upland" south of the escarpment. In the latter area, livestock farms are similar to those across south-central Ontario. The main crops of hay, corn, wheat and oats make up about 60 percent of the cultivated land in the Niagara Peninsula.

There are minor, but significant differences in the environments of the sub-regions. Soils on the lake plain are lacustrine in origin and include some which are almost ideal for peach trees; in contrast, soils south of the escarpment are glacially deposited and include some thin and relatively poor soils in the southeast near Fort Erie. Differences in micro-climates are quite significant to fruit growing: on the lake plain, the proximity of cool water usually delays blossoming in the spring beyond the danger of the last spring frosts. The average frost-free season is 10 to 15 days longer on the lake plain than on the upland south of the escarpment. In winter, severe temperatures which can damage or kill fruit trees are possible south of the escarpment, but are rare on the lake plain.

Over a period of many decades of trial and error adaptation to this physical environment, farmers learned that fruit trees, vineyards and small fruit bushes survive and produce better on the northern lake plain than on the southern part of the peninsula. This narrow plain became Ontario's major source of grapes, cherries, peaches, plums and pears. Farms are generally small and intensively used.

The Lake Ontario plain is also a favourable environment for people as well as for crops. At opposite ends of this plain are two of Canada's ten largest cities — metropolitan Hamilton (see p. 161) and the merging urban complex of St. Catharines-Thorold-Niagara Falls. These growing, industrial cities have expanded their residential areas over the valuable adjoining fruit lands. The mapping of this outward areal pattern of urban growth during 1966-1971 recorded that for every 1,000 persons added to the city population more than 700 acres of agricultural land disappeared near St. Catharines. Many transportation lines also follow the level land of the lake plain. Thousands of acres of fruit land disappeared for the wide swath of an expressway from Hamilton to St. Catharines and internal north-south rural movements were disrupted by the east-west "barrier" of that highway.

In the central section of the lake plain, the small towns with fruit, vegetable and vineyard processing plants also grew in population and in area. Around each city, former valuable farmland became even more valuable when subdivided into residential lots. The total regional scale of this land use conversion became quite apparent in the 1970s. The following table indicates the scale of the decline in tree fruit acreage in the Niagara Peninsula and also the increase in grape acreage. These acreage figures are not the same as production statistics; the latter are influenced by climate and other conditions.

Table 1

CROP/IN ACRES	1951	1971	1981	CHANGE/1951-81
Peaches	14,100	9,300	6,900	−6,200
Other tree fruits	18,500	15,600	9,400	−9,100
Grapes	20,400	21,900	22,300	+1,900

This increasing conflict between urban and agricultural uses is common near most growing cities in Canada, but it is critical on the lake plain of the Niagara Peninsula. It is a man-land problem in which concepts of geography can contribute toward understanding. Who is responsible for the decisions as to whether land shall be kept in agricultural use, even though the farmer-owner wants to sell it at a profit and retire? People who want to work in urban occupations also need land near their work on which to build their houses and apartments. If most of the fruit land disappears into urban uses, will this mean greater imports of fruit from the better climates of the United States — an increasing drain of Canadian foreign exchange? Geographical considerations of position, area, land use and physical environments are central to these discussions. Finally, however, decisions are political and democratic.

Summary:
   The methodology in these preceding sample regional studies considered the interplay of physical and human factors in explaining the location of certain agricultural crops. They illustrate the continuing theme of man-land relationships in particular places. In addition, concepts of internal sub-regional differences and of scale variations were also developed.

CITIES AND INDUSTRIAL REGIONS

Introduction

   The greatest concentration of industrial production and manufacturing in Canada is located around the western end of Lake Ontario. The core of this region is the zone of interconnected industrial plants and cities, sometimes called the "Golden Horseshoe," extending from Oshawa on the east, through Toronto, Hamilton and St. Catharines, to Niagara Falls.

Adjoining this strip and connected with it by supply linkages and business management is the industrial region along the Grand River in the cities of Brantford, Cambridge, Kitchener, and Guelph (see map below). In most of these cities, in the "heart of the Heartland," manufacturing employment constitutes more than 50 percent of the labour force. Nearly every type of manufacturing listed in the census of manufacturing is produced somewhere within these two connected industrial regions. Much of the production is meant for consumption within the Great Lakes-St. Lawrence Lowlands, but products are also shipped to hinterlands across Canada and some items enter foreign trade. The area around the western end of Lake Ontario is an example of a functional, industrial region.

URBAN AREAS AROUND THE WESTERN END OF LAKE ONTARIO

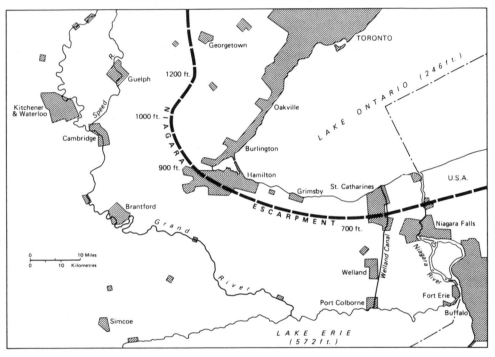

There is a great deal of internal movement and linkages within the region. Industries are well supplied with the necessary ingredients of labour, capital and power, but many raw materials are imported from other parts of Canada and much machinery and technology comes from the United States. Very importantly, these "consumer-type" industries have the greatest concentration of consumers in Canada nearby. Internally, products often move from one plant to another and from one city to another for further processing and assembly, and finally are transported again for consumption.

159

Therefore, most of south-central Ontario is tied together by a close network of roads and railways linking industrial plants and city populations. Although the many industries are both concentrated and dispersed throughout the region, they are connected by an elaborate transportation and management system into a functioning, operating industrial region.

Manufacturing and Raw Materials

Manufacturing in southern Ontario can be classified in the same way as discussed for Montreal:

1.) some industries are based on local raw materials;
2.) some on materials brought from elsewhere in Canada;
3.) some are supplied by imported raw materials.

In this type of organization, manufacturing can be studied as part of the heartland-hinterland concept.

1.) Manufacuring based on local raw materials consists mainly of food products such as fruit and vegetable canning and butter and cheese processing, and the processing of local non-metallic minerals such as sand, gravel, salt and limestone. The Great Lakes-St. Lawrence Lowland does *not* have a wide variety of natural resources.

2.) Raw materials from central and western Canada are moved to the consumer markets and processing machinery of southern Ontario. For example, some of the grain of the Interior Plains is processed and consumed in the heartland, although most of it passes through the region via Great Lakes water transport en route to European markets. Cattle, other livestock and semi-processed livestock products from the Plains also move either to southern Ontario feed lots or directly to meat processing and packing plants in the large urban markets. Most minerals of the Canadian Shield are semi-processed at or near the centres of production, but final processing and fabrication of metal products is done in the Lowland cities (as well as in foreign consuming markets). Do any raw materials move from the Atlantic Provinces to Southern Ontario?

3.) It would be incorrect, however, to think of southern Ontario as manufacturing only local or Canadian raw materials. Many of the industrial occupations in the cities are based on the assembly, further processing and packaging of many products previously manufactured in the United States.

The obvious industrial development in the cities of southern Ontario should not obscure the fact that the region (and Canada) imports large quantities of manufactured products from other countries with lower production costs.

Iron and Steel

The iron and steel industry is discussed here as an example of methodology in the study of a large industry in Ontario. It is not the purpose of this book to present factual information about all of the many industries in Ontario. Others may be chosen by readers for local analysis. For example, study the location of auto parts and equipment plants, the location of auto assembly factories and the movement between these industries. Or what are the geographical patterns of the petrochemical, furniture or meat-packing industries? Comments on iron and steel production are an example of geographical patterns of supply which are basic to most industries and an illustration of "spatial interaction" as a basic concept in geography.

Many of the products manufactured and consumed in southern Ontario are made of iron and steel. Two of the large companies which produce primary steel are located on the waterfront of Hamilton. The three main raw materials needed to produce steel are iron ore, coal and limestone; only the latter is obtained locally from the Niagara escarpment. During the first half of this century, the iron ore for the Hamilton mills came almost entirely from the Mesabi area of the United States, west of Lake Superior; this region also produced most of the iron ore used in the American steel industry located on the south side of the Great Lakes.

The pattern of movement to Hamilton was similar to that in the American iron and steel industry where iron ore was transported by long, narrow lake freighters down the Great Lakes during the nine-month open season to the American steel plants on or near the south sides of the lakes. Iron ore going to Hamilton had the additional transport cost of being carried north through the Welland Canal. The opening of the new steel plant in the late 1970s at Nanticoke, on the Lake Erie side of the Niagara Peninsula, permitted American iron ore to be consumed directly there, avoiding canal tolls.

After World War II, numerous large deposits of iron ore were found in the Canadian Shield (discussed in Chapter 7). The steel companies in Hamilton gradually shifted to Canadian sources of iron ore. The ore of the Labrador-Quebec boundary region could be shipped directly from Sept Iles to Hamilton after the St. Lawrence Seaway was completed in 1959. During the 1970s, iron ore moved to Hamilton from several mines in the Canadian Shield in northwestern and northeastern Ontario, as well as from the Labrador-Quebec region.

There are no coal supplies in southern Ontario. Coal came to the steel industry in Hamilton as part of a broader pattern of coal movement from

161

central United States to southern Ontario (see p. 165). Although Cape Breton coal could be carried as far inland along the St. Lawrence River as Montreal, transport costs west of Montreal were prohibitive or required subsidies.

Production of primary iron and steel at Hamilton and Nanticoke is the result of interplay between the locations of raw materials, markets, power and labour; these are measured by costs. The markets, power and labour are all available locally; therefore, it is economical to move the raw materials to them. The primary iron and steel is then converted in other factories throughout the nearby industrial region into a myriad of products, from automobiles to dishwashers. If consumers do not buy these products, steel production declines. The Niagara Peninsula steel plants are the nodal centre of a sub-regional network of interlinked fabricating and assembling plants all connected by ample transport lines. The ultimate consumers are mainly in southern Ontario, but they may be anywhere in Canada.

American Ownership of Industry

The pattern of concentration of American branch plant manufacturing in southern Ontario can be analyzed as a geographical topic and it can also be studied by others from business or political viewpoints. One of the reasons for the concentration of industry in southern Ontario is its location adjoining the nearby and larger American manufacturing belt. Because Canada raised tariffs early in the century to protect some of its younger and smaller (than in the United States) manufacturing plants, many American companies placed branch plants or subsidiaries in Ontario to supply and serve this growing consuming population. (British firms had done the same across Canada on a smaller scale in the late 19th century.) Business trends in Ontario are linked closely with prosperity or recession in central United States, particularly in the automobile industry. One of the obvious disadvantages of foreign-controlled manufacturing plants is their lack of interest in developing export trade in competition with American parent plants and therefore helping to reduce Canada's foreign exchange payments. There are also many economic and political implications related to the high percentage of foreign ownership in certain Canadian primary industries in other regions of Canada, such as forestry in the Canadian Shield and mining in the Interior Plains. ("Ownership" and "control" are business terms that need exact definitions as to how they are implemented. Similarly, "foreign" may mean British, German or Japanese in some parts of Canada.)

Individual American companies decided on the location of their branch plants in southern Ontario by balancing at least two locative facts—the relative location in the United States of the ownership firm and the location of their main market in Ontario (or Canada). For example, most firms with headquarters in Detroit find it both convenient and economic to locate across the Detroit River in Windsor; similarly, plants in Buffalo are most likely to build branch plants nearby in Niagara Falls, St. Catharines or Hamilton. But American companies farther away from the international border in, for example, Chicago, St. Louis or Pittsburgh, are likely to choose an Ontario location in the middle of the market (that is, Toronto), rather than proximity to the home firm. Although Toronto and Montreal are about the same distance from New York, twice as many New York companies have located branch plants in Toronto as in Montreal. The distribution of American branch plants and subsidiaries in Ontario is therefore similar to a map of all manufacturing in that province. The greatest concentration is in Toronto and the nearby Golden Horseshoe, and across the southwestern peninsula. Eastern Ontario has fewer American plants; this latter region is also one of less prosperity in the province. Does this latter areal association suggest a cause and effect relationship between American branch plants and relative prosperity? What other factors are involved?

Windsor, International City

Windsor, Ontario, is an example of an international city, influenced in its urban growth and character by the establishment of American branch plants. Windsor's industries are directly dependent on the location of Detroit, north (sic) of it. Because the Detroit River is only about a half-mile wide there, 19th century transport lines found this site a convenient and direct place to cross from Ontario to Michigan. Early in this century, the newly-established automobile industry in Detroit placed branch plants across the river in Windsor, and with them came a myriad of auto parts and accessory plants. In the 1930s, Windsor called itself the "automobile capital of the British Commonwealth."

The two cities of Windsor and Detroit functioned together in many ways. Before immigration regulations were tightened in the 1960s, several thousand Windsorites crossed the river daily by tunnel and bridge to work in Detroit. Almost 10 percent of Detroit's population is reported to be Canadian-born; this is more than the present total population of Windsor. As Detroit's residential area spread outward in the 1950s, many American businessmen moved to Windsor because they were closer to their offices in downtown Detroit if they lived one or two miles away in Windsor rather than 10-15 miles away in the Detroit suburbs. It has been reported that more than 10 million vehicles cross between Detroit and Windsor in a year and about half of this traffic is generated by the residents of the two cities. In the 1970s, about 75 percent of Windsor's labour force worked in American-owned plants. The industries of both cities polluted the Detroit River almost beyond hope of recovery—and, of course, Canadians blamed Detroit for this pollution, since it has ten times the population of Windsor! These above-noted facts simply illustrate how the two cities function together. But despite these strong economic links, Windsor remains a strongly "Canadian" city—one would not dare to state in Windsor that it is a "suburb" of Detroit!

Energy and Power

Electric power, and energy in other forms, are needed in great quantities in the operations of industries and in homes of southern Ontario. Except at Niagara Falls, southern Ontario was lacking in local water power prior to 1940, and the supply of energy from small natural gas fields north of Lake Erie was minor. Fortunately, electric power generated at Niagara Falls was central to southern Ontario and could be transmitted as far away as Windsor (about 300 kilometres) and to eastern Ontario. Although Ontario has been the main manufacturer of industrial products in Canada throughout this century, its great expansion came after 1940. As a result, Ontario became power deficient during the 1950s. In order to support increased industrial production, Ontario Hydro had to find new and bigger supplies. These came from five different sources.

Internal Water Power:
The only two major hydro power sites in the Great Lakes-St. Lawrence system were expanded:

a.) a larger generating station was built downstream on the Niagara River, at.the base of the gorge rather than at the base of the falls; the power of Niagara Falls is shared with New York state, which also built a generating station on the American side of the river;
b.) the construction of the St. Lawrence Seaway included a power dam and canals around the rapids in the international section of the river at Cornwall. The turbines in this dam supply electricity to both eastern Ontario and adjoining New York state.

Canadian Shield Water Power:
Physical conditions for water power are different in the southern Shield in Ontario compared with Quebec (refer to Chapter 7). Whereas the industries of Montreal and southern Quebec could be amply supplied with power generated from the many rivers tumbling over the nearby Shield edge, the Ottawa is the only large Shield river near southern Ontario. With the agreement of the Quebec government, which shares the Ottawa River political boundary, a series of dams were built in the 1950s along that river, generating power which could be transported to the Toronto area. The outward areal expansion to power sources continued during the 1960s when the tributaries of the Moose River flowing to James Bay were further dammed. Such development became technically feasible after it became

possible to transmit electric power over longer distances. Whereas Quebec Hydro went farther and farther along the Canadian Shield outer edge to obtain power for Quebec industries and homes, Ontario Hydro has not harnessed the unused power of the rivers of northwestern Ontario which flow to Hudson and James bays (see Chapter 7). What is your opinion about the use of these rivers rather than increasing the production of nuclear power in Ontario?

Coal-Based Thermal Power:

The use of thermal sources increased after 1950. A political decision was made to build coal-burning plants on the Ontario shores of the Great Lakes fueled mainly by imported American coal, even though Ontario Hydro was aware of the vulnerability of depending on foreign coal and the danger of loss of supplies through foreign labour strikes. Can the vast supplies of surplus thermal coal in Alberta and Saskatchewan be transported economically to power producing facilities in Ontario? Is Cape Breton coal consumed in Montreal and Ontario?

Petroleum and Natural Gas from the Interior Plains:

Prior to the mid-1950s, Ontario obtained its petroleum from American oil fields south of the Great Lakes, transported mainly to oil refineries at Sarnia. After petroleum was discovered at Leduc, Alberta in 1947, and later in other large oil fields near Edmonton, surplus oil, and later, natural gas, could be transported by pipeline to markets in midwest United States and southern Ontario. Both petroleum and natural gas have many industrial uses, as well as home heating, and also they can be used as alternative sources of thermal power. Although the natural gas pipeline across northern Ontario also served Montreal, the petroleum pipeline was built through the United States only to Sarnia and later to Toronto. In the late 1970s, it was extended to Montreal, and later to Quebec City. Will natural gas and petroleum pipelines be extended to the Maritime Provinces in the 1980s or will the latter be supplied by offshore wells?

Nuclear Energy:

Despite attempts to increase power and energy supplies from external sources, these were not sufficient to meet the enormous demand of the industries and urban populations in southern Ontario. Ontario Hydro turned to nuclear power generating stations at Douglas Point on Lake Huron, and near Toronto, to supplement other conventional sources. Canada has enormous supplies of uranium in the Canadian Shield to fuel these atomic reactors. Increased use of nuclear power to feed industrial and urban demands in southern Ontario is controversial there, as it is elsewhere in North America, centring on problems of atomic waste disposal. If Ontario continues to be the industrial and urban heartland of Canada, from where will it get its major power and energy supplies? What is your opinion on this controversial matter? Can some of the concepts and themes of geography contribute to this discussion? One of the problems in reading the scientific literature and popular press on this topic is to determine which are "facts" and which are "opinions".

Summary:

The industrial heartland of Canada in southern Ontario is dependent on, and vulnerable to, power sources from outside the region. Knowledge of the distribution pattern of these sources and their transmission lines helps in the understanding of industrialization in southern Ontario. A heartland-hinterland theme is illustrated by the flow of raw materials, power and energy into the heartland from dispersed sources through the hinterland; in turn, manufactured goods move outward from the heartland cities to smaller hinterland settlements.

CITIES: POPULATION GROWTH AND AREAL EXPANSION

Southern Ontario is the most urbanized region in Canada. The following statistics which illustrate this statement are not meant to be memorized; they are simply the evidence which quantifies the concept that population is concentrated in southern Ontario. Study the distribution of southern Ontario cities in terms of population size and their spacing relative to one another. Name the cities represented by dots on the following map.

In 1981, nine of the 27 largest metropolitan cities in Canada were located in southern Ontario; these nine cities had a total population of 5,635,000 or about 64 percent of the provincial population. Four of these cities are spread around the western end of Lake Ontario with very little agricultural land left between the urban land uses. In addition, southern Ontario had one-third of Canada's medium-size cities with 30,000-100,000 population (excluding those cities which are classified as part of larger metropolitan areas). Most of these ten cities were distributed in a semi-circle outside of the metropolitan concentration of St. Catharines-Hamilton-Toronto-Oshawa. Place a dot on a map for each of these cities in the outer ring: Welland, **Brantford,** Cambridge, Guelph, Orillia, Barrie, Peterborough, Belleville.

In addition, the region had six smaller cities of 20,000-30,000 population in 1981. Two of these, Fort Erie and Port Colborne, are just south of the St. Catharines-Niagara urban complex; three other cities—St. Thomas, Woodstock, Stratford—are on the edges of metropolitan London. Only one small city, Owen Sound, is located in the less-urbanized area between Georgian Bay and Lake Huron. Compare the number and distribution of medium-size cities in southern Ontario with those in southern Quebec. One should also recall that about 80 percent of the people in Ontario live in cities which are larger than all but five cities in the Atlantic Provinces.

166

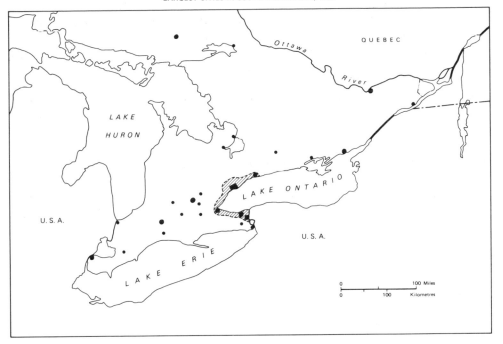

Population Increase

The increase in population in Ontario has been concentrating in the large cities. For example, in the 1971-1976 period, the population *increase* (*not* total population) of five metropolitan cities, Oshawa, Toronto, Hamilton, St. Catharines, Kitchener, totalled 282,000 persons, about 67 percent of the total population increase in Ontario in that period, but most of this was in Toronto. This figure is a quantitative measure of the scale of population concentration in southern Ontario. For comparison, the increase (only) in five years in these five large cities was greater than the present *total* population of Victoria, B.C. or Halifax. However, the growth rate in large cities slowed during the 1976-1981 period. For example, the *total* population increase in the four metropolitan cities of St. Catharines, Hamilton, Kitchener and Oshawa was only 50,000 persons in that period.

Ontario cities did not grow equally from 1971-1976. Ninety percent of the population increase was recorded by eight of its ten largest cities; almost half of the population increase was concentrated in metropolitan Toronto. As is noted later (p. 171), one has to be careful with the definition of "Toronto." Population actually *decreased* in the original political unit of Toronto, as in other central cores of metropolitan areas, but increased greatly in the adjoining suburban cities. If one analyzes birth rates and death rates in

167

Toronto, it is apparent that the increased population there is *not* due to natural increase, but to immigration. Toronto's average increase of 40,000 persons per year (equivalent to the present *total* population of Chatham, Ont. or Fredericton, N.B.) throughout the whole period of 1971-1981 was mainly the result of migration from other parts of Ontario or Canada, as well as immigration from abroad.

Since most of the increased urban population was concentrated in eight of the largest cities, and actually mainly in suburban Toronto, population increase was minor in the medium-size cities. Between 1976-1981, Windsor actually *declined* in population and St. Catharines grew only by 3,000 persons. Two of the cities along the St. Lawrence River in eastern Ontario—Cornwall, and Brockville—experienced a decrease in population during 1971-1976—a reminder that eastern Ontario did not experience the same favourable rate of economic growth as central Ontario in the early 1970s. Analyze the population increase in Ontario medium-size cities from 1976-1981 to determine if rapid urban population growth has finally levelled off. Watch the trends in the 1980s.

City Distribution

The ten medium-size cities (30,000 to 100,000 population, excluding those in southeastern Ontario) are dispersed across the southern Ontario Lowland (Table 2, page 170). Each is a city with many types of manufacturing, but also they are sub-regional service centres for surrounding agricultural areas. This areal pattern of regional centres is one of the spatial differences compared with the southern Quebec Lowland which has eight cities of this population category outside of metropolitan Montreal (refer back to chapter 4, p. 113). Only four of Ontario's medium-size cities are located in the southeastern area—a reminder that this sub-region has different geographic patterns than the rest of southern Ontario. Three cities, Brantford, Cambridge and Guelph, are on the western edge of the expanding urban crescent around the western end of Lake Ontario and can be considered as part of that metropolitan complex. Only the area east of Lake Huron is without a large regional service centre and a manufacturing city. This sub-region is just off "Main Street, Canada."

Study the geometric spacing of cities across southern Ontario and in a broader context, across the Great Lakes-St. Lawrence Lowlands (refer to map, p. 167). For example, note that Chatham is about halfway between Windsor and London, and Brantford is halfway between London and Hamilton. Does the population size of these cities relate to the area and population of the surrounding agricultural hinterlands that they serve? This geographical concept of Central Place Theory—i.e., city-hinterland relationships—is discussed further in Chapter 8. In southern Ontario, a city's service and supply occupations may be difficult to separate from its industrial employment; the latter may have no connection with the surrounding hinterland.

For example, in the dominantly agricultural area northwest of Guelph and Kitchener-Waterloo, the relationships between service-centre towns and surrounding agricultural hinterlands show two opposite growth trends.

1.) Many small villages and small towns have declined in service population because farmers now drive their cars to the larger towns and cities to obtain their food and consumer goods and professional services. The number and size of service-centre small settlements declined as the population became more mobile, particularly if there were no local manufacturing industries.

2.) On the other hand, the population of certain other villages or small towns increased as they became "dormitories" for people seeking a quieter residential setting outside the larger cities. During the 1960s and early 1970s, when gasoline was relatively inexpensive and seemed to be ample, many workers were willing to drive up to an hour each way daily to their work in the growing cities in order to have less expensive homes in a different social environment of small towns. The area north and west of Toronto and the Grand River cities provides an excellent example of the distributional trends in growth and decline of small towns. Will these trends continue into the 1980s if gasoline is no longer as inexpensive or ample as before? What is happening to population trends in the small towns or villages near where you live?

Areal Expansion of Cities

Population increase has always been accompanied by areal expansion of urban land uses (refer back to Chapter 2). In many parts of Canada, this urban expansion is taking place on the most productive agricultural land in the country. About one-half of the first class agricultural land in Canada lies within 50 miles of Canada's 20 largest cities; this valuable land is vulnerable to the spread of urban uses as city population increases. Across Canada, about 87,000 hectares (200,000 acres) of agricultural land disappeared into urban uses in the period 1966-1971 and 63 percent of this land was good agricultural soil. This rural-urban conversion declined to 63,000 hectares in 1971-1976, suggesting that the rate of outward areal growth of cities was slowing slightly. However, the rate of land conversion related to urban population change increased from 60 hectares per 1,000 persons in 1966-1971 to 72 hectares per 1,000 in 1971-1976. Almost half of the disappearing agricultural land (1966-1971) was in Ontario (40,000 hectares) and another 18,000 hectares was converted in Quebec. The problem (if it is a problem) is therefore concentrated in the Great Lakes-St. Lawrence Lowlands. The annual removal of agricultural land into urban uses there is about equal to the area of the city of Hamilton. This is a very small percentage of the total area of Canada, but a noticeable amount of the productive land of Ontario.

It is well known that the best land for urban uses should be flat, well drained and have adequate soil depth and soil stability; these physical characteristics also describe land of high agricultural capability. Some of these best farmlands are around southern Ontario cities where they were first developed to feed the people in these nearby cities. Among the growing cities, St. Catharines had the highest rate of land converted into urban use for every 1,000 persons of increased population. This urban-rural conflict, requiring political decisions about land use, was noted on p. 157 in the discussion of agriculture in the Niagara Peninsula. If one converts these land-population ratios to actual decreased acreages, the 1966-1971 figures reported that Toronto, for example, converted about 12,000 hectares into urban uses and Kitchener removed 2,000 hectares. Do you consider these areas to be "large" or "small"?

Table 2

Population of Major Urban Metropolitan Centres of Central and Southwestern Ontario, 1981

CITY	1976	1981	METROPOLITAN AREAS	CITY AREAS 1976	METROPOLITAN AREAS 1981
Metro Toronto	2,804,000	3,000,000	St. Catharines/Niagara	302,000	304,000
Toronto	633,000	600,000	Kitchener-Waterloo	272,000	288,000
North York	560,000	560,000	London	271,000	284,000
Scarborough	388,000	444,000	Windsor	248,000	246,000
Etobicoke	297,000	300,000	Oshawa	135,000	155,000
Mississauga	250,000	266,000	Kingston	91,000	115,000
York	142,000	135,000	Peterborough	65,000	86,000
Brampton	104,000	135,000	Sarnia	81,000	84,000
East York	107,000	102,000	Guelph	70,000	78,500
Markham	56,000	77,000	Cambridge	73,000	77,000 (city)
Oakville	68,000	75,000	Brantford	69,000	74,400
Richmond Hill	34,000	37,000	Barrie	50,000	61,300
Newmarket	25,000	30,000	Chatham	40,000	47,200
Milton	21,000	28,000	Belleville	35,000	46,400
Ajax	20,000	25,000	Welland	45,000	45,500 (city)
Metro Hamilton	530,000	542,000	Orillia	25,000	31,000
Hamilton	312,000	306,000			
Burlington	104,000	115,000	CITY AREAS		
Stoney Creek	30,000	36,000	St. Thomas	27,000	28,000
Dundas	19,000	19,600	Woodstock	27,000	27,000
			Stratford	25,000	26,000
			Fort Erie	25,000	24,000

When changing urban-rural land use figures become available for the 1976-1981 period, determine if these trends have continued. For example, select a large city near you and map the amount of agricultural or formerly unused rural land that has been taken over for urban uses in recent years. How many 150-acre farms would this area contain? These figures should indicate why urban-rural "sprawl" is a serious planning problem around most Canadian cities, and particularly in southern Ontario where urban population increase is the largest. When one sees future population figures reporting increases, put these figures into an *area* context. One knows, however, that some population increase is accommodated by going *up* (in apartments) as well as going *out* (to the suburbs). In southern Ontario, the large increases in urban population around the west end of Lake Ontario have changed many of the geographical patterns of land use there. Toronto is an example of how urban land uses change as population increases and expands outward and upward.

TORONTO

Introduction

Although metropolitan Toronto was about equal in population to metropolitan Montreal in 1976, it became the most populous Canadian city in 1981 with about three million people. Toronto had previously replaced Montreal as the country's leading manufacturing city, and is also Canada's main financial and commercial city. Decisions made in the head offices of businesses and industries in Toronto influence and direct much of the economic activity in Canada. Much of Toronto's population growth occurred after 1951; in that year, the city held a million people—ten years after Montreal reached one million population. In comparative terms, Toronto added the equivalent of almost two Vancouvers to its population in 30 years after 1951! The increasing concentration of population and economic activity in Toronto resulted in a restructuring of the urban area. The changes in the urban forms and areal patterns that took place there can also be studied in other Canadian cities if the factual information is available.

Definition of Toronto

The urban unit called "Toronto," like other cities, can be defined in several ways. Many large metropolitan cities in Canada were once smaller in area and population and were surrounded by other small towns. As the larger city grew outward, it often annexed or absorbed the smaller towns or villages into the original urban political unit. The five boroughs of York, East York, North York, Etobicoke and Scarborough were added to the early city of Toronto. These constitute the present political area of Toronto for most administrative and government purposes. Outward of these units, other municipalities such as Mississauga, Brampton and Oakville are included within metropolitan Toronto by the federal census (refer to Table 2). It is necessary to know which of these "Torontos" is being referred to when one reads about the city. The same definition problem is met when referring to Montreal or Vancouver.

In addition to different political definitions of Toronto, the geographical areas of all cities have various definitions. Geographers often refer to the *central core* of a city when discussing its area of highest density of commercial (and sometimes industrial) activity. On a different areal scale, one may refer to the whole *urbanized area* in which urban land uses such as commerce, industry, residential, institutional, parks, and transportation corridors occupy a continuous, built-up area. In an expanding city, this urban area is continually moving outward and absorbing former rural villages, agricultural land and vacant land held by speculators. This dynamic, changing zone is called the *urban-rural fringe*. The "hinterland" of a city lacks exact definition; cities such as Oshawa, Guelph and Brantford (and their surrounding agricultural people) are partly served and supplied directly by people and organizations in Toronto, and are therefore part of Toronto's hinterland; but Toronto also has a "distant" hinterland which could include North Bay, for example, or even Vancouver or Halifax under certain conditions.

Land-Use Patterns and Areal Expansion

Toronto was founded in 1793 because its protected harbour was one of the few good ones along the north shore of Lake Ontario. The small town was called York until 1834. At that time, the urban area extended back from Toronto harbour to Bloor Street and occupied the lower, former glacial shores west of the Don River to present Dufferin Street (see map, p. 174). The main urban functions of the town as the capital of Upper Canada were governmental and administrative. Toronto's commercial and industrial activities increased about the middle of the 19th century when railways were built outward from the city throughout south-central and southwestern Ontario; these railways also connected to the United States, maintaining the strong connections between the economies and people of midwest U.S.A. and southern Ontario. Railways also helped to focus the dispersed economic activities of southern Ontario into Toronto. Toronto became a land-based city; the port was not of major importance. Ocean shipping could not penetrate west of Montreal because of the rapids in the St. Lawrence River and Canadians did not develop much shipping on the Great Lakes, as did the Americans. Toronto's site was adjoining a good harbour, but little use was made of it.

Toronto became a central node, or focus, of economic activity for southern Ontario in this century. Wholesaling and commercial services supplied other cities of the Ontario Lowland. Within the city, industrial buildings occupied the land along the railways adjoining the waterfront because raw materials were brought into Toronto by these transport lines. As the number of manufacturing and processing plants increased, the industrial areas expanded outward along the railways. The business and commercial centre of the city was established on Yonge Street, just north of the railway, and south of the government area, and it gradually expanded a few blocks east and west of that street. The residential areas were laid out in rectangular blocks in a semi-circle around these industrial and commercial places of work. Some of the more expensive and larger homes were located in the "suburbs" on the higher ground of a former glacial beachline to the northeast and northwest of the city centre. The general land-use patterns of 19th century Toronto were quite similar to other Anglo-American cities of that time.

By the beginning of this century, Toronto had a population of 200,000 and was Canada's second largest city after Montreal. The area occupied by urban land uses had expanded outwards only about a mile, mainly to the west or northwest of the original commercial core, and northward into the adjoining farmlands (refer to the following map). Even by 1930, the area then occupied by urban land uses in Toronto was less than one-third of the urban area of the metropolitan region in 1981. Whereas in 1930, the residential edges of Toronto were about eight or nine kilometres from the city centre, by 1981 the built-up city area had expanded outward to 32 to 40 kilometres from the downtown core. The internal movement of people within this large area had become a serious problem.

As Toronto expanded areally after 1950, several processes of urban change took place concurrently. The land uses of the older city were duplicated in the outer fringes. For example, new industries were located along the rail lines in the outer edges of the city, but more frequently along the highways and expressways which, like the railway pattern, also focused on Toronto. When old industries near the waterfront of the original city wanted to replace their old buildings, many owners decided to build again in the less congested outer areas. Did industries move outward to be near the labour of the growing residential suburbs or did people move out to the suburbs to live closer to the outward-moving industries? Probably both reasons applied since these were concurrent areal processes.

While residences were being built farther and farther out from the city centre, the commercial functions of the city core were also duplicated in the outer areas. Vast suburban shopping centres offered ample and convenient parking areas and a wide range of retail stores and professional offices. Yorkdale, Fairview and Sherway were examples of this type of shopping mall that was built in almost every large city in Canada during the 1960s. Other city centre urban functions such as The University of Toronto were also duplicated in the newly-occupied outer sections of the city when the

new universities—York, Scarborough and Erindale—were located amid the
increasing teenage populations of the middle-class residential suburbs.

AREAL GROWTH OF TORONTO

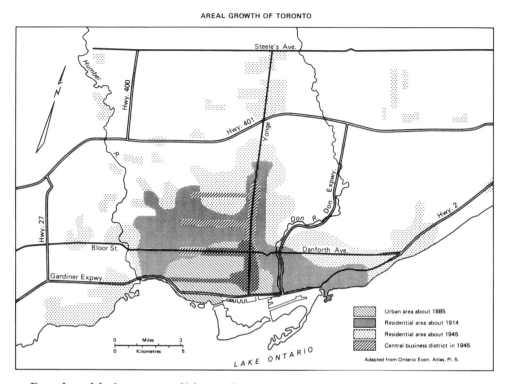

But the old city centre did not die. It also expanded areally and renewed
itself internally. Although some of its commercial establishments providing
local services were duplicated on the city's edge, the city centre became of
national importance as the financial and business "capital" of Ontario and
of Canada. Commercial areal expansion to the northwest was confined by
the large area occupied by government offices and the university campus,
but could spread eastward by replacing old and poorly-kept low income
residential areas. Commerce also grew outwards in linear patterns along the
streetcar lines. In addition, the original small commercial and financia¹
buildings were replaced by larger buildings of different building materials
and architectural styles. Daytime population densities of workers increased
as the commercial core expanded upwards into some of the tallest office
buildings in Canada and the density of shoppers also increased as stores
went underground into a maze of interconnected pedestrian and shopping
malls. Twice a day, these thousands of people have to be transported from
their "sleep places" to their work and shopping places. Many old, single-
family houses near the city centre were demolished and replaced with
apartments in which mainly young adults could live close to their non-

industrial work and close to the concentration of evening entertainment. These physical changes were not unique to Toronto, but were also occurring in Montreal and Vancouver and on a smaller scale in other large Canadian cities.

Transportation both promotes and responds to change. Wide multi-lane highway 401 was built in the 1950s on the (then) north edge of the city to take through regional traffic away from the congestion of the city centre. Now this throughway is a "river" which bisects the urban area and heavy north-south travel has to be funnelled into "bridges" or overpasses. The building of multi-lane expressways into the city centre became controversial. The need to bring more workers and their cars to the stores and offices of the city centre was balanced by the land-use problem of where to park these cars in an already congested commercial core. So a subway system was built to move people from the suburban residential areas to the downtown work places. Wherever the major new transportation lines crossed or terminated, clusters of high-rise apartments appeared, increasing suburban densities. Should planning decrease the number of city centre work places? The spatial arrangement of activities and the location of transport lines were geographical problems that were occurring in every large Canadian city during the 1970s. Will Toronto's decisions be copied by other cities if they reach Toronto's large population size and urban area?

Social Geography

A city is made up of people and not only industrial, commercial and residential buildings occupying land. Prior to 1940, Toronto was known as a city of people who were dominantly of British ancestry, Protestant religion, and rather conservative and quiet. Post-1945 immigration, mainly from Mediterranean Europe, changed many of these general socio-economic characteristics. Immigrants created new internal geographical patterns as they clustered into sectors mainly northwest of the original city centre. Italians, Jews, Greeks and Portuguese virtually created their own "cities" within Toronto; they have their own shopping streets, entertainment centres and local community social establishments. The past concentration of immigrants into certain areas of the city was followed by dispersal of their adult, Canadian-born children to other areas of the city. Social geography is just as dynamic in Toronto as are changing land-use patterns. Compare the location of ethnic groups in Toronto with those in Montreal, Winnipeg or Vancouver. Are such concentrations consistently close to the original city centre? Why? Will dispersal be common in the 1980s?

Summary:
Within about 40 years, a new and larger urban landscape emerged in metropolitan Toronto. A polynucleated urban form was created in which

high density land uses and clusters of people expanded within the old city centre and were duplicated in several nucleii throughout the suburbs. At the broad city-region scale, the general land-use patterns are relatively simple and apparent, but within local areas diversity is complex and ever-changing. Residents within metropolitan Toronto try to understand these geographical patterns and may prepare for future changes; residents in other large Canadian cities can learn from the experiences in Toronto and prepare for a time when their cities may reach a population of more than one million people with an urban area more than 80 kilometres across.

REGIONAL DIFFERENCES WITHIN SOUTHERN ONTARIO

Southern Ontario, like other large regions, differs from place to place in its landscapes and intensity of use, but also has general similarities. The region is characterized by a mixture of large and medium-size cities having a wide variety of manufacturing and assembling industries and by a well developed, prosperous agriculture, producing a wide variety of crops. The region is both city-industrial and rural-agricultural, but within it there are regional differences in these characteristics.

The sub-region around the western end of Lake Ontario has the most industries and commerce, resulting in the highest population densities of Ontario and of Canada (refer to map, p. 159). The areal extent of these characteristics has spread north towards Georgian Bay, west to the cities in the Grand River valley, and south into the Niagara Peninsula. It is the core of the Heartland of Canada. These intensities of activity present advantages and opportunities for economic and social life, but also have some negative attributes, such as excessive pollution and crowded transportation lines. Past urban growth, measured by both population and occupied area, greatly changed internal geographic patterns and changes are continuing. Urban and regional planning and public viewpoints have been based on 40 years of continuous growth and expansion; how might geographical patterns change in a period of declining economic activity and prosperity?

The southwestern peninsula has fewer large industrial cities than the Toronto-centred sub-region and they are more dispersed (refer to map, p. 154). The attractive rural landscape, based on a very prosperous agriculture with specialty crops, is relatively more important than agriculture in the south-central core. The four counties around London may be the most productive agricultural lands in Canada and to many may represent the best characteristics in Canada of the merger of urban and rural activities and economies. This southwestern sub-region, at the western end of "Main Street," is greatly influenced by nearby American activites.

The sub-region east of Lake Huron is just off the main track of southwest-northeast movement in the Great Lakes-St. Lawrence Lowlands. The dairying-livestock agriculture is prosperous there, but is less intensive than in the lands south of it and has fewer specialty crops. There are no large cities in the sub-region, but small industries produce a wide range of consumer goods in many of the towns. This part of rural Ontario, with its small service-centre towns, still maintains many of the reputed pleasant characteristics of Ontario life and economy of several decades ago; life there is a little less hectic and intense, particularly in comparison with the heartland south of it.

The Frontenac Axis of the Canadian Shield and the eastern Ontario Lowland are less developed sub-regions of Ontario (refer to map, p. 109). Agriculture is scanty and poor on the thin soils amid the rocky landforms of the Shield which extends south to the St. Lawrence River east of Kingston. This forested, lake-dotted extension of the Shield breaks the continuous agricultural landscapes of southern Ontario. However, the different physical environment is intensively used in another way—for recreation by people in the Lowlands. The fragmented, patchy, areal patterns of economy form a transitional zone between the general characteristics of intensity on the Lowlands and the dispersed patterns of the Shield.

The dairy-livestock farms of eastern Ontario are part of the food hinterland of Montreal and Ottawa and function as part of the Quebec Lowland (see Chapter 4). The area has the greatest number of French-speaking people of any part of southern Ontario. The few cities in this sub-region have not had as much economic growth as the industrial cities to the west. The St. Lawrence Seaway, which was once looked upon as an economic stimulator to this less prosperous area, did not help as much as was hoped; traffic and products may now go *through* the area rather than stopping. Compare the geographical location and less-developed economies of southeastern Ontario, southeastern Quebec (Gaspé), southeastern British Columbia (Kootenays) and southeastern Alberta. Can geographical determinists explain what is "wrong" with a southeastern relative location? This is a provocative and non-serious question!

REFERENCES

Atlases:

"Toronto Planning Atlas" edited by S. Chamberlain, Ontario Planning and Development Dept. Toronto, 1980. 107 pages.
"Economic Atlas of Ontario" edited by Wm. Dean, cartography by G.J. Mathews, Univ. of Toronto Press, 1969. 385 maps.

Periodicals:

Ontario Geography, published by Dept. of Geog., Univ. of Western Ontario, London, Vol. 1, 1967 to Vol. 20, 1982.

Cahiers de Géographie du Québec. For example:
"Industrial Change in Old Port Areas: The Case of Toronto" by G.B. Norcliffe, No. 25, Sept. 1981, pp. 237-253.

Annals of Assoc. of Amer. Geographers. For example:

Vol. 70, No. 1, March 1980. "Local Industrial Complexes in Ontario" by G.B. Norcliffe and L.E. Kotseff, pp. 68-79.

Monograph Series:

Many geography departments in Ontario publish monograph series on research topics of concern to their faculty and often about local problems. Write to the geography department of a regional university. For example:
"Industrial Development in Southern Ontario" edited by Jim Bater and David Walker, Dept. of Geog., Series No. 3, Univ. of Waterloo, Waterloo, 1974. 306 pages.
"The Countryside in Ontario" edited by M. Troughton et. al., Dept. of Geog., Univ. of Western Ontario, London, 1975. 260 pages.
"The Climate of the Essex Region: Canada's Southland" by Marie Sanderson, Dept. of Geog., Univ. of Windsor, Windsor, 1980. 78 pages.
Various urban geography reports from the *Centre for Urban and Community Studies*, Univ. of Toronto, Toronto.

Government:

"The Impact of Industrial Incentives on Southern Georgian Bay Region" by Maurice Yeates and Peter Lloyd, Geog. Paper No. 44, Policy and Planning Branch, Dept. of Energy, Mines and Resources, Ottawa, 1963. 85 pages.

"Urban Growth, Infrastructure and Land Capability: A Windsor Example,"
Lands Directorate, Environment Canada, Ottawa, 1980. 78 pages.
"The Climate of Southern Ontario" by D.M. Brown, Atmospheric Environment Services, Environment Canada, Toronto, 1980.
"The Economics of Soybean Production in Ontario, 1980" by G.A. Fisher,
Econ. Information Series, Ontario Ministry of Agriculture and Food,
Toronto, 1981. 40 pages.
"Design for Development," several volumes on Ontario regions such as
Niagara, Midwest, Northeast, etc., Regional Development Branch, Ont.
Dept. of Treasury and Economics, Toronto; about 1970 on.

Books:

"Toronto: An Urban Study" by R. Baine and A.L. McMurray, Clarke, Irwin,
Toronto, 1970. 126 pages.
"Four Cities: Studies in Urban and Regional Planning (Windsor, Sarnia,
London, Waterloo)" by Peter Nixon and Maurice Campbell, Curriculum
Resource Book Series No. 26, McClelland and Stewart, Toronto, 1971.
120 pages.
"Urban Development in South Central Ontario" by Jacob Spelt, McClelland
and Stewart, Toronto, 1972. 296 pages.
"Toronto" by Jacob Spelt, Collier-Macmillan, Toronto, 1973. 183 pages.
"Toronto: A Photo Study of Urban Development" by Ben Vass, McGraw-Hill
Ryerson, Toronto, 1971. 93 pages.

Some relevant articles in *The Canadian Geographer* between 1970-82, Can.
Assoc. of Geog., Burnside Hall, McGill Univ., Montreal:

Vol. 26, No. 4, 1982.   "Loss of Farmland in South-Central Ontario, 1951-71"
by D.M. Crewson and Lloyd Reeds, pp. 355-360.
Vol. 26, No. 2, 1982.   "Problems of Slow Growth in the Niagara Region"
by Hugh Gayler, pp. 165-172.
Vol. 26, No. 1, 1982.   "Zoning and Neighbourhood Change: The Annex in
Toronto, 1900-1970" by Peter W. Moore, pp. 21-36.
Vol. 25, No. 4, 1981.   "The Diffusion of Grain Corn Production through
Southern Ontario, 1946-71" by Alun Joseph and
Phillip Keddie, pp. 333-349.
Vol. 25, No. 2, 1981.   "Hierarchical and Functional Stability and Change in
a Strongly Urbanizing Area of Southwestern Ontario,
1871-1971" by Lorne Russwurm and B. Thakur, pp.
148-166.
Vol. 24, No. 2, 1980.   "The Impact of Investment Incentives on Manufacturing Change: The Georgian Bay Region" by James
Cannon, pp. 131-148.

Vol. 23, No. 3, 1979.   "The Recent Evolution of Ontario Central Place Systems in Light of Christaller's Concept of Centrality" by Richard Preston, pp. 201-221.
"Occupation and Job Location Patterns in Toronto" by S. Gera and P. Kuhn, pp. 266-276.

Vol. 22, No. 4, 1978.   "Structure of Urban Systems: London, Ont." by Russell Muncaster, pp. 306-318.

Vol. 22, No. 3, 1978.   "Urbanization of the Niagara Fruit Belt" by Ralph Krueger, pp. 179-194.

Vol. 22, No. 1, 1978.   "The Dynamics of Growth in a Regional Urban System: Southern Ontario, 1851-1971" by John Marshall and W.R. Smith, pp. 22-40.

Vol. 20, No. 4, 1976.   "A Comparison of Three Central Place Systems: Guelph, Barrie and Owen Sound" by Fred Dahms and James Forbes, pp. 439-444.

Vol. 20, No. 2, 1976.   "Forest Regeneration in the Urban-Rural Fringe in the Niagara Peninsula" by Michael Moss, pp. 141-157.

Vol. 19, No. 4, 1975.   "Migration and Population Change within Metropolitan Toronto, 1966-71" by David Ingram, pp. 340-346.

Vol. 16, No. 3, 1972.   "Multivariate Analysis of Social and Physical Space in Metropolitan Toronto" by Larry Bourne and R.A. Murdie, pp. 211-229.

CHAPTER 7

THE CANADIAN SHIELD

CHAPTER 7

THE CANADIAN SHIELD

INTRODUCTION

The Canadian Shield, the largest region in Canada, includes about half of the land area of mainland Canada. For such a large area, the generalizations and scale of detail may be different than those discussed in the smaller areas of eastern Canada. Despite the variety that can be expected over its large area, there is a great deal of uniformity or similarity in many physical environmental conditions. Diversity and similarity are, of course, *perceived* generalized characteristics which are "seen" by the eyes of observers and may exist in the "real world" to varying degrees. The Canadian Shield does not seem to have the characteristics of diversity apparent in the small regions in the Atlantic and Gulf region, nor does it have the heavy concentration of people and economic activity known in the St. Lawrence Lowlands. Despite its large size, the region holds only about 10 percent of Canada's population. It is, however, our "storehouse" of natural resources.

A major theme of this chapter is the evolution of geographic patterns of resource uses and associated settlements. In order to deal with the scale problem of the large area of the Shield, think of the region as bounded by two semi-circles centred on Hudson Bay; this locational concept permits a discussion of an "inner" and "outer" part of the Shield. Much of the resource development has taken place in the outer part of the Shield. A main geographical concept is that of an outward-moving distribution pattern of resource uses from central cores in the southern Shield.

THEMES

1.) To describe distribution patterns of various elements in the physical, economic and human geography of the Canadian Shield.

2.) To analyze areal and functional interrelationships between the natural environment, natural resources and people.

3.) To describe regional variations in the resource use distribution patterns and the evolution of transportation patterns related to resource developments.

4.) To compare and contrast the character and function of single-industry, resource-based towns in the Shield with other urban centres in eastern Canada.

5.) To analyze the areal links and functional relationships between the Shield as a source of raw materials and natural resources and their use by people and industries in the Great Lakes-St. Lawrence Lowlands.

DEFINITION OF THE REGION

As previously discussed, there are problems in defining the boundaries of most regions. For the Canadian Shield, the main physical criterion is geological; it is underlain by Precambrian rock exposed at the surface of mainland Canada. This criterion arbitrarily excludes large areas of surface Precambrian rock of Baffin Island and other eastern Arctic Islands and the smaller areas of Precambrian rock in the Appalachians and Cordillera. This geological definition of a landform region has been used in Canada throughout this century, although the region has been given other names, particularly outside Canada, such as the "Laurentian Plateau."

The Canadian Shield forms a huge horseshoe-like, semi-circular upland around Hudson Bay. Its structure can be likened to that of a saucer: its outer rim is highest in the mountains of northern Labrador and in the Laurentide and Laurentian hills north of the St. Lawrence River in Quebec; in the northwest, rocky hills rise above the Mackenzie River lowland. Much of the Shield slopes down toward the shallow water of Hudson Bay in the centre of the saucer.

In terms of landform and geology criteria, the area underlain by flat, younger, Paleozoic rocks south and west of Hudson and James bays is different from the Canadian Shield and should be classified as another physical region. However, the poorly-drained, lake-covered, mosquito-plagued (in summer) lowland has very few people and little economic activity; very little can be said about the sub-region if one is discussing the geographical themes of man-land relationships and distribution patterns of resource use. This Hudson-James Bay Lowland is a little-known part of Canada, seldom appearing in the literature, news or discussions. Although the area is included here as a sub-region of the Canadian Shield for organizational convenience, there will be little discussion of it, except to call attention to the negative and restrictive aspects of its physical environment for man's utilization.

The northern parts of the Shield present another problem of regional definition. In this book, the "North" has been arbitrarily defined by political criteria as being the two Territories. (The reasons, pro and con, are discussed in Chapters 1 and 10.) In summary, the northern parts of the Canadian Shield are different from the southern sections in two significant physical criteria—vegetation and climate. The northern Shield is treeless and has no summers as defined in climatic terms. It is also inhabited by a different people—the Inuit or Eskimo. Because of this political definition of the North, the Shield northwest of Hudson Bay is discussed as part of the Northwest Territories in Chapter 10; whereas the similar treeless area of northern Quebec, with its Arctic climate and Inuit inhabitants, is included as part of the Canadian Shield. This organizational arrangement of keeping Arctic Quebec within the province and in the Shield region is open to debate; some people may be more comfortable in thinking of Arctic Quebec as part of the North region.

These comments concerning the problems and alternatives for regional boundaries are not meant to be confusing. There are different ways of dividing Canada into manageable units for discussion of its geographical characteristics. Canadian geographers have not agreed as to how this should be done; there is no "right" or "wrong" way. A debate about regional boundaries can become bogged down into individual subjective choices as to what are the most meaningful criteria and how many regions are desirable; such arguments are seldom productive. Regional boundaries are chosen for convenience of study and analysis after a careful consideration of alternatives. Our main task is to know and understand the environmental characteristics, man-land relationships and areal patterns of resource developments in the area of Canada defined here as the Canadian Shield.

PHYSICAL ENVIRONMENT RELATIONSHIPS

Because the Canadian Shield occupies so much of Canada, many of the general characteristics of its physical environmental conditions were described in Chapter 2. The methodology of this chapter is to *use* information about the elements of the physical environment and their regional differences in a discussion of natural resource development, rather than to describe environmental patterns again. For example, the Shield's landforms define the size of drainage basins and the direction of river flow and therefore can be linked into a discussion of water power. Climate has affected both positively and negatively the growth of forests and the development of agriculture, and also it has influenced the recreational attractiveness of the Shield.

The links between natural (physical) environments and natural resources have been previously discussed in Chapter 3. In the Shield, these themes can be illustrated again. For example, differences in the geological characteristics of the Precambrian rocks have directed the search for areas where ore bodies may be found and also the later direction of mining development. Similarly, the distribution of types and species of trees and areal differences in their density have indicated particular distribution patterns of forestry use. The character of Shield soils—their areas of accumulation and of sparcity—along with differences in patterns of climatic elements have indicated the location and amount of agricultural settlement. Thus, our understanding of where people live in the Shield and what they do can be aided by a study of the areal and functional connections between the physical environment, natural resources and peoples' uses of these resources and environments.

The concept is, however, not as simple in operation as stated above. We are still learning about how the human mind *perceives* the natural

185

environment in different ways. People see, feel and react differently to each element in the natural environment—and to the environment in totality—depending on their backgrounds, cultures and aspirations. One has to be cautious, therefore, in generalizing about man-land relationships as related to the use of the physical environment. For example, some people may think of trees as raw materials for lumber or pulp, whereas other people see the same trees as scenery or the habitat of wild animals. Who decides what use of these trees is proper or "right"?

When one discusses water in the Canadian Shield, it can be thought of mainly as a source of electric power to be used in homes and industries, but there are many other uses of water. Near the high population densities of the St. Lawrence Lowlands, people have conflicting viewpoints as to the use of water for power and/or for recreation. The conflicts between the perception and use of water for power and/or fish are not as significant in the Shield as they are in British Columbia because Shield rivers are not fish producers on the same scale as rivers in B.C. One must continually remember that the concepts of "multiple use" of natural resources also entail decisions about *priority* of use.

The natural environment of·the Canadian Shield has changed very little in the past two centuries. It was considered a barrier and a hindrance in the 19th century and is now an important "resources storehouse" in this century. How will Canadians assess the natural environment of the Canadian Shield in the 21st century?

MINING

Introduction

Several terms and concepts probably need clarification prior to comments on the evolution of areal patterns of mining in the Shield.

1.) Geologists use the term "mineralization" to describe any occurrence—large or small—of the dozens of minerals which are found throughout the Precambrian age rocks of the Shield whereas the words "mineral deposit" or "ore body" signify a concentration of certain minerals. Whether or not the ore body is of sufficient size and value ever to be developed into an operating *mine* depends on numerous external conditions which are measured by costs. A mine is the tangible end of a long and expensive process of exploration, development and facility construction. The following section discusses the *location* of mines and groups of mines, but our interest should be with the people who operate and service the mines and with the "character" of their settlements.

There is a direct areal association between certain types of rock in the Shield and mining. Shield rocks are not equally mineralized. Large areas consist mainly of granite and gneiss which are not likely to contain minerals in concentrated quantities. Metallic mineralization has been found in useful amounts in specific areas of ancient sedimentary and volcanic rocks which are called "greenstones." Most present mines are in these greenstone areas and seldom in the granites and gneisses. (Consult a recent edition of the map of Principal Mineral Areas of Canada, Map 900A, Geological Survey of Canada, Ottawa. It also shows geological sub-regions.) Thus, in the first stage in the geographic methodology of *areal association,* mining is most likely to occur in particular areas which are underlain by volcanic rocks of Precambrian age.

2.) The *geography* of mining may need clarifying. A theme in this section is the distribution patterns of mining activity and the significance of relative location of mining to other economic activity and settlements. Such study may *use* some knowledge of geology of the rocks, as well as an understanding of business and economics; the latter determines the costs of transforming metallic minerals in rocks into useful metal products. These geological or economic influences—important as they are—will not be discussed in detail.

Perhaps more than in any other natural resource development, the areal patterns of mining are continually changing. Almost every year, a few new mines begin production within the Shield and a few older or non-economic mines close; in turn, closed mines may reopen if internal or external costs and markets change. Because there may be as many as 100 mines operating in the Canadian Shield in any one year, it seems preferable to think of mining *regions,* or groups of mines within certain areas, rather than the characteristics and distribution of particular mines.

3.) One of the themes of this chapter is the association between evolving transportation patterns and mining (and other) settlements. Most of the ore bodies discovered in the Shield in this century were in areas with no previous permanent European settlement. New transport lines (usually railroads) had to be built to these places to bring out the mineral products in semi-processed form to markets outside the Shield. The original ore body had to be large enough and rich enough to pay for the cost of transport by guaranteeing enough tonnage and freight revenue for a period of years. Once this transport was created, development costs for other marginally economic mines (or other resource potentials) were reduced and additional mines could be opened nearby. In other words, once the initial transport and other infrastructure was provided for one big producing mine, it was possible for three or four more mines to come into production nearby— providing that mineralization was present.

4.) The influences and effects of world-wide competition are not discussed in this chapter. Emphasis is on *internal* patterns within Canada, whereas it is well-known that markets for the mineral (and forest) products of the Shield (and other parts of Canada) are mainly *outside* of Canada. These external conditions are undoubtedly important. Whether or not Shield iron or copper, for example, sells in the United States or Europe may depend on the costs of production of mines in Africa or Australia. Canada is part of a world economy that changes every year and it has little control over the external factors that influence the resource-based economy.

Evolution of Areal Patterns of Mining Development

The complex interaction of the preceding factors and influences resulted in a distinct distribution pattern of mines and mining in the Canadian Shield. This pattern changed and expanded over the years, particularly after approximately 1950. The core of the areal development has been, and is, the cluster of mines in the south-central part of the Shield on both sides of the Ontario-Quebec boundary. From this central core established early in this century, mining spread outward to the east and west, principally near the outer parts of the Shield. In later years, penetration began *into* the Shield from these outer developments.

Can one predict that the future distribution pattern will be similar, but more intensified, to that of the present, because markets will continue to be near, but outside of, the southern edge of the Shield? Will there be only minor, and not spectacular, penetration of the mining frontier into the inner, and northern, parts of the Shield—a view contrary to what you may read or hear elsewhere about the "vast, untapped resources" of northern Canada (see Chapter 10)? Is there a geographical pattern of mine closures which is comparable to past patterns of mine openings?

The South-Central Edge of the Shield:
Only a few mines were producing in the Shield prior to 1880. Several small mines produced industrial minerals and minor metals intermittently during the last part of the 19th century in the Grenville geological region of the Laurentian Hills of Quebec and the Frontenac Axis of Ontario. These mines on the Shield edge had locative advantages near the small industrial market being established then in the St. Lawrence Lowlands. No large deposits were ever found, but new mines came into production as others closed, and this section along the south-central edge of the Shield has remained a mining region throughout this century. The type of mineralization is not spectacular; e.g.—graphite, mica, dolomite, talc, silica—but the minerals are used in a wide range of industries; their geographical location permits relatively low transportation costs.

The Ontario-Quebec Metals Region:
Mining penetrated into the south-central Shield by the turn of the century.

188

The rich copper-nickel ores near Sudbury were discovered in 1883 by workmen clearing and blasting a route through the rocky hills for the Canadian Pacific Railway. A cluster of mines and a smelter were operating there by 1900, but no new mines were discovered outside of the Sudbury geological basin because the geology (as known then) was not suitable for mineralization. The next major discoveries—of silver and cobalt ores near Cobalt—were also the result of railway construction in 1903. For the next 20 years, the many small silver mines in and near Cobalt made this area one of the richest mineral producers on the continent. The "boom" town of Cobalt spread haphazardly among low rocky hills and small lakes and along a twisting main commercial street.

By the 1920s, a prosperous, resource-based economy had evolved in northeastern Ontario. From the business and supply centre of Cobalt (an early example of Central Place Theory in a non-agricultural context?) prospectors and mining companies fanned out into the surrounding area and discovered some of Canada's most productive gold mines at Timmins, Porcupine and Kirkland Lake in 1909 to 1912. In this regional economy, the rocks supplied minerals, the forests were used for lumber and pulp and paper, the rivers provided electricity and the small areas of lacustrine soil produced some of the food needs for the growing settlements. The sub-region was tied together by roads, railways, transmission and communication lines into a functional, operating unit. As new mines came into production outward from the central area, chiefly in adjoining northwestern Quebec, they in turn were connected with the central core. By 1940, the few dots on the mining map of 1912 had evolved into an expanded, integrated mining region.

After 1950, mining increased within the core on both sides of the Ontario-Quebec border and expanded outward to the northeast in Quebec. By the 1970s, the several lead, zinc, copper, silver and gold mines of the Chibougamau-Matagami area had formed another mining region linked by new rail and road connections to the older settlements in the Lac St. Jean and northwestern Quebec areas. A small mining region had become a large one.

Although many of the old mines in the central core closed after 30 to 50 years of production, most of the old towns remained as residential centres to serve new mines that opened nearby. Timmins, for example, seemed destined to die as one by one the old gold mines closed during the 1960s; then very rich lead-zinc deposits were discovered north of the city and a large smelter-refinery was built eastward. The city revived, and new housing and shopping centres soon contrasted with the unattractive physical appearance of the old city.

New types of single-industry resource-based towns were established after 1950 throughout the mining frontier across the central part of the Shield. They were attractive, well-planned communities with curved streets, modern housing and recreational facilities, and usually located amid the forests and lakes a few miles from any pollution and noise from the mine. In many parts of the Shield, these towns are the *only* settlements in thousands of square kilometres of little-used area. In the 1950-1980 period, many new place names appeared on the map of "Middle Canada" such as: Chibougamau, Matagami, Joutel, Temagami, Manitouwadge (see map following). Some of these communities may disappear in a few years, and other new names will appear. Study the distribution pattern of these planned communities and the mines which they service; many parts of the Shield still have no mining settlements and are "empty."

SOME RESOURCE-BASED TOWNS IN THE CANADIAN SHIELD

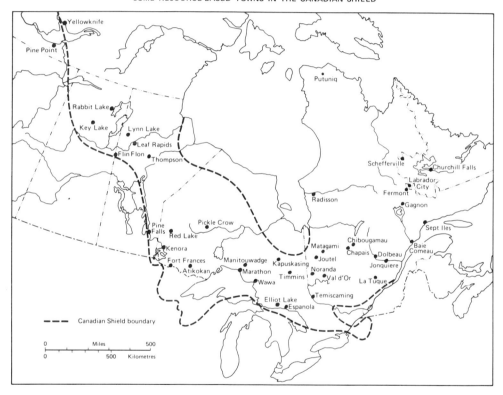

Can one predict that future areal patterns of mining will continue an outward expansion northward into the area east of James Bay? New geology maps record several areas of greenstone volcanics in this region; this information can be perceived in a new light because accessibility changed during the 1970s. A road built north of Matagami to bring in supplies for the hydro power development near the mouth of La Grande (formerly Fort George) River improved accessibility; it may encourage prospecting in the region and reduce the cost of bringing in exploratory equipment. An extension of the central mining region could evolve if all the many "ifs" are positive: if mineral deposits are large and rich enough; if capital investors believe there is a profit in extracting the ore; if costs of production are less than those in the established mining areas farther south; if there is a demand for the mineral and no competition from similar ores better located. This latter factor becomes of prime importance if world demand declines in the 1980s. These are a lot of "ifs"—but they are the same kind of conditions that were satisfied in other parts of the Canadian Shield, particularly after 1950. When will these conditions become favourable for mining in the region east of James Bay?

Northwestern Ontario:

Small areas of greenstone volcanic rocks are dispersed north of Lake Superior and across northwestern Ontario and, therefore, mines are also dispersed. Several types of metal mines have opened and closed across northwestern Ontario and adjoining eastern Manitoba. In a locative sense, the uranium mines at Elliot Lake, the iron at Wawa, and the base metals at Manitouwadge can be considered as "outliers" to the west of the main mining core. They are located near the outer edge of the Shield. Transportation has been less of a problem in this region because the transcontinental railways and highways pass through this "transit" area, connecting the population concentrations of southern Ontario and southern Manitoba.

The Red Lake gold producing area was north of the main east-west transport lines; it was connected by road, rather than rail, because the product being shipped out—gold bricks—was not bulky for its high value. With no major industrial consumers nearby in Canada, the mineral production of northwestern Ontario goes mainly to markets in the United States. The area does not have the number, density or value of mines as in the core of the south-central Shield.

The Northwestern Shield:

The Precambrian rocks in the Nelson Trough of northern Manitoba are lower than the surrounding hills and are mantled with marine deposition of a larger, glacial Hudson Bay and by lacustrine deposition of a larger, former glacial Lake Agassiz (its remnant is present Lake Winnipeg). Because of this soil covering, the rocks were not well-examined in the first half of this century when prospectors had to look directly at the rocky surface for signs of mineralization.

Westward, where the rocky hills of the Shield are exposed at the surface along the Manitoba-Saskatchewan border, mining developed near Flin Flon in the 1930s. After 1950, prospecting fanned out from the mining core of Flin Flon-Chisel Lake, similar to the areal pattern which developed outward from Cobalt-Timmins-Kirkland Lake core 30 to 40 years before. Because the area was sparsely inhabited, the new mines had to be linked by new transport lines. After a nickel deposit at Lynn Lake proved large enough to pay for the cost of building a new railway from the old mining area at Flin Flon, then other mineralization near Lynn Lake became economic to develop.

The resulting mining communities of Thompson, Leaf Rapids and Lynn Lake in Manitoba, and Key Lake in Saskatchewan, mark the outer limits of the mining frontier of this region in the northwestern Shield (excluding the mining towns in the Shield of the Northwest Territories). In Leaf Rapids, for example, the new type of buildings designed for northern living is illustrated. Most commercial, service and institutional facilities are under one roof to conserve heat during the cold winters and to permit office workers and shoppers to be concentrated in one place. Most recent single-industry resource-based mining towns across the Canadian Shield are relatively small in population, with about 2,000 to 5,000 inhabitants, but Thompson was different, growing into a small city of almost 20,000 people at its peak of the early 1970s.

This western mining region lacks the integrated resource developments of the Ontario-Quebec metals region. The northwestern Shield has no agriculture and no forestry; fishing is a minor occupation. Water power production is adequate for the mines, but is confined mainly to the Nelson River. The native Indian population has not been well integrated into the regional wage economy — in some cases, by their own choice. The lesser economic development of the northwestern Shield illustrates the geographical concept of decreasing density of use outward from the south-central core of the Shield.

Mining is penetrating into the interior of the northwestern Shield from gateways such as Thunder Bay, Flin Flon and La Ronge. Although the mining region has had past locative disadvantages of being farthest away from the industrial markets of the Great Lakes-St. Lawrence Lowlands and northeastern United States, it may have future locative advantages of being nearer than other Shield areas to markets around the North Pacific Ocean.

A similar geographical pattern of mining extends northward along the outer edge of the Canadian Shield into the Northwest Territories, along the eastern edge of the Mackenzie Valley. The few mines there are a reminder that intensity of use is less in the northwestern outer edge of the Shield. The area is far from markets and has high transport costs; mineralization must be very rich to overcome these locative disadvantages. This part of the northwestern Shield is discussed in Chapter 10.

The Eastern Shield:

Mining developed later in the eastern Shield. Whereas several transportation lines crossed northern Ontario and one crossed northern Manitoba early in this century, no land routes penetrated into eastern Quebec and Labrador until the 1950s. The high grade iron ore deposit reported at the turn of the century on the present Quebec-Labrador boundary had to await several changes in external conditions before development could begin. When American steel companies began to run out of high grade iron ore from the Precambrian area in the United States near Lake Superior, they turned to other sources of supply; one of those areas was along the Labrador-Quebec border. Once the iron deposit was proven large enough to pay for infrastructure costs, a railway was completed in 1954 from the port of Sept Iles on the Gulf of St. Lawrence to a new town of Schefferville.

Transportation linked interior mines with external markets. After the railway was in operation, the lower grade iron ore at Labrador City-Wabush could be brought into production because transport costs had been reduced. In addition, changing technology permitted the use of lower grade iron ore in pellet form. In the meantime, the St. Lawrence Seaway had been built and Labrador-Quebec iron ore could be transported directly by lake freighter to the steel mill at Hamilton and to American mills along and south of Lake Erie. Another rail line penetrated into the eastern Shield from Port Cartier to iron ore deposits at Gagnon and, later on, to other ore bodies at Fermont near the Labrador border. The distributional concept is that of transportation from the outer edge of the Shield linking with mining centres within the southeastern Shield.

One of the distinguishing characteristics of urban development in Canada is the distribution of resource-based towns across "Middle Canada" and particularly across the Canadian Shield (refer to map, p. 190). Life is quite different, and more comfortable, in these single-industry resource-based towns compared with the rough mining towns in northeastern Ontario early in this century. But isolation from the urban activity and cultural and sports events of southern Canada is still real and felt; despite high wages, labour turnover is high, particularly among single male workers who may spend only a few months or years in these places. These dispersed, isolated resource-based towns in the eastern Shield, like others across the mining frontier of the Shield, have distinct internal social characteristics.

The eastern Shield does not have the integrated resource development of the core region in the south-central Shield. Unfavourable physical environmental conditions prevent agriculture near the Quebec-Labrador border, and forestry activity is limited to the forested strip near the Gulf of St. Lawrence. Water power is more than ample for the local mines and towns and a large surplus is exported to southwestern Quebec (see pp. 203-204). The geological conditions favourable to iron mineralization extend northward to Ungava Bay and, some day, it may be economical and desirable to send these reserves of iron ore to external world markets. Whether or not the areal pattern of inward penetration of the mining frontier will continue depends greatly on external market conditions.

Summary:
The preceding discussion did not attempt to list all of the many mining centres in the Canadian Shield. A map of current mines will do this; mines open and close every year. The theme developed is that of a changing, outward-evolving, areal pattern of mining activity. The geography of mines is illustrated by a semi-circular pattern near the outer edges of the Shield with regional differences in densitites and linkages.

Mining towns arose first in the south-central part of the Shield, closest to the markets and transportation of the Great Lakes-St. Lawrence Lowlands. Other mining communities were established later to the west of this central core and along or near the outer edge of the Shield. Penetration into the Shield, aided by new tranport lines, accelerated after 1950 from several entrances, or gateways, around the outer semi-circle of the Shield. Most of the inner and northern parts of the Shield, despite some known mineralization, are geographically still too far away and economically expensive to be developed for mining.

FORESTRY

Introduction

The conquest of the forest has been a persistent theme through Canada's economic history. The vast size of the forest area impressed early explorers and later visitors. To most settlers of the 19th century in eastern Canada, the forest was a nuisance and a hindrance, delaying the clearing of farms. Other people, however, saw the forest as a raw material, a natural resource and a source of income. The conflict between farmers and loggers for the use of the land is part of our history of settlement and still exists in some areas. On the southern edge of the Canadian Shield these two major land uses sometimes conflicted, but were often complementary. Both types of land uses expanded across the south-central Shield in the early part of this century (see p. 210). Forestry activity spread outward around the edge of the Shield, creating a peripheral settlement pattern similar to that of mining, but not functionally related.

If one travels from southern Quebec or southern Ontario across the Canadian Shield to southern Manitoba, one passes through or over more than 1,600 kilometres of almost continuous tree cover. This is the best forest area of the Shield. There are, however, regional differences in the type and extent of forests.

Character of the Forest

The type and density of forest cover are related to local and regional environmental conditions. As the ice front of the continental icecap melted

194

back about 8,000 to 10,000 years ago, vegetation became established in the coarse gravelly soils of the valleys and in greater density on the finer deposits of former glacial lake bottoms. The spread and survival of various tree species were related to the various physical environmental conditions of the postglacial centuries.

The Mixed Forest across the south-central Shield consists of both deciduous and coniferous species (see map p. 39). The deciduous trees, such as maple, elm, poplar and birch, give the bright fall colours so popular with camera-carrying visitors to the recreational areas across the southern Shield. The red and white pine of the Mixed Forest stocked some of the finest lumber stands in eastern Canada in the late 19th century. This forest region has the warmest summers, on the average, in the Shield and the less severe winters permit deciduous trees to survive. All of these forests are south of the drainage divide and, therefore, accessible from south-flowing rivers.

The Boreal Forest, consisting mainly of coniferous species, extends across the southern part of the Shield from southeastern Quebec to north-central Saskatchewan. Whereas most of past lumbering took place in the Mixed Forest zone, much of the present pulpwood cutting is in the Boreal Forest. The latter has cold winters and cool summers; the eastern part receives more annual precipitation than does the west and, therefore, has generally higher densities and some different coniferous species. Although forest cover is generally continuous, there are many small areas without trees due to lakes, poor drainage and bare, glacially-scoured rock outcrops.

To the northward, the coniferous trees are smaller and farther apart. A transitional zone of vegetation lies between the Boreal Forest and the Arctic Tundra. This open forest extends from southern Labrador to James Bay and westward to northern Manitoba where it is often called "the land of the little sticks." The northern part of the Shield has probably been ice-free for more than 7,000 years, but forest cover has migrated northward slowly. Temperatures are cool there in summer because of the proximity of the cold water in Hudson Bay. In addition, warm air masses from the south seldom penetrate into the northern Shield.

The northern part of the open forest is a transitional zone in which slow-growing coniferous trees are interspersed with large areas of low, tundra vegetation and numerous bogs and muskegs. Local physical environmental conditions such as depth of soil, kind of drainage and amount of bare rock surface become very critical to tree growth and only the hardiest species survive. As a result of several unfavourable environmental conditions, trees have not been able to grow in northern Labrador, northwestern Quebec (Ungava Peninsula) and the Shield area in Keewatin District west of Hudson Bay. This treeless, tundra area coincides with the Arctic climate area. It is obvious that there will be no forestry settlements in the northern Shield where the forest resource is sparse or lacking.

The Evolution of Areal Patterns of Forest Use

The location of forestry activity is the result of the interplay of three main conditions: the natural resource (forests), the market demand and accessibility (transportation). The forests of the southern Shield were known for 200 years, but used only for the production of fur from the wild animals of the forest habitat. A demand for forest products arose in external consuming centres, particularly in Britain and eastern United States. In the middle and late 19th century, only the southern Shield forests were accessible to water transport on the Great Lakes or from tributaries of the St. Lawrence River. In the early part of this century, land transport brought more forest of the south-central Shield into the "resources hinterland" of the industrial regions of eastern Anglo-America.

The Logging Frontier:
The logging frontier moved across the southern Shield from east to west. By the 1850s, thousands of loggers and many sawmills operated in the Saguenay, St. Maurice and Ottawa river valleys, cutting down the white pine (and other) forests. Much of this timber was rafted down these rivers to Montreal or Quebec City for export by sailing ships to North Atlantic markets. This exciting and sometimes dangerous life was attractive to many sons of French-Canadian farmers for whom a fling at life in the woods was a part of youthful activities. Although the southern Shield was a region of forest-cutting, few permanent settlements were established.

The lumber frontier crossed the Frontenac Axis of Ontario during the 1870s and 1880s following the building of trails, roads and railways. Farmers and loggers were intermixed on the Shield fringe and sometimes were the same people; winter work in the forest was a major source of income for farmers on the thin and marginal soils of the Frontenac Axis.

By the 1890s, most of the good forest, for lumber purposes, had been cut near Georgian Bay, and the cutting frontier jumped Lake Superior early in this century to begin using the Mixed Forest west of that lake. By 1914, lumbermen had removed most of the usable trees across the south-central Shield. The new market for lumber in the settlements arising across the Prairie Provinces could be supplied by bigger trees then being cut in British Columbia.

Forestry activity never reached the Shield of northern Manitoba and Saskatchewan. The usable forests of those provinces, adjoining agricultural settlement on the grasslands, are on the Interior Plains (see Chapter 8). Within the northwestern Shield, the scrubby trees provide a wildlife habitat, but they are not a significant resource.

Although the southern Shield forests became important as the main source of pulpwood in Canada after the beginning of the century, logging for lumber did not disappear. Hundreds of sawmills, large and small, still produce some lumber for the urban needs of people in the Great Lakes-St. Lawrence Lowlands. These mills are often an "industrial base" of the small service-centre towns in the pockets of agricultural land dispersed across the south-central Shield from the Lac St. Jean Lowland to the Rainy River-Lake of the Woods area of northwestern Ontario.

Pulp and/or Paper Mills:

The market for pulp and paper expanded rapidly early in this century, mainly in eastern United States. Aided by changes in technology, the spruce and other coniferous trees, which had been bypassed by lumbermen, could be looked upon as new raw material. By the 1920s, the pulp and paper industry had become a significant part of the Canadian economy. Shield forests supplied the raw material and Shield rivers supplied the transportation and generated electric power for the mills.

The best combination of environmental and locative conditions for the establishment of pulp and/or paper mills was along the outer edges of the south-central Shield. Many of the mills were placed at, or near, the mouths of southward-flowing rivers. The drainage basins of these rivers contained the best stands of trees in the southern Shield; the outward-flowing rivers carried logs towards ultimate markets in eastern United States; the rivers dropped over an outer "fall line" of the Shield where dams could be placed to produce the large amounts of electrical power needed; the outer edge of the Shield was served by ample road or rail transport from the Lowlands or water transport on the Great Lakes or St. Lawrence River. Rivers were the functional links between the producing areas and the processing plants (see p. 200). These environmental and locative conditions were more favourable in the Quebec part of the Shield than in Ontario, so the greatest concentration of pulp and paper mills in Canada extends through Quebec, north of the St. Lawrence and Ottawa rivers.

The first paper mills were built in the Great Lakes-St. Lawrence Lowlands near the small local urban markets. By the end of the 19th century, paper companies decided to place their mills near the source of supply. In Ontario, the first pulp and paper mills in the Shield were located north of Georgian Bay at Sault Ste. Marie, Sturgeon Falls and Espanola. In Quebec, the first Shield mills were placed along the southern edge at Mont Rolland, Grand Mère, Chicoutimi and Jonquière. This dispersed pattern filled in during the first part of this century, resulting in a line of pulp and paper mills extending along the southern edge of the Shield in Quebec, mainly on the Lowland, from Clarke City on the north shore of the Gulf of St. Lawrence to Temiscaming on the upper Ottawa River. The major cluster within the southern Shield was in the Lac St. Jean-Saguenay Valley (refer to following map).

Locative conditions were different in northern Ontario. There were no long, outward-flowing rivers to encourage penetration into the Shield as in

Quebec. Some of the mills in northwestern Ontario, near the United States border, were located on railways. The western extent of the line of pulp and paper mills across the southern Shield fringe was at Pine Falls in southeastern Manitoba. A different distribution pattern evolved in northeastern Ontario as a result of using northward-flowing rivers, for the first time, to get access to the vast, solid stands of spruce in the Clay Belt. The products of these mills had to be carried out by railroads. The Shield forests of Ontario supported fewer forestry-based mill towns than in Quebec. Name some of the forestry-based towns shown by dots on the map below. Compare with the map on p. 190.

PULP AND PAPER MILLS IN AND NEAR THE SHIELD

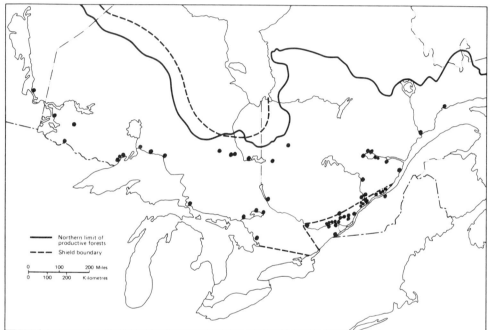

By 1940, the distribution pattern of pulp and paper mills was established. Most forest areas had been granted in concessions of various types to large forestry companies; many of them were American-owned and their main product, newsprint, was consumed by American newpapers. After World War II, new mills were built along the north shore of Lake Superior, filling in the linear distribution pattern along the southern edge of the Shield. Although production of pulp and paper increased greatly after 1950, this increase was achieved by expanding and improving facilities at existing plants rather than by building at new locations.

The peripheral distribution pattern of mills remained constant throughout this century, except for the few interior mills in the Clay Belt. However, some of the original locative factors no longer apply. Hydro power plants need not be near the mills because of improvements in power transmission technology; rivers are still used for log transport, but transport by roads and logging trucks is now more important.

Some forest areas of the Shield are not yet used for pulpwood. The largest area of less-utilized forest is in northwestern Ontario. This unsettled area is crossed by rivers flowing in the "wrong" direction — to shallow Hudson and James bays. Logging areas, therefore, have to be opened up by roads from the south in order to transport the pulpwood to mills along the edge of the Shield. The lower density, slow-growing forests of the northwestern Shield in Manitoba and Saskatchewan are not likely to be used; the quality and quantity of trees are not suitable and, in addition, these forests are located north of better, more accessible trees on the Interior Plains. Similarly, the large area mapped as forest cover across central and northern Quebec is really not of suitable quality to be considered as a forest resource in the near future. Trees in the marginal forest of southern Labrador, if used more in the future, are likely to be moved to mills on Newfoundland Island rather than being processed in Labrador.

Forestry Settlements

Unlike the numerous single-industry mining communities dispersed across the Canadian Shield, only a few settlements have forestry as their sole economic activity. However, because the forest is a renewable resource, unlike minerals, and must be managed under provincial government regulations, forestry settlements are more permanent than mining towns.

Single-industry forestry towns show the same range of visual appearance as mining towns, depending on their age. The pulp and paper industry penetrated into unsettled forests in the first quarter of this century and several resource-based towns were established then to house mill workers and loggers. Some of the earliest examples of attractive, planned communities in Canada were built about 1920 at Kapuskasing and Temiscaming and later at Baie Comeau (refer to map, p. 190). However, the old "company" towns at La Tuque and Espanola, for example, were less attractive and were similar to some of the scruffy mining towns of the early part of the century. The modern communities, such as Marathon and Terrace Bay, with their curving streets, neat bungalows and shopping centres, look little different from suburban facilities in most southern Canada cities.

These single-industry forestry towns increase the density of the distribution pattern of resource-based towns across the Canadian Shield and are one of the distinguishing characteristics of the region. However, single-industry forestry towns are also part of the landscapes in the Atlantic and Gulf region and in the Cordillea. Are they similar all across Canada? In addition to the forestry towns, many of the pulp and paper mills are in towns and cities with diversified industries around the southern edge of the Shield or in the adjoining Lowlands, such as Jonquière, Trois Rivières, Sault Ste. Marie and Thunder Bay. These industrial cities are similar to those in the urban Lowlands.

HYDRO-ELECTRIC POWER

Introduction

Rivers were important in the exploration of Canada by Europeans. In the 18th and early 19th centuries, certain Shield rivers, along with the Great Lakes, provided water routes for canoes and shallow-draft vessels going to the Interior Plains from eastern entrances to Canada through the St. Lawrence River and Hudson Bay. The use of Shield rivers declined in significance after the mid-19th century when the economy required the movement of greater volumes of material by land transport. However, railways were not built across the Canadian Shield as rapidly as across the plains and lowlands of the United States south and southwest of the Great Lakes because of difficult physical characteristics of the Shield and the lack of known resources or settlement attractions within the region. Southward-flowing Shield rivers became important again in the 19th century when they were used by lumbermen for access to southern Shield forests (see p. 196). Use of the rivers in the 20th century for their vast water power had to await technological advances in the production and distribution of electric power.

Physical Environmental Conditions Affecting Water Power Potential

A number of physical environmental conditions are favourable to the concentration of water power in certain Shield rivers, but there are regional differences in these characteristics. The following comments are further examples of the theme that natural resources are derived from the natural (physical) environment.

Drainage Patterns and Landforms:
The saucer-like character of Shield landforms produces three types of drainage patterns. Refer to the following map. These have different internal climate conditions.

1.) The longest rivers flow *inward* toward Hudson and James bays, along the gentle slopes to the lowlands around this large central water body, or northward to the Arctic coasts. Although the rivers are long, their volumes are not great because of the low amount of annual precipitation received in the central and northwestern Shield (recall Chapter 2, p. 38).

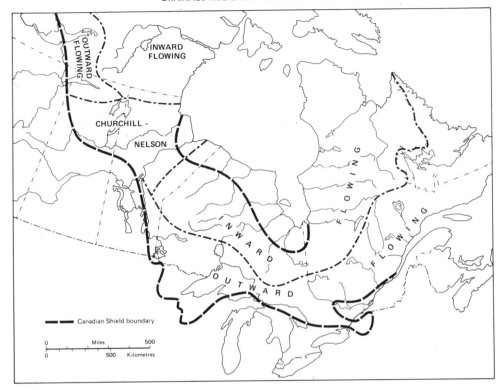

2.) Shorter rivers flow *outward* through the upturned outer edge of the Shield, dropping down to lowlands along the St. Lawrence and Great Lakes, Lake Winnipeg and the Mackenzie Valley. The drainage divide is shown on the map above. These outward-flowing rivers are longer in Quebec than they are in Ontario or the Northwest Territories. Because of decreasing annual precipitation across Canada from east to west, Quebec river basins receive much more precipitation—and therefore more run-off—than those in the northwestern Shield.

3.) Rivers flow *across* the Nelson Trough, or Lowland, in northern Manitoba, dropping from the higher Interior Plains to the flat lowland adjoining Hudson Bay. These rivers drain an enormous area, but one which receives very little precipitation.

The Fall Line:
The potential for water power is determined by the "head" of a river, i.e., the gradient or number of metres that water drops from its source to its mouth, plus its volume (which is related to precipitation). The eastern

201

Shield has two "fall lines" which concentrate the gradient in a short distance. The outer fall line is the geological escarpment which marks the sharp southern boundary of the Shield so noticeable above the Lowland in Quebec. Outward-flowing rivers in Quebec and Labrador head in a lake-dotted, gently rolling upland averaging 600 to 1,000 metres above sea level; they have many lake broadenings along their routes which provide natural storage to balance seasonal differences in precipitation; the water descends through several falls and rapids where rivers have cut into the outer edge of the Shield.

An inner fall line around Hudson and James bays is not as high or sharp as that to the southeast. The Paleozoic rocks of the Hudson-James Bay Lowland are lower than the Precambrian rocks of the Shield and, therefore, rivers tumble down 20 to 40 metres from the Shield in northern Ontario to the flat Lowland. East of Hudson and James bays, the headwaters of rivers are 300 to 600 metres above sea level, dropping to the westward gradually through several rapids and lakes.

Temperatures:

All lakes and most rivers of the Shield freeze over during winter. The length of the freezing period increases from three or four months in the south to seven or eight months in the north. During this time, the water still flows beneath the ice in all but the small and shallow rivers, but volume is greatly reduced. Run-off is rapid in the spring when the precipitation stored as snow during the winter melts and the rivers are swollen with spring rains. Storage dams are therefore necessary on all rivers to even out the seasonal differences in water flow, to concentrate the "head" in one place and to house the turbines which generate electric power.

Summary:

The regional differences in physical environmental conditions noted in the preceding section indicate that some parts of the Shield have more favourable combinations of conditions for water power than others. The largest amounts of potential water power are in Quebec, but for centuries this potential power was unused.

Evolution of Patterns of Development

The distribution pattern of the development of water power resources is similar to that previously discussed for mining and forestry. A peripheral pattern evolved around the outer edge of the Shield, except for the use of some inward-flowing rivers in northeastern Ontario. The first water power sites for the generation of electricity were developed in the south-central Shield, closest to the large urban and industrial markets of the St. Lawrence Lowland. Later utilization, often associated with mining and forestry activity, followed an outward-moving, generally peripheral pattern from this central core. After most of the large, outward-flowing rivers had been harnessed, continually increasing power needs directed the provincial government power commissions to inward-flowing rivers.

Hydro-electric power is used both within and without the Shield for different purposes and developments are of different sizes.

1.) *Within* the Shield, power was used early in this century for local resource processing, particularly in mining and forestry. These power developments were generally small and seldom interconnected into· the Lowlands' distribution network. The evolving internal areal pattern was similar to that already discussed for mining and forestry facilities—namely, first in the south-central Shield and then outward along or near the outer periphery of the Shield.

2.) Power produced by Shield rivers was used *outside* of the region in the cities and industries of the Great Lakes-St. Lawrence Lowlands. These power developments for the external market were generally large and they increased in size over time as the technology of power generation and transmission improved. This areal pattern evolved outward to the northeast along the Shield edge in Quebec, but was different in Ontario where physical conditions and markets were different.

In Quebec:

The functions and principles of location of Shield water power sites in Quebec were established right from the beginning of this century on the St. Maurice River. The power plant at Shawinigan supplied electric energy to internal industries such as a pulp and paper mill, aluminum plant and a chemical industry; in addition, surplus power was carried by one of the (then) world's longest transmission lines (about 130 kilometres) to the urban and industrial markets of Montreal. A similar pattern developed in the Saguenay Valley from 1920-1930. The Saguenay River and its tributaries were dammed to produce electric power for several local pulp and paper plants, an aluminum industry and the home needs of urban and rural residents. By that time, transmission technology permitted the export of surplus electric power more than 200 kilometres to Quebec City and into the power distribution grid in the Quebec Lowland. Some of the world's largest (then) power plants were built in the Saguenay Valley at that time.

Power production spread eastward. After 1950, when the south-central rivers such as the St. Maurice and Saguenay were almost completely utilized, the increased demands of growing industries and cities in the Quebec Lowland required that power be obtained farther and farther away to the east. As a result, the outward-flowing Bersimis (Betsiamites) River was dammed during the 1950s and the Manicouagan-Outardes rivers during the

1960s. The main purpose of these enormous developments was to supply electric power to the Quebec Lowland, but the power also assisted industrial growth along the North Shore, such as pulp and paper mills and another aluminum plant. Shield rivers continued to play their part as the resources hinterland for the Lowland heartland.

The last of the major outflowing rivers of the eastern Shield—the Churchill (formerly Hamilton) River in Labrador—was developed during the 1970s as a result of a contract to supply power to Quebec. Its power is transmitted more than 1,600 kilometres to markets in southern Quebec. The lower (eastern) section of the Churchill River is the last large unused source of water power in the eastern Shield. If there are no internal demands for large blocks of power within Labrador, what could its external markets be? The Newfoundland government wants to renegotiate the low power rates given to Quebec and would also like to transmit power across Quebec to markets in the Atlantic Provinces and perhaps in eastern United States. Although petroleum and natural gas may be transported in pipelines across provincial borders, why is it more difficult, politically, to transmit electric power on wires through (or over) another province?

What scale concepts do you have of the power-producing capacities of Shield rivers? What are the relative sizes of the hydro-electric power developments in the Quebec Shield compared with those in the Cordillera? Table 1 lists the installed generator capacity of the major power dams on Shield rivers. This table does *not* record the production of electric power which varies daily, monthly and annually. The total generating capacity of these river basins is larger than recorded in Table 1 because many small power plants are omitted. Note the enormous hydro-electric power capacity of Quebec rivers.

With no other large outward-flowing rivers available in the Quebec Shield, the Quebec government had to look ahead in the 1970s to find other sources of electric power for expected increasing industrialization. It was decided to develop the first of the inward-flowing rivers in Quebec—La Grande (formerly Fort George) River which empties into James Bay. When completed with several river diversions and power plant dams, the integrated river system could be the largest electric power producer in North America. Even if mines are discovered nearby, there will be no local demand for such vast amounts of electric power in the James Bay area; therefore, the power must be transmitted to the St. Lawrence Lowland and on to power-deficient northeastern United States. Such power export requires federal government approval and will cause political bargaining.

Table 1

Installed Generator Capacity in Hydro-Electric Power Dams in the Canadian Shield, 1981
(Larger than 75,000 kws. and Listed by River Basin)

RIVER	POWER PLANT	GENERATOR CAPACITY (000 KWS.)	
Churchill	Churchill Falls	5,225	5,225
Manicouagan- Outardes	Manic 1, 2, 5. Outardes 3, 4 McCormick	2,500 1,400 300	
	Total		4,200
Betsiamites	Bersimis 1, 2	1,500	1,500
Saguenay	Shipshaw Chute des Passes Isle Maligne Savanne Diable Caron	720 750 340 190 190 180	
	Total		2,370
St. Maurice	Shawinigan 2, 3 La Trenche Beaumont La Tuque Rapide Blanc Grand Mere La Gabelle	310 290 240 220 180 150 130	
	Total		1,520
Ottawa	Carillon Des Joachims O. Holden Chenaux Chats Tributaries in Quebec Tributaries in Ontario	650 360 200 125 100 670 670	
	Total		2,775
Moose-Mattagami	Abitibi Wells Otter Aubrey Harmon Kipling	235 200 175 130 130 125	
	Total		995
Nipigon	Pine Portage	130	130

205

Winnipeg-English	Seven Sisters	150	
	Slave Falls	140	
	Great Falls	130	
	Pine Falls	85	
	Caribou	75	
	Total		580
Nelson	Kettle Rapids	1,225	
	Kelsey	235	
	Total		1,460
Churchill (Sask.)	Island Falls	105	105
La Grande (Que)	LG 1, 2	5,300	5,300

In Ontario:

The areal patterns of hydro power development in the Ontario Shield were different as a result of different landforms and drainage patterns. Outward-flowing rivers are quite short in Ontario. These were harnessed early in this century in the Frontenac Axis, on tributaries of the Ottawa River and north of Georgian Bay and North Channel to supply local mines and forestry facilities. As was noted in Chapter 6 (p. 164), for the first half of this century, industries and cities of southern Ontario were amply supplied with electric power from Niagara Falls, which was a central source within the Lowland region. The Quebec Lowland had no such large internal power source.

Another characteristic of the pattern of power development in Ontario which was different from that in Quebec was the early use of northward-(inward) flowing rivers. Before 1914, the headwaters of the Mattagami (Moose) River were dammed to produce electric power for the Timmins-Porcupine mines. Other power plants were built after 1920 on other tributaries of the Moose River, such as the Abitibi, to supply power to the pulp and paper mills of northeastern Ontario and for the urban residents.

In the south-central core in both Quebec and Ontario, tributaries of the Ottawa River were utilized prior to 1940 to produce power for several local pulp and paper mills and for the Ottawa-Hull urban market. The main river was little used, however, because it was the interprovincial boundary with shared authority for development. It was agreed after 1950 that development would be done by Ontario Hydro to help reduce the electric power deficit caused by increasing industrial demand in southern Ontario. By the 1970s, the water of the Ottawa River, similar to other rivers of the south-central Shield, was used over and over again as it passed through a series of power dams along its course to Montreal.

In the 1970s, Ontario took advantage of the inner fall line to increase electric power production on tributaries of the Moose River and to transmit the power about 1,000 kilometres to southern Ontario. However, the other long, inward-flowing rivers of northern Ontario are unused for power (except for diversions southward to Lake Superior) and the water tumbles undisturbed to Hudson and James bays. These rivers can not be dammed on the flat, broad lowland near the bays; any future power plants would have to be built within the Shield and near the inner fall line. Should such rivers be developed in preference to building nuclear power plants? Which will be more costly? How do you measure "costs"?

The Western Shield:

The pattern and purposes of electric power development on the outward (westward)-flowing rivers near the Ontario-Manitoba border were similar to those elsewhere in the Shield. The Winnipeg River was the longest outward-flowing Shield river near the growing city of Winnipeg. Like other Shield rivers, it was dammed at several places prior to 1940 to supply the internal local needs of mines and pulp and paper mills in northwestern Ontario, and also its power was used externally in Winnipeg. The Winnipeg River, therefore, had a similar relative position and function to northwestern Ontario-southeastern Manitoba and Winnipeg as the St. Maurice River had to the Quebec Lowland and Montreal.

The Nelson-Churchill rivers are different from other Shield rivers in that they flow completely *across* the Shield. When the power of the Winnipeg River was almost completely in use, Manitoba had to turn to its northern rivers in the 1960s. Electric power from the Nelson first supplied the internal needs of the mines and urban residents at Thompson, and then surplus power was transmitted southward to Winnipeg and southern Manitoba. A future integration of the flows of the Churchill and Nelson rivers will permit the production of large amounts of electric power for any needs in the eastern part of the Interior Plains, with a surplus available for export to the United States. Will there be any political problems?

Settlements:

In the preceding discussion of areal patterns of water power development, little was said about the establishment of settlements within the Shield. Although power plant, dam and transmission facilities employ large numbers of workers during a few years of construction, they require few permanent employees once the power production and distribution system is in operation. Construction workers usually live in nearby towns or in temporary camps. One of the few examples of a single industry, resource-based town depending solely on the production of hydro power is Churchill Falls, Labrador. The power of Shield rivers is very important in supporting and strengthening settlements both within and outside of the Shield, but does not in itself create settlements. ◄

Summary:
Throughout the history of power development, the *relative location* of the outward-flowing rivers of the Shield has been important. Not only did these rivers have the physical attributes of ample volume, natural storage, fast flow and sufficient head, but also they were located near the places where electric power was needed and where competing sources of coal, petroleum and natural gas were lacking locally. Nearly all of the power plants, except those in northeastern Ontario and northern Manitoba, were located at or near the outer edge of the Shield; development progressed outward along the Shield periphery from the first plants built in the south-central core. Now that most outward-flowing rivers are almost fully used, additional water power supplies must be obtained mainly from the long, inward-flowing rivers. An alternative for consumers in the heavily-populated Lowlands, outside of the Shield, is to turn to thermal, nuclear or solar sources of power produced within the consuming region.

Shield rivers have been available and important in the industrial and urban development of the Great Lakes-St. Lawrence Lowlands. They were transportation arteries for the forestry industry and they are the main source of electric power for more than half of Canada's industries located in the Lowlands. The theme of functional connections between the Shield and Lowlands has been further illustrated.

There have been no major conflicts in multiple resource use. Sport fishing activities on the Shield rivers, and recreational needs, have successfully adjusted to, and often benefited by, control of the rivers for hydro power development. The flooding of agricultural land behind the power dams has been only a minor problem because few of the valleys were settled by farmers. Compare the lack of such problems there with the many multiple use conflicts over the rivers in the Cordillera. There has been, however, disruption of the hunting and trapping activities of the Indian population near those rivers flowing into James Bay in Quebec, in northwestern Ontario and near the Nelson-Churchill rivers of Manitoba. What arrangements have been made with native peoples to reduce or settle these conflicts in multiple resource use?

AGRICULTURE

Introduction

When eastern Canada was being settled during the first half of the 19th century, the Canadian Shield was a formidable barrier to the north. Settlers coming to Canada in the 19th century had a wide choice of land with varying physical environmental conditions all across Canada (and also they could move on to central United States). The Shield was a region for trapping, hunting and fishing, but not one for traditional ways of farming. As the better and more accessible lands of the Great Lakes-St. Lawrence Lowlands were occupied, the sons and daughters of Quebec and Ontario farmers, and new immigrants, began to look for land nearby in the south-central part of the Shield. By the later part of the 19th century, it was known that small areas of level land with suitable soils were available amid the rocky hills and lakes of the Shield. Although such areas had to be cleared of their forest cover, this process was the same as that faced by earlier settlers on the forested Lowlands.

Unlike the use of the other natural resources in the Canadian Shield, agricultural activity is *not* expanding areally. Decreasing farm acreage and population had become typical throughout eastern Canada by the mid-20th century (discussed in Chapter 2) and this trend was accelerated within the Shield. Although urban population increased in the resource-processing cities of the Shield, providing an increased local market for food, it usually has been cheaper and more reliable to obtain these food products from the adjoining Lowlands. The latter region has a more favourable physical environment for food production and a better-organized marketing system.

Physical Conditions Affecting Agriculture

The influence of continental glaciation was both negative and positive for agriculture. For example, erosion by moving ice sheets removed soil cover from large areas of the Shield. Although this erosion made it easier to prospect for minerals over the bare rock hills, the growth of forests was inhibited and agriculture was impossible. On the other hand, mixtures of gravel, sand and clay were deposited in valleys and lakes providing some soil potential for agriculture—if other physical and economic conditions were favourable.

Most of the large areas of level land within the Shield are the result of deposition of fine-grained sediments into large glacial lakes which occupied structural depressions (refer to the map following). These lakes formed along the front of the retreating icecap when the land was still depressed as a result of the weight of the enormous ice mass. The lakes drained as the ice front retreated northward about 7,000 to 10,000 years ago and the land began to rise. The bottoms of these former glacial lakes are the only large areas of level land with sufficient depth and quality of soil for crop production. The largest of these are: the lowland around Lac St. Jean; the so called Clay Belt across the Ontario-Quebec border (the soils contain less clay than was originally believed); the Nipissing lowland north of Georgian Bay; dispersed small pockets west of Lake Superior; and areas east and north of Lake Winnipeg. Only the latter has not been occupied by some farmland.

In addition, there is much level land around Hudson and James bays. These lowlands are the slowly-emerging bottom of an arm of the sea which occupied central Canada in the later stages of the Ice Age. However, they do not have suitable drainage, soils or climate for normal farm production.

The physical environment requirements for agriculture are more than level land, suitable soil and reasonable drainage; weather and climate conditions must permit the maturing of crops. The level areas across the south-central Shield lack summer heat and a long frost-free season. Cold air masses from the northwest or from across Hudson Bay may cause frosts across the southern Shield late in the spring or early in the fall (refer to Chapter 2, p. 37). Although the presently-occupied farmlands of the Lac St. Jean Lowland and the Little Clay Belt in Ontario have an average frost-free season of 100 to 120 days, the western part of the Clay Belt and much of northwestern Ontario may experience only 50 to 70 days without frost. Across the rest of the central and northern Shield, cool summers and a very short frost-free season prohibit agriculture, except for vegetable gardens.

AREAS COVERED BY FORMER GLACIAL LAKES AND POST-GLACIAL OCEANS

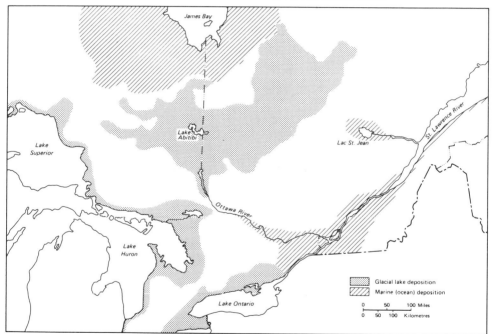

Evolution of Areal Patterns of Agricultural Settlement

The overflow population from the densely-populated (for that time) farmlands of the Great Lakes-St. Lawrence Lowlands penetrated into valleys along the southern edge of the Shield in the middle and late 19th century. The British colonial government placed Irish settlers on marginal soils in narrow river valleys between the St. Maurice and Rivière du Nord early in the 1800s, but they began to abandon these farms by the middle of the century. French-Canadians took over these lands and also came to the head of the Saguenay estuary at Grand Baie by the middle of the century. (Recall the discussion of the areal expansion of French-Canadians in Chapter 5, pp. 128-129.) By 1880, most of the strips and patches of good land in the valleys of the southward-flowing rivers within the Shield from Quebec City to Hull were occupied and, after 1880, new waves of settlers poured into the lowland around Lac St. Jean.

The landform boundary between the Frontenac Axis and the Lowland is less sharp in Ontario. Farmers and loggers moved into this Shield fringe in the middle of the 19th century. Many of the farms were abandoned by the 1880s when the loggers moved on to other forests to the northwest.

By the 1880s, settlers had reached the Little Clay Belt around Lake Temiskaming in both Ontario and Quebec and were beginning to agitate for a railroad to permit them to ship their products south to the urban centres on the Lowland. The influence of this railway on mining was noted on pp. 188-189. Following the construction of an east-west railroad through the area en route to the Interior Plains, patches of land were settled in the Great Clay belt during the 1920s and 1930s in a broad zone from Senneterre to Amos in Quebec and to Cochrane and Hearst in Ontario.

The physical environments of the Clay Belts across the Ontario-Quebec border were perceived differently in the early part of this century. Optimistic literature of that time appealed to and encouraged (probably in all honesty) agricultural settlers to take up free land in the area. Provincial and federal government agencies, colonization companies, the Catholic church in Quebec and even preliminary soil reports, all commented on the "millions" of acres of potential agricultural land available across the south-central Shield. Although the natural environment has not changed, peoples' perception of it, and use of it, has changed very much. What will people think about the environment for agriculture there in the 1990s if urban population continues to expand over the farmlands of the Lowlands?

Cultivated acreage and farm population decreased rapidly after 1950 on the dispersed farmlands across the southern Shield. By 1981, there was less cultivated land in the Clay Belts than in all of tiny Prince Edward Island. Farm population had decreased to about 20,000 in 1981 in the two largest areas of cultivation—Lac St. Jean Lowland and the Quebec-Ontario Clay Belt—compared with 120,000 recorded in 1951. Refer to Tables 2 and 3 which illustrate these trends in population and improved acreage. Write a few paragraphs to describe the trends. What are some explanations for them? This type of information may be obtained from the census for other parts of Canada.

Although farm consolidation and mechanization are responsible for some of the population decrease as in the rest of eastern Canada, it is obvious that farm abandonment is also common in order to cause such an enormous decrease in farm population. In seeking reasons for decreased farming in the Shield, how much relative weight must be given to influences of marginal physical environments, to economic conditions of low annual incomes and to cultural factors of lack of personal satisfaction in such occupations?

Table 2

Population and Acreage Trends in the Clay Belts of N.W. Quebec and N.E. Ontario

| CENSUS DIVISION | YEAR | — POPULATION — | | | RURAL NON-FARM | FARM | NO. OF FARMS | IMPROVED LAND | |
		TOTAL	URBAN	RURAL				ACRES	HECTARES
Abitibi,	1931	23,700	2,200	19,000		11,100	2400	80,000	32,400
Que.	1941	68,000	15,000	52,000		36,000	7300	213,000	86,200
	1951	87,000	33,000	54,000		38,000	6960	290,000	117,400
	1956	100,000	40,000		19,000	41,000	6400	329,200	133,200
	1961	108,000	49,000		37,000	22,000	3400	269,000	108,900
	1966	115,000	62,000		34,000	19,000	2500	278,000	112,600
	1971	112,000	65,000		39,000	8,000	1235	185,000	74,900
	1976	88,000	48,000	42,000	38,000	3,800	825	171,000	69,200
	1981	94,000	47,000	46,000			875	179,000	72,500
Temisca-	1931	20,000	9,000	11,000		7,730	1350	73,000	29,600
mingue,	1941	40,000	16,000	24,000		14,000	2500	100,000	40,500
Que.	1951	55,000	30,000	25,000		15,700	2760	155,000	62,800
	1956	57,000	31,000		11,000	15,000	2400	165,000	66,800
	1961	60,000	35,000		14,500	11,500	1800	155,000	62,800
	1966	60,000	35,000		14,000	11,000	1460	169,000	68,000
	1971	55,000	33,000		15,000	6,000	1010	151,000	61,100
	1976	53,000	31,000	22,000	19,000	3,000	575	127,000	51,400
	1981	53,000	30,000	23,000			550	127,000	51,400
Cochrane,	1931	58,000	25,000	33,000		10,678	2500	75,000	30,400
Ont.	1941	80,000	44,000	36,000		14,000	3060	117,000	47,400
	1951	84,000	50,000	34,000		11,700	2200	124,000	50,200
	1956	87,000	57,000		19,000	10,600	1770	116,000	47,000
	1961	96,000	64,000		27,000	5,000	900	81,000	32,800
	1966	97,000	67,000		25,000	4,800	680	75,000	30,400
	1971	96,000	71,000		23,000	1,500	340	45,000	18,200
	1976	97,000	68,000	29,000	26,660	1,100	285	53,000	21,500
	1981	97,000	67,000	30,000			325	56,000	22,700
Timiska-	1931	37,000	12,000	25,000		8,500	1950	100,000	40,500
ming, Ont.	1941	51,000	26,000	25,000		8,000	2000	115,000	46,600
	1951	50,000	30,000	20,000		8,000	1600	125,000	50,600
	1956	50,000	30,000		12,000	8,000	1550	137,000	55,500
	1961	51,000	34,000		12,000	5,000	1070	122,000	49,400
	1966	47,000	30,000		12,000	4,600	900	133,000	53,800
	1971	46,000	31,000		12,000	3,400	700	121,000	49,000
	1976	44,000	30,000	14,000	11,900	2,100	555	127,000	51,400
	1981	41,000	27,000	14,000			660	152,000	61,500

Table 3

Population and Acreage Trends in the Lake St. Jean-Saguenay Region, Quebec, 1931-81

Chicoutimi County

| | | —POPULATION— | | | | | |
YEAR	TOTAL	URBAN	RURAL	NON-FARM	FARM	NO. OF FARMS	IMPROVED ACREAGE
1931	56,000	37,000	19,000		13,000	1,700	145,000
1941	79,000	53,000	26,000		16,000	2,100	154,000
1951	116,000	84,000	31,000		17,000	2,000	157,000
1961	157,000	124,000	34,000	24,000	10,000	1,400	140,000
1971	163,000	128,000		29,500	6,000	850	105,000
1976	166,000	132,000	34,000	31,165	2,850	541	84,000
1981	174,000	131,000	44,000			647	95,000

Lac. St. Jean East County

YEAR	TOTAL	URBAN	RURAL	NON-FARM	FARM	NO. OF FARMS	IMPROVED ACREAGE
1931	20,000	10,000	10,000		8,000	1,000	100,000
1941	25,000	10,000	15,000		10,000	1,200	108,000
1951	31,000	16,000	15,000		8,000	1,100	110,000
1961	44,000	30,000	14,000	7,000	7,000	1,000	100,000
1971	45,000	33,000		8,000	4,500	700	100,000
1976	46,000	35,000	10,000	7,500	2,500	517	88,000
1981	48,000	36,000	12,000			523	94,000

Lac St. Jean West County

YEAR	TOTAL	URBAN	RURAL	NON-FARM	FARM	NO. OF FARMS	IMPROVED ACREAGE
1931	30,000	9,000	21,000		18,000	3,000	150,000
1941	39,000	11,000	28,000		21,000	3,100	116,000
1951	51,000	17,000	34,000		21,000	3,000	200,000
1961	62,000	27,000	35,000	21,000	14,000	2,000	200,000
1971	57,000	31,000		20,000	7,600	1,100	175,000
1976	58,000	29,000	29,000	25,000	4,000	775	154,000
1981	63,000	31,000	32,000			755	157,000

Regional Total (As Defined by 3 Census Divisions)

| | —POPULATION— | | | |
YEAR	TOTAL	URBAN	FARM	CULTIVATED ACREAGE
1931	106,000	56,000	50,000	400,000
1941	143,000	74,000	47,000	378,000
1951	198,000	117,000	46,000	467,000
1961	263,000	182,000	31,000	440,000
1971	265,000	192,000	18,000	380,000
1976	270,000	196,000	9,300	326,000
1981	285,000	198,000		346,000

Note: 61% of the cultivated acreage in the region in 1981 was in tame hay, oats and barley.

Agricultural expansion within the Shield ceased about 1950. However, the period of decreasing acreage seemed to have stopped or levelled off by 1981. Perhaps most of the marginal land has now been abandoned. Large areas of level land with usable soils and marginally permissible climate still remains unoccupied and could grow a limited range of crops. Are such lands better used if they grow a "crop" of trees?

OTHER RESOURCES

Regional geography cannot be an inventory of *everything* in a region; certain themes are developed and other topics are omitted. This chapter says little about three other resources: fish, fur and scenery. The first two are less important than the resources already discussed, but the latter is of increasing relevance. Brief analysis of the areal patterns of fish and fur resources and their associated human activities results in no discussion of geographical aspects of the native Indian population—a topic which has not been well studied by Canadian geographers.

Fisheries

Fishing is of more importance in the water bodies *around* the outer edge of the Canadian Shield than those within it. Offshore fishing is significant to the few thousand residents of coastal Labrador, but the shallow banks are used more intensively by fishermen who come from northern Newfoundland Island during the summer. The fish resources in Georgian Bay, Lake Superior, Lake Winnipeg and Lake Athabasca have been greatly depleted. The commercial fishery of the other rimming lake, Great Slave Lake, is discussed in Chapter 10. Despite the large area of water in Hudson Bay, its scanty fish resources are sufficient for only the small local population.

Fish are, however, a part of the natural environment that is important to the recreation or tourist industry. Sport fishing, therefore, is of some significance in the many lakes and rivers of the south-central Shield nearest the areas of high population density in the adjoining Lowlands.

Trapping and the Fur Trade

The furs of animals in the Shield first brought Europeans into the region and trapping has remained a major support of the native Indian population. The fur-trapping industry actually covers more *area* of the Shield than the other resource-oriented activities; over large parts of the sparsely-settled central and northern Shield hunting and trapping are usually the *only* occupations or resource uses. Furs were, and are, for export outside of the region, similar to the use and function of the other natural resources.

The areal pattern of the development of the fur trade was different from that of the other resources in that it was the only one to export products from the inner ring of the Canadian Shield, as well as from the south-central outer edge. From posts on Hudson and James bays, fur traders and explorers pushed into the Shield in the 18th century along the inward-flowing rivers. By the early 19th century, trading posts dotted the forested parts of the Shield and had spread to the Mackenzie River valley in the Northwest. In terms of permanent settlement, however, the fur trade period had minor impact upon the landscape of the Canadian Shield.

Scenery—The Recreation or Tourist Industry

This chapter has emphasized the concept that the natural environment ("Nature") becomes a natural resource when used by people. As discussed throughout, each element of the total physical environment is used by people as *their* resource. It is apparently difficult to comprehend the *totality* of the natural environment—that which may be called scenery. People perceive differently the total environment and the interrelations among the elements. Conflicts in perception, and use, are common.

The natural environment of the Shield—its lakes, rivers, trees, rocks and cool temperatures—is in demand by people in the adjoining Lowlands, similar to the demand for the Shield's water power, pulpwood and minerals. However, an element of the natural environment which the tourist literature does not usually describe are the myriads of biting black flies and mosquitoes. These annoying pests breed very well everywhere in the lake-dotted Shield and are a negative element of the environment to which both residents and visitors must adapt for a few months of the summer.

Unlike the other natural resources of the Shield, the scenery resource cannot be transported out of the region—except on film or in one's mind. The scenic environment brings people into the Shield for varying lengths of time and supplies income to workers within the Shield who operate services and facilities for the seasonal visitors. The functional and areal relationships between the rural scenery of the Shield and urban dwellers of the Lowlands should be apparent.

The areal patterns of resource use for recreation or tourism are similar to the distributions discussed for the other natural resources. The earliest developments took place along the edges of the south-central Shield, closest to the cities and high population densities of the Great Lakes-St. Lawrence Lowlands. The highest densities of parks, campsites, picnic tables, summer cottages, etc., extend across the southern Shield from the Laurentides, north of Quebec City, westward to Georgian Bay and beyond to southeastern Manitoba. Intensity of use has been spreading outward around the outer edge of the Shield and penetrating farther and farther northward from the south-central core. Similar to the development of other natural resources, a transportation system evolved along with areal expansion; new areas of scenery were opened up with paved highways, airports or landing strips, and canoe portage facilities. Heavy use of the physical environments of the south-central Shield has also given rise to problems of abuse and pollution, as is common with other resource developments. With wise management and control, however, scenery probably can be classified as a *renewable* resource—a product which can be "used" and enjoyed by Canadians for many decades to come.

SETTLEMENTS

Industrial Cities

Although most people live in urban settlements in the Shield, only three of the large metropolitan cities of Canada are in the region—Sudbury, Chicoutimi-Jonquière and Thunder Bay. Each is a service and supply centre for a small, surrounding sub-region, as well as being a resource-processing city like others in the Shield (refer to Table 4, p. 217).

These industrial cities differ little in appearance or function from similar cities in the Lowlands. The merged cities of Chicoutimi-Jonquière house workers in pulp and paper mills, an enormous aluminum smelter and the usual consumer goods industries and occupations required in the Saguenay-Lac St. Jean sub-region. Sudbury is the largest mining-based and mineral-processing city in the Shield and in Canada, but it is also a commercial centre for other settlements in the Sudbury geological basin, a university centre and a transportation hub for north-central Ontario. Thunder Bay is the gateway to northwestern Ontario and therefore has important supply and service functions and occupations, but also it is a resource-processing city with pulp and paper mills, and is a resource-transfer centre for nearby iron ore and pellets, other minerals and grain from the Interior Plains.

Single-Industry Resource-Based Towns

Throughout this chapter, the importance of single-industry resource-based towns has been noted (see map p. 190). These are found in other regions of Canada, but they are particularly numerous in the Shield and can be one of the distinguishing characteristics of the region. Mining towns are the most common; they are both old and new. Even though mineral resources are non-renewable and are expected to be depleted at any one site sometime, it may be surprising that most mining towns have survived for a long time. Because the southern Shield appears to be well-mineralized, mines have been developed in clusters; although individual mines open and close, most of the mining communities have survived. Pulp and paper mill towns are even more permanent and should continue to process the wood of well-managed areas which are supported by timber concessions. Another type of resource-based town not discussed is that based on the use of the environment for recreation. Ski resort villages dot the edge of the Shield in the Laurentian Hills and service and accommodation centres for tourists and cottagers are dispersed along the roads across the south-central Shield. If the Canadian Shield is the "resources storehouse" of Canada, then it is not surprising that its settlements are mainly concerned with the extraction, processing, transporting, managing and servicing of those natural resources.

Table 4

Population of Cities in the Canadian Shield, 1981

	1976	1981		1976	1981
Newfoundland:			Ontario:		
Labrador City-Wabush	16,000	14,700	Sudbury	157,000	150,000
Happy Valley-			Thunder Bay	120,000	121,400
Goose Bay	8,000	7,000	Sault Ste. Marie	85,000	87,000
			North Bay	52,000	57,000
Quebec:			Timmins	45,000	46,000
Jonquière-Chicoutimi	129,000	135,000	Kirkland Lake	14,000	12,200
Shawinigan-			Kapuskasing	13,000	12,000
Grand Mère	52,000	62,700	Kenora	12,000	11,600
Sept Iles	31,000	29,300	Haileybury-		
Rouyn-Noranda	28,000	26,000	New Liskeard	10,000	10,000
Alma	26,000	26,300			
Val d'Or	20,000	21,400	Manitoba:		
La Baie	20,000	21,000	Thompson	17,000	14,300
Hauterive	15,000	14,000	Flin Flon	10,000	10,000
Baie Comeau	12,000	13,000			
La Tuque	12,000	11,500			
Chibougamau	11,000	10,700			

Gateway Settlements

Because most resources move out of the Shield, many settlements are involved in transportation activities. Much of this transport is north-south, linking the complementary economies of the Shield and the Lowlands. In Chapter 8, the geographical concept of "gateways" across middle Canada is discussed; certain places have a significant geographical position through which products and people pass between "northern" and "southern" Canada. In the Shield, for example, North Bay is a gateway from southern Ontario into the multiple-resource region of northeastern Ontario; Thunder Bay is a transit centre for traffic to and from northwestern Ontario; La Ronge is an entry point into the Saskatchewan Shield.

Similar gateways have not developed to the same degree in Quebec,

217

probably because areal patterns of resource development are more dispersed. For example, Port Cartier and Sept Iles share gateway functions to the iron ore region near the Labrador border; no city has emerged in the Saguenay Valley as the "jumping off place" or collecting centre for the resources frontier in central Quebec; no major resource-use region developed along the St. Maurice Valley north of Shawinigan or Trois Rivières; traffic to northwestern Quebec may be beginning to funnel through the Clay Belt city of Val d'Or. Is the apparent lack of dominant gateway cities between the Lowlands and Shield of Quebec due to the dominance of Montreal? Many of the hinterland products in middle and northern Quebec seem to move directly in and out of Montreal and Quebec City.

REGIONAL DIFFERENCES WITHIN THE SHIELD

The Canadian Shield as defined in this book is the largest region of Canada; one should not expect to find complete uniformity or similarity over this large area. The preceding sections have been organized *topically* with each of the natural resources discussed in turn. Within this topical discussion, *regional differences* in the amounts and uses of the natural resources were emphasized. These conditions and patterns were not uniform throughout the Shield. The dichotomy of *topical* versus *regional* is a continuing problem in the organization of geographical information. In reality, geographers use both methods. In a sense, the Shield has been studied by a series of horizontal slices across it; one should also try to look down vertically to see how the various slices of space function together within any one sub-region. Some of the sub-regions are shown on the following map.

The Eastern Shield

The Eastern Shield includes Labrador and the so called "North Shore" of Quebec, north of the estuary and gulf of St. Lawrence. Settlement patterns are of two types:

1.) coastal settlements are mainly small fishing villages or larger towns which process and/or transport the natural resources, chiefly minerals, from the interior Shield;
2.) widely dispersed interior settlements represent penetration of resource development, mainly iron ore mines, into the Shield. Most of the interior area is literally empty and unoccupied.

The range and quantity of resources in the Eastern Shield are not as great as to the westward: iron ore and water power are the basis of the main developments; forestry takes place near the coasts; agriculture is lacking, except for gardens at the settlements; fur-trapping is minor among the few Indian inhabitants; the scenery resource is seldom seen, except from ships in the Gulf of St. Lawrence. Transportation consists of a few single lines to a few particular resource centres. Resource development is relatively recent—coming after the 1950s.

REGIONAL NAMES IN THE CANADIAN SHIELD

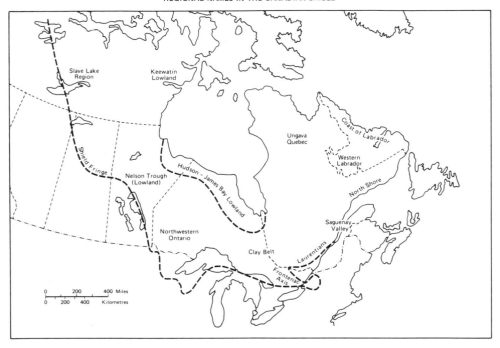

The South-Central Shield

The South-Central Shield is the core of settlement and resource development; it adjoins and supports the Heartland of Canada in the Lowlands. Its resources were developed first because they were located near the high density population of the Lowlands; the sub-region has the greatest diversity and number of settlements and resource utilization because of the continuing and expanding demands of the Lowlands economy. The South-Central area has the largest number of mines within the Shield and most of the pulp and paper mills; its rivers are almost completely used for the generation of electric power; its cities are surrounded by the largest areas of cultivated land within the Shield; its recreational resources are heavily used. Its settlements are tied together by an efficient, linking network of all types of transportation.

The South-Central Shield has many of the same human characteristics of population and economy as the Great Lakes-St. Lawrence Lowlands, except less density. There are fewer large cities and less variety of manufacturing in the Shield compared with the Lowlands; there is more empty or less utilized open space between the settlements. Forests are the dominant landscape element in this part of the Shield, in contrast to the farmland seen everywhere throughout the Lowlands. The adjoining Shield and Lowlands both complement and supplement one another. They are different in landscapes, population density and economies, but they function together. As the high density characteristics of the Heartland penetrate into the South-Central Shield, the boundary between the regions becomes transitional and blurred.

The Northwestern Shield

The Northwestern Shield shows dispersed patterns of people and resource use. Mining is scattered throughout the outer sections of the whole sub-region, but forestry, agricultural and recreational activities are confined to the section between lakes Superior and Winnipeg. Water power sites are available throughout the sub-region and more could be utilized if resource developments (mainly mining) should increase. Fur and fish resources are only of local significance to the Indian population.

The area north and west of Lake Superior has a greater variety of resource developments with more integration and better transportation facilities than the Shield areas of Manitoba and Saskatchewan. This part of north-western Ontario has characteristics similar to those of the South-Central Shield, but there is very little direct interaction with northeastern Ontario, except for through traffic along the Trans-Canada Highway. In some regional classifications, this part of the Shield in northwestern Ontario could be a separate sub-region.

The lowland of the Nelson Trough in northern Manitoba looks different from most of the Shield. The rocky hills are lower and large areas of level land left behind by glacial Lake Agassiz are covered with lakes, swamps and muskegs. The beginnings of mineral and water power development only reached the physically unattractive area in the 1960s. Although the outer edge of the Shield from Chisel Lake through Flin Flon to La Ronge has some mining settlements, there seems little likelihood of integrated multi-resource development or many new settlements across the rest of northern Manitoba and northern Saskatchewan.

The Hudson-James Bay Lowland

The Hudson and James Bay Lowland has different geology and landform characteristics from most of the Canadian Shield. The flat-lying Paleozoic rocks are buried under marine deposition of a larger post-glacial Hudson Bay; the flat surface is poorly drained, lake-covered and mosquito-plagued. Except for the railway terminals of Moosonee and Churchill at the two ends of the sub-region, there are virtually no inhabitants in this part of Canada — within an area larger than the Maritime Provinces.

Arctic Quebec

Arctic Quebec is a part of the Shield which is similar in landforms, climate and population to the eastern Arctic Islands and the Arctic area northwest of Hudson Bay. A regional classification of Canada which included an Arctic region based on climate, vegetation and population criteria (rather than a "North" defined politically) would probably include northwestern Quebec.

The northern treeline extends from the northern part of James Bay to Ungava Bay; the treeless, upland interior of northwestern Quebec is unoccupied but a few thousand Inuit (Eskimo) live along the coasts of Hudson Bay and Hudson Strait. Most of the physical environment of the interior of northern Quebec seems to offer little of interest or value to people in southern Canada, except for the possible future use of the water in its long rivers.

Comparison with Other Regions

If regional geography is concerned with similarities and differences from place to place, then the large area of the Canadian Shield can be expected to have areas which are similar to other parts of Canada. As discussed in this chapter, the Shield differs in many ways from the main characteristics of the Great Lakes-St. Lawrence Lowlands, but it has similarities to some characteristics of the Atlantic and Gulf region and the Cordillera. An emphasis on resource-based economies is similar in the Atlantic and Gulf region, the Canadian Shield and the Cordillera, although the internal geographical patterns of development are different in each; many settlements in all three regions are single-industry resource-based towns. The forest dominates the landscapes of each region and agricultural clearing occupies a very small fraction of each area. These resource-based regions are part of the hinterland of Canada in the heartland-hinterland geographical concept, but their links and dependence vary from region to region.

The Cordillera of British Columbia (Chapter 9) can be considered as a smaller duplicate of the geographical patterns and functional interrelationships of the Great Lakes-St. Lawrence Lowlands and the Canadian Shield together. The Lower Fraser River valley and lowlands of southwestern British Columbia are a smaller "heartland" with comparable characteristics of high densities of population, industry and agriculture on a smaller scale than in the Great Lakes-St. Lawrence Lowlands. The remainder of the Cordillera is a "resources hinterland" which functions within British Columbia as the Shield does for the Lowlands. When reading Chapter 9, consider the similarities in geographical patterns and functions of the Cordillera compared with many aspects of various parts of eastern Canada.

REFERENCES

Atlases:

"L'Atlas Régional du Saguenay-Lac Saint Jean" edited by M.J. Gauthier, Univ. du Québec à Chicoutimi, Chicoutimi, 1981. 98 pages.
"Ontario Arctic Watershed" by C.L.A. Hutton and W.A. Black, Map Folio No. 2, Lands Directorate, Environment Canada, Ottawa, 1975. 107 pages.

Government:

"Earth Sciences of the Hudson Bay Lowland: Literature Review and Bibliography," Working Paper No. 18, Lands Directorate, Environment Canada, Ottawa, 1982.
"The Ecological Land Classification of Labrador: A Reconnaissance," Ecological Land Classification Series No. 4, Lands Directorate, Environment Canada, Ottawa, 1978.
"James Bay Hydro-Electric Project: Environmental Concerns and Recommendations," Environmental Assessment Studies No. 4, Environment Canada, Ottawa, 1975.
"Mining, Land Use and the Environment," Land Use in Canada Series, No. 22, Lands Directorate, Environment Canada, 1982.
"Science, History and Hudson Bay" edited by C.S. Beals, Dept. of Energy, Mines and Resources, Ottawa, 1968, 2 vols.

University Series:

"Les Villes du Saguenay: Etude Géographique" by L.M. Bouchard, Dept. of Geog., Univ. du Québec à Chicoutimi, Chicoutimi, 1973. 212 pages.
"Canadian Resource Towns: A Heartland-Hinterland Perspective" by Larry McCann, *Essays on Canadian Urban Process and Form, II*, Dept. of Geog. Series No. 15, Univ. of Waterloo, Waterloo, 1980, pp. 209-267.
"The Impact of the Mining Industries on the Canadian Economy" by R.W. Broadway and J.M. Treddenick, Centre for Resource Studies, Queen's Univ., Kingston, 1977. 115 pages.
"The Transportation Impact of the Canadian Mining Industry" by Iain Wallace, Centre for Resource Studies, Queen's Univ., Kingston, 1977. 153 pages.
Various publications of the Subarctic Research Station, Dept. of Geog., McGill Univ., Montreal; up to No. 35 in 1981.

Books:

"Mid-Canada Development Corridor—A Concept" by Acres Research and

Planning Co. Toronto, 1968.

"Little Communities and Big Industries" edited by Roy T. Bowles, Butterworth's, Scarborough, 1982. 232 pages.

"National Resources in US-Canada Relations; Vol. 2, Patterns and Trends in Resource Supplies and Policies," C.D. Howe Institute, Montreal, 1980. 625 pages.

"Resources of the Canadian Shield" by J. Lewis Robinson, Methuen, Toronto, 1969. 136 pages.

Some relevant articles in *The Canadian Geographer* between 1970-82, Can. Assoc. of Geog., Burnside Hall, McGill Univ., Montreal:

Vol. 21, No. 1, 1977.   "The Changing Rural Economy of Gatineau County, Quebec" by Helen Parson, pp. 22-31.

Vol. 14, No. 2, 1970.   "Changes in the Number of Farms in the North Part of Central Ontario" by E.B. Macdougall, pp. 125-138.

CHAPTER 8

THE INTERIOR PLAINS

CHAPTER 8

THE INTERIOR PLAINS

INTRODUCTION

The main characteristics of the Interior Plains probably are perceived as a series of stereotypes. Its landforms may be dismissed with one word — flat; its climate is notorious — namely, dry and cold; its agricultural economy is simple — wheat; its significance to Canada is probably also handled with one word — oil; the occupations of its people are well-known — they are farmers or ranchers. All of these characteristics are partly correct, but in each case the generalization is too simple and the words do not tell of the variety within the Interior Plains. The region has diversity and differences in density in each of these characteristics.

Although the Interior Plains has large areas of flat land, it also has a variety of minor landform features. Although the climate is very dry in some years, some places can receive heavy rainfall for a few days and spring flooding can be a problem at times in other places. Although wheat has been the backbone of the agricultural economy, the region now produces a variety of other grain crops, along with legume and oil seeds. Although discussions about the wealth generated by, and the use of, Plains petroleum are common in national news, one should not forget other mineral resources such as natural gas, coal and potash. Although the problems and characteristics of Prairie farmers may seem to be well-known, they now constitute a minority of the Plains population, which is mainly urban.

There are major differences in the characteristics of the economy of each of the three Prairie Provinces and they should not be lumped together by "easterners" as similar. The Canadian Shield occupies more than half of the area of Manitoba and, therefore, the mining and water power developments and settlements of the Manitoba Shield are not duplicated in Alberta. Winnipeg holds half of the population of Manitoba — an urban concentration not found elsewhere in the other Prairie Provinces — and supports a diversified manufacturing economy much different from other Plains cities. The dominance of the urban economies of the twin cities of Edmonton and Calgary in Alberta is not duplicated in Saskatchewan's twin cities of Regina and Saskatoon. The social, economic and political similarities and linkages are probably greater between Alberta and British Columbia than between Alberta and Manitoba.

The Interior Plains region is no longer as dependent a part of the hinterland of Canada as it was prior to 1940. The raw materials of the region — petroleum, natural gas, coal, potash, wheat, meat — have greater markets now in foreign countries than in Eastern Canada. The political and economic links of each of the Prairie Provinces are more international than they are interprovincial with Ontario and Quebec in the Heartland. More Plains products flow out through Vancouver than Montreal. The financial dominance of Toronto is being reduced by the increased financial services in Calgary. Although the Plains region still depends on the Heartland for many of its manufactured goods, the Heartland, in turn, now depends on the Plains for its energy sources of petroleum and natural gas. The heartland-hinterland concept is weakening in Western Canada.

The Interior Plains is a land of diversity and it is also a land of change. The areal patterns and economies established in the first half of this century have been changing. The "uniformity" which the average person may think to have existed over the vast Plains was never that real and it certainly is less so now.

THEMES

1.) To describe the distribution of the major elements in the physical environment and to discuss areal associations among these physical patterns.

2.) To evaluate influences of the physical environment upon the distribution of types of agriculture and to discuss the changing character of agricultural patterns after 1950.

3.) To comment on the areal patterns of mineral and other natural resources and their impact upon the regional economy.

4.) To analyze the effects of decreasing rural and village population on the distribution and functions of town and small city service centres.

5.) To describe the areal growth of metropolitan cities and their subregional functions.

DEFINITION OF THE REGION

Some of the problems of defining regions in this part of Canada are discussed in Chapter 1. Some geographers, and most of the general public, describe the area as the "Prairie Provinces," a group of three political units. The vegetation term "prairie" is a historical misnomer which was meant to describe only the southern part of the three provinces. It remains a misleading descriptive word for about half of the Plains section of the political units; the northern part of the Plains is covered with forests and not prairie grassland. Some people also misuse the word "prairie" as a landform term, meaning flat. The term, Prairie Provinces, has been in use for so long, however, that it is unlikely that any new regional name will be given.

Another locative and descriptive problem is caused by people in Eastern Canada who often call this region "the West"—a vague term which is disconcerting to people in British Columbia who are usually *not* included in this eastern definition of "the West." Perhaps British Columbia is the

"Far West" to people in central Canada, in the same way that the Atlantic Provinces can be the "Far East" to people in British Columbia. The crux of the regionalization problem in the Prairie Provinces is whether or not to include the Canadian Shield. There are good reasons for placing the Manitoba and Saskatchewan Shield in either region. On the one hand, it is similar to the Ontario and Quebec Shield to the east and it contrasts with some of the Plains features to the south. On the other hand, there is no escarpment or land use boundary between the Shield and Plains as there is in Eastern Canada; the geological boundary, hidden beneath glacial deposits and coniferous forests, is not a major observable landscape feature. If the region is defined politically as three provinces, there could be a tendency to neglect discussion of the Canadian Shield sections because they have few people. The functional relationships which operate so well between the Canadian Shield and St. Lawrence Lowlands are *not* as well developed in Manitoba and Saskatchewan. The academic debate need not concern us further. In this book, the Canadian Shield is discussed in Chapter 7 and this chapter is concerned with the Plains part of the Prairie Provinces.

Within this landform region, there can be other subdivisions:

1.) the northern part is the Mackenzie River valley; it is discussed in Chapter 10 as part of "The North" region;

2.) within the Prairie Provinces, the Plains can be subdivided into forested and cultivated parts. The northern section is forested; population density and economic activities are sparse and spotty;

3.) the southern part of the Plains was formerly grassland and parkland; now most of this vegetation region is either cultivated or used for ranching;

4.) this southern area can be further subdivided into agricultural regions or urban-centred regions.

THE PHYSICAL ENVIRONMENT

The characteristics of the physical environment were important to both the original Indian population and to incoming European agricultural settlers. This man-land theme was introduced in Chapter 2 and was a background concept running through discussions of agriculture in Eastern Canada. As part of a policy of illustrating different approaches to the study of regional geography in this book, the physical environment—its areal patterns and process relationships—will be described more specifically in this chapter. The Plains environment is, of course, different from other regions of Canada, and people react to it in varying ways. These environmental differences and contrasts are not specifically stated in the following sections, so readers should make the comparisons based on knowledge of Eastern Canada environments.

Landforms

Areal associations have been noted in preceding chapters between bedrock geology and landforms. On the Interior Plains, these have been modified by a variety of deposition resulting from continental glaciation. For example:

1.) the coincidence of Paleozoic rocks and the Manitoba Lowland is direct, but other geology-landform relationships are less apparent westward, except for the Cypress Hills;
2.) deposition into large post-glacial lakes evolved into some of the most fertile soils and also created some of the extensive flat areas, such as the bottom of former glacial Lake Agassiz across southern Manitoba and the very flat plain around Regina;
3.) although the geological escarpment between the Manitoba Lowland and the Saskatchewan Plain is quite noticeable in Riding Mountain National Park, to the west the plain slopes up gently. As a result, the level areas in southern and central Alberta are notably higher above sea level than those in southern Manitoba.

Internal landform variety throughout the Interior Plains results from two features:

1.) the entrenchment of post-glacial rivers into the gently rolling glacial deposits and even down into bedrock in some places; most of these rivers are now small streams that meander across broad, flat-bottomed valley floors which indicate where a larger glacial river once flowed. The Assiniboine and Battle rivers are examples;
2.) the erosion-resistant remnants of harder rock which rise above the Plains as flat-topped hills or "mountains," such as Turtle Mountain and the Cypress Hills.

In general, landform features were *not* impediments to the broad flow of agricultural settlement across the Plains. They do, however, have influences upon the distribution of some elements of climate and land use.

Areal Patterns of Climate

The Interior Plains climate is *not* a favourable one for agriculture compared with that of the Lowlands of southern Quebec and Ontario. A belief that the Plains have one of the "best" climates for wheat or grain production is not correct. Ask a Prairie farmer about his problems with the weather and his chances of producing a good crop every year. Wheat and other grains *can* be produced in the marginal climates of the Plains, even though yields per acre are lower than in more favourable environments for wheat elsewhere in the world; many other crops cannot be grown at all in the Plains region.

Precipitation:

Precipitation is the climatic element of critical significance to agricultural settlers. Fortunately, usually more than two-thirds of the annual precipitation falls as rain during the spring and summer months when it is needed for crop growth. Winter snowfall is normally light. But, unfortunately, there is great variation in the amounts that fall from month to month, season to season and place to place. Maps can show the *average* amount of precipitation that may fall in an area, but a farmer has to produce a crop on the *actual* amount that falls during a particular season. Undoubtedly, droughts—both long and short—have reduced yields and farm incomes from place to place and in different years.

On the average, the least amount of annual precipitation, 250 mm., is recorded in the Dry Belt on both sides of the southern Saskatchewan-Alberta border; the greatest amounts, 500 mm., fall on the Red River plain of southern Manitoba and the southern foothills of Alberta. Average annual precipitation decreases to the north into the Mackenzie Valley, but this decrease is partly balanced by less evaporation in the cooler summers. One of the main sources of moisture is the warm, moist air masses from the Gulf of Mexico which are pulled into the region in the cyclonic circulation system. Because precipitation can vary so much from season to season and from place to place within the season, a study of the relationships between precipitation and crop production requires specific annual and seasonal records at specific places.

Surface and Groundwater:

Surface and groundwater supplies are equally as important to farmers as the more obvious precipitation that falls from above. Since most of the surface water available in the North and South Saskatchewan drainage basin falls in the narrow belt of their headwaters in the Alberta Foothills, the total amount is limited and needs to be managed carefully. Precipitation may be stored in the many shallow lakes, ponds, sloughs and glacial depressions across the Plains, but such surface water evaporates rapidly in the hot summers and may disappear. The amount of groundwater storage depends on porosity of the soils and underlying glacial or bedrock conditions. For example, sand plains usually have good groundwater discharge and a more

231

dependable flow from springs, whereas clay plains have poor groundwater supplies because of rapid run-off during storms or spring snowmelt. The large and small irrigation projects across the southern Plains are the result of cooperative efforts of people and companies, aided with financial support by governments, to manage the relatively small amounts of water. Problems of conflicting demands between agricultural and urban uses for the limited water supplies are frequent. Who makes the decisions about such water uses?

Frosts:

Frosts are another major climatic hazard of the Interior Plains. Because the region has no mountain barrier to the north, it is open at any time of the year to the southward penetration of cold air masses from the Arctic Ocean or from the Yukon and Alaska. Because the number and intensity of these cold air masses in the spring and fall can vary greatly from year to year, the frost-free season also varies from short (70 to 90 days) to long (100 to 120 days). Since there is no certain way to predict these air mass movements months ahead of their arrival, a farmer can not know the length of the frost-free season for the year when he plants his crop.

Maps of average frost-free seasons indicate where the chances of a longer frost-free season are best. On the average, the longest frost-free seasons are experienced in southern Manitoba and southeastern Alberta — about 120 days. The shortest frost-free seasons, of 90 days or less, are recorded across the forested parts of the plains in central Saskatchewan and central and northern Alberta. However, short average frost-free seasons are also known in the higher, hilly sections of the plains, such as the Cypress Hills and Riding Mountain.

Summer Temperatures:

Summer temperatures during the short growing season are usually not a problem for farmers. Most days are warm and some days may seem "hot" to some people. The accumulation of heat (called "degree days") varies across the Plains. In areas where there are more than 3,000 degree days, such as southern Manitoba, corn can be grown.

Winter Temperatures:

Winter temperatures are cold; some days and weeks may be severely cold, similar to winter conditions in the Canadian Shield. Such temperatures prevent the growing of crops that can be winter killed, such as orchards, but otherwise winter conditions do not affect distribution patterns of agriculture. Average monthly temperatures in winter are less cold in southwestern Alberta, partly because the averages are raised by the inflow of warm Chinook winds descending on the east side of the Rocky Mountains. Do you question why some books state that Chinooks are warm air *descending* from the Rockies, whereas meteorologists say that warm air is supposed to *rise?* Long and cold winters do cause longer periods of home and business heating compared with southwestern Ontario. People on the Plains adapt to cold winters in various ways; undoubtedly "blizzards" can be miserable to people and traffic, and even dangerous, but such negative aspects are balanced by the "invigorating" clear air and bright sunshine.

Natural Vegetation and Soil Patterns

There are ecological and areal relationships between climate, vegetation and soils. Nature's way of indicating the long-term effectiveness of precipitation is illustrated by the areal patterns of vegetation. The latter, in turn, are mirrored by the soil regions. Natural vegetation and soil regions are mapped in atlases as semi-circular patterns across the southern part of the Plains.

For example, the driest part of southwestern Saskatchewan and southeastern Alberta was covered with short grass when first seen by Europeans. The soils in this south-central area are classified as Brown. In a semi-circle around the Brown soil zone are the coinciding zones of Dark Brown soils, mixed-grass prairie and somewhat higher annual precipitation. The more effective precipitation resulted in a more luxuriant grassland vegetation and, in turn, the grassland added darker-coloured organic matter to the soils. Farther outward in the semi-circular pattern are Black soils, parkland (aspen grove) vegetation and more annual precipitation. These original natural vegetation patterns are, of course, now greatly changed by clearing, ploughing and cultivation. To the north, the less fertile Grey Wooded soils have developed under deciduous and mixed forests in a zone of decreased precipitation, cooler summers and shorter frost-free seasons. The High Lime soils of central Manitoba are not part of this concentric pattern and are due more to glacial history than to climate and vegetation.

As settlers moved into the Plains in the early part of this century, their adaptations to these natural environment zones resulted in a semi-circular pattern of agriculture:

1.) most of the land was used for ranching in the short grass area with Brown soils, although grain cultivation was also attempted in some places and it was soon realized that irrigation was needed;

2.) wheat farming was dominant on the prairie grassland with its Dark Brown soils;

3.) mixed grains and livestock farms characterized the parkland vegetation zone with Black soils;

4.) grain and livestock farming penetrated with difficulty into the less favourable environmental conditions of the forest-covered Grey Wooded soils.

The areal and process relationships between climate, vegetation and soils—and their significance to agriculture—are themes worthy of further discussion. The concept has been introduced here to encourage further reading and analysis. Exact ecological relationships should be studied on a local scale rather than as regional generalizations.

THE EVOLUTION OF AREAL PATTERNS OF AGRICULTURAL SETTLEMENT

Introduction

Indians used the grassland and its animals in a different way than the later-arriving Europeans. Much of Indian economy and way of life evolved around the hunting of the bison (buffalo). These herds were greatly depleted following the introduction into the region of horses and guns—used by both Indian and white hunters. The Plains tribes occupied loosely defined territories in carrying on their hunting activities; their settlements were less permanent than those of the Indians in southern Ontario, who had more sedentary occupations. When European fur traders came into the grassland and parkland late in the 18th century, they encouraged the Indians to think of the animal population as a "resource" suitable for trading or sale, rather than as items for food or clothing.

The Interior Plains were settled by Europeans later and much faster than Canada's other major level area in the Great Lakes-St. Lawrence Lowlands, but with lower population densities. Settlers came to a relatively empty area to build homes and establish farms in environments which differed from those that they knew in southern Ontario and Quebec or in western or central Europe. Despite the enormous quantity of "free" land, it was a difficult and capricious natural environment for agricultural settlers not accustomed to a treeless landscape.

The preceding section (pp. 229-234) noted that the physical environment was not uniform; it had regional variations. Some areas were semi-arid grassland and others were wet and forested; some were flat to the horizon, others had "badlands" caused by the erosion of river banks. In some years the coincidence of many favourable conditions of the environment could mean excellent crops, while in other years "everything could go wrong" and total or partial crop failure could be the result.

The areal patterns of rural settlement were related to the evolution of a railway network. Settlement progressed from east to west; highest densities were first established in southern Manitoba. A belt of higher rural density extended westward over the Black soil belt from Winnipeg to Saskatoon to Edmonton; sparser settlement spread west of Regina into the dry, short grass area.

By 1940, most of the land suitable for agriculture on the Interior Plains had been settled. Only a small part produced food for the internal population in the growing cities; most products were grown to be consumed outside of the region, either in areas of higher population density elsewhere in Canada or in parts of the world which had food deficiencies and money to pay for our surplus food. From more than 40 years experience of relying on the undependable physical environment, farmers learned some hard lessons about adjusting to the variations in climate from year to year and from place to place. Farming methods and technology changed greatly. They also learned of their vulnerability in selling their surplus products in a world market where prices also fluctuated from year to year. The risks and instability of Plains farmers contrasted sharply with the more conservative circumstances of farmers in the Great Lakes-St. Lawrence Lowlands where food was produced in a much more favourable environment and for a larger, nearby market. Did these different environmental and marketing conditions encourage Plains farmers to think "differently" about Canada and the world?

While reading the following discussion of patterns of agriculture, keep in mind that an *urban* settlement pattern was evolving at the same time. The small service-centre towns and villages were directly dependent on their surrounding agricultural hinterlands. This is a major theme of the chapter.

AGRICULTURAL REGIONS AND SETTLEMENT

The agricultural frontier pushed westward across the Plains before and after the beginning of the 20th century. Once the land had been transferred from the historic Hudson's Bay Company to the new Dominion of Canada in 1870 and the native Indian population had been confined to reservations, there was "unlimited" agricultural land available. By the last decades of the 19th century, most of the good land in southern Ontario was occupied and farmers' sons and daughters then had to move to "the West" (or to the United States) to obtain free or cheap land. Fewer settlers came from the Quebec Lowland because they found sufficient land close to their homeland in the Canadian Shield and in the Appalachians (recall Chapter 5). The greatest number of farm immigrants came from Europe during the period 1900-1930, encouraged and attracted by advertising of the Canadian government and the railways. The land survey system laid out farmland in large squares and rectangles which are still so apparent to people who now fly over the region.

Railways were built concurrently with the arrival of settlers and had a great influence on the areal patterns that developed. The main rail line of the Canadian Pacific preceded settlement because its primary purpose was to cross the region and get to the West Coast. However, by the early 1920s, a close network of branch lines of the C.P.R., and other companies later to become the C.N.R., were built to serve local farmers. If possible, most farmers settled within five to ten miles of a railroad, to which they brought their wheat by horse and wagon. The railway companies sold land along their routes to farmers who would need the railroad to transport their wheat crops. These new settlers also became consumers of the increasing volume of manufactured goods carried west by the railways from the cities in the St. Lawrence Lowlands (and from central United States). In contrast to southern Ontario where much of the land was settled in blocks, both farm and village settlement across the Plains was linear, along and near the rail lines.

SUB-REGIONS OF THE INTERIOR PLAINS

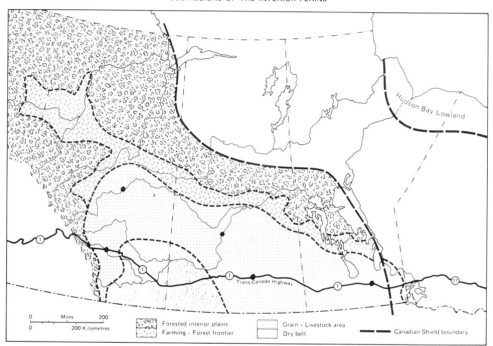

Physical environment patterns influenced settlement. Because most settlers were familiar with the time-consuming and difficult process of clearing forest to obtain viable farmland, they first chose the tall prairie grasslands. Others chose the parklands where groves of trees could be used for fuel or building material. Within a year, the grassland could be ploughed under and commercial crops produced. Climate limited their selection of crops to those which could mature within about 100 frost-free days; this limitation narrowed the choice mainly to wheat and the feed grains. The latter were fed to livestock which could be transported to meat-consuming cities of the Heartland.

The Grain-Livestock Farming Area

Crop specialization developed in particular areas from experience gained partially by trial and error experimentation and the struggle with good and bad years (see map, p. 236). A belt of more prosperous farming and higher rural population densities extended across southern Manitoba and through Saskatoon to the Edmonton area. It coincided with the Black soil belt and tall prairie grasslands; it had groves of deciduous trees on its northern edge and shorter grassland to the south. Crops produced consistently better on these fertile Black soils than in the drier areas to the south.

A mixed farming region developed in which individual farmers decided whether to:

1.) produce only, or mainly, wheat;
2.) grow some wheat, but primarily other grains such as oats, barley and rye;
3.) raise livestock, mainly beef cattle, but also pigs and poultry, to be fed from nearby grain farms.

Although these three main types of farming are intermixed within the Winnipeg to Edmonton agricultural area, some areas of specialization evolved. For example, most farmers in south-central Saskatchewan prefer to raise wheat; in this area, about 80 percent of crop acreage is in wheat production. Very large farms spread over miles and miles of level land around Regina. In most classification of agricultural regions, this part of southern Saskatchewan is known as the Wheat Belt. To many Canadians, the wheat farms of this area are probably the stereotype of Prairie agriculture.

When viewed from the air the rural landscape of southeastern Saskatchewan differs in appearance from the flat farmland of the Regina plain or south-central Manitoba. The glacially deposited ground moraine of southeastern Saskatchewan is pitted with many small lakes, ponds and sloughs, most of which are circled with a strip of small trees or shrubs. These circular patches of non-cultivation contrast with the unbroken fields of the Red River plain.

In southern Manitoba at the eastern end of the mixed farming zone, diversification came early. Southern Manitoba has the advantage of a longer frost-free period which permitted a greater choice of crops. Prior to 1940, it had the biggest local market within the Plains region — the city of Winnipeg. Southern Manitoba became a specialized livestock area; cattle were transported from the western plains to its feed-grain farms and fattened there before further transport to the meat packing plants in Ontario and Quebec. The large livestock yards along the railway in St. Boniface are visual evidence of the continuing significance of livestock in southern Manitoba. Other crops gradually became more important than wheat; barley and oats acreages increased and speciality crops such as sunflowers, sugar beets, canning vegetables and corn became part of the rural landscape. Dairy farms increased in number as the urban population of Winnipeg increased. To what degree is the agriculture of southern Manitoba similar to the livestock-dairy farming of southern Ontario?

Farmers in central Alberta developed diversity of crops and new farming methods later than in Manitoba. Wheat is still important there, but the other feed grains are also grown; livestock farms which convert the grains to meat are numerous. There are more beef cattle raised in the Edmonton area than in the better-known ranching region of southern Alberta which has lower carrying-capacity on its grasslands. Feed lots are as much a part of the rural landscape in central Alberta as are grain elevators in southern Saskatchewan. In the 1970s, central Alberta farmers turned to new cash crops such as rapeseed, flaxseed and legumes. Unlike the large wheat farms in south-central Saskatchewan where one crop covers a large area on each farm, the farms of southern Manitoba and central Alberta have many fields, each growing a variety of crops. Seen from the air, the smaller rectangular field patterns in the mixed farming areas of Manitoba and Alberta are much different from those of Saskatchewan. Flying over the Plains can be interesting if one looks for the diversity of field patterns and land uses in the landscape.

The Northern Fringes of Agriculture

Farming penetration was slower north of the main agricultural zone and was characterized by lower population densities. The agricultural frontier pushed northward into the forested areas after World War I; many of the settlers were European, particularly from the Ukraine, Germany and Scandinavia. Although natural grassland clearings were usually occupied first, particularly in the Peace River area, throughout most of the "pioneer fringe," it took almost a generation of hard work to hack away the forest to create a viable farm of more than 100 acres. In this farmland-forest region (map, p. 236) the natural fertility of the Grey Wooded soils is not high and crop yields may decrease after five or six years unless commercial fertilizer is added. Although precipitation is generally adequate, the frost-free season is shorter and more irregular than it is farther south. In addition, social and community life in the pockets of farming amid the forest is not as attractive as in the longer settled grasslands. Service-centre villages are far apart and towns are few. Transportation is supplied by single lines of rail or road rather than a network.

This "pioneer agriculture" which penetrated north-central Saskatchewan and Alberta prior to 1940 was similar to settlement in the Clay Belts of Ontario and Quebec in having dispersed distribution patterns, subsistence living (often supplemented by local fish and game food supplies), feed grain and livestock production and isolation from urban amenities. And the result was much the same as in the Clay Belt—farm abandonment. Farming is difficult in this environment and markets are farther away. The agricultural frontier is no longer moving northward in Canada.

Forest clearing is, however, still going on *within* the farm-forest frontier aided by modern mechanical bush-clearing equipment. Abandoned farms are being consolidated into larger farms. In the decade 1961-1971, about four million acres of new cropland were added along the northern edges of farming across the three Prairie Provinces. About half of this increase in cultivated acreage was reported in northern Alberta. The expansion of agricultural acreage is particularly apparent in the Peace River district of Alberta and northeastern British Columbia. There, exploration for and development of petroleum and natural gas have given both increased road access and have increased the local urban population. Improved and extended rail and road connections to Vancouver in the 1960s gave the Peace River area better access to world markets, and farmers have responded to this external change.

Unlike in Eastern Canada where farm acreage had been steadily decreasing, new land is still being brought into agricultural use on the Interior Plains. The scale of this increased cultivation, 1961-1981, is recorded in the following table of improved acreage in the census divisions across the northern sections of agricultural land. Have the percentages of land occupied by each crop changed? Consult the census of agriculture.

Table 1

Changes in Improved Acreage Across the Northern Sections of Agricultural Areas of the Prairie Provinces (in 000 Acres)

YEAR	ALBERTA[1]	SASKATCHEWAN[2]	MANITOBA[3]	TOTAL
1961	10,000	8,800	2,300	21,100
1971	12,000	9,800	2,700	24,500
1976	12,600	10,500	3,000	26,100
1981	13,300	10,300	3,600	27,200

1. Alberta: Census Divisions 10-15
2. Saskatchewan: Census Divisions 14-18
3. Manitoba: Census Divisions 12, 14-18 in 1961-71; Census Divisions 16-22 in 1976-81.

The Dry Belt

South of the grain and livestock belt, the boundary between ranching and grain farming has been a fluctuating one, never clearly defined. The natural grasslands have been used for cattle ranching since the 1880s. Because the area receives little and very irregular rainfall, the carrying capacity of the land is low in terms of the number of hectares needed to feed one cow; ranches are therefore very large. Less precipitation, on the average, is partly balanced by an average frost-free season which is two weeks longer in the central dry belt than in the adjoining grain-livestock area northward. Farmers who ploughed these grasslands harvested adequate grain crops in a few "wet" years, but the "dry" years and poor harvests were more numerous. The top soil was sometimes blown away and crop failures were common. During the "dirty thirties" (1930s) when successive years of low rainfall came at the same time as the loss of world markets due to the economic depression, thousands of farmers had to leave the dry belt; many moved north to areas of more adequate precipitation in the farm-forest fringe, particularly to the Peace River area. After 1945, both the federal and provincial governments helped to restore the environment by developing community pastures, providing facilities to store groundwater and building more irrigation systems.

Cultivation of the Dry Belt increased after 1950, assisted by technological advances and stimulated by frequent high grain prices. The resulting areal expansion of cultivation was due to two important techniques:

1.) strip agriculture by dry farming methods;
2.) irrigation.

Strip Farming:

Using strip farming methods, alternate rectangular strips are cultivated while the others are left in fallow; the fields are rotated each year. Two years of rainfall, therefore, can accumulate in the soil to produce a crop in one year. Although fallowing is used through the grain producing areas, often constituting 20 to 30 percent of the total farm acreage, in the Dry Belt about 50 percent of the cultivated land remains unused in any particular year. This successful technology resulted in the addition of large areas of grain cultivation across southern Alberta, northwest and northeast of Lethbridge, and in Saskatchewan, west of Regina. Such increased production was only possible, however, when world markets could pay for the crops.

These alternate long narrow rectangles of brown soils and green or gold grain make interesting patterns when seen from the air during the summer. There is great variety in the field patterns. Some rectangles are long and narrow; others are wider. Most extend north-south, at right angles to prevailing winds, but other strips can be diagonal. Individual farmers still make personal choices about the shape and direction of their fields. Within the strip farming area, large blocks of land remain uncultivated; since the climate is essentially the same across south-central Alberta, either some other factor in the environment is less favourable, such as poor soils, or farmers have made individual choices to use the land less intensively. In some places, a careful observer can see large circles of cultivation amid the rectangles, indicating that a farmer is using central pivot irrigation. In the man-land equation, the "land" has not changed; man is simply using it differently.

Irrigation:
Irrigation increases the intensity of land use in the Dry Belt and also results in higher population densities. Both farms and fields may be smaller. Because irrigation requires high capital costs, irrigated land must produce crops which are more valuable per acre than those grown by dry farming methods. Service-centre towns are numerous in the irrigated areas because of the higher rural population densities nearby. In contrast, the ranching areas have low densities of farm population and very few towns.

Two types of irrigation are practiced in different environments:

1.) Small-scale irrigation is common throughout the grain and livestock areas of Alberta and Saskatchewan. In this system, small dugouts excavated into the rolling glacial deposits collect groundwater into small ponds; in other places, earth dams placed across small intermittent streams hold back spring run-off. Wells may also be used, if groundwater is available. These adaptations to the semi-arid environment are really water conservation methods and are used mainly for watering stock. Such small scale irrigation can be done by individual farmers, whereas large scale projects require group cooperation and government financial help.

2.) The other method of irrigation involves building large dams within the Dry Belt. Annual precipitation stored in lakes behind these dams is transported by aquaducts to farms where summer rainfall is insufficient or unreliable. Most of these large irrigation works are in southern Alberta, obtaining water from headwater tributaries of the South Saskatchewan River, but there is one storage and power dam on that river in south-central Saskatchewan.

Although it is possible for more of the Dry Belt to be irrigated to produce food or feed crops, there are environmental and economic limitations. The average total amount of precipitation which falls on the Foothills of south-western Alberta is small—500 to 635 mms. If more surface water is to be used in the area, it may have to be diverted from the North Saskatchewan or Athabasca rivers; the water of these latter rivers is not needed for irrigation locally because northern farms usually receive adequate summer precipitation, but it may be needed in the future for urban industrial, domestic or power uses. Water is a valuable commodity.

Entrenched rivers in the western Interior Plains present another physical problem for irrigation expansion. It is costly to pump water from the river bottoms to irrigate the flat lands above the deep-cut rivers. In addition, not all soils across the Plains are suitable for irrigation; many of the glacial deposits are too coarse to hold moisture near the surface. These various physical environment limitations restrict irrigation possibilities to only about one million hectares across the southwestern plains. The present and potential irrigated area is a small share of the 36 million hectares (90 million acres) that are in cultivation and fallow each year on the Plains.

The areal expansion of irrigation is also limited by market conditions. The regional population of about four million people is a relatively small market for irrigated crops such as sugar beets and vegetables, and these are not likely to be exported outside of the region to compete with vegetable producing areas in southern Ontario or southern British Columbia. However, increasing urban population in the large cities of Alberta will certainly make a larger local market. The external price of wheat influences whether it is economic to cause higher production costs by growing wheat by irrigation. Some of the irrigation crops, such as alfalfa and other legumes, are used for cattle feed. Irrigation agriculture is therefore areally associated and functionally linked with the ranching industry which surrounds the irrigated districts.

Summary:

The general pattern of agriculture consists of a broad belt of mixed livestock and grain farming extending from Winnipeg to Edmonton from which expansion is taking place southward into the Dry Belt and northward into the forest region. Increased cultivation within the Dry Belt has been aided by the technology of strip farming and irrigation; consolidation within the forest frontier has been aided by mechanical bush-clearing equipment. These changes in areal patterns have been possible because of good markets for grain and meat products outside of the region. Further land use changes can be expected as populations increase in the Plains cities; "urban oriented" food crops should increase, similar to those in the Great Lakes-St. Lawrence Lowlands, but within the limitations of the local climate.

The spread of agricultural settlement was parallelled by an evolving pattern of supporting small towns and villages supplying the goods and services needed by the farm population. The greatest number of these urban settlements dotted the landscape between the large regional cities of Winnipeg, Saskatoon, Regina and Edmonton, and then arced southward to Calgary and Lethbridge.

CHANGES IN URBAN-RURAL PATTERNS

The system of small urban places established along with agricultural settlement was functionally tied to the railroads. The towns and villages illustrate the concept of Central Place Theory which is concerned with city-hinterland relationships. This theory, developed in rural Germany early in this century, was noted in Chapter 6 with comments about an urban network of regional cities and service-centre towns in the Great Lakes-St. Lawrence Lowlands. In Chapter 3, the service-centre functions of small towns in the Annapolis Valley and St. John River valley of the Maritimes were described. The concept of the location, spacing and functions of central places is well-known in geographic literature; the principles apply quite well on the Interior Plains.

Central Place Theory states that goods and services are supplied in urban places to people in a surrounding rural and agricultural hinterland. Empirical studies have indicated how many persons in a surrounding area are needed to maintain grocery stores, drug stores, gas stations, doctors' offices, barber shops, accountants' offices, etc. in a village or town, i.e., a "central place." "Low-order" goods and services are those needed frequently and are therefore usually available close to the consumer. "Medium-order" goods and services are required less frequently and can be located farther away. "High-order" goods and services, such as hospitals, medical or business specialists, furniture stores, etc., are needed only occasionally, and therefore people may travel longer distances for them. Such high-order goods and services are located in medium to large cities where there is both a larger local population and a larger surrounding area of rural population. This central place, service-centre relationship applies mainly to towns and villages in dominantly agricultural areas.

Because agriculture is not commonly considered an "industry," the service-centre towns of the Interior Plains tend *not* to be classified in the geography literature as single-industry, resource-based towns. However, they *do* depend on one occupation, so they can be compared with resource-based towns of the Canadian Shield. Although these settlements are different types in internal form and distribution patterns, they have similarities in functions. The agricultural towns of the Plains and the mining and forestry towns of the Shield differ from the commercial and manufacturing towns and cities of the Great Lakes-St. Lawrence Lowlands.

A linear pattern of central place service towns evolved across the Interior Plains, controlled and directed by the railways. As the railways were built and lands occupied for grain and livestock farms, stations were established five to ten miles apart to which farmers could transport their grain. These stations provided a *service* function. Thousands of grain elevators rose above the flat prairie landscape marking the sites of villages or towns. Villages might have one or two elevators, whereas towns might have four or five elevators lined along the railway and adjoining small commercial "cores." Near some of these railway stations, but not all, stores were opened to supply consumer and household *goods* to the nearby farmers. In principle, the greater the number of farmers in the surrounding area, the greater the number of stores in the central place. In some of these places, "medium-order" stores would be located, expecting to supply a larger hinterland containing more people. A hierarchy of size of towns evolved in which the medium-size towns were approximately evenly spaced along the railroads, with several small villages between them. The geometry of location, size and spacing of these service centre towns is one of the interesting geographical patterns on the Plains. Study this pattern in the Yorkton area, Saskatchewan, on map, p. 245. Enlarge the symbols for the different sizes of towns and comment on the distribution pattern of the larger places.

The form and structure of small Plains towns were quite similar. The commercial section was usually about one or two blocks in length along the "main street" and adjoining the railway station. This business and service strip was either parallel to the railway track or was at right angles, leading away from the railway station. As the village grew, both forms could be combined into a "T-shaped" commercial core. Some towns might have some agricultural processing buildings, but usually industrial functions were lacking. Residences were built with a rectangular street pattern around the commercial section, but were nearly always only on one side of the railway tracks. Even in larger Plains towns, most of the urban area is still only on one side of the railway, creating one of the distinctive regional urban forms in Canada. In this sense, the railroad is almost as much of a physical barrier to urban movement and land use expansion as is a river.

By about 1940, this distribution pattern of agriculture and accompanying small towns and villages was established across the Plains. Towns were more numerous along the railways in the grain-livestock belt from Winnipeg to Edmonton and fewer in the sparsely occupied grasslands to the south and in the forest frontier in the north. This linear pattern is illustrated on the map of the Yorkton region.

Changes have been occurring in this urban-rural pattern as a result of several concurrent developments:

1.) Farms have become larger and more mechanized. As farmers expand their cultivated acreage, they need more equipment to operate their farms efficiently. In turn, mechanized farms require less part-time labour. Larger farms, therefore, mean fewer farmhouses per square mile and mechanization means fewer people per farm. Thus, the geographic significance of changing farming methods is a reduction in rural population densitites.

2.) Because specialized grain farms usually have little or no livestock, they need not be staffed during the winter and can be operated with only a few people during the short summer growing season. As a result, many wheat farm families have moved to the larger towns where there are better medical, social and educational facilities; the farm can be worked during the summer by absentee owners. A result of these changing social and family arrangements was further decreases in farm population densities. This type of decrease is more apparent in the dominant wheat growing areas of south-central Saskatchewan and southeastern Alberta than in the livestock areas of the other parts of the Plains.

TOWNS, VILLAGES AND RAIL LINKS OF EAST - CENTRAL SASKATCHEWAN

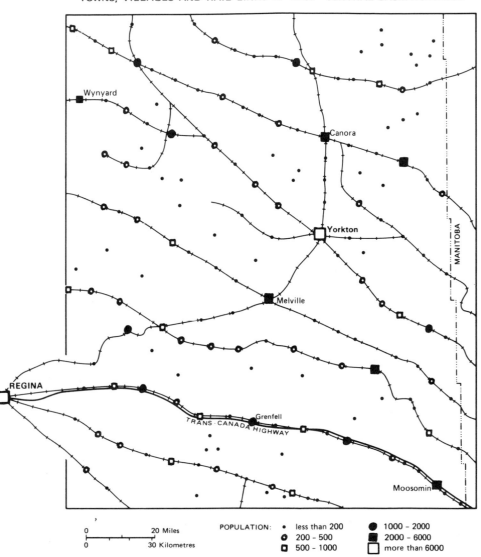

	POPULATION:	
	• less than 200	● 1000 - 2000
0 ⟼ 20 Miles	◉ 200 - 500	▨ 2000 - 6000
0 ⟼ 30 Kilometres	▣ 500 - 1000	☐ more than 6000

3.) Because of lower farm population densities, fewer people came to the small local villages for goods and services. Some stores and offices were therefore abandoned because their services were no longer needed; hamlets supplying only low-order goods or services simply did not have enough customers to survive economically. Village populations decreased. The viability of local social and educational facilities decreased. As commercial and professional people moved from the villages to the cities, the process of village decline and city increase was accelerated.

4.) Increased use of trucks and cars after 1945, parallelled by improved and paved roads, permitted people to travel farther to large towns for a wider choice of goods and services, bypassing the limited services of the local village. Similarly, the use of trucks instead of horses for hauling grain widened the tributary area for the local grain elevators; they no longer needed to be a few miles apart. Many small grain elevators closed and larger storage facilities with better grading capacities were built in larger towns. The closing of the grain elevator was often the final blow to a tiny settlement. The various sizes of the tributary areas around grain collection centres is illustrated by the following map of the Yorkton area.

Whereas the railway lines across the Plains were built by external capital and interests, the highway system was created by internal decisions of provincial governments. The roads had more specific local uses and they tended to focus traffic and products into the larger urban centres. Railways created the original linear settlement patterns, but roads accelerated the growth of certain places in the size hierarchy.

Decreased farm and village populations lessened the need for maintenance of the costly road network in which local roads were about a mile apart. Local and provincial governments faced awkward political decisions as to which roads to close to reduce costs and which ones to leave open to appease voters. Recognizing changing geographical patterns forces difficult political decisions!

The disappearance of some hamlets and villages resulted in the abandon-ment of some branch rail lines. Sometimes the process was initiated by the railways when they decided to abandon certain unprofitable, short branch lines and to close the little-used grain elevators along that line. The continuation of this process is controversial: the railways wish to abandon more branch lines to make their collection and transport of grain more efficient and less costly; many small towns and villages are fighting politically to maintain their elevators, railways and existence. Older people, in particular, are loathe to leave their village homes. (Recall the similar controversy over economic and social values involved in the centralization of fishing and fishermen in Newfoundland.) Political decisions that have to balance economic and social values are difficult to make. The problem has a geographical (i.e., distributional) aspect.

GRAIN DELIVERY POINTS AND TRIBUTARY AREAS IN EASTERN SASKATCHEWAN

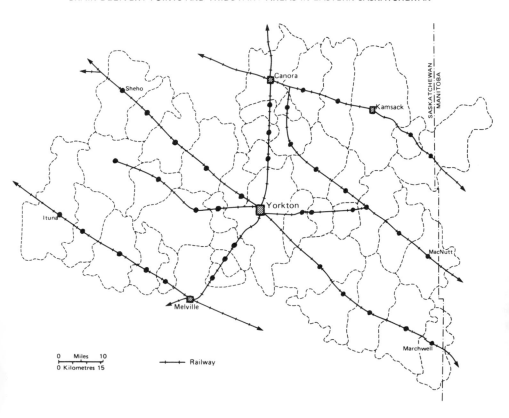

There were some exceptions to the pattern of decreased village population. Although some of the villages and small towns near large Prairie cities almost disappeared when their service and supply functions were bypassed, others revived in the 1970s as "dormitories" for overflow city populations. (This changing pattern in southern Ontario is noted in Chapter 6.) The attractiveness of small-town living brought people to certain places outside the metropolitan cities where they could commute to work, recreation and cultural events. Study the 1966-1981 census of population of villages near several of the large cities and note which places have increased in population.

247

Towns of 3,000 to 10,000 population illustrate an irregular pattern of growth or decline. Some of these are still needed to perform central place service-centre functions for their agricultural hinterlands, but not as many as before. Most medium-size towns grew at the expense of local villages and hamlets. They are still present in all agricultural areas and offer the farm population a choice of goods and services. For example, rural depopulation seemed to level off in southern Manitoba after 1971 and nearly all of the market centres began to increase in population. This trend is different from that of southern Saskatchewan. The growth or decline of Plains towns is not easy to explain or generalize without individual investigation and field work. Some towns have obvious locational advantages for serving people, such as being at crossroads or at a convergence of transport routes. Other towns are "saved" by the energy and enthusiasm of local business leaders.

Governments also influence the growth of certain towns. Government services such as secondary schools, regional hospitals, court houses, public work yards and facilities, etc., have to be located in central places to serve the population. Governments make political decisions whether to "save" certain towns by locating government service facilities (and their workers) in these places or to accelerate the centralization process by placing the facilities in "growing" towns.

Other towns have the good fortune to be located above or near deposits of petroleum, natural gas, coal or potash. When these minerals were brought into use, such towns could then add processing and industrial facilities (and the people who perform these activities) to their previously established service functions. With a few exceptions, the discovery of petroleum, natural gas and potash came *after* the urban network had been established for the agricultural economy. Individual oil and gas wells had little impact upon farm population densities or villages; there was no local processing and the products were transported by pipelines to certain urban centres. Therefore, few resource-based towns like those in the Canadian Shield were created in the Plains region. The arrival of new industrial workers, such as in the potash mines, simply added houses and industrial buildings to a nearby agricultural town. Because the major non-metallic and fuel resources are spread across southern Saskatchewan and Alberta, such urban growth has been more common in these provinces than in Manitoba.

The distribution, hierarchy and spacing of settlements in the Yorkton region of east-central Saskatchewan are shown on the map on p. 245. Enlarge the symbols for each size category of settlement on the map and study the distribution and spacing of each size category as you do this.

Population trends of settlements in this region are recorded in the following table. Obtain a detailed map of the area from a nearby map library or use the Canada Gazetteer Atlas, p. 61 and make a map which will show the location and spacing of those settlements which have increased in population; with another symbol show the location of settlements which have decreased in population. How will you symbolize those settlements which fluctuated in population?

Table 2

Population Trends in Settlements in the Yorkton Area of East-Central Saskatchewan, 1966-81

CITIES, OVER 5,000 POPULATION

CITY	1966	1976	1981
YORKTON	12,600	14,400	15,400
MELVILLE	5,700	5,200	5,100

TOWNS, 1,000 TO 5,000 POPULATION

TOWN	1966	1976	1981
Canora	2,730	2,700	2,670
Esterhazy	3,190	2,900	3,065
Fort Qu'Appelle	1,600	1,770	1,830
Foam Lake	1,170	1,390	1,450
Grenfell	1,370	1,360	1,310
Indian Head	1,890	1,720	1,890
Langenburg	1,270	1,200	1,025
Kamsack	2,980	2,720	2,690
Moosomin	2,140	2,500	2,580
Preeceville	1,200	1,170	1,250
Wadena	1,400	1,380	1,500
Whitewood	1,070	1,070	1,000
Wynard	1,950	2,050	2,150

VILLAGES, 500 TO 1,000 POPULATION

VILLAGE	1966	1976	1981
Balcarres	750	730	740
Broadview	1,050	860	840
Cupar	590	610	670
Churchbridge	915	930	970
Ituna	975	910	870
Norquay	530	520	550
Quill Lake	580	530	510
Qu'Appelle	550	550	650
Raconville	630	870	930
Sturgis	700	700	790
Springside	—	470	530
Saltcoats	600	490	550
Wolsley	1,050	890	900

HAMLETS, 250 TO 500 POPULATION

HAMLET	1966	1976	1981
Abernethy	310	300	300
Bredenbury	570	440	470

Buchanan	445	435	390
Dysart	—	235	275
Grayson	285	260	265
Invermay	440	400	350
Kelliher	500	410	400
Lemberg	440	420	415
Lipton	450	350	360
Lestock	450	415	400
Neudorf	505	395	425
Pelly	470	350	390
Rhein	330	285	270
Stockholm	370	330	390
Sheho	—	310	285
Spyhill	345	350	355
Theodore	—	460	470
Wapella	610	450	490

Summary:

These rural to urban movements and trends have made the Plains region more urban in its regional characteristics, and these changes have implications upon the local economies. Compared with 1940, the Plains urban system now has fewer places, larger ones, and they are farther apart. As the urban population increases and incomes rise above national averages, these Plains people can become greater consumers of manufactured goods that can increasingly be produced locally rather than transported from the Great Lakes-St. Lawrence Lowlands. The Plains urban system now serves fewer rural people than in 1940 and more internal, city dwellers.

Geographical changes in the patterns of agricultural and small-town settlement are an integrated, on-going process. There are many reasons for people to be "pushed" from the farms, and different reasons for people to be "pulled" to the cities. The process is called rural depopulation and urban concentration. The distribution and types of agriculture have influenced the pattern and functions of small urban settlements. An evenly-spaced pattern across a uniform plain envisioned by the models of Central Place Theory, with a hierarchy of towns related to population size, has been modified into linear patterns because of dependence on the railroads. Further changes in the distribution and density patterns resulted from adjustments to road transport. A theme of this chapter has been the areal relationships between service towns and agricultural hinterlands which are determined by characteristics of area, population densities and transportation.

POPULATION

When population was mainly rural and agricultural, it was possible to study the geographical patterns of ethnic groups. The "Ukrainian belt," for example, extended east and southeast of Edmonton, and Scandinavians tended to settle in the northern parts of several agricultural areas. Some particular cultural and religious groups, such as Mennonites and Hutterites, still maintain distinct communities in southern Manitoba and southern Alberta. Their landholding systems and communal dwellings add variety to the Plains cultural landscape. Although French-Canadians settled in groups in certain communities in the early part of the century, their descendants have generally been absorbed into the social and economic mosaic of the region, unlike the French-Canadians in some parts of Ontario and New Brunswick.

Most immigrants, however, dispersed themselves throughout the Plains region. The early ethnic patterns have generally been lost in the migration to the cities where people with different ethnic and national backgrounds became intermixed in the high-rise apartments and suburban neighbour-hoods. It can be misleading now to think of Plains people as illustrating the cultural characteristics of European people who settled the area in the early part of this century. In fact, more than 90 percent of Prairie province inhabitants are Canadian-born and the young people of the region are probably second or third generation descendants of original European immigrants. Their cultural heritage is still remembered, however, in local festivals and museums.

OTHER NATURAL RESOURCES

Introduction

The economy of the Prairie Provinces began to change after petroleum was discovered at Leduc, south of Edmonton, in 1947. The internal use and export of petroleum and other mineral resources brought diversity; no longer were employment and prosperity so dependent on agriculture and its external markets as they were prior to 1940. But these "other resources" have always been present; their new prominence is due to discovery in larger amounts and because technology has developed other uses for them. However, one big problem still remains: Plains natural resources have a relatively small, although growing, local market. Unlike the concentrated consumer market at the western end of Lake Ontario, the urban consumers on the Plains are dispersed into three, or five, major centres. Profits are obtained by transporting and selling resources outside of the region in centres with more industry and larger population.

Forestry

A "forest crescent" arcs across the central Interior Plains, north and west of the parklands and livestock-grain agricultural region. Agriculture penetrated into it slowly and with difficulty. The cutting and processing of the forest resource offered alternative employment to farmers on these marginal lands on the agricultural-forest frontier, similar to such opportunities in parts of the Clay Belt and in the Atlantic and Gulf region. Forestry activities also helped to broaden the economic base of such agricultural service towns as The Pas, Nipawin, Prince Albert and Grande Prairie.

Small amounts of lumber are cut for local use all across the forest crescent, but the small size of trees does not produce the quantity or quality of lumber that can be obtained from British Columbia. This forest is primarily a pulpwood reserve to be used if more accessible forests are depleted. The few pulp and paper mills in the region were not established until after 1950; they have higher export transportation costs than the mills in British Columbia, Ontario and Quebec, which are closer to markets.

On a Canada-wide scale, the functional relationships and areal associations between agricultural and forestry activities have been common all across the marginal lands from the Atlantic Provinces, through the southern Canadian Shield, and across the central Interior Plains. Forests have delayed agricultural clearing, but have also given supplementary incomes to farmers. This part-time way of life is fast disappearing as occupations become more specialized.

The forest has another significance to the Plains region. Like the forest across the southern Canadian Shield, it is a recreational resource—a change in environment for the rural and urban dwellers on the Plains. Saskatchewan residents and people from the High Plains of central United States visit the lakes and forests north of Prince Albert; Albertans can go to the forested Foothills and the spectacular mountain scenery of the Rockies. The Rockies have a position and function for Calgary residents that the Canadian Shield edge has for people in Montreal.

The forests are also the natural habitat of animal wildlife and fur-bearers which still support the trapping economy of the native Indians. These native people live in a different physical environment than the white residents of the Plains—an environment which is a difficult one in which to make a living now; their difficulties can be compared to those of agricultural settlers on the grassland plains a century ago.

Fisheries

Fisheries play a minor part in the Interior Plains economy. In terms of distribution patterns, there is essentially no fishing and few large, deep lakes in the grassland area; however, there is some sports fishing and a little commercial fishing in the lakes of the forest area. Most commercial fishing uses the line of large lakes—Winnipeg, La Ronge and Athabasca—along the boundary between the Shield and Plains. Despite the long distance to markets, much of the catch is consumed in central United States; the price commanded by good quality fish produced in cold water offsets the high cost of transportation.

Minerals and Mining

Metallic minerals are located in the Canadian Shield parts of Manitoba and Saskatchewan and are discussed in Chapter 7. The Pas is the transportation gateway to the Shield mining region which developed north of Flin Flon. This mining region had past locational disadvantages, being far from the industrial and consuming markets of eastern North America and northwestern Europe, but these disadvantages have been decreasing due to improved access to central United States industrial consumers and the likelihood of increased markets westward around the Pacific Ocean rim.

The discovery and use of non-metallic minerals and fuels brought enormous changes to the economy and prosperity of peoples on the Interior Plains. As discussed in Chapter 7, the *geography* of mineral resources is difficult to analyze; the distribution pattern is directly related to geological conditions and development is controlled by economics. Factors in geology and economics, therefore, influence the geographical patterns.

Coal:

The use of coal resources illustrates the problems of poor location with regard to external markets. Most of the vast coal deposits in the western part of the Plains were used locally prior to 1950 for home heating, steam power generation or as fuel for the railways. These local, internal uses declined for about 25 years when consumers switched to petroleum; but with the reduction or disappearance of low-cost petroleum during the 1970s coal reserves revived in importance. Coal has many uses: some types can be a raw material in industry, such as coking coal for the steel industry; other kinds are an alternative to oil or natural gas for steam power generation; coal by-products have many chemical and industrial uses. An increase in coking and thermal uses resulted in the revival of the coal mining towns particularly in western Alberta (and in eastern British Columbia). A question to be answered in the future is whether the quality and location of coal will attract future industry to the western Plains. Will this resource continue to be exported from the region to industrial and consuming markets elsewhere?

Petroleum and Natural Gas:

Some of the same locational problems apply to the production and use of petroleum and natural gas. Supplies of the latter were known in Alberta early in this century and were used for local heating in several cities, such as Medicine Hat. When large reserves were discovered during the 1950s, it became possible to export gas by pipeline to consumers in higher density regions outside the Plains. Locally, some people were employed by the extraction and export of large amounts of sulphur from the natural gas. As the use of other chemical by-products increased, more industries employed people in the larger cities. Discoveries of deeper natural gas fields in the late 1970s improved the reserves estimates, particularly in comparison with declining petroleum reserves. Natural gas has been significant within the Interior Plains for inexpensive domestic heating in the cold winter climate and also as a raw material for some urban industries. However, these same useful characteristics also became available to other Canadian (and American) regions when the gas was exported.

The areal patterns of petroleum discovery and production on the Plains can be compared with the outward-evolving patterns of metallic mineral production in the Canadian Shield. Excluding the early Turner Valley field which was significant in attracting capital and oil companies to Calgary, the evolving areal pattern of petroleum production spread outward from Edmonton after the late 1940s. Whereas in the Canadian Shield the metal mines were linked to external markets by railroads, in the Plains transportation was by pipelines. As external demand increased, petroleum fields farther and farther from Edmonton, such as beneath the plains of northeastern British Columbia, were linked by longer pipelines to central refineries and to an external distribution system.

As known light and "conventional" petroleum reserves began to dwindle and external demands elsewhere in North America increased, it became necessary to develop some of the marginal (in location and economically) oil reserves of the Athabasca Tar Sands of northeastern Alberta and the "heavy" oils near Lloydminster. There are many technological and financial problems to overcome before the oil sands can be fully developed. The high cost of extracting petroleum from the oil sands must be balanced against costs of obtaining oil from underwater wells in the Beaufort Sea or off the Atlantic coast.

The village of Fort McMurray had been a small trans-shipment point between the north end of a railway and the shallow-draft water transport facilities on the Athabasca River serving the Mackenzie Valley. In the 1970s, a whole new city of several thousand persons was created to house and service the people developing the oil sands for petroleum. Fort McMurray is now a large single-industry resource-based city, like many others to its east in the Canadian Shield. The construction of large, local processing facilities, transportation lines and services, plus the housing and feeding of thousands of workers and commercial and service personnel, had an enormous impact on the settlement pattern of this previously almost empty part of northeastern Alberta. The "multiplier effect" appeared in the form of many high-rise office and management buildings and supply and maintenance facilities in Edmonton.

Although a small petrochemical industry developed in Alberta using petroleum and natural gas as raw materials, the relatively small size of the consuming market in the Interior Plains remains a problem. As a result, much of the petroleum is shipped out of the Plains region in crude form and is processed elsewhere in consuming centres which are longer established. As population increases across the western Plains and in the Cordillera, a local threshold may be reached in which regional petrochemical and allied industries may expand. Such development will further increase urban population.

Although petroleum and natural gas greatly changed the economies of the Plains region and gave enormous revenues to the provincial governments, they did not really change the settlement distribution pattern. Except for examples such as Fort McMurray and Drayton Valley, few *new* settlements were created to develop these mineral resources. However, the management, servicing and processing of these extractive industries were located in the large cities, offering new urban employment which accelerated the rural to urban population flow. Thus, although the distribution pattern of settlement did not change, densities did; rural depopulation continued and urban concentration increased. These areal trends were most noticeable in Alberta and had the least impact in Manitoba.

It is not forgotten by provincial governments and Plains residents that the 1970s boom in the regional economy was greatly based on a declining natural resource, petroleum. Abandoned mining towns in the Shield and Cordillera are reminders of the danger of depending on non-renewable resources.

Potash:

Potash, the fourth of the main non-metallic minerals, helped to bring diversity and prosperity to central and eastern Saskatchewan. Many of the small agricultural towns there added mining and processing facilities to their service-centre functions. Potash, therefore, has had a similar impact upon the urbanization process in eastern Saskatchewan as petroleum had on the cities of Alberta. The potash reserves are some of the largest known in the world, but like the other natural resources, they are exported out of the Plains region to become fertilizer in other parts of the world.

Summary:

Many of the changes in the Plains regional economy are related to changing uses of its natural resource base. The region has become an important supplier of fuel and raw materials to Canadian, American and Japanese manufacturers and consumers. Much of the urban growth in large cities after 1945 can be attributed to the employment generated by the extraction, processing, management and transportation of mineral resources. This growth was superimposed on an established urban system which had evolved to serve the agricultural economy.

CITIES

Introduction

The development and areal growth of most Plains cities was similar to that of eastern Canadian cities, but there were also some differences. One of the fundamental differences is in age and the resulting visual appearances. Prairie cities are new; they began growing almost a century after many eastern Canadian cities were founded. Much of this population growth and areal expansion came after 1950. Plains cities have generally been well planned; their growth came at a time when urban planning had become an accepted part of city government (unlike the uncontrolled growth of many eastern cities prior to 1940). In addition, western city planners were able to avoid the earlier mistakes made in eastern cities. The ubiquitous high-rise office and apartment buildings in the downtown cores of Plains cities look the same as in eastern cities, but residential housing tends to lack the diversity of eastern cities; in the latter, houses were constructed over a longer period of time and experienced various architectural trends and fads. Western streets are usually wider than in eastern cities and parking facilities were built during the automobile age, unlike the older, crowded central sections of eastern cities.

The spacing, hierarchy and functions of large cities on the Interior Plains are related to their local hinterlands. These areal patterns and location principles are similar to those previously noted for small towns in agricultural settings. Each of the five metropolitan cities (Table 3, p. 268) serves a regional hinterland of a different size. Although these large cities supply the same types of central place and service functions as small towns, they have a greater variety and number of them. In addition, cities have larger numbers of industrial and processing activities and, of course, supply goods and services to a much larger local population within the urban area. The large cities of the Interior Plains are not integrated into a functioning "urban system" like those around the west end of Lake Ontario and across south-central Ontario. Plains cities tend to be separate entities and they compete with each other.

Manufacturing in the cities of the Interior Plains is much like that in the cities of the Atlantic and Gulf region. It is based on the processing of regional natural resources, mainly for export, in addition to the production of consumer goods for the local urban population. Manufacturing in the Plains serves a larger number of metropolitan city consumers, with generally higher incomes, compared with the Atlantic and Gulf region. When comparing the Plains with the Great Lakes-St. Lawrence Lowlands, the latter has fewer natural resources, but a larger consuming market (but with resources nearby in the Canadian Shield), whereas the Interior Plains has a wide range of natural resources, but a small consuming population. In many cities of the Great Lakes-St. Lawrence Lowlands, manufacturing can be the employment occupation of more than 50 percent of the labour force, whereas in the Plains cities about 66 percent of the labour force is engaged in tertiary activities. These employment differences suggest different urban lifestyles. Consider what the manufacturing economy and urban patterns may be like in Alberta if its population doubles in a few years.

Distribution and Hierarchy

Is there some significance to the size and spacing of Plains cities in which Saskatoon is about halfway between Winnipeg and Edmonton and one-quarter of the population of these two larger cities? Similarly, Regina is halfway between Winnipeg and Calgary and has one-quarter of the population. Does this spacing and urban population tell something about the size of the direct hinterland served by each city?

On a different scale, in the next order of city size, Lloydminster and North Battleford are about halfway between Edmonton and Saskatoon; Medicine Hat halfway between Calgary and Regina; Red Deer about halfway between Edmonton and Calgary; and Brandon midway between Regina and Winnipeg. Is this spatial concept of "geometric determinism" (similar to environmental determinism of the 1920s) of interest? Recall a similar spacing and hierarchy of large cities in southern Ontario (p. 168). This evenly spaced arrangement of settlements and progressive hierarchy of city size does *not* apply, however, to the resource-based towns and cities in the Canadian Shield. Most Shield cities, and those in the Cordillera, depend on local resources rather than on surrounding agricultural hinterlands. The concept expressed here is that of regional differences in the distribution patterns of Canadian cities.

Internal Areal Patterns and Functions

Some of the concepts of urban geography may be studied through examples of Plains cities. Outward areal expansion of the large Plains cities has been mainly concentric from a central business district which was located beside the railway. However, in each city urban growth has been encouraged or restricted by specific local conditions such as the railroads or rivers. In four of the five metropolitan centres, the downtown commercial and business cores became constricted between the railway and the river. The exception is Regina, which is the only major city not bisected by a river. In all cases, the local functions and purposes of the railway, which gave birth to the city, are no longer necessary in the city centre. Saskatoon has taken the expensive step of removing the railroad and its accompanying industrial facilities from the downtown core; despite high costs, this change in transportation and land use is being studied in the other large Plains cities. After 1950, the outward areal expansion of industries in Plains cities followed the highways as well as the railways, similar to urban patterns in eastern Canadian cities. The peripheral location of suburban shopping centres was similar to that of eastern cities and was related to distance, area and population density. As residences were built outward, shopping centres were established in suburban neighbourhoods to supply convenience goods to local residents. This areal expansion was directed by planning authorities in each Plains city. Compare these general distribution patterns of land use with those of a city in your local region.

The functions of shopping centres in a large city are similar to those discussed in preceding pages for villages and towns in an agricultural area (pp. 243-248). Compare the "corner store," supplying low-order convenience goods to a neighbourhood, with the supply-service functions of a hamlet in an agricultural region. On a larger scale in the central place hierarchy, compare a regional shopping centre, supplying a wider range of goods and services, with the functions of a town supplying a large surrounding farming area. Finally, the high density "downtown" core has a similar functional relationship within a metropolitan city as does a sub-regional city to its hinterland. The geography of service and supply functions of villages and towns in a region is similar to the patterns and functions of business centres in a city. If cities are, in fact, small-scale *regions,* are there other principles and concepts of regional geography which apply to them?

Gateway Cities

Several cities across the Interior Plains are central nodes, collection and distribution centres, or "gateways," between the well-settled livestock-grain belt and the dispersed and varied economies of the farming-forest frontier. Edmonton, for example, performs this function on a grand scale, being the gateway to all of northern Alberta and also to the Yukon and the western part of the Northwest Territories. Goods, services, people and ideas flow out of Edmonton into its northern hinterland; the products and people of the North funnel southward into Edmonton en route to other parts of Canada or the world. On a different scale in this hierarchy of gateways, Grande Prairie and Dawson Creek serve similar entrance and exit functions for the Peace River area. Prince George provides a comparable gateway function between southern British Columbia and the Plains region of northeastern B.C. It, therefore, competes with Edmonton in supplying goods and services to the Peace River area. The efficiency and number of these north-south links along the settlement frontier are related to the amount and quality of transportation. (Recall the discussion of this topic in Chapter 7.)

In Saskatchewan, Prince Albert is called "the gateway to the North." The city has its own central place functions for agriculture in central Saskatchewan, but also it is a focus for people and products moving into and out of the forestry, fishing, mining, trapping and recreation frontiers scattered across northern Saskatchewan. Prince Albert has a smaller size in the hierarchy of gateway cities than does Edmonton because its direct, occupied hinterland in northern Saskatchewan is smaller and has fewer economic activities than the whole of northwestern Canada in the hinterland of Edmonton. Compare Prince Albert's geographical position in "Middle Canada" with that of North Bay in northeastern Ontario.

The geographical pattern and functions of gateway cities are not as well developed in Manitoba because the transitional zone between agriculture and forests is broken by the large area occupied by the "Great Lakes"— Winnipeg, Manitoba and Winnipegosis. South-north movement is directed by the physical barriers of the lakes on the lowland east of the escarpment. The "jumping-off" point to the North is The Pas, from where roads and a railway lead north to the Shield mining region and to the ocean outlet at Churchill on Hudson Bay. The Pas does not have as large a surrounding agricultural area to serve as does Prince Albert and Edmonton and therefore is smaller in population. The Pas is often bypassed, particularly by air traffic coming directly out of Winnipeg. Flin Flon is a secondary gateway at the southern edge of the Canadian Shield on the Manitoba-Saskatchewan border.

Is Winnipeg a gateway and focus of activity for northern Manitoba as it used to be for the West? Can Winnipeg's geographical position and functions with relation to the Manitoba Shield be compared with those of Montreal to the Quebec Shield, but on a different scale? Early in this century, Winnipeg was the entrance (or exit) to the funnel that led to (or from) the Interior Plains. It was the transportation and communications hub and the supply, service and wholesale centre through which goods and services from the Heartland of southern Ontario flowed into the developing West. In turn, the products of the Interior Plains were assembled into Winnipeg on their way to the Heartland. Although some of these functions remain and Winnipeg is still a major transportation node, many of the supply-service functions for people of the Interior Plains are now provided regionally by the four metropolitan cities west of Winnipeg.

NODAL SUB-REGIONS

The earlier discussion in this chapter regionalized the Interior Plains based on land use and vegetation criteria (pp. 233-242). It is also possible to subdivide the area into a set of nodal, city-centred regions. As the urban population steadily increases and the metropolitan cities become larger in area, they dominate the economy of their nearby regions. These urban influences, in terms of trade and services, are equally as important as are differences in livestock or grain production. The concept of urban-centred regions may be more significant to some readers than subdividing the region by land use criteria.

More than half of the people in southern Manitoba live in metropolitan Winnipeg. Because of the wide choice of goods and services available in Winnipeg to so many people within a reasonable travel distance, there is little need for other large cities in southern Manitoba. Winnipeg dominates the region. In a hierarchy of sub-regions, the Interlake area is less developed than the remainder of southern Manitoba and can be considered as different from the agricultural lowland directly around Winnipeg. The Interlake area has fewer people, less resource development and more environmental hazards than the rest of southern Manitoba. Although on a smaller scale, Winnipeg is a similar nodal centre for southern Manitoba as Montreal is to the lowland of southwestern Quebec. On a provincial scale, Winnipeg is a small scale heartland and northern Manitoba is its hinterland. However, the Manitoba Shield lacks the resource development and potential of the Quebec Shield.

Southern Saskatchewan is a bi-nodal region. Regina and Saskatoon have about equal-size hinterlands to which to supply goods and services. Because these cities are smaller than the other three metropolitan cities, there is still a need and place for smaller service-centre cities in southern Saskatchewan. Interaction and movement between Regina and Saskatoon are frequent and significant because many urban functions are either split or shared.

The settled parts of Alberta can be thought of either as bi-nodal—similar to, but on a larger scale than, southern Saskatchewan—or as two separate city-centred regions around Edmonton and Calgary. Each of these cities has more than a half-million population and can supply a complete range of goods, services and consumer products to their internal populations and to residents of nearby areas. Whereas Edmonton has no large cities within its immediate service area, some of Calgary's central place functions are duplicated in Lethbridge. Can one think of the Edmonton-Calgary-Lethbridge "corridor" as an evolving "Western heartland"? How does it differ from the Eastern Canada heartland?

The cities of southeastern Alberta and southwestern Saskatchewan are smaller because the region has fewer resources. Medicine Hat is growing more slowly than other Plains cities, suggesting that some of its urban functions are being gradually taken over by Calgary and Regina. The urban-centred regions based on these two latter cities may be strengthening and expanding.

No single major sub-regional centre has emerged in the Peace River area. The urban functions of collection and distribution and of supplying goods and services are still split between three small cities: Grande Prairie, Dawson Creek and Fort St. John. In predicting which of these three cities might experience the most growth in the next decade, consider geographical location, accessibility and urban-rural relationships. However, one cannot predict the influences of local businesses or industrial decisions or the impact of a discovery of a large mineral resource.

METROPOLITAN CITIES

The following comments describe mainly the origins of land-use patterns in the five metropolitan cities. Present internal geographical patterns evolved from these beginnings. Various themes are presented here to stimulate thought about some of the geographical patterns in each city, but there is no attempt to discuss all the present internal functions or planning problems. As stated elsewhere in the book, its purpose is not to describe the detailed urban geography of each major Canadian city.

Winnipeg

Winnipeg is the only Plains city which has a lengthy history of settlement comparable to some eastern Canadian cities. Different sites at or near the junction of the Red and Assiniboine rivers were occupied by trading posts of the Hudson's Bay Company early in the 19th century. At the same time, agricultural settlers created a linear pattern along the Red River, similar to the long-lot farms near the St. Lawrence River. A few French-Canadians had settled near St. Boniface by the middle of the 19th century, well before the major outflow of French-Canadians from the Quebec Lowland. Winnipeg was still only a village of a few hundred people when Manitoba became a province in 1870.

Winnipeg's growth was accelerated by the railroads, similar to the other Plains cities. The first trains came northward from St. Paul in the United States reaching the city in 1878. The Canadian Pacific Railway was persuaded with grants to build its line through Winnipeg in 1881. As a result, the population of the city boomed to 25,000 in 1884 and Winnipeg became the largest city in western Canada.

The main urban land-use patterns were established in these early years. A few stores clustered north of the Fort Garry trading post around the corner of Portage and Main streets, and this area developed into the commercial core of the city. Industries located along the river and railway, north and east of the commercial core, in the Point Douglas area and across the river in St. Boniface. The bigger and better homes were built west of old Fort Garry and south of the Assiniboine River in Fort Rouge; the smaller, poorer houses of workers were located east of Main Street and north of the railroad. The north end of Winnipeg developed a different economic and social character from the rest of the city. These original land-use patterns persisted and spread outward from the central core during the next 50 years (see map, p. 262).

Winnipeg grew rapidly in population and area in the early decades of this century when settlers poured into the Prairie Provinces. It then established its transportation and wholesale functions, illustrated by rail-yards, hotels and warehouses. St. Boniface established its own separate commercial centre. Winnipeg's industrial development came later, as local western markets became available and the Plains were occupied. Winnipeg is still the leading manufacturing city in the region, although its early

AREAL GROWTH OF WINNIPEG, 1872 - 1914

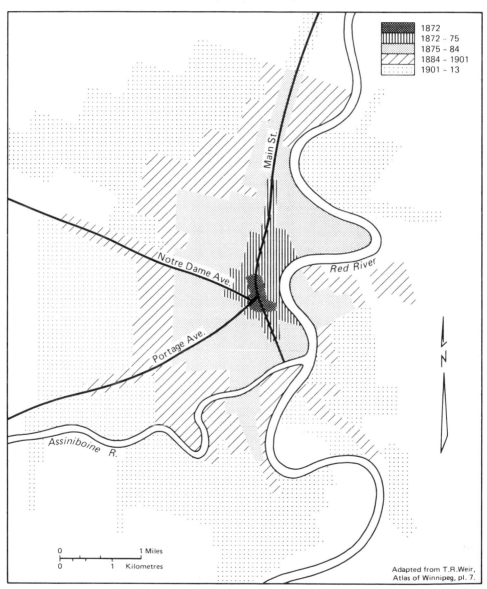

1872
1872 - 75
1875 - 84
1884 - 1901
1901 - 13

Main St.

Notre Dame Ave.

Red River

Portage Ave.

Assiniboine R.

0   1 Miles
0   1 Kilometres

Adapted from T.R.Weir,
Atlas of Winnipeg, pl. 7.

N

dominance is being reduced by increased secondary manufacturing in Edmonton and Calgary. The rivers were bridged to permit urban expansion, but most of Winnipeg's residential area spread to the northwest; only small residential clusters were built east of the Red River and south of the Assiniboine River.

Because of its central location, Winnipeg can supply most of the high-order goods and services needed by the small town and rural residents in southern Manitoba. As a result, southern Manitoba has only two sub-regional cities— Brandon and Portage La Prairie—compared with six small cities in southern Saskatchewan.

Regina and Saskatoon

These cities were also created by the railways. The site of Regina, selected in 1882, was no different from hundreds of other railway stations which the Canadian Pacific placed along its route across the grassland plains. The site had no natural advantages: it lacked a good water supply, had no nearby trees to produce local lumber for buildings and there were no landscape attractions to break the monotonous horizon. But people who owned land there persuaded the federal government to locate the capital of the (then) Northwest Territories at Regina. It also became the headquarters of the North West Mounted Police (R.C.M.P.). The small town might have had an even better beginning if the C.P.R. had made it a divisional centre for railway yards and maintenance facilities instead of choosing Moose Jaw for these services.

Saskatoon had a more attractive site on the high banks of the South Saskatchewan River, but it lost the fight to become the capital of the new province of Saskatchewan in 1905. In 1909, however, Saskatoon's institutional functions were established when it became the site for the provincial university and agricultural college.

Both cities grew rapidly in the first decades of this century as service centres. Their population increase and areal expansion were directly related to the amount of land taken up by settlers on the nearby flat plain; prosperity in each city fluctuated annually with the price of wheat in the world market. Neither city developed much of an industrial base beyond the production of the usual small scale consumer goods.

Regina and Saskatoon have higher percentages of employees in wholesale and retail trade than the other metropolitan cities. The cities are close enough together that these trade functions are sometimes complementary as well as competitive. Regina has a high per capita number of government employees; it is therefore like Halifax, Quebec City and Victoria in being classified as a dominant government-institutional city. Saskatoon has a higher density of rural population around it than Regina and therefore supplies more goods and services to people in central Saskatchewan.

Regina lacks the variety of housing seen in the other Plains cities. Because a high percentage of the residents were civil servants without wide ranges in salaries, little wealth was accumulated and reflected in superior residences as in Winnipeg and Calgary. The central part of the city was laid out in 25-foot lots which resulted in block after block of similar small houses. The poorer homes on the east side of the city were often occupied by incoming immigrants of mixed national backgrounds. The economic and social characteristics of eastside Regina (and northside Winnipeg) are repeated in east Vancouver and discussed in Chapter 9.

In addition to the inflow of former farm residents into the city, both Regina and Winnipeg became havens for Indians who left the reservations. In both cities, low income areas with social and economic problems developed near the city centre. Are these small replicas of the Negro ghettos of some American cities? Is the geography of urban poverty in Canada related to ethnic and racial backgrounds? Are the Negro areas in Halifax and Windsor, Ontario similar to the Indian concentrations in Winnipeg and Regina?

Calgary

In 1875, the North West Mounted Police selected the site of Calgary for one of its forts to control American whiskey traders. A tiny commercial settlement developed outside the fort to serve the surrounding ranchers. When the C.P.R. reached the settlement in 1883, there were already several hundred people living there, but the railway created a new townsite west of the old fort. Calgary's nodal position in southwestern Alberta was established after railroads were built north to Edmonton and south to Fort MacLeod in the early 1890s. The livestock and grain products of the surrounding agricultural hinterland were brought to Calgary for processing or further transportation. When the city was incorporated in 1893, it already held 4,000 people. At the turn of the century, Calgary and Edmonton were the only "large" cities in Alberta—a status which has never changed.

Early industries located along the railway on the east and southeast side of the city and industrial workers lived in small houses nearby. In contrast to Regina, early wealth—often obtained from land speculation and later from oil—was shown by large, elaborate homes on the river bank slopes south and southwest of the downtown commercial core. These subdivisions for the wealthy in the boom period of 1909-1913 gave parts of Calgary curved streets and large view lots, so different from the drab rectangular pattern of streets and similar small wooden houses in other Plains cities. (The same type of elite residential development was promoted by the C.P.R. in Vancouver at the same time. See p. 301-302, Chapter 9.) Calgary was another example of the social and economic differences between the east and west sides of many Canadian cities prior to 1940. Do you have a satisfactory explanation for this repeated geographical east-west urban pattern?

During the 1920-1940 period, population increase in Calgary and the other Plains cities was relatively slow compared with eastern cities. Calgary's residential area spread mainly to the southwest, over the gentle hills between the Bow and Elbow rivers. Rapid urban growth came after 1950, and new subdivisions were planned and developed outward in all directions. Suburban Calgary, and the suburbs of the other Plains cities, looks no different from the new suburbs of other Canadian cities. The homes may have different styles of architecture, but collectively they are nearly all the same; the shopping centres have the same forms and the same types of stores; the schools seem to have come from one mold.

Some of the characteristics of Calgary's population illustrate the rural to urban migration going on in other Plains cities. The 1971 census reported that 80 percent of Calgary's population was born in Canada and 63 percent was born in Alberta. The latter figure indicates that many of the city's residents had moved from nearby places. Immigrants were few and the largest number of these came from the United States. Does the census indicate that other Plains cities are different in their ethnic population mix? Winnipeg, for example, is well-known for its ethnic variety and ethnic newspapers, but what percentage of its residents were born in Manitoba? Does the 1981 census show a change in the percent of locally-born residents in Calgary as a result of the westward migration of eastern Canadian labourers, businessmen and service workers to partake of the material prosperity of Alberta during the 1970s?

The growth of Calgary and Edmonton was based on sharing activities related to the petroleum and natural gas industries. Calgary has most of the head offices, management and financial companies; whereas Edmonton has the refineries, fabricating, transportation, maintenance and servicing facilities. Calgary is the administrative centre of the oil industry and Edmonton is the operations centre. The flow of people between these cities is enormous. Calgary's commercial and financial core has a greater density of high-rise, "prestige" office towers than has Edmonton; commercial activity is more dispersed in Edmonton and its central core has more diversity as a result of government buildings and activities. The city centre of Calgary looks more like "downtown" Toronto and Montreal than does central Edmonton.

On a large scale, one can think of Edmonton and Calgary as one large, "dispersed" city in which many urban functions are shared. If this concept is valid, then one should expect increased urban activities in Red Deer which is a "suburb" of both cities.

Although on a different scale of area and population density, the urban corridor of Edmonton-Red Deer-Calgary-Fort MacLeod-Lethbridge is comparable to "Main Street" in the Great Lakes-St. Lawrence Lowlands stretching from Quebec City through Montreal, Toronto and London, to Windsor. Will the similarities increase in the next decades? Will Calgary

THE URBAN POPULATION CORRIDOR IN ALBERTA

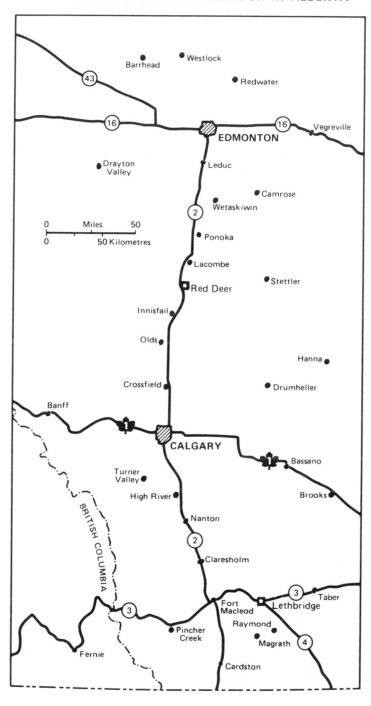

occupy the financial position in the West that Toronto does in the East and will Edmonton be the gateway to the Northwest that Montreal was to Central Canada in the 19th century?

Edmonton

Edmonton's origins were like those of Saskatoon and Winnipeg in that two settlements were originally occupied on opposite banks of the river. The Hudson's Bay Company built Fort Edmonton nearby in 1795, but the present town on the north side of the river was not surveyed until 1882. When the railroad was built north from Calgary in 1891, the town of Strathcona was the terminal on the south side of the North Saskatchewan River. These settlements and their functions were little different from many others across the Plains until Edmonton was selected as the capital of Alberta in 1905. In the same year the second transcontinental railway (later to become the C.N.R.) arrived from the east and its station was built on the north side of the river. Edmonton's early functions were similar to those of Regina — it held employees in the provincial civil service and was a service centre for agricultural lands being occupied around it. Edmonton's direct hinterland had higher rural population densities in the mixed livestock-grain farms than did the wheat farms and ranches around Calgary.

Edmonton's period of rapid population increase and outward areal spread came after 1940. Its position as the gateway to northwestern Canada became evident during World War II; Edmonton became the assembly centre and supply focus for military operations and construction throughout north-western Canada and Alaska. This boom was followed immediately by the activity generated by the discovery of large quantities of petroleum at Leduc, a few miles south of Edmonton, in 1947. Then, major oil discoveries at Redwater to the northwest and Pembina to the west placed Edmonton in the centre of oil field activity.

Urban land uses expanded from original patterns. The commercial core spread outward, replacing the old, small wooden houses in the city centre, and rose upward in the same type of office towers found in all large North American cities. The smaller, duplicate commercial core on the south side of the river near the university did not expand as rapidly. Refineries were built on the east side of the city to be on the lee side of the prevailing winds and to use river water *after* it had flowed through the city. Other secondary industries and plants fabricating a wide range of products needed in the exploration, production and transportation of petroleum located along the railways on the east side of the city. Industrial land use extended as far east as Fort Saskatchewan. New residences were laid out in planned neighbour-hood units all around the edge of the occupied urban area, similar to the controlled building in each of the Plains metropolitan cities.

As in the other Plains cities, political boundaries were extended outward successively in order to control and administer urban land uses. The sharp line between urban and rural land uses has always been maintained in Plains cities, unlike the sprawl so notorious on the urban-rural fringe in eastern cities. Separate, satellite communities were able to evolve around Edmonton, similar to those around Winnipeg, but such were never created on the edges of Calgary.

Table 3

Population of Cities in the Interior Plains, 1981

ALBERTA	1976	1981	SASKATCHEWAN	1976	1981
Metropolitan Edmonton	555,000	657,000	Regina (metro)	152,000	164,300
Edmonton city	460,000	532,000	Saskatoon (metro)	135,000	154,200
Strathcona	42,000	52,000	Moose Jaw (metro)	33,000	36,000
St. Albert	24,000	32,000	Prince Albert (metro)	28,500	38,400
Sturgeon	13,000	17,000	North Battleford (metro)	14,000	18,700
Fort Saskatchewan	8,300	12,200	Swift Current	14,000	16,600
Calgary (metro)	470,000	593,000	Yorkton	13,000	15,400
Lethbridge	47,000	54,000	Lloydminster	10,400	15,000
Medicine Hat (metro)	33,000	50,000			
Red Deer	32,000	46,400	MANITOBA		
Fort McMurray	18,000	31,000			
Grande Prairie	16,000	24,300	Winnipeg (metro)	560,000	585,000
Camrose	10,000	12,600	Winnipeg (city)	558,000	562,000
Leduc	10,000	12,500	Brandon	35,000	36,200
			Portage La Prairie		
BRITISH COLUMBIA			(metro)	13,000	20,700
			Flin Flon	10,300	10,000
Fort St. John	11,000	14,000	Selkirk	10,000	10,000
Dawson Creek	9,000	11,400			

INTERNAL REGIONAL DIFFERENCES

If one thinks of the Prairie Provinces as a political unit, the first level of regional distinction is between the Canadian Shield in the northeast and the Interior Plains in the southwest. The Plains area can be characterized by large areas of level land, by grassland, agriculture, productive forests and by non-metallic minerals and fuels. In contrast, the landscapes of the Shield have an abundance of low rocky hills and poorly drained muskeg and lake cover, scrubby forest or tundra, no agriculture and a wealth of metallic minerals.

Within the Interior Plains, one may use land use and vegetation criteria to divide it into three sub-regions (map, p. 236):

1.) the forest-farming frontier;

2.) the livestock-grain belt;
3.) the dry belt.

Forests cover the northern parts of the Interior Plains and within this vegetation region population densities are lower than in the agricultural zones and economic activities are dispersed. Primary resource extraction in the forest zone is mainly fishing, fur trapping and, in some particular places, petroleum production and cutting of trees for lumber or pulpwood. The servicing of recreational activities such as hunting, fishing and camping can also be classed as primary resource utilization, if not "extraction." Large urban settlements are few within the forested areas; however, the penetration of the petroleum frontier resulted in the city of Fort McMurray and the forest frontier is represented in B.C. by Fort Nelson.

The southern edge of the forest area is a transitional zone into which agricultural clearing has penetrated. The extensive farmland and urban development of the Peace River area is different from the rest of the forest zone and could be considered an "outlier" of the agricultural zone. In the Peace River sub-region, agriculture, forestry, mining, hydro-electric power and recreation activities are combined into a functional regional economy which can be compared with that of the Clay Belt sub-region of the Canadian Shield.

Both similarities and sub-regional differences characterize the rural landscapes and urban settlements within the agriculturally occupied Interior Plains. The belt of livestock-grain farming on Dark Brown and Black soils has higher densities of farm population, more varieties of crops and more supporting urban centres than does the short grass, Brown soil, dry belt. Some people may consider that the more uniform characteristics of the wheat belt of southern Saskatchewan are sufficiently different to consider it as another sub-region. The crescent of mixed farming containing the largest cities, from Winnipeg to Edmonton to Calgary is a small scale "Main Street" of the Prairie Provinces.

A boundary between the dry belt and the livestock-grain regions is a changing, transitional one; its fluctuations are related to precipitation, technology and economic conditions. When world demand, and prices, have been high, the grain frontier has penetrated into the dry belt, particularly using strip-farming techniques. Fluctuations in annual yield and grain acreage are not as great now as in earlier years, due to increased use of fertilizers and better land management. When drought and/or low wheat prices have persisted, wheat acreages have declined in the short grass areas. Areal diversity is now apparent in the dry belt as the use of irrigation for special crops increases in particular areas.

There is spatial interaction and functional integration between the dry belt and the livestock-grain belt around it. The feed grains of the livestock-grain belt are transported into the short grass zone to help feed cattle on large ranches there; the irrigated crops move out of the dry belt to become feed for the livestock area or food for the cities within the livestock-grain belt.

If agriculture continues to expand into the dry belt, sub-regional land-use differences will become less apparent and one may be able to think of the Interior Plains as having only two sub-regions—the forested north and northwest, and the populated agriculture area. Then, in terms of human geography, the city-centred nodal regions may be a better organizing sub-regional concept.

REFERENCES

Atlases:

Atlas of Alberta, edited by Wm. Wonders, Dept. of Geog., Univ. of Alberta, Edmonton, 1969. 172 pages.
Atlas of Manitoba, edited by Thomas R. Weir, Manitoba Dept. of Natural Resources, Winnipeg, 1983. 317 maps, 157 pages.
Atlas of Saskatchewan, edited by Howard Richards and K.I. Fung, Dept. of Geog., Univ. of Saskatchewan, Saskatoon, 1969. 244 pages.
Atlas of the Prairie Provinces, edited by Thomas R. Weir and G. Mathews, Oxford Univ. Press, Toronto, 1971. 31 maps.
Atlas of Winnipeg, edited by Thomas R. Weir, Univ. of Toronto Press, Toronto, 1978. 150 maps.
Atlas des Francophones de l'Ouest, edited by Armand Bédard, Centre de Recherches du Collège Universitaire de Saint-Boniface, Winnipeg, 1979.

University Serials and Monographs:

The Albertan Geographer, Dept. of Geog., Univ. of Alberta, Edmonton, Vol. 1, 1964 to Vol. 18, 1982.
Manitoba Geographical Studies, Dept. of Geog., Univ. of Manitoba, Winnipeg, Vol. 1, 1972 to Vol. 7, 1981. For example:
  No. 2, 1974, "A Geographical Analysis and Classification of Canadian Prairie Agriculture" by Peter Laut. 202 pages.
  No. 7, 1981, "The Prairies and Plains: Prospects for the 80s" edited by John Rogge. 148 pages.
Canadian Plains Research Centre Studies, Univ. of Regina. For example:
  No. 1, 1973, "A Region of the Mind: Interpreting the Western Canadian Plains" edited by Richard Allen. 209 pages.
  No. 6, 1976, Proceedings, "Man and Nature on the Prairies" edited by Richard Allen.
Prairie Forum, Journal of the Canadian Plains Research Centre, and also the *Canadian Plains Bulletin*, Univ. of Regina, Regina.
"Background Papers; Southern Prairies Field Excursion" edited by A. Paul and E. Dale, Dept. of Geog., Univ. of Regina, Regina, 1972. 350 pages.
Regina Geographical Series, Dept. of Geog., Univ. of Regina, Regina.
  No. 1, 1977, "Saskatchewan Rural Themes."
Canadian Ethnic Studies, Research Centre for Canadian Ethnic Studies, Dept. of Sociology, Univ. of Alberta, Edmonton. For example:
  Vol. 9, No. 2, 1977 was devoted to geographical research.
Western Geographical Series, Dept. of Geog., Univ. of Victoria, Victoria. For example:
  No. 12, 1975, "Calgary: Metropolitan Structure and Influence" edited

by Brenton Barr. 271 pages.
No. 15, 1978, "Edmonton: Emerging Metropolitan Pattern" edited by
  Peter Smith. 291 pages.
No. 18, 1980, "Regina: Regional Isolation and Innovative Development"
  edited by Edmund Dale. 238 pages.
B.C. Geographical Series, Tantalus Research Ltd. Vancouver. For example:
No. 30, 1980, "The New Provinces: Alberta and Saskatchewan, 1905-1980."
  "Scandinavian Homesteaders in Central Alberta" by Wm. Wonders,
  Ch. 7, pp. 131-171.

Government:

Environment Council of Alberta, Edmonton. For example:
  "Agriculture and the Environment," 1981. 45 pages.
  "The Agricultural Land Base in Alberta," 1981. 111 pages.
  "Urbanization of Agricultural Land," 1981. 77 pages.
  "Irrigation Agriculture in Alberta," 1982. 74 pages.
  "Selected Issues in the Economics of Agriculture," 1982. 148 pages.
Lands Directorate, Environment Canada, Ottawa.
  Reports on Urban Land Use Monitoring Programs: No. 1, Calgary;
  No. 3, Regina; No. 4, Edmonton, 1981.
Economics Branch, Agriculture Canada, Regina.
  "Prairie Regional Studies in Economic Geography," Vol. 1, 1967
  to Vol. 27, 1975. *Reports discussing small towns and possible railway
  abandonment.*
Policy, Planning and Research Branch, Sask. Dept. of Environment, Regina.
  "Land Use in Saskatchewan" by P.C. Rump and K. Harper, revised,
  1980. 185 pages.
Atmospheric Environment Services, Environment Canada, Toronto.
  "The Climate of the Prairie Provinces" by R.W. Longley, 1972. 79 pages.

Books:

"Town and City: Aspects of Western Canadian Urban Development" edited
  by Alan Artibise, Canadian Plains Research Centre, Regina, 1981. 445
  pages.
"The Landscapes of Southern Alberta: A Regional Geomorphology" by
  Chester Beaty, Dept. of Geog., Univ. of Lethbridge, Lethbridge, 1975.
  95 pages.
"Western Canada's Coal: The Sleeping Giant," Canada West Foundation,
  Calgary, 1980. 208 pages.
"Nature's Lifeline: Prairie and Northern Waters," Canada West Foundation,
  Calgary, 1982. 467 pages.
"Southern Alberta: A Regional Perspective" edited by Frank Jankunis, Univ.

of Lethbridge Press, Lethbridge, 1972. 123 pages.
"The Viability and Livability of Small Urban Centres" edited by Frank Jankunis and B. Sadler, Environment Council of Alberta, Edmonton, 1980. 114 pages.
"Urban Indians: The Strangers in Canada's Cities" by Larry Krotz, Hurtig Publishers, Edmonton, 1980. 157 pages.
"Winnipeg, 1874-1974: Progress and Prospects" edited by Tony Kuz, Man. Dept. of Industry and Commerce, Winnipeg, 1974. 248 pages.
"Man's Impact on the Western Canadian Landscape" by J. Gordon Nelson, Carleton Library Series No. 90, McClelland and Stewart, Toronto, 1976. 205 pages.
"Saskatchewan: A Geographical Appraisal" by J. Howard Richards, Div. of Extension, Univ. of Saskatchewan, Saskatoon, 1981. 225 pages.
"The Agricultural Economy of Manitoba Hutterite Colonies" by John Ryan, McClelland and Stewart, Toronto, 1977. 306 pages.
"The Edmonton-Calgary Corridor" by Peter Smith and Denis Johnson, Dept. of Geog., Univ. of Alberta, Edmonton, 1978. 159 pages.
"By Section, Township and Range: Studies in Prairie Settlement" by John L. Tyman, Assiniboine Historical Society, Brandon, 1973. 250 pages.

Periodicals:

Annals of the Assoc. of Amer. Geographers. For example:

Vol. 71, No. 4, Dec. 1981.	"Residential Land Use Change in Inner Edmonton" by Peter Smith and Larry McCann, pp. 536-551.
Vol. 69, No. 2, June 1979.	"Log Dwellings in Canadian Folk Architecture" by Wm. Wonders, pp. 187-207.

Some relevant articles in *The Canadian Geographer* between 1970-82, Can. Assoc. of Geog., Burnside Hall, McGill Univ., Montreal:

Vol. 26, No. 3, 1982.	"Edmonton's Wholesale Relationships with Northwest Canada" by R.G. Ironside and D.D. Peterson, pp. 207-224.
Vol. 23, No. 4, 1979.	"Centre Pivot Irrigation: The Canadian Experience" by Tom McKnight, pp. 360-367.
Vol. 23, No. 1, 1979.	"Ethnicity and Urban Residence: Winnipeg, 1941-71" by Peter Matwijiw, pp. 45-61.
Vol. 22, No. 3, 1978.	"A Canadian Skid Row: Winnipeg" by Gwyn Rowley, pp. 211-224.
Vol. 21, No. 3, 1977.	"Ethnicity and the Rural Economy in Southern Manitoba, 1961-71" by D. Todd and J.S. Brierley,

237-249.

Vol. 17, No. 4, 1973. "A Comparative Factorial Ecology of Three Prairie Cities" by Wayne Davies and G.T. Barrow, pp. 327-353.

Vol. 15, No. 4, 1971. "Growth and Distribution of Apartments in Prairie Metropolitan Areas" by George Nader, pp. 307-317.

Vol. 14, No. 1, 1970. "Landforms and Glacial History of the Upper North Saskatchewan Valley, Alberta" by H.J. McPherson, pp. 10-26.

CHAPTER 9

THE CORDILLERA OF BRITISH COLUMBIA

CHAPTER 9

THE CORDILLERA OF BRITISH COLUMBIA

INTRODUCTION

British Columbia is a mountainous province. Great contrasts within small areas are characteristic of the natural environment and there are also wide contrasts in population densities. It is a region of urban people with agriculture entirely lacking over large areas or confined to certain narrow valleys or floodplains. This urban population is concentrated in one small area, the southwestern corner of the Cordillera, where 70 percent of the people live.

In the middle of the 19th century, cut off by the mountain barrier and the empty Interior Plains from the other colonies in eastern Canada and far from "Mother England" by sea around Cape Horn, the Pacific colony experienced isolation. Even today, its people often exhibit degrees of independence and non-conformity. The belief that British Columbia is distinctly "different" (interpreted in coastal B.C. as "better") than the rest of Canada is sometimes promoted with annoying (to easterners) smugness.

British Columbia was in the distant hinterland of the British Empire in the mid-19th century and far from the Heartland of Canada during the first half of the 20th century. But the concept of being part of the hinterland of "eastern" Canada is now weakening. Even more than Alberta, most of British Columbia's raw materials—lumber, fish, minerals—go to external, foreign markets and not to the consuming areas of the Great Lakes-St. Lawrence Lowlands. Manufactured goods from heartland industries must now compete in B.C. with imported Japanese goods. Economic, social and travel links are strong between British Columbia and the west coast American states to the south. British Columbia is a Pacific province; East Asian influences have been strong since the time Chinese labour was used to help build the railway to the present inflow of Japanese capital.

Throughout its history, much of the economy of the Cordilleran region has been determined by external decisions. Together with Alberta, the two western provinces now expect to have more to say about their national and international destinies.

In contrast to both the Interior Plains and the Canadian Shield, where environmental conditions are similar over large areas, the Cordillera is a region of small scale diversity. The one element common throughout the region, and providing the physical characteristics so different from the rest of southern Canada, is its rugged, mountainous landforms. Although mountains dominate the landscape, people do not live directly *on* these mountainous slopes; the important physical features are the linear valleys and coastal plains. People live in these lowlands and transportation lines

277

funnel through certain valleys; economic activities have clustered and/or linear patterns in the lowlands and valleys similar to those in the Atlantic and Gulf region.

The human patterns of occupance contrast in intensity of use outside of the southwestern core. In the valleys of the southern interior and northward along the coast, most residents occupy small settlements; their locations are the result either of the utilization of local resources or are service centres along transportation routes. Economic activities developed in local regions at different times in response to expanding external markets for their desired resources. Most of the northern valleys are almost empty and throughout the Cordillera most of the mountain and upland areas are completely lacking in permanent residents. Few people live on farms, but in terms of occupied area, large sections of the south-central interior are used for grazing. Throughout the southern two-thirds of the Cordillera, extensive tracts of forest are utilized under various tree-farm management licenses where controlled cutting should maintain a continuous harvest. Similar to other regions, the number of primary workers in the farms, forests, mines and fisheries is small compared to the number of people employed in the wide range of occupations in the large urban centres.

Vancouver is the "heartland" of the Cordillera—similar, but on a smaller scale, to the Great Lakes-St. Lawrence Lowland being the Heartland of Canada. Much of the economic activity, with its interactions and flows of people and products, is concentrated in the Vancouver heartland; the rest of the Cordillera is its hinterland.

THEMES

1.) To emphasize contrasts in physical environment elements within the region.

2.) To describe the changing patterns of resource use in the Cordillera over the past century and the significance of resource-based towns in the settlement patterns outside of the southwest core.

3.) To discuss the dominance of Vancouver and the urban region around Georgia Strait as the heartland of the Cordillera.

4.) To compare and contrast the geographical characteristics of the two major sub-regions of the Cordillera—the Coast and the Interior—and to describe internal variations within each.

DEFINITION OF THE REGION

Most regional discussions treat British Columbia as a political unit. In

Note: To the dismay of editors and other purists, throughout this chapter British Columbia will be called "B.C.," the affectionate name by which the province is known both to local residents and across the rest of Canada.

this chapter, using the Cordillera as a landform region places the Peace River area of B.C. into the Interior Plains. The rolling plains, mixed forests and patches of grassland in northeastern B.C. are similar to the environments of the Plains. The economy of the Peace River area, like that of the rest of the Plains, is based on livestock-grain and natural gas-petroleum. Dawson Creek and Fort St. John have urban landscapes and functions similar to Interior Plains towns. Further research is needed, however, to discover whether these cities, which interacted predominantly with Edmonton prior to 1960, are now linked mainly with Prince George and Vancouver. Economic and political ties may now be stronger than the separation by physical barriers.

The physical characteristics of the Cordillera extend northward through Yukon Territory and on into Alaska. The mountain masses and linear valleys and the vegetation and climate of the Yukon are much the same as those of northern British Columbia. There is, therefore, sound environmental support for including the Yukon in the Cordillera region. In addition, Whitehorse, with more than half of the Territory's population, is a smaller replica of Vancouver in terms of its dominance over the Yukon economy; Whitehorse is tied economically to the Pacific through the port of Skagway in Alaska. However, there seems to be little political support within the Yukon for a future addition of the Territory to British Columbia.

Resource development is different in the Yukon. The differences are partly the result of its very small population, and also are due to its political status in which certain decisions are influenced by, and need the financial support of, the federal government. These factors favour a decision to discuss the Cordillera of the Yukon as part of the North region along with the other "colonial" political unit, the Northwest Territories. This is another of those subjective decisions concerning regional boundary definition. Should a political boundary be used to subdivide a landform region? Is it defensible to use a political boundary to define the North and to neglect political units in other Canadian regions?

THE PHYSICAL ENVIRONMENT

Landforms

The physical landscape of the Cordillera has great variety and its scale is impressive. Comparable spectacular landforms are found only in mountainous Baffin and Ellesmere islands in the northeastern Arctic, but their extent is not as great as the width of 1,000 kilometres of peaks, ridges and valleys across the southern Cordillera. Although the mountains seem to be a jumbled mass of peaks locally and stretch endlessly to the horizon when viewed from the air, they have quite specific areal patterns and are subdivided into smaller subregional units.

The Coast Mountains present striking landform variations in their numerous rugged offshore islands, protected alongshore channels, linear fiords twisting inland into jagged alpine peaks, narrow coastal lowlands, low marine terraces and the broad flat delta of the Fraser River. The Insular Mountains on Vancouver Island and the Queen Charlotte Islands are not as high and have wide lowlands on their east sides. The visual attractiveness of these coastal features to tourists in summer cruise ships is very apparent and of economic value to the province. The coastal features contrast with the level horizons of the broad interior plateaus with their deep canyons and valleys.

LANDFORM REGIONS OF BRITISH COLUMBIA

Despite maps published outside of Canada which spread the name "Rocky Mountains" across much of British Columbia and even into the Yukon and Alaska, the Rockies are a specific line of mountain ranges extending northwest from Montana along the southern and central Alberta-British Columbia border and terminating at the broad plain of the Liard River. The western boundary of the Rocky Mountains is the Rocky Mountain Trench, one of the longest, continuous valleys on the earth's surface extending from Flathead Lake, Montana to the Liard Plain in the Yukon. Other mountain systems to the westward, such as the Columbia and Cassiar-Omineca mountains, are separate landform regions. They have similar internal characteristics of high, sharp peaks and narrow U-shaped valleys. The official landform regional boundaries are shown on the previous map.

In contrast, the Interior and Stikine plateaus are undulating interior basins with generally level horizons; in some places, however, rivers have cut deep canyons into the plateau edges. Interior river valleys usually have narrow strips and terraces of level land above the entrenched rivers; most settlements and transport lines are confined to these narrow terraces. One is always aware within the Cordillera how little level land there is at low elevations.

The character of Cordillera landforms influences settlement and resource development. The positions, directions and interconnections of the interior valleys are particularly important; they are the inhabited parts of the Interior sub-region and the routes of land transport. Can one assess how important the Rocky Mountain Trench might be as a future through-route from Montana to the Yukon and Alaska? Has the "barrier effect" of mountains been overemphasized? Are mountain ranges barriers to jet airplanes flying at 10,000 metres altitude? Can one compare the costs to the taxpayer of building roads along the steep sides of Cordillera valleys with the costs of roads on the flat Interior Plains or the St. Lawrence Lowlands? In brief, how does one assess the *significance* of mountains to the people of B.C.?

Climate and Vegetation

Contrasts in climate are characteristic of mountainous regions and B.C. is no exception. Because most of the weather stations are in the valley bottoms where settlements are, vertical contrasts have to be inferred from vegetation differences or other indirect environmental information.

The greatest amounts of precipitation recorded in Canada — more than 3750 mm. (150 inches) annually — fall on some of the west-facing slopes of the Insular and Coast mountains. But only 400 kilometres eastward in the southern interior valleys, some of the driest stations outside of the Arctic report less than 250 mms. (10 inches) of annual precipitation. Most of the precipitation falls on the coastal lowland settlements as rain during the winter months, while, at the time, snow blankets the higher elevations of the nearby mountains. Although long-time residents of Vancouver are wont to boast that it "seldom snows here," a cold air mass from the Interior Plateau can spill westward along the Fraser Valley, raising and chilling the usual mild, moist Pacific air masses and resulting in great amounts of snow being dumped on the coastal cities for a few days.

Another regional characteristic of B.C. is the mild coastal climate, the warmest in Canada, with January averages of about 0°C (30 to 35°F). But the linear valleys of the Interior are open to the southward penetration of cold air masses from Alaska and the Yukon, and settlements there record many days of below zero winter temperatures. Indeed, winter temperatures in the interior of the Cordillera are similar to those experienced across the Interior Plains.

In summer, the southwest coast is normally cool, about 15°C (60°F) average in July, and sunny for many weeks when high-pressure ridges form over it and deflect storms northward. This cool summer climate characteristic is another element which is unique in southern Canada. But a few hundred kilometres eastward, residents and visitors in the southern valleys can experience some of the hottest temperatures recorded in Canada. The coastal climate is therefore different from that of the rest of Canada, whereas the remainder of the Cordillera has some climates which are similar to those east of the mountains.

Vertical contrasts in climate are shown by the horizontal zonation of vegetation on mountain slopes. The mild and wet coastal climate has nourished the largest trees known in Canada. However, temperatures decrease with altitude and steep, rocky slopes have little soil; therefore, tree size and density decrease at about 1,500 metres and generally the alpine slopes above 2,000 metres are treeless. In northern British Columbia, the upper treeline can be about 1,000 metres above sea level, leaving only narrow strips of forest along the river valleys. Although the presence of grassland is obvious to travellers through the dry valleys of the southern Cordillera, it occupies only narrow strips or small basins and the total grassland area is not large. Cattle ranching in the Interior operates more in a parkland vegetation environment than does ranching on the grassland of southeastern Alberta.

Drainage Basins

Water is one of the valuable natural resources of the Cordillera. Its distribution patterns of abundance and scarcity can be studied both as precipitation upon the surface and as run-off in the major river basins. Climate and landforms are functionally related. The Cordillera of B.C. has six interior river basins and several small, separated river basins along the coasts. The position of these river basins and the variations in their amounts of annual and seasonal run-offs are important in understanding both the distribution of hydro-electric power and the problems and possible conflicts with salmon fishing. These river basins are not described here, but the information is *used* later in the chapter.

References have been made throughout this book to people's *perception* of their natural environment. How do we think about river valleys and the possibility of floods? What are our perceptions of river valley floodplains as desirable or dangerous places on which to live? Is flooding in the Cordillera an accepted "natural hazard" because of the wide regional and seasonal variations in river run-off? Floodplains, such as along the lower Fraser River, have been recognized as attractive for agriculture because of the level land and fertile soils, but residents seem less aware that the natural flooding that deposited the good soils is a continuing process. Can man control this aspect of Nature by dikes, levees and upstream dams?

EVOLUTION OF SETTLEMENT PATTERNS

Introduction

The Cordillera is a land of contrasts with little uniformity over large areas in either the physical landscape or in man's occupation and use of the land and its resources. The variety in the natural environment offered a wide choice of natural resources for Europeans who entered the region in increasing numbers near the close of the 19th century. Except for the large cities in the southwest, settlements were based mainly on the exploitation of a particular natural resource. This resource-based economy was similar to that in many settlements in the Canadian Shield and the Atlantic and Gulf region.

The exploitation of Nature's endowment came gradually and to different places at different times. For about 50 years, while the towns and cities of eastern Canada were growing as commercial and manufacturing centres serving a relatively dense agricultural settlement, European settlement of the Cordillera remained minor and dispersed. The spotty and discontinuous settlement pattern that evolved contrasted with the broad, westward-moving frontier which subdued the Interior Plains. From the beginning of European settlement, a dual pattern evolved:

1.) coastal settlement which slowly penetrated inland;
2.) interior settlement from the east which was connected outward to the coast.

After the middle of the 19th century, small sea-oriented settlements were established in the southwestern corner, but at the same time older dispersed settlements of the interior persisted as remnants of the land-based fur trade or mines. A distinction between "the Coast" and the vaguely defined area known as "the Interior" has persisted in Cordilleran geography and economy. Present geographical patterns evolved through increasing functional connections which tied the urban areas of the coast with the small centres of the interior, and the province as a whole with the rest of North America, Europe and the Pacific Rim countries.

Settlement in the Cordillera, and elsewhere in Canada, can be discussed in at least three different ways:

1.) agricultural;
2.) resource-based, single-industry towns;
3.) large cities.

Some of the processes of agricultural settlement were discussed in Chapter 8; resource towns were a theme in Chapter 7; the growth of metropolitan cities was part of Chapters 2, 5 and 6. Each of these approaches to settlement can be illustrated again in the Cordillera.

Early Resource Utilization

Fur bearing animals of the forests were the first natural resource utilized by Europeans. Fur traders crossed the Interior Plains and made contact with Indian groups in the interior early in the 19th century. Trading posts were established at such places as Kamloops, Fort (later Prince) George and Fort St. James. A few decades later, traders arrived by sea; the appeal of their trade goods increased the hunting and trapping activities of coast Indians. Coastal trading centralized in such posts as Fort Langley, Victoria and Nanaimo.

Gold was the next natural resource to attract settlers to the Cordillera. The Coast-Interior resource-use patterns that were to become dominant in the Cordillera were established then. The Gold Rush of 1858 brought prospectors, miners and transport facilities to the central Fraser River and to the western slopes of the Cariboo Mountains; at the same time, commercial activity and administrative and governmental control were located on the coast — in Victoria and New Westminster. New transport lines, such as the Cariboo Road, linked the separated exploitation and management regions. The heartland-hinterland relationships in the Cordillera had their beginnings in the 1860s.

In this type of resource-based economy, mining centres such as Barkerville ultimately closed when ores were exhausted, but the management and consuming centres on the coast survived because the people in them found other resources to develop in the interior or coastal hinterlands. When B.C. became part of Canada in 1871, the largest clusters of European population were concentrated on the southwest coast; this geographical pattern remained the same for the next hundred years — although, of course, numbers greatly increased.

AGRICULTURAL SETTLEMENT AND LAND USE

Although the Cordillera is not a major agricultural region, some parts were originally settled solely for agricultural purposes. In other places, however, farming was closely related to, and supported, other resource developments, particularly in forestry and mining. Some early settlers probably came to B.C., as to other parts of Canada, for the main purpose of owning a piece of land and rearing a family in a rural setting. These may still be the reasons for some farming settlement west of Prince George on the Nechako Plateau and in some of the Kootenay valleys in southeastern B.C.

Most farm settlers, however, intended to develop commercial agriculture as quickly as possible, selling surplus food to mining and forestry workers or to the increasing urban population in southwestern B.C. and elsewhere in western Canada. Farmers who settled near mining and forestry towns throughout the Cordillera made only a marginal living by producing food for people engaged in natural resource extraction, management and transportation. Many of the narrow strips and pockets of farmland in the Kootenay valleys were of this type, .as were the dispersed farms and ranches of the upper and central Fraser River. Agriculture flourished or faltered in these places as the resource-based towns grew or died. The regional distribution of cultivated land in B.C. is recorded in Table 1. The largest block of farmland is on the Interior Plains section.

Table 1

Improved Acreage, by Region, in British Columbia, 1981
(Regions Defined by Combinations of Census Divisions)

REGION	ACRES	NO. OF FARMS	CENSUS DIVISIONS
Peace River	930,000	1,870	55
Prince George-Skeena	320,000	1,640	47, 49, 51, 53
Okanagan	255,000	5,300	5, 7, 35, 37, 39
Thompson	250,000	950	31, 39
Cariboo	225,000	1,020	41, 45
Lower Mainland	200,000	6,130	9, 11, 13, 15, 27, 29
Kootenay	90,000	1,020	1, 3
Vancouver Island	65,000	2,075	17, 19, 21, 23, 25

The Okanagan Valley

The most successful of the Interior farmers were those in the Okanagan Valley who used irrigation to transform the dry environment to grow fruit which had markets throughout western Canada. Okanagan Valley settlements were much like the agricultural villages on the Interior Plains in form and function, although in a different environment and growing different crops. Small fruit farms were established at the north end of the valley in the early decades of the century, sometimes by wealthy British immigrants. Orchards occupied narrow, former glacial lake terraces and small deltas and alluvial fans deposited by tributary rivers—in other words, farms were developed on small patches of level land to which irrigation water could be brought from the small lakes and streams of the upland above the valley. Within a few years, orchards were producing apples, cherries, peaches, pears, etc.

Amid each agricultural area, a small service-centre town arose. These towns were evenly spaced along the Okanagan Valley, each supplying and serving a surrounding agricultural hinterland similar to the service-centre relationships on the Interior Plains. The grading, processing and marketing of the fruit crop is done by workers in the towns. Rural-urban settlement in the Okanagan Valley is therefore similar in pattern and function to the two other major fruit-producing areas of Canada—the Niagara Peninsula and the Annapolis-Cornwallis Valley.

The economy of the Okanagan Valley diversified after the 1950s when highway transportation to the southwest coast was greatly improved. (A similar change in accessibility and geographical patterns was noted in Chapter 3 when better highways linked the Annapolis Valley and Halifax.) The warm summer temperatures and attractive sandy beaches of the Okanagan became part of the recreational hinterland of metropolitan Vancouver. This seasonal activity, which conflicted with the summer labour needs of the fruit industry, was expanded to winter occupations with the opening of ski lodges on the snow-covered slopes above the valley. In addition, the agricultural economy was diversified by planting increased acreages of grapes for the wine industry and by more production of vegetables.

As a few manufacturing industries came to the Okanagan cities, urban expansion led to problems of urban-rural land use conflict, similar to those in the Niagara Peninsula, but on a smaller scale. With limited amounts of water and limited amounts of level land available for both city and farm use, future urban or rural growth requires planning decisions by local governments and the public. If the Lower Fraser Valley near Vancouver becomes filled with urban residences, will the Okanagan Valley become even more a part of the food hinterland of metropolitan Vancouver, similar to the position and function of the Annapolis-Cornwallis Valley to Halifax? There are many similarities in the geographical patterns of Atlantic and Pacific Canada.

Southwestern B.C.

Agricultural settlement in the Lower Fraser Valley and on southeastern Vancouver Island is directly related to the establishment and growth of the two metropolitan cities, Vancouver and Victoria. As these cities increased in population, the area of farmland expanded on the nearby lowlands. These relatively small areas of level land with suitable soils not only have the advantage of nearby large markets, but also they have the longest frost-free season in Canada. Although the West Coast is known, perhaps is even notorious, for the heaviest rainfall in Canada, it falls mainly in winter and on west-facing slopes. Heavy winter rainfall, therefore, helps tree growth, but has little effect on summer agriculture. In fact, farmers of the southwest lowlands can sometimes have summer drought problems.

Some of the crops of the Lower Fraser Valley fit local environmental conditions. For example, dairying and vegetable production are concentrated on the fertile, floodplain lowland along the lower Fraser River, whereas poultry and small fruit are located about 100 metres above the river on the poorer soils laid down on an older, raised glacial delta. Cranberries and blueberries are grown in the acidic soils of the bogs after peat is removed.

Service centres, such as Chilliwack and Langley, having the same functions as agricultural, service-centre towns all across Canada, arose amid the farmland of the Lower Fraser Valley. And similar to formerly quiet towns outside of Toronto or Montreal, the Fraser Valley towns have taken on commuter and industrial functions as part of the outward spread of metropolitan Vancouver.

Although the agricultural crops on the eastern side of Vancouver Island are similar to those in the Lower Fraser Valley, they have different distribution patterns and smaller local markets. Most Island soils are derived from glacial and alluvial deposits carried eastward by short rivers flowing out of the mountains; soils vary greatly in quality within short distances. Good soils are thus dispersed in small pockets. Because urban markets are also dispersed, small agricultural clearings are located mainly near cities such as Victoria, Nanaimo and Courtenay.

Central Interior

The wide range of crops that can be grown in the southwestern corner contrasts with the limited choice of crops on the Interior Plateau near Prince George where the frost-free season is usually less than 100 days. The Interior Plateau and southern valleys are open to cold air masses that flow southward in early and late summer along the north-south grain of the topography. For example, many "soft" fruit trees have been lost in the northern Okanagan Valley as a result of killing frosts.

Although agricultural acreage is relatively small in the Cordillera compared with the vast area of little-used mountains, additional farmland is still being cleared and cultivated. Most of the new farmland in B.C. is being occupied on the Interior Plains of the northeast rather than in the Cordillera, but new acreage is also being cultivated on the Nechako Plateau, west of Prince George, as increased forestry activity promotes the growth of interior cities. Interior expansion is partly balanced by decreasing farm acreage in the Lower Fraser Valley as a result of the urban growth of metropolitan Vancouver. This latter problem is similar to those discussed in other parts of Canada in Chapters 2 and 6.

Although rural agricultural settlement was significant in some small parts of the Cordillera, much of the settlement of the region was "urban" in the sense that people clustered into towns and small cities to extract, process and transport natural resources. The purpose of settlement was therefore similar to that in the Canadian Shield.

NATURAL RESOURCE UTILIZATION AND SETTLEMENTS

Elements in the physical environment of the Cordillera have supported resource-based settlements similar to those in the Canadian Shield and in Atlantic Canada. The varied and contrasting physical environment became a basis for primary resource utilization.

Forestry

Variety in the Cordilleran landscapes is intensified by the contrasts in vegetation. Extensive stands of tall, green conifers clothe the lower slopes of the Coast and Insular Mountains and the west-facing slopes of interior mountain ranges; smaller trees spread endlessly across the Interior Plateau. In the lee of the mountains, however, and in the dry southern interior valleys, tawny bunch grass and even cactus indicate the sparseness of the vegetation cover. In winter, the green of trees, grass and shrubs on the mild and wet coast contrasts with blue skies, cool temperatures and snow-covered landscapes of the interior. Man's impact upon the natural vegetation in terms of agricultural clearing and forest logging has modified only small parts of the total natural landscape, but in local areas these patterns of utilization constitute significant geographical changes.

Forestry is the main segment of British Columbia's economy. The areal pattern of utilization was first that of dispersal along the coast, followed by concentration in the southwest. Utilization of the large trees for lumber started in the southwest and the wood-processing industry is still concentrated there. In the Georgia Strait region, transportation facilities were available for assembly and export to world markets and the region was also a market in itself.

The forests on the coastal lowlands near Vancouver, Nanaimo, and Victoria were first processed in local small mills for export. As forests farther away along the coast were cut, a water-based, log-transporting technology was developed to carry logs to large mills in or near the cities around the Strait of Georgia. Improvements in transport technology—from the Davis rafts of the 1930s to modern self-dumping log barges—permitted the exploitation of a longer coastal hinterland to supply the urban sawmills. The hinterland supplied the raw materials and the southwest heartland did the processing. The mills and settlements around the Strait of Georgia and lumber camps northward along the Inside Passage became part of an integrated, functional region linked together by movements and services related to the forestry industry. Similar to the changing areal pattern of sawmills in Atlantic

288

Canada, the number of mills decreased after 1950 and the remaining ones became larger. The enormous sawmills in the southwest now produce most of the lumber and plywood in Canada.

Pulp and paper mills were established on the west coast about 1910, more than a decade later than the first mills in the Canadian Shield. They used inexpensive coastal water tranportation to assemble raw materials and to move their finished products. The locations of the early mills were determined by the availability of forest concessions (similar to the pattern in the Canadian Shield)-and were not then directly tied to lumber production. The market for B.C. pulp and paper was mainly in California—a much smaller one than the market in eastern United States for eastern Canadian mills.

The pulp and paper mills at Powell River, Ocean Falls and Port Alice were placed in areas without nearby agricultural settlement and work forces were imported, creating single-industry resource-based towns similar in form and function to those in the Canadian Shield and in the Atlantic and Gulf region. These older mill towns contrast in visual appearance with the attractive new pulp and paper mill towns such as Gold River and Mackenzie. Other mills were built in or near the industrial and commercial cities of the heartland, such as at Port Alberni, Nanaimo and northwest of Vancouver. These mills have positions and functions similar to the pulp and paper mills located near the south edge of the Canadian Shield in the industrial cities of the St. Lawrence Lowlands.

Corporate and functional integration of the wood product industry was one of the major developments in the coastal forestry industry after 1950 and this affected distribution patterns. Pulp and paper mills, sawmills, plywood operations and the manufacture of other wood products could be integrated into one large plant or in adjoining mills. Much of the forestry activity was concentrated into the Georgia Strait region: logs were brought from as far north as the Queen Charlotte Islands by rafts and barges; lumber moved from sawmills to the major coastal ports; wood chips and sawdust from sawmills were carried by barges to pulp and paper mills within the region; newsprint rolls were picked up at the mills by coastal or ocean ships. The many operations of the coastal forestry industry were linked together over the sheltered, calm waters of Georgia Strait.

Prior to 1940, because wood products were mainly for export by water to California, northwestern Europe or eastern United States, the forest industry concentrated on the coast and mainly near the ports in the south. After 1950, increased world demand, plus improved rail and road transport into the untapped forest reserves of the Interior, permitted areal expansion of the industry into the Interior. Another impetus for the increased use of interior forests was the possible depletion of some coastal forest species such as Douglas fir.

The geographical patterns of forest utilization were different in the

Interior. Most of the early sawmills were located in linear patterns in the valleys at settlements on or near the few railways. The forest industry of the Interior seldom used rivers for transportation, as was done in eastern Canada. Because population was sparse in the Interior, local demand was minor, except near the mines and mining settlements, such as in the southeast.

SOME RESOURCE-BASED TOWNS IN THE CORDILLERA

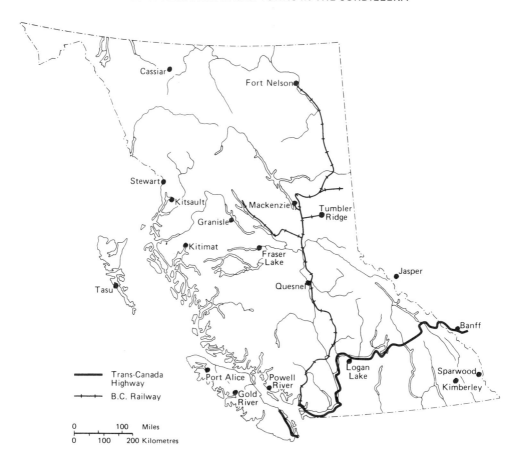

The forest industry, along with mining in some places and agriculture in a few other places, became the economic base of much settlement throughout the Interior. Some former mining towns, such as Grand Forks and Nelson, survived by finding a new resource base in forestry after the old mines closed. The major expansion of sawmilling in the central Interior came after 1950 as a result of the extension of the B.C. Railroad (then called the Pacific Great Eastern Railway), north of Quesnel to Prince George and beyond to the Peace River area. Similar to the areal patterns on the Coast and across Canada, the small, often portable sawmills in the woods gradually closed; bigger sawmills were built at transport junctions, such as at Prince George and Kamloops, and in cities in the southeast, such as Cranbrook. The latter were close to direct-shipping markets on the Interior Plains and in west-central United States.

The Interior forestry industry became more diversified and centralized with the addition of pulp and paper mills after 1961. It went through a similar type of corporate and functional integration as had occurred earlier in the coastal industry. Compared with the concentration of mills on the southwest coast, the distribution pattern of the Interior pulp and paper mills is still dispersed because of the spread of the areas for which the companies have cutting rights. There are only a few single-industry resource-based pulp and paper mill towns in B.C. compared to the Canadian Shield. Some of these new towns such as Gold River and Mackenzie are located on the previous map.

The lumbering and pulp and paper aspects of the forest industry seem to be more integrated in place and function in the Cordillera than in the Canadian Shield. However, the geographical, economical and settlement patterns of resource utilization are similar in the two regions. In both regions, mining and forestry generally take place in different communities, and agriculture is minor and only locally supportive.

Fisheries

The geography of the west coast fishery is different from that of the Atlantic coast. Five main species of Pacific salmon constitute most of the west coast fish catch and the industry has adapted to the natural habits and migrations of these fish. Halibut, herring and other fish are also caught in lesser numbers and value. Salmon enter river mouths in late summer heading for spawning waters in the interior lakes and shallow headwater tributaries; fishermen assemble off these river mouths to catch the salmon en route. Salmon canneries were established at or near the mouths of many rivers along the coast late in the 19th century, but the greatest concentration was near the Fraser and Skeena rivers which have the largest drainage basins and therefore usually the most fish production.

As fishing technology gradually improved, larger and faster fishing vessels, with better gear and greater carrying capacities, could harvest a larger area away from the river mouths. As the catching area which supported a processing cannery increased, fewer canneries were needed. The number of canneries in a linear pattern along the coast decreased from about 100 early in the century to about 10 in the 1970s. The central coast has no salmon canneries left. Similar to the forest industry, the changing areal pattern of fisheries has been the result of both corporate integration and new fishing technology. The lifestyles of fishermen have changed accordingly. This distribution trend is now about complete on the west coast, whereas the process is still in progress on the east coast.

Salmon caught near the mouths of the central coast rivers, plus those obtained offshore as they migrate toward the Skeena and Fraser rivers, are now transported in refrigerated boats to a few large canneries near Vancouver and Prince Rupert. The canneries at the delta mouth of the Fraser River are not only near the migration of salmon to the whole Fraser River basin, but also they are near the metropolitan area which attracts transportation to carry fish to world markets. In addition, the city's suburbs can supply the needed seasonal labour. Prince Rupert is at the mouth of the second largest salmon-producing river of the Canadian Cordillera, but the port does not attract as frequent nor the variety of transportation services as does metropolitan Vancouver. In addition, its very rainy, cloudy climate is not perceived as a desirable residential location by fishermen or cannery workers compared with the urban amenities and natural environment of the southwestern heartland.

A number of conflicts are of concern to the fishing industry. For example, some of the fishery is shared with American fishermen. Commercial fishermen also compete with an important sport fishery which is part of B.C.'s valuable tourist industry. Indians claim rights to catch fish along interior rivers after the fish are permitted to escape the coastal nets. Because salmon live part of their lives in the ocean and part in the inland rivers, the maintenance of the fishery is complicated by regulations of both federal (for offshore) and provincial authorities. Conflicts in interpretation and purposes between fishermen and governments seem to be inevitable on both coasts.

One of the dormant, but potential conflicts is with the hydro-power industry for use of certain rivers. For example, the Fraser River is not only the largest producer of salmon in its many tributaries, but also it is the largest potential generator of hydro power, if dammed in its lower canyon or upstream north of the junction of the Thompson River. Provincial government policy has given priority to fish production in the river since electric power may be obtained from alternative sources and sites. Similarly, the Skeena and Stikine rivers have been maintained as salmon producers, although both could produce large quantities of hydro power for future industries along the northwest coast. In addition, future use of the Stikine River is complicated by the need for political agreements with Alaska through which the river empties. These political problems may be greater than the engineering ones.

Mining

Mining has been significant in the economy of the Cordillera since the time of the Cariboo Gold Rush after the middle of the 19th century. The changing distribution patterns of mining in the Cordillera were not the same as the outward-expanding patterns of the Canadian Shield. The Cordillera has a wide variety of rocks of almost the complete range of geological ages. For example, young, tilted sedimentary rocks contain coal in the Rocky Mountains, whereas nearby in the Purcell and Selkirk mountains, old Precambrian rocks produce lead, zinc and other metals. Because mineralization has been widespread, mining has been dispersed. The concept discussed in Chapter 7, that mines open and close but mining regions endure, is further illustrated in the Cordillera.

From 1890 to 1905, the Kootenay region of southeastern B.C. was one of the first and most important mining areas of Canada, while the rest of the province was struggling to create a viable economy. It was an exception to the generalization that economic development and settlement in eastern Canada usually preceded the "opening" of the West by several decades. The mines and their supporting communities in the southeast were linked together by rail and water transport; local agriculture on narrow river terraces produced food for the mining towns; local forestry supplied building material for the towns and mines; the rivers were dammed early in the century to supply electric power to industries and residents. This interrelated regional economy was well developed before the mining region of Cobalt-Timmins-Kirkland Lake was established in the Canadian Shield in the 1920s. As a mining region, it still functions around the large smelter-refinery at Trail, to where a variety of metal ores are taken for processing, both from nearby and from as far away as the Yukon and the Northwest Territories.

This early Kootenay economy was not well integrated into the rest of the Cordillera; it was not connected by direct rail to the coast until 1915. By that time, the mining boom there was about over. The Kootenay region then had closer economic links with the adjoining mining region in the American Cordillera. Southeastern B.C. has gradually been brought into closer economic relations with the southwest core, particularly after highways were improved after 1950. These links were strengthened in the 1970s when coal from the southern Rocky Mountains was tranported by unit trains to a new, artificial port created off the mouth of the Fraser River for export to Japan. For almost a century, mining has been a major impetus in the economy of the Kootenays; abandoned mines, slag piles and decaying houses—as well as modern efficient mines and new planned towns—are significant elements in the regional landscape.

Because minerals are produced for export outside of the region, the mineralized areas of the Coast and Insular mountains, accessible to ocean transport, continue to support producing mines. As in other mining regions, individual mines close and new ones open, but the coastal area as a whole remains a producer. In the early 1970s, the capital and markets of Japan provided the stimuli for the opening of small iron mines on the coast and copper and molybdenum mines along the edges of the Interior Plateau.

Unlike most metal mines elsewhere in Canada, the more recent Cordilleran mines are enormous open-pit mines where low-grade ore is extracted by the use of improved technology in equipment and facilities. Such pits leave scars on the landscape, but they are generally in areas which have no other people nor significant competing forestry or agricultural land uses.

Mining has been a continuous activity throughout the Cordillera in this century. In the southwestern Interior Plateau, mining towns that flourished and died near Princeton early in this century have their modern counterpart in the planned town of Logan Lake (see map. p. 290). The differences in physical appearance and in amenities between the old and new mining communities are remarkable; these contrasts are like those old and new mining towns in the Canadian Shield. On the northwest coast, mines have opened and closed in the Portland Canal area for more than 70 years; similarly, mining of different minerals at different places has been continuous on Vancouver Island for more than 120 years. This dispersal of mining and its associated towns is characteristic of much of the resource-based, single-function activity throughout the Cordillera outside of the southwestern Heartland. Whereas some of the mineral resources of the Shield are consumed in the adjoining Lowlands, none of the Cordilleran mineral resources go to the eastern Heartland. Cordilleran mineral production may depend upon eastern heartland companies for some capital, but not for consuming markets.

The development of petroleum and natural gas in northeastern B.C. is part of the pattern of fuel production in the Interior Plains (Chapter 8). The flow of oil and natural gas from the Interior Plains to markets in the Cordillera is seen in the landscape as oil refineries in the industrial sections of Prince George, Kamloops and Vancouver (and in other refineries in adjoining northwestern United States).

Hydro-Electric Power

The Cordillera has the fortunate natural endowment of heavy precipitation, sloping landforms, lakes for water storage and numerous rivers. Together, these environmental conditions are excellent for the production of hydro power. To these natural elements, companies and provincial power authorities have added dams, turbines and transmission lines to the urban and industrial markets. Despite the vast amount of precipitation that falls on the Cordillera, only two of the interior river basins are well used—the Columbia and Peace—and also the northwestern part of the Fraser River system. The dispersed, separated, small river basins of the Coast region were the first to be harnessed; most of those in the southwest suitable for hydro development are now almost completely utilized.

Water power development has shown one pattern of clustered concentration and another of dispersal (refer to following map). Throughout the history of B.C. settlement, the largest cities, major rural population and most industries have been concentrated in the southwest corner. Hydro-electric power for these markets was supplied from small sites in the Coast Mountains near Vancouver or on short rivers on southern Vancouver Island. As transmission technology improved, power could be produced at more distant sites, such as Bridge River east of the Coast Mountains. This outward-evolving pattern was therefore similar to that in the Quebec Shield, but on a smaller scale, since the Vancouver market was a smaller one than Montreal (Chapter 7). A cluster of relatively small power plants evolved in the southwest near urban and industrial markets.

MAJOR HYDRO-ELECTRIC POWER DEVELOPMENTS

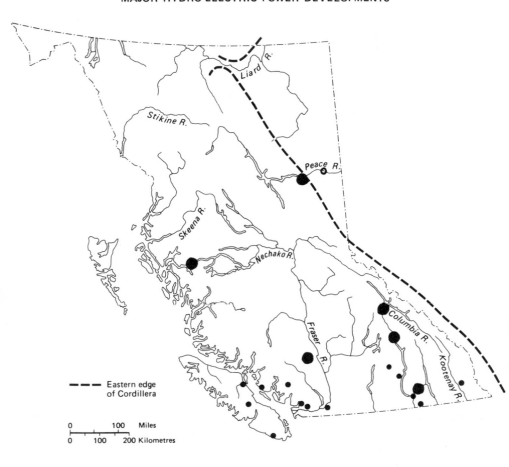

Elsewhere, power developments were dispersed in the three other corners of the province and at first supplied only local needs. As in the Canadian Shield, the availability of relatively inexpensive hydro-electric power throughout the Cordillera aided other resource developments. For example,

295

power for the large smelter-refinery at Trail, and for cities in the southeast, came mainly from several plants on the Kootenay River. Later, power and water-control dams were built at Castlegar, Revelstoke and Mica Creek on the Columbia River to supplement power production in Washington State and for transmission to Vancouver. In the northwest, the Nechako River was dammed in the early 1950s and diverted through a tunnel beneath the Coast Mountains to produce power at Kemano for the large aluminum smelter at Kitimat. In the late 1960s, power was developed in the fourth corner of the province, on the Peace River of the northeast, partially as a result of improvements in long-distance transmission technology. More power can be obtained from the Peace River in the 1980s, since this river has no conflicting fishing industry. However, downstream changes in the water levels near the mouth of that river in Alberta are not appreciated by local residents there. The largest power dams in B.C. are shown by larger circles on the map on p. 295.

In the 1970s, the two areal patterns of concentration in the southwest and dispersal in three other sections of the province became part of one large provincial distribution network. Because there are no large under-developed water power sites near the growing industrial and urban markets of the southwest, future increased power may have to be supplied from local thermal or nuclear plants or from low-grade coal deposits near the junction of the Thompson and Fraser rivers. However, a parallel scenario to the power deficit of the industrial Ontario Lowland in the 1950s is not likely to be repeated in the B.C. heartland in the near future.

The development of hydro-electric power in four sections of the Cordillera did not directly affect the settlement pattern. This lack of direct settlement impact was noted in Chapter 7. Workers who built the power dams usually lived in temporary construction camps near the site or commuted from nearby towns. Few people are needed to operate power plants once they are in operation.

Recreation and Tourism

The varied and spectacular natural environments of the Cordillera may prove to be one of the region's most valuable "natural resources." As in the Canadian Shield, the "empty" areas of B.C. should have increasing value as population densities increase in the rest of the continent. As noted as a concept in Chapter 7, the greatest intensity of recreational use—and of abuse—is in the southwest, near the large local centres of population and accessible to still greater numbers from the west coast American states. This topic is noted only briefly here, despite its high economic value, because it has little influence on the development of settlement patterns.

Probably the best known tourist and resort centres are Banff and Jasper in the Rocky Mountains of Alberta. They were originally promoted by the railroads to bring visitors from afar to the spectacular mountains and valleys. The natural environments of these mountain areas are, in fact, duplicated in many other parts of the Cordillera, such as in the Coast Mountains north of Vancouver.

As road transport improved in the Interior (there is still no continuous road along the coast of B.C.), other interesting environmental areas became available to visitors, such as the Okanagan Valley and the Cariboo. However, many parts of west-central and northern B.C. are still without roads and can be seen only by occasional hardy visitors seeking "wilderness" environments.

Resource-Based Settlements

As discussed in the preceding sections, many settlements in the Cordillera, as in the Canadian Shield, are dependent on the extraction, processing and transporting of natural resources. Some of the characteristics of these single-industry resource-based towns were noted in Chapter 7. Both regions have a mixture of old, "company" towns and new, attractive, planned towns.

Mining towns have been a continuous part of the settlement landscapes of the Cordillera. Some disappeared when ores were exhausted; others, such as Grand Forks, Nanaimo and Nelson found a new resource base in forestry; others were replaced by new towns, such as the coal-mining town of Sparwood replacing Michel in the East Kootenays. When mines were established in areas without nearby settlements, new towns had to be created, such as Logan Lake and Granisle (see map, p. 290). Trail is an example of a city that has persisted as a mineral processing centre; it smelts and refines base metals from the whole Cordillera.

Many towns have a forestry base. Some of these, such as Port Alberni, Prince George, Quesnel and Castlegar, increased in population when pulp and/or paper mills were added later to the original sawmills. Prince George, however, grew beyond the stage of being only a single-industry resource-based forestry town as it added central place commercial, wholesaling and service functions for the north-central Interior. Prince George is, therefore, comparable in function to Corner Brook in western Newfoundland as a sub-regional centre. The former, however, serves a much larger region, with a greater variety of consumers and resources than Corner Brook has in western Newfoundland.

Fishing villages and temporary workers' housing near the canneries almost disappeared following the centralization of fish processing. Now most of the central coast is virtually unoccupied for much of the year. In the Cordillera, there are no single-industry, fish processing towns like those along the east coast of Canada; fish processing is now part of a broader industrial mix in metropolitan Vancouver and Prince Rupert.

METROPOLITAN VANCOUVER

Introduction

Much of the resource-based activity throughout the Cordillera is focused directly or indirectly upon metropolitan Vancouver. This city, and others in the Georgia Strait urban region, grew as the Cordillera's natural resources were developed. The raw materials and power of the interior and coastal hinterlands either supplied the industries of the southwestern heartland or they were funneled through the southwestern ports to markets elsewhere. Although resource-based extractive industries are dispersed throughout the Cordillera, head offices, management and financial activities are concentrated in metropolitan Vancouver. The following comments are concerned mainly with the evolution of land-use patterns *within* the city, but it should be understood that these internal patterns are due in part to forces and trends in the coastal and interior hinterlands of the city.

Almost half (46 percent) of the population of British Columbia lives in Greater Vancouver and another 25 percent lives nearby in the Lower Fraser Valley and on southern Vancouver Island, including the capital, Victoria. Vancouver is the focus of an urban system which evolved around the shores of Georgia Strait—a functioning multicentred urban region. In this concept, Georgia Strait links the urban centres rather than separating them. The urban system in itself is *not* discussed here since this topic is illustrated in Chapter 6.

In many ways, Vancouver has the same internal urban landscapes as cities of eastern Canada: high-rise office buildings and apartments, rows of ranch-style homes, suburban shopping centres and low sprawling factories and warehouses along the outer highways. In other ways, the urban patterns within the metropolitan region are distinct and its natural setting of the spectacular North Shore mountains and the sheltered harbour give it a reputation as one of Canada's most attractive cities. As noted for Montreal and Toronto, the term Vancouver is used for a larger metropolitan area which includes other political units with other names. The city is discussed here as an example of urban historical geography with emphasis on land use.

Origins of European Settlement

Indians had selected several sites near the mouth of the Fraser River and along Burrard Inlet for their camps, based mainly on harvesting sea resources. When British Columbia became a British colony in 1858, the strategic site of New Westminster was chosen as the capital; this fort and administrative centre on the main channel of the Fraser River could control the water entrance to the colony and to the Interior gold fields. New Westminster became the chief "central place" in the Lower Fraser Valley during the 1870s after sawmills and fish canneries expanded its industrial base and stores and offices supplied commercial goods and services to farmers who settled nearby on the Fraser delta. The expected future growth of New Westminster, based on the apparent advantages of its site and geographical position, ceased after 1886 when the nearby tiny sawmill-based village of Granville, on Burrard Inlet, was chosen as the western terminal of the Canadian Pacific Railway. The large land grants given to the C.P.R. by the new city of Vancouver—similar to such land ownership in other western cities along the route—were to be influential in the areal growth of the city for the next century.

Vancouver and Victoria were competing cities during the last decade of the 19th century. Their functions, and their rivalry, can be compared with Quebec City and Montreal in eastern Canada in the early 19th century (see Chapter 5). Victoria was the ocean gateway to the Cordillera, a cultural centre and the political capital, like Quebec City in the east; Vancouver became the industrial and commercial city, closer to the interior markets, parallelling the position and functions of Montreal. Vancouver became the transshipping point and main port for western Canada in the same manner that Montreal became a major transportation hub of eastern Canada. The main difference has been, and is, in the scale of population and industrial and commercial development; Quebec and Montreal are each about three times the size of Victoria and Vancouver respectively. Similar to Toronto replacing Montreal as the eastern financial centre, will anyone predict that coastal Vancouver will be replaced by inland Calgary as the western financial centre by the end of the century?

The spatial separation of political and commercial-management functions between Victoria and Vancouver is repeated elsewhere across Canada. Both the links and the separation have been previously noted between Edmonton-Calgary, Regina-Saskatoon, Montreal-Quebec and Saint John-Fredericton. Each of these "twin cities" are bi-nodal urban centres of larger sub-regions. In contrast, these functions are concentrated into one urban node in St. John's, Toronto and Winnipeg.

Early Land-Use Patterns

By 1900, the future urban land-use patterns of Vancouver were established (map p. 300). An industrial zone expanded along the C.P.R. tracks and along the harbour, being more concerned with supplying and assembling goods for regional resource developments and for local consumers than with a trans-Pacific trade which did not materialize as expected. This waterfront strip has remained in industrial land use ever since. Directly south of the city's commercial centre, a second industrial zone spread around False Creek which was too shallow to be used by ocean vessels; the protected water was ideal, however, for log booms and it became the focus of Vancouver's sawmill industry. The outward areal spread to the east and west of the city's residential areas is shown on the following map.

Throughout the next decades, Vancouver's economic base, except for the sawmills, was *not* based on primary processing of the natural resources of the Cordillera hinterland. Much of the salmon canning industry and its management remained in Victoria until the turn of the century; other canneries were located along the channels of the Fraser delta rather than in Vancouver itself. None of the mineral resources of the southeast or those northward along the Coast was processed in Vancouver. As thousands of people flooded into the city early in this century, some manufacturing developed to supply local consumer goods. These industries were protected, in one sense, by the transportation costs of goods imported from eastern Canada by rail or from Britain by sea.

The commercial section of the original village of Granville remained the business centre of early Vancouver. As the city's population (and consumers) increased, this commercial core spread south and west, replacing the original small wooden residences which had been built on narrow lots on the edges of the original business district.

AREAL GROWTH OF EARLY VANCOUVER

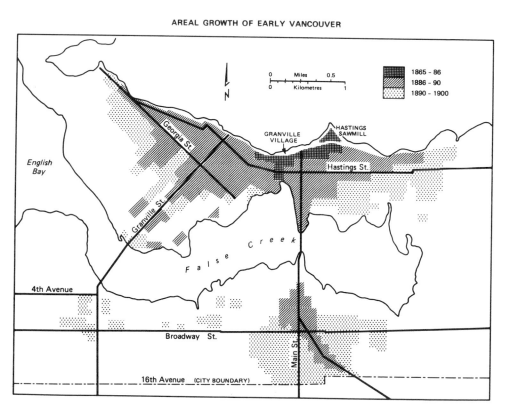

The commercial core developed two nodes—the older, eastern section catered to the lower income population in the East End and new specialty stores served higher income people in the West End. From these early days, working class people lived in small houses on narrow lots in the eastern parts of the city, near industrial areas, whereas commercial and management people built their larger houses on larger lots west of the city centre. This income and social areal differentiation between east and west has remained in Vancouver and is still apparent in local and provincial politics. Compare the following historical geography comments with the growth patterns of a large city near you.

Evolution of Urban Land-Use Patterns

By 1920, most of the area within the political boundaries of Vancouver of that time was occupied. Much of the early outward areal expansion followed a radial pattern from the central core and was aided and directed by the routes of the streetcar lines. This radial pattern was common in other Anglo-American cities of that time. Bridges across False Creek permitted residences to be built south and west of that water barrier. "Suburban sprawl" (using our modern terminology) was already taking place into the adjoining municipalities of South Vancouver and Point Grey in the 1920s.

Vancouver's outward residential growth was different from that of eastern cities in at least two ways:

1.) expansion was *not* on to agricultural land like that which surrounded most eastern cities, but spread into low value forest land which had been cut-over in the 1880s;

2.) people were able to build, or buy, their own homes; tenements were few and the city had a high percentage of single-family detached homes; workers were higher paid and probably felt more independence than eastern industrial labour.

In the suburbs, small "villages" with a cluster of stores and offices were established along the streetcar tracks and at junctions of routes across the stump-covered upland of Burrard Peninsula. The settlement pattern of nodes and strips on the south side of present-day Vancouver was therefore different from the radial patterns that settled the original city near the harbour.

During the inter-war years, 1920-1940, east-west social and economic distinctions also became evident in South Vancouver and Point Grey. Much of the land in the latter was owned by the C.P.R. which did *not* develop subdivisions in a usual outward pattern. Point Grey was laid out with some wide boulevard streets; many parks and golf courses added green areas;

houses were built back from the streets with attractive flower gardens decorating front lawns. Point Grey residents had among the highest average incomes in Canada in the late 1920s. Did other Canadian cities have this type of suburban subdivision at this time?

In contrast, many of the residences of South Vancouver were designed and built by construction companies. Rows of houses looked much the same; lots were narrow; houses were close together and very near the street; the small backyards were used to grow vegetables rather than flowers. Streets were narrow and often unpaved, since the tax base of South Vancouver was poor. These urban landscape differences between former South Vancouver and Point Grey are still apparent in the present city. Both municipalities still had large blocks of unoccupied land when they were annexed to Vancouver in 1929. The residential filling-in process took place during the 1950s and 1960s and these later homes look the same as those all across Canada.

The main urban land uses — industrial, commercial and residential — which had been established by 1900 had solidified by 1920; they expanded areally in the next 60 years, but did not change their relative positions.

The industrial zone along Burrard Inlet spread eastward during the 1920s when grain elevators and oil refineries were built along the eastern parts of the harbour. Transport, storage and transshipping facilities and other industries spread to the North Vancouver waterfront in the 1950s and later. Many of the raw materials of western Canada, such as wheat, oilseeds, lumber, mineral concentrates, coal, potash and sulphur, now flow through the port facilities of metropolitan Vancouver en route to world markets. Vancouver's port is the international outlet for western Canadian products, similar to the functions of Montreal in the east. Although people no longer have to live close to their work as they did early in this century, the eastward migration of industrial areas increased the industrial worker component of the population of eastern Vancouver and adjoining Burnaby. The second industrial zone around False Creek also expanded eastward, occupied by land transportation-oriented industries and facilities. Similar patterns of industrial location along highways were common in most large Canadian cities.

A third industrial zone, along the Fraser River, began in the last century with the establishment of sawmills and fish canneries. The industrial strip was being filled in during the 1930s and the process accelerated after the 1950s. It is now the main wood-producing area in metropolitan Vancouver.

The outward areal expansion of suburban shopping centres in Vancouver is similar to the patterns in other large Canadian cities. The first ring of shopping centres, with ample area for parking, was established in the 1950s. As population continued to spread outward, a second ring of shopping and service complexes was built in the 1960s and 1970s in the suburban municipalities of Richmond, Surrey and Coquitlam. Although on a different scale, these suburban shopping centres have the same relative position and function now as did the corner grocery stores and the commercial strips along the streetcar tracks in South Vancouver and Point Grey in the 1920s.

The economic character and functions of Vancouver are changing; the city is now classified as a commercial, service and management city. Policy decisions concerning resource development throughout the hinterland of the Cordillera are made in the high-rise office towers west of the commercial core. Industry has steadily declined in relative significance; many industrial plants have moved outwards to the suburbs where there is cheaper land, more accessible transport and a nearby work force. These same patterns are characteristic of Montreal and Toronto.

Vancouver's urban land uses were established early in its settlement history and they were related to transportation facilities; later areal growth expanded from these original patterns. Are the expanding urban land uses in other cities different from or similar to those in Vancouver?

OTHER CITIES OF THE SOUTHWESTERN CORDILLERA

Victoria was the first major European settlement along the west coast of Canada; it was selected by the Hudson's Bay Company in 1843 as a trading post and chief administrative centre. Its commercial and governmental population grew when it became the sea entrance to the gold rush to Interior B.C. in 1858-1862. Victoria remained the largest city in southwestern B.C., with its government and business residents, until surpassed by Vancouver in the 1890s.

Victoria is still classified as a government and institutional city, but it is also a service centre for residents on southern Vancouver Island. The city has attempted to maintain an "old English" charm in its business centre and in some residential sections to attract tourists. Its mild winter climate, with less rainfall than the coastal areas on the east side of Georgia Strait, has attracted retired people in great numbers from the Prairie Provinces and eastern Canada.

North of Victoria, Nanaimo is the chief wholesale and distribution centre for central Vancouver Island. Forestry is its industrial base, with both sawmills and a pulp and paper mill. Both Nanaimo and Victoria are closely linked to Vancouver with frequent daily ferry and air service. The complementary urban functions of these cities and the high degree of interaction between them encourages the concept of considering the communities around southern Georgia Strait as one large urban region. Compare this area with the urban complex around the west end of Lake Ontario. Geography studies similarities and differences across Canada.

SUB-REGIONS OF THE CORDILLERA

The other cities of the Cordillera outside of the southwest heartland are sub-regional centres. The service-centre functions for resource-based activities in the dispersed valleys of the Interior are usually focused in one main city. The linkages between these cities and Vancouver were continually strengthened after 1950, illustrating a regional heartland-hinterland concept.

As in other regions of Canada, the Cordillera can be subdivided in various ways for different purposes. Within British Columbia, the heartland-hinterland concept is known by the terms of "the Coast" and "the Interior." To the 70 percent of the population of B.C. who live around Georgia Strait, the term "Coast" usually means only the southwestern coast. To those residents, the central and northern coast is undoubtedly part of the hinterland of the southwestern heartland.

Prince Rupert is the only major city on the north coast. The city and its interior hinterland has had many decades of hopes, but little development. It was laid out as the northern terminal of the (now) Canadian National Railway early in this century—the closest port to the expected trans-Pacific trade with East Asia. But the port and terminal could not compete with the volume of products that moved through Vancouver; traffic and trade remained minor. The hinterland east of Prince Rupert had minor forestry and agricultural settlement along the railroad prior to 1950. Local processing of fish and forest products, plus aluminum smelting at nearby Kitimat, have maintained the sub-regional economy, but this northern gateway never became a duplicate of Vancouver. Prince Rupert may yet become the northern outlet for which it was created, if minerals and forest products of the northwest are joined by coal and grain from the northeast. The need for incoming traffic, however, will still remain.

There is little agreement about the number of sub-regions in Interior B.C. Questionnaires to some residents of the southwest indicate that they are unclear about environmental and geographical differences within the vague area known as "the Interior." There are no defined regional names for locative purposes in the Interior similar to county names in eastern Canada. Some of the regional names used in B.C. are shown on the following map. Lines are dotted around the regions because boundaries are not clearly defined. The regions are concepts, not administrative or political units. On one scale, every valley could be a sub-region, since it differs in landscape and economy from nearby valleys; the amount of interaction among valleys varies greatly.

One method of regionalizing the varied Interior is to use a framework of city-centred regions—as was suggested in the Interior Plains—instead of the valley landform features. The two largest regional centres in the Interior Plateau are Kamloops in the south and Prince George in the north. Kamloops occupies a strategic transportation position at the junctions of the North and South Thompson rivers, the Canadian Pacific and Canadian National railways and the Trans-Canada and Yellowhead highways. It is a service and supply hub and a processing centre for a nearby hinterland which includes mining, ranching and forestry. Many branch offices of the provincial government are located in this central place. A regional name, Cariboo, is applied loosely to the area, but many residents of the southwest think of "the Cariboo" as being centred on Williams Lake, northwest of Kamloops. Local regional natural environments include dry grasslands, wet forested uplands, gently rolling plateaus and deeply-cut river canyons. The growth and functions of Kamloops are examples of using the advantages of central geographical position amid diverse environments and economies.

REGIONAL NAMES IN BRITISH COLUMBIA

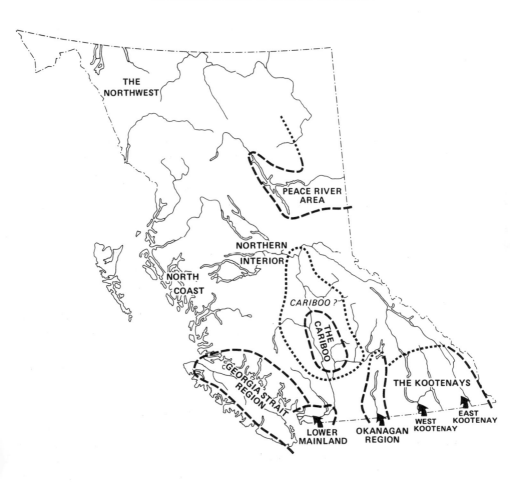

Prince George also occupies a crossroads position. River, rail, road and air routes all meet there. Its economy is based mainly on the forest-processing industry, consisting of large sawmills, wood-working and pulp and paper mills, but it is also the service centre for the forestry and agricultural activities of the central Interior Plateau (refer back to p. 297).

Prince George occupies a gateway position for northern B.C. Products and people from the Peace River area funnel through Prince George to and from heartland Vancouver. The future will reveal whether resource development — probably in mining — in empty northwestern B.C. will focus on Prince George, because of railroad extensions, or on Prince Rupert, because of highway extensions. The little-occupied northern Cordillera has yet to be well-integrated into the economy of southern B.C.

The Okanagan Valley is the most populated of the southern interior valleys. Its three evenly-spaced cities, Penticton, Kelowna and Vernon, vie for dominance of central place and agricultural processing functions (refer back to p. 286). The former grassland environment of the valley was modified by irrigation to become one of Canada's leading fruit regions. The regional environment, with lack of rainfall (compared with the coast) and a high percentage of sunshine, became a retirement haven for Plains residents as well as temporary summer campers. It is challenging to predict that the locational advantages of Kelowna will be used to make it the future largest "central place" in the Okanagan Valley.

The southeastern valleys are collectively known as "the Kootenays." Both clustered and linear settlements in each valley have been concerned with mining and forestry and supported by local agriculture and water power. The amount of level land for urban land use has been limited at the sites of each town and city. The group of settlements from Trail to Castlegar to Nelson, near the junction of the Columbia and Kootenay rivers, is beginning to take some sub-regional dominance; a secondary node of Cranbrook-Kimberley is the focus in the East Kootenay(s). Southeastern B.C. has not been well-integrated into the provincial economy in the past and its rate of economic growth has been slower than in other parts of the Interior hinterland.

There was little coordinated integrated development in the Cordilleran hinterland prior to 1940. Resource development came at different times, at different places, for different purposes. The Kootenays was a mining region; the Cariboo was a ranching region; the Okanagan was a fruit region; the Northwest Coast was a fishing region; the Central Interior was a forestry region. Towns were established in several places in each region and their growth, or decline, depended on the success or failure of the local mine, forest or fish industries. Interior settlements had much more interaction with Vancouver than with each other. These resource developments and urban functions were much like those in the Canadian Shield. However, regional isolation slowly changed to functional integration as interior transportation improved. Like the functional relationships between the Canadian Shield and the Great Lakes - St. Lawrence Lowlands, the hinterlands of the southwestern heartland of B.C. have been brought closer together into an economic system.

Table 2

Population of Largest Cordilleran Cities, 1981

CITY	1976	1981	CITY	1976	1981
Metro Vancouver	1,167,000	1,268,000	Metro Victoria	220,000	233,500
Vancouver	411,000	414,000	Victoria	62,000	64,400
Surrey	117,000	147,000	Saanich	74,000	79,000
Burnaby	133,000	137,000	Oak Bay	17,700	17,000
Richmond	80,000	96,000	Esquimalt	15,000	16,000
Delta	65,000	73,000	Metro Kelowna	52,000	77,500
North Van. Dist.	64,000	65,000	Kelowna	52,000	59,000
Coquitlam	56,000	61,000	Prince George	60,000	68,000
New Westminster	39,000	38,600	Kamloops	59,000	65,000
West Vancouver	37,000	36,000	Metro Nanaimo	41,000	57,700
North Van. (city)	32,000	34,000	Nanaimo	40,000	47,000
Port Coquitlam	24,000	27,500	Metro Vernon	36,000	42,000
			Vernon	22,000	20,000
			Metro Chilliwack	37,000	41,000
			Metro Port Alberni	26,000	32,600
			Port Alberni	20,000	20,000
			Penticton	21,000	23,200

SUMMARY

Peripheral west coast location has always affected British Columbia's development, similar to the locational disadvantages of east coast Canada. When eastern Canada was being settled by people from across the Atlantic Ocean looking for farmland, B.C. was unknown. Westward migration reached it much later. The heritage and influence of large numbers of farmers, who were part of Eastern Canada's population, were never significant in the Cordillera. The Cordillera's population has always been mainly urban— whether "urban" meant a fur-trading post, a mining town, logging camp or a fish cannery early in the century, or the present urban complex around Georgia Strait in the southwest.

Isolation from Britain was a social and economic problem in the 19th century and separation from the heartland of eastern Canada was equally real for the first half of the 20th century. Without a large consuming market, the development and use of the regional raw materials from the forest, sea and rocks were usually dependent on markets, transportation and capital investment supplied from external places. Secondary manufacturing came

307

very slowly and was often by branch plants opened by eastern Canadian manufacturers. Only in the 1970s did British Columbia and Alberta reach a threshold of population density and strategic resource potential to become more economically independent.

The Cordillera of British Columbia has distinctive variety within small areas in climate, vegetation, soils, land use and settlement. Its heartland in the southwest is functionally connected with coastal and interior hinterlands. The regional economy stresses the development of natural resources and, as such, it has many characteristics similar to the Canadian Shield region and the Atlantic Provinces. The urban development of the southwestern Cordillera is like that of metropolitan Montreal and Toronto, but it lacks the wider network of interconnected large cities that is one of the regional characteristics of the Great Lakes-St. Lawrence Lowlands. Within the Cordillera, the two main sub-regions are the Coast, with its distinctive climate and urban concentration, and the growing resource-oriented settlements of the Interior. These regional sub-divisions were fundamental in the past history of areal occupation, but improved transport after 1950 decreased the effects of separation. New sets of areal patterns are evolving.

REFERENCES

Atlases:

"Atlas of British Columbia: People, Environment and Resource Use" by Albert L. Farley, Univ. of B.C. Press, Vancouver, 1979. 135 pages and 60 maps.

University Geographical Series:

Western Geographical Series, Dept. of Geog., Univ. of Victoria, Victoria, Vol. 1, 1970 to Vol. 18, 1980. For example:
No. 12, "Victoria: Physical Environment and Development" edited by Harold Foster, 1976. 334 pages.
No. 16, "Vancouver: Western Metropolis" edited by Len Evenden, 1978. 277 pages.
No. 17, "Vancouver Island: Land of Contrasts" edited by Charles Forward, 1979. 349 pages.
B.C. Geographical Series, Occasional Papers in Geography, Tantalus Research Ltd., Vancouver, No. 1, 1960 to No. 36, 1982. For example:
No. 24, "The Urban Hierarchy of Central Vancouver Island" by Elizabeth Forrester, 1977, pp. 121-134.
No. 31, "The Functional Structure of the B.C. System of Ports and the Interactions with the Primate Port, Vancouver" by Charles Forward, 1981, pp. 75-92.

Government:

Lands Directorate, Environment Canada, Geographical Papers Series, Ottawa.
No. 41, "Waterfront Land Use in Metropolitan Vancouver" by Charles Forward, 1968.
No. 43, "Land Use of the Victoria Area" by Charles Forward, 1969.
No. 56, "Water Resources and Related Land Uses, Strait of Georgia-Puget Sound Basin" by Mary Barker, 1974.
No. 57, "The Urbanization of the Strait of Georgia Region" by Edward M. Gibson, 1976. (Map of Georgia Strait Urban Region by L. Skoda enclosed.)
Lands Directorate, Pacific Region, Environment Canada, Vancouver.
"Coastal Resources Folio—East Coast of Vancouver Island," 1982, 2 vols.
B.C. Government, Dept. of Economic Development, Victoria.
"The Manual of Resources, Including Physical Environment," 1977. 62 pages.
A series of regional reports. For example:

The Northeast, 1975. 123 pages.
The Mid-coast, 1976. 175 pages.
The Central Interior, 1976. 174 pages.
The Northwest, 1977. 250 pages.
B.C. Dept. of Industrial Development, Trade and Commerce, Victoria.
A series of regional economic studies. For example:
Cariboo-Chilcotin, 1969. 118 pages.
Okanagan-Shuswap, 1971. 177 pages.
Lillooet-Nicola, 1972. 163 pages.
Skeena-Queen Charlottes, 1973. 159 pages.
B.C. Dept. of Mines and Petroleum Resources, Victoria.
"Landforms of British Columbia" by Stuart Holland, 1964. 138 pages and enclosed map of landform regions.

Books:

"Natural Resources of British Columbia and Yukon" by Mary Barker, Douglas and McIntyre, Vancouver, 1977. 155 pages.
"British Columbia in Books: Annotated Bibliography" by M.L. Cuddy and J. Scott, J.J. Douglas, Vancouver, 1974. 144 pages.
"British Columbia: Landforms and Settlement" by Angus Gunn, Smith Lithography, Richmond, 1968. 48 pages.
"Vancouver" by Walter G. Hardwick, Collier-Macmillan, Don Mills, 1974. 214 pages.
"The Climate of Vancouver" by John Hay and Tim Oke, Dept. of Geog., Univ. of B.C., Vancouver, 1976. 49 pages.
"The Climate of British Columbia and the Yukon Territory" by W.G. Kendrew and Don P. Kerr, Meteorological Branch, Dept. of Transport, Toronto, 1956. 222 pages.
"British Columbia: One Hundred Years of Geographical Change" by J. Lewis Robinson and Walter G. Hardwick, Talonbooks, Vancouver, 1973. 62 pages.
"Ranching in the Southern Interior Plateau of B.C." by Tom R. Weir, Geog. Branch Memoir No. 4, Dept. of Mines and Technical Surveys, Ottawa, 1964. 165 pages.

Periodicals:

Some relevant articles in *The Canadian Geographer* between 1970-82, Can. Assoc. of Geog., Burnside Hall, McGill Univ., Montreal:
Vol. 25, No. 2, 1981.   "Inner-City Revitalization in Canada: A Vancouver Case Study" by David Ley, pp. 124-148.
Vol. 17, No. 3, 1973.   "Intrametropolitan Manufacturing in Greater Vancouver" by Guy Steed, pp. 235-258.

CHAPTER 10

THE NORTH

CHAPTER 10

THE NORTH

INTRODUCTION

The North means different things to different people in Canada. Since most Canadians inhabit a narrow strip across the southern part of the country, most of the area of Canada lies north of them. Thus "the North" can be a vast region in the minds of Canadians; and in such a large area one might expect a wide variety and range of physical environmental conditions. The geographical characteristics that are probably best known are its cold climate, scanty population, and its Eskimo (Inuit) inhabitants.

The North is the only Canadian region to have a larger native population than non-native. Although it is a region in which the characteristics of the physical environment can be overpowering, one should look carefully at the human characteristics of the scanty population. The local Indian and Inuit population had their traditional way of life changed greatly after 1940—a reminder that similar disruptions were experienced by Indians in southern Canada one to two centuries ago.

The resource potential and development of the North are controversial and probably not well understood. The concept of a "northern frontier" probably brings forth images of economic opportunity to some and physical hardships to others. The North was touted to be the land of promise in the second half of the 20th century, comparable to the opening of the West in the first half of the century. This image did not prove to be as accurate as was hoped. The resources frontier of the North is more developed in the northern parts of the provinces rather than in the two Territories.

The North is a politically defined region which has been called "colonial" because of the varying degrees of federal government control. The region fits the heartland-hinterland concept, except that its resources have been developed by people directly southward in addition to those in the Great Lakes-St. Lawrence heartland. There is only limited east-west interaction among the separated sub-regions of the North. Most of the North's economic and transportation links are with areas directly south; the North is the hinterland of regional "sub-heartlands" as much as it is the hinterland of political control from Ottawa.

THEMES

1.) To describe physical environmental conditions in the North, particularly similarities to and differences from southern Canada environments.

2.) To contrast and compare environments, peoples and resources between the northwestern Subarctic regions and the northeastern Arctic region.

3.) To discuss the limited natural resource base of the Territories and the physical environmental and economic difficulties affecting their development.

4.) To discuss changes in lifestyles and adaptations to environment of the native Inuit (Eskimo) people.

This chapter is organized along more "traditional" lines of regional description, partly because accurate information sources about the North may be less available to readers than for other parts of Canada, and partly to continue the theme of using different approaches to the study of regions.

DEFINITION OF THE REGION

The North has been arbitrarily defined as the political area of Yukon Territory and the Northwest Territories (recall Chapter 1). As so defined, it covers a land area of about 4,000,000 square kilometres (1,512,000 square miles) which comprises about 40 percent of Canada's total land area. This area does not include the thousands of square kilometres of water between the Arctic Islands, nor the vaguely defined, pie-shaped wedge of ice-covered Arctic Ocean shown on some Canadian maps to extend to the geographical North Pole.

The name, Northwest Territories, in itself, can be misleading because it is now only *one* territory and most of it is in north*eastern* Canada rather than in the northwest. The Northwest Territories (also spelled North-West Territories in the past, and still abbreviated as N.W.T.) is an example of an historical name no longer serving as an accurate locative description of the place.

To some people, "the North" may have a specific connotation, meaning the Arctic part of Canada. The word "Arctic" also has conflicting definitions; it is usually used in a climatic sense, and is properly defined as an area with no summers. In Canada, this area is north of the 10°C (50°F) isotherm for July—a line extending from Churchill, Manitoba, northwest to the mouth of the Mackenzie River, and also including northwestern Quebec and northern Labrador. Some people, and some popular books, have defined the Arctic as the area north of the Arctic Circle—a latitude line, north of which there are 24 hours of daylight near the end of June; the Arctic Circle has no direct connection with climatic conditions. On the other hand, the area of Arctic climate extends far *south* of the Arctic Circle on the east side of Hudson Bay. If one uses a political definition of the North, the region has both an Arctic climate in the northeast and a Subarctic climate in the northwest. Sub-regions of the North, as used in this chapter, are shown on the following map.

A geographer, Louis Hamelin, suggested that neither the political nor climatic definition of the North is appropriate, and he devised a numerical index based on weighted values of many characteristics of "nordicity." His formula results in three "Norths," with different degrees of "northness."

Middle North extends across the northern parts of the provinces, and is similar to a vaguely defined east-west zone sometimes called "Middle Canada;" it is a transitional zone between settled "southern" Canada and empty "northern" Canada. In Hamelin's "Middle North," the Mackenzie Valley and the Clay Belt of Ontario are in the same region; this concept is not acceptable to some regionalists. Hamelin's "Far North" generally coincides with the Arctic climatic region; and his "Extreme North" refers to the most northern Arctic Islands. The latter are nearly uninhabited.

REGIONS OF NORTHERN CANADA

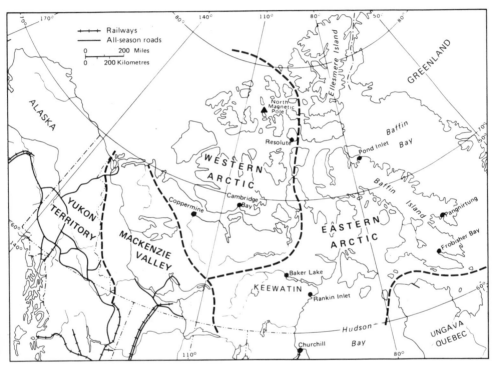

When defined politically as two Territories, the North has no similarity of landform characteristics as has been used for criteria for the definition of other regions of Canada. The North includes the northern extension of other landform regions: the Yukon covers the northern Cordillera extending north of British Columbia; the Mackenzie Valley is the northern part of the Interior Plains; Keewatin District, west of Hudson Bay, is underlaid by the Canadian Shield, and most of Baffin Island also has Precambrian rock similar to the Canadian Shield on the mainland. The common physical element of the Arctic Islands is their island character—their landform features range from high mountains to flat plains.

Because these different landform characteristics may influence future

315

settlement and resource developments, other geographers may wish to incorporate the mainland parts of the political North into southern Canada regions. Such an organization would leave only the Arctic Islands as a separate "North" region. Because the northern mainland areas are similar in several ways to adjoining southern regions, there have been occasional suggestions that they be annexed to the adjoining provinces. (Arctic Quebec was added to that province in 1912.) Such suggestions have had no enthusiastic support from people in the Territories.

THE PHYSICAL ENVIRONMENT

Many of the unfavourable (to people) physical conditions in the North are probably well known, but they are perhaps exaggerated by southern Canadians. The Arctic part is characterized by no trees, virtually no soil, much bare rock, some icecaps, and long cold winters. These physical conditions have repelled potential European settlers and therefore the Arctic area is occupied mainly by its original inhabitants, the Inuit. More favourable physical conditions for settlement and resource development are found in the northwestern part of the two Territories, which is inhabited both by Indians and people of European ancestry who migrated there from southern Canada.

Landforms

The North has a complete range of landforms. High, alpine peaks with many permanent icecaps and discharging glaciers extend along eastern Baffin Island, through Devon Island, and terminate at the Arctic Ocean in northern Ellesmere Island. This spectacular mountain scenery with beautiful fiorded coastlines—like that of Norway and British Columbia—may someday be a major tourist attraction. This line of mountains rimming the eastern part of the North is comparable to the position (but with different physical characteristics) of the Appalachian Mountains along the east coast of southern Canada.

Northwestern Canada is occupied by the broad Cordilleran mountain system. The distribution of landform regions within the Yukon Cordillera is similar to those in British Columbia with high mountains on the east and west around a central plateau. The eastern ranges, collectively called the Mackenzie Mountains, extend along the Northwest Territories-Yukon boundary and then arc westward near the northern Yukon coast into Alaska. These rugged, high mountains were little known and seldom traversed prior to 1940, and there is still only one road through this landform barrier between the valleys of central Yukon and the northern Mackenzie Valley. The line of mountains across southwestern Yukon is crowned by Canada's highest mountain, Mount Logan. Unfortunately for people in south-central

Yukon, this high, ice-capped mountain barrier keeps out most mild Pacific Ocean air masses, which are able to cross the Coast Mountains farther south in B.C.

Between these surrounding mountains, the Yukon Plateau slopes down into Alaska and is cut into by broad, flat-bottomed valleys of the Yukon River and its tributaries. Most people, and resource-oriented activities, are located in the valleys of south-central and west-central Yukon Territory, and transportation follows these lower routes, as in the adjoining Cordillera of B.C.

The Mackenzie River valley has different landform characteristics from the rest of the North. The Interior Plains slope down to the north, reaching sea level in the wide delta of the Mackenzie River. The broad, flat valley is mantled with tens to hundreds of feet of glacial and alluvial deposition into which the Mackenzie River has cut, flowing between high, steep gravel banks. The large area of flat land is little used and all settlements are along the river or on the edges of Great Slave and Great Bear lakes. Can one speculate about a future Mackenzie Valley which might be settled as the St. Lawrence Lowland was settled in the 19th century?

Low, rocky hills of the Canadian Shield rise above the eastern side of the Mackenzie Valley; the geological boundary is buried beneath Great Slave and Great Bear lakes. The visual appearance of the Shield in the North — rounded hills and innumerable lakes — is similar to the Shield in the provinces, except for diminishing tree cover northward. Bare, frost-riven rock is exposed at the surface over thousands of square kilometres in Keewatin District, west and northwest of Hudson Bay.

The western Arctic Islands have a different geological base than the Precambrian eastern mountains; the former's young, gently folded sedimentary rocks appear as flat plains and low plateaus and hills. More importantly, some of these rocks are a source of natural gas and petroleum similar to those in the Interior Plains.

Climate

The contrast between the Arctic climate in the northeast and the Subarctic climate in the valleys of the northwest was noted on p. 23-24. The main difference between these climatic regions is in summer conditions.

Summer:

In late June, when there is a long period of daylight throughout the North, the mainland coast and Arctic Islands are still surrounded by land-fast sea ice. The heating effect of long days is balanced by cool air from the ice cover. When the sea ice melts during July and into August, the Arctic northeast remains surrounded by cold water moving through the islands toward Davis Strait; this nearby cold water keeps temperatures low at the coastal settlements where the weather stations are. Therefore, warm temperatures are seldom recorded and the northeast has an Arctic climate without a "summer." Daily summer temperatures are, however, well above 0°C (32°F) and the snow melts from the land throughout all of the region.

In contrast, the large land mass of northwestern Canada—distant from the Arctic Ocean and channels—can heat up during the summer and the valleys become moderately warm during July and August. In addition, occasional warm air masses from the Interior Plains or the Pacific can penetrate northward into the Mackenzie Valley or southern Yukon, raising average monthly temperatures there. As a result of warmer summers in the northwest valleys, trees can survive and a limited range of crops can be grown. Average monthly temperatures in the southern Mackenzie Valley are as warm as those recorded in the Ontario Clay Belt.

Some people have incorrectly attributed the summer warmth of the Northwest to the long duration of daylight in these northern latitudes. Because the number of hours of daylight received in a day is determined by latitude (and the inclination of the earth's axis), southern Yukon has the same number of hours of daylight as southern Baffin Island and southern Greenland, yet there are major differences in summer warmth at these places. One can conclude, therefore, that hours of daylight do not necessarily result in warm temperatures. Other factors must be involved, such as the temperatures of air masses crossing over these areas and the nearness of cold ocean water.

Winter:

Winters are long and cold throughout the North, since the duration of daylight is short in late December. In addition, cold air masses are continually crossing the area from the Arctic Ocean or Siberia and Alaska. The lowest minimum temperatures recorded in North America have been experienced in northwestern Canada, but the lowest *average* monthly temperatures are in the central Arctic Islands. This severe and continuous cold makes it costly and difficult to operate and maintain machinery and vehicles in the North. Southern Canadians who enter the region in winter can adapt to the extreme cold for a few hours or a few days with special clothing, but the duration of continuous cold and little daylight for several months is psychologically difficult for many "southerners."

Precipitation:

Although all of the North receives small amounts of annual precipitation (refer to p. 38, Chapter 2), there are regional differences across this vast area. The least precipitation in Canada is recorded at the few weather stations in the central Arctic Islands. The fine, granular snow (usually not in flakes as in southern Canada) blows about during the long winter and can become hard-packed; it does not melt until June. Although the officially recorded amounts are low, snow does accumulate in sufficient depths to be used for snowhouses by the Inuit and it banks up against modern houses as useful insulation. Throughout the region, some of the precipitation falls in the form of drizzle rain during the summer when temperatures are above 0°C.

Greater amounts of precipitation fall on the eastern mountains, as is shown by the permanent icecaps on Baffin, Devon and Ellesmere islands. The gradual retreat of these icecaps indicates that the amount of precipitation received in a year is less than the amount which melts during the summer. The retreat, or advance, of icecaps is therefore related to seasonal temperatures, as well as precipitation. More precipitation is also received in the St. Elias Mountains in southwestern Yukon; although no permanent climate stations are maintained there, the amount of precipitation is indicated by the accumulation of snow which has become ice in the icecaps and glaciers near the Pacific coast. However, in the valleys of the Northwest, on the lee side of the mountains, summer precipitation is generally low and drought is one of the environmental problems of agriculture.

Permafrost

Permafrost is an additional environmental hazard not known in southern Canada. An understanding of the characteristics of permafrost and the process of its formation help to comprehend some of the special environmental problems of northern residents, particularly in building houses and in road or pipeline construction. The land which was unprotected by vegetation, and the underlying rock, became permanently frozen long ago to a depth of several hundred metres. During the summer, when daily temperatures are above 0°C, the surface thaws to a depth of a few inches or a few feet, while the ground and rock beneath remains frozen. If the surface consists of unconsolidated materials, it can become a soggy, spongy mass which makes overland travel by foot or vehicles very difficult. Because underground drainage into the frozen material is lacking or impeded, water collects on the surface during the summer, forming innumerable irregular lakes, swamps or muskegs. Travel is therefore much easier during the winter when the surface is frozen and snow-covered.

The designing of suitable foundations for buildings erected in areas with permafrost is a serious construction problem in the North. Buildings may settle differentially into the permafrost if there is unequal heating beneath them. To protect the permafrost from melting, most buildings are erected on piles which are sunk into the permafrost and frozen in place. If pipelines were buried in the North, they would probably break if the permafrost melted differentially; any future pipelines will likely be laid on, or above, the frozen surface. The construction problems are easier to handle in the Arctic with present techniques because the permafrost is stable, but adaptation is more difficult in the Subarctic due to seasonal fluctuations and irregular, non-continuous distribution of permafrost.

Vegetation

One of the most visible environmental distinctions between the northwest and northeast is vegetation cover. The Arctic northeast is treeless, whereas the Subarctic northwest is forested in the valleys. With warm summers, trees can grow slowly in the lowland and valley soils of the northwest, whereas in the northeast tree growth is inhibited in the more recently glaciated area, which has much bare rock with very little soil, with strong winds and a lack of summer heat. However, low tundra vegetation, consisting of grasses, sedges, mosses, etc., does survive on some Arctic lowlands, particularly near the treeline, and in sufficient amounts to support herds of migrating caribou. The animal population on the land of the northeast—if dependent on the vegetation for food—is much less, and different, from that of the northwest. Undoubtedly, the past adaptations of the Inuit in an Arctic climate and treeless tundra had to be different from those of the Indian and European of the Subarctic, forested northwest. Eskimo of past generations depended mainly on the animal resources in the sea for their food and clothing, in addition to animals on the land, and, therefore, lived along the coastline. In contrast, Indian groups in the northwest lived much like other Indians across forested southern Canada prior to the arrival of Europeans.

Sea Ice

Sea ice is a physical environmental characteristic not discussed in the regions of southern Canada. There are regional differences in the amount and duration of this ice cover. Hudson Bay, the coasts of Labrador and northern Alaska, and the channels of various widths between the Arctic Islands, are frozen over for different lengths of time for much of the year. For example, Hudson Bay and Strait may be navigable for about three months of the year (from mid-July), whereas the channels west of Lancaster Sound may be ice-free for only about one month (August). The channels between the far northwestern Arctic Islands never break up, except for narrow open water strips along the shores; these islands, joined together by virtually permanent sea ice cover, can be considered as one large "land" mass (see following map). Ships have not penetrated to the shores of these northwestern Arctic Islands such as Axel Heiberg, Meighen and Ellef Ringnes islands. Petroleum and natural gas exploration there is carried on entirely by air transportation. Because there are no railroads or roads (except for short local roads within some settlements) in the Arctic regions, the significance of sea ice is fundamental in understanding the difficulties and costs of water transportation.

The amount of sea ice cover in a particular summer in the Arctic is influenced by temperatures and prevailing winds. Average conditions in a mild summer are illustrated on the following map. These conditions indicate accessibility, or lack of it, for summer water transportation in particular areas. There should be only minor problems with sea ice during August in the white areas on the map.

SEA-ICE COVER, MILD SUMMER

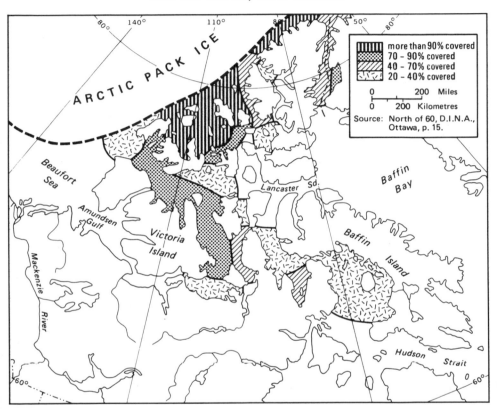

EVOLUTION OF SETTLEMENT PATTERNS

Introduction

For about two centuries, Anglo-Americans moved west across the continent; a number of phrases, such as "go west young man" or "westward the course of Empire," illustrated these themes in the 19th century settlement history of the United States. A later westward movement filled in the agricultural lands of western Canada in the early part of this century. After World War II, some Canadians tried to create a northern image of themselves with slogans such as "Canada's destiny is in the North" and "Canada is a northern nation." Just as people moved into different physical environments on the Interior Plains, compared to what they knew in eastern Canada, so do Canadians now have to face different physical environmental conditions in the North. Does the northern environment offer more, or less, than that of the Plains early in this century?

Despite a small increase in the number of people moving into the two northern territories and increased natural resource utilization, the northern population flow is but a trickle compared with the numbers concentrated into the cities across southern Canada or compared with the major resource developments in the "Near North" or "Middle Canada" in the northern parts of the provinces. Yukon Territory, for example, increased in population from 5,000 in 1941 to 23,000 in 1981. This impressive *percentage* increase does indicate that something is happening in the North—but the total numerical increase of about 18,000 people in 40 years is less than the *annual* increase in population in a few large Canadian cities. The North is still sparsely settled. Similarly, although the population of the Northwest Territories doubled between 1961 and 1981, the *total* population of 46,000 in 1981 was equal to that of only an average medium-size Canadian city.

POPULATION DISTRIBUTION AND SETTLEMENTS

The population of the Territories is of mixed ethnic origin—Inuit, Indian and non-natives who are mainly of European ancestry. The latter totalled about 45,000 people in 1981—slightly more than 25,000 people in the Northwest Territories and less than 20,000 in Yukon Territory. Most of the non-natives are Canadians who moved north after 1940 and in greater numbers after 1960. They are urban dwellers.

In the Yukon, about 60 percent of these former "southerners" are concentrated into the capital, Whitehorse, whereas, in the Northwest Territories, most are dispersed into several settlements along the Mackenzie Valley. The seven largest settlements in the Mackenzie Valley in which both Indians and non-natives live hold about two-thirds of the population of the Northwest Territories. Yellowknife, the capital, is the only large community (9,500 population in 1981), and the other settlements each have 1,000 to 3,000 population (Table 1, p. 323).

There are three types of settlements in the North (map on p. 328):

1.) The largest urban places are administrative centres—Whitehorse, Yellowknife, Inuvik, Frobisher Bay. Most of their residents are government employees who are paid by external capital and not by local resource development. The government services which they operate are found in most southern Canadian cities, but these become more apparent in these northern towns where there are few other positions or opportunities. Government services, and the infrastructure that goes with them, are supplied to local residents at a high per capita cost by southern Canadian taxpayers.

2.) A second type of settlement are the few single-industry, resource-based mining towns, such as Pine Point, Norman Wells, Elsa, Faro and Tungsten. Their residents are almost entirely non-natives and they have the social and economic characteristics found in similar towns in the Canadian Shield. An exception to this pattern is Nanisivik, on northern Baffin Island, which has a local Inuit population. Mineral products are shipped out of the region and usually face higher transportation costs than more southerly resource towns.

3.) A third type of settlement are the smaller centres occupied mainly by native people. Most of these have less than 1,000 residents and are therefore not "urban" in the census. The Inuit villages of the Arctic are coastal (except Baker Lake) and accessible to water transport in the short summer season. They include place names such as Pond Inlet, Pangnirtung and Cambridge Bay. Villages with mainly Indian populations along the Mackenzie River include Forts Resolution, Simpson and Good Hope.

Table 1

Population in the North, 1981

Northwest Territories	45,800		Central Arctic	3,100
			Cambridge Bay	800
Mackenzie Valley	30,000		Coppermine	800
Yellowknife	9,500			
Inuvik	3,200			
Hay River	3,000			
Fort Smith	2,300		Yukon Territory	23,200
Pine Point	2,000		Whitehorse	14,900
Rae-Edzo	1,400		Faro	1,600
Fort Simpson	1,000		Watson Lake	750
			Dawson	700
Baffin Island	8,300			
Frobisher Bay	2,400			
Pangnirtung	850			
Cape Dorset	800			
Igloolik	750			
Keewatin Dist.	4,400			
Rankin Inlet	1,000			
Eskimo Point	1,000			
Baker Lake	1,000			

The Inuit and Indian populations are separated by the northern tree-line; Inuit live north and east of the treeline and Indians live south of it. The northern people of Asiatic ancestral origin now prefer to call themselves Inuit, meaning "the people," rather than Eskimo. The latter was a derogatory term meaning "raw meat eater" given to them by the Indians, with whom they traditionally fought in the past. The Inuit are the *chief* inhabitants of the treeless Arctic region, whereas the Indians are a minority group in the forested Subarctic northwest region. The Mackenzie Valley Indians prefer to call themselves, Dene, a term which also means "the people."

More than 12,000 Inuit are coastal dwellers in the Arctic part of the Northwest Territories, and about 5,000 Inuit live in northern Quebec and Labrador. Most live in small villages dispersed along the northern mainland coast and around the coasts of the southern Arctic Islands. Many of these communities are unincorporated and community services and facilities are supplied, or subsidized, by the federal and territorial governments.

The Indian population is difficult to discuss locatively because the census records only those who are "registered," and does not include a few thousand Metis. Perhaps one-third of the Indian population of the Territories is nonregistered. More than 7,000 registered Indians are dispersed thinly throughout the Mackenzie Valley—a larger group than the 3,000 Indians registered in the Yukon. The number of Indians is not large (perhaps 15,000 Dene and Metis) compared with the larger Indian population in the provinces, but they are *relatively* more significant in the sparsely populated territories. There are few Indian reserves in the Territories, as in southern Canada, but a few hundred square kilometres have been set aside in small parcels throughout both Territories for use primarily by Indians. Discussions have been taking place for several years as to native "rights" and "ownership" of hunting and trapping areas on crown land in the Territories.

EXPLORATION AND EARLY SETTLEMENT

Northern Canada and Alaska were probably the first parts of the continent to be inhabited. Asiatic people migrated across Bering Strait to Alaska several thousand years ago. Archaeologists are still working to discover enough evidence to prove the exact times and routes they followed. The ancestors of people now called Indians probably came into Canada through the valleys of Yukon Territory and/or along the south coast of Alaska. Inuit were later migrants; they first moved along the northern Alaska coast in search of land game and sea mammals about 5,000 years ago. They spread thinly across Arctic Canada and reached western Greenland before 1,000 A.D.—about the same time that the Norse were "discovering" North America for Europeans.

Early exploration of the North was part of the futile search for a Northwest Passage—a route by which it was hoped to get trading ships around North

America to East Asia. Slowly, the map of the North was unrolled. Ships from northwestern Europe entered the eastern Arctic during the 16th and 17th centuries. These brief summer voyages charted the coasts of many of the southern Arctic Islands and the shores of Hudson Bay; sea captains reported on the unfavourable and lengthy ice conditions and the barren landscapes. The Arctic northeast remained unoccupied by Europeans until early in the 20th century. There was no easy way through it and nothing of apparent value in it.

Most of the exploration along interior rivers of the northwest took place early in the 19th century and was stimulated by a search for new fur-trapping areas. Such fur-bearing animals inhabited the northwestern forests, as in the Canadian Shield, but were scarce in the treeless northeast; the fur trade was essentially the only resource utilization of the northwest during the 19th century. The Mackenzie Valley was occupied in the early 1800s with a string of fur-trading posts along the river, which was the main route for transport. Fur traders did not penetrate into the less accessible Yukon valleys, however, until the middle of the 19th century.

Mineral wealth brought Canadians into the North in this century. The story of the gold rush of 1898 to the Klondike area of Yukon Territory has been told many times—and, over the decades, facts and legends have become intermixed! The boom city of Dawson arose at the turn of the century at the junction of the Yukon and Klondike rivers as a service and supply centre for about 25,000 people in the area. Within a few years, because much of the alluvial gold could not be recovered easily by primitive hand methods, the Yukon lapsed into about 40 years of economic stagnation; its population dropped to less than 5,000 people, about half of whom were native Indian.

Mining awakened the Mackenzie Valley in the 1930s—later than in the Yukon. Pitchblende—a source of valuable radium and later of uranium—was discovered then on the eastern shore of Great Bear Lake, and gold was found on the northeast side of Great Slave Lake. Petroleum reserves, which had been known previously, were then brought into production at Norman Wells to supply these few northern mines. These petroleum resources became of strategic importance during World War II when they were the only nearby source of petroleum products for military machines in Alaska.

World War II also brought non-natives into the Canadian Arctic in large numbers for the first time. Airfields were constructed in northeastern Canada and Greenland across the short polar route to Europe; weather stations which were dispersed through the eastern Arctic Islands for the first time advised flyers of the movement of air masses across northern Canada. In the 1950s, the "cold war" brought a line of radar stations into the North along the Arctic mainland coast and across Baffin Island at about latitude 65 degrees North. Much was learned about transportation difficulties in the Arctic environment during these military installations.

Prior to 1940, the few Europeans who settled in the Canadian Arctic were usually *sent* there by their southern organizations; they were fur traders, missionaries or policemen. After 1950, government personnel became more numerous in facilities such as hospitals, schools and welfare offices; government research employees, such as meteorologists and transport specialists, also were sent North. Most of these "southerners" or "outsiders" now stay for only a few years and then return to positions in southern Canada. In the Northwest, however, there are a small number of non-natives with small businesses, professions, or running transport facilities, who are attempting to make the North their permanent home.

THE INUIT

The impact of the externally stimulated activity upon the native Inuit was profound. For centuries, these few thousand people lived a primitive life of hunting, plus some trapping early in this century; they lived in close harmony with their environment, adapting to the seasons as they changed. Starvation was undoubtedly frequent when caribou failed to appear or when seals were scarce. There were few other resources on the land or in the sea upon which the Inuit could depend for a living. The close relationship of a people to their environment is described in many elementary school textbooks throughout the English-speaking world, often as an example of a "happy" primitive society. Although there were happy and peaceful moments for a people unknowing or unconcerned about the problems of the rest of the world, their lives were, in reality, hard. The fact that, in 1940, the one million square miles of Canadian Arctic environment supported only about 9,000 Inuit suggests that scarcity of food and other resources had limited past population increase. In context, one should recall that only about one-fifth of the Inuit live in Canada; they are more numerous in Alaska and Greenland.

Because of the past publicity given to them as a "different" people, the number of Inuit is sometimes overestimated in Canada, and elsewhere. It is, in fact, becoming a little difficult to define "Eskimo"—which is both a people and a language—as more and more of them become English-speaking. The 1971 census used the term "Eskimo" and recorded about 15,000 of them in Canada, of whom almost 10,000 lived in the Northwest Territories. There were none in Yukon Territory, but more than 3,000 lived along the coasts of Arctic Quebec, and less than 1,000 inhabited the rugged coast of northern Labrador. Perhaps a surprising figure, and possibly indicating a future trend, about 1,000 Inuit were dispersed through seven provinces in 1971, about half of them in Ontario. What is the distribution of Inuit reported in the 1981 census?

Within the Northwest Territories, about half of the Inuit (5,000) lived in settlements around the coast of Baffin Island, excluding the unoccupied west coast. The largest Inuit community in the Arctic is at Frobisher Bay. The few "Caribou Eskimo," who once inhabited the interior of Keewatin District, have all moved to coastal settlements, including Baker Lake. This interior part of north-central Canada is now virtually unoccupied. There are no Inuit in the far northern Arctic Islands, except for those brought to work at the air base and scientific station on Cornwallis Island, and those moved to the game resources at Grise Fiord on Ellesmere Island.

After 1940, the construction activity related to air bases, weather stations and social facilities provided greater employment opportunities for the Inuit. Although the external demand declined for the one fur-bearing animal in the Arctic environment, the white fox, this loss of income was balanced by increased markets for handicrafts such as paintings, print-making and soapstone and walrus ivory carvings. These activities, mostly initiated and managed by people from "outside," were encouraged only in certain places; as a result, the Inuit moved to these centres of economic and government activity. Their former migratory way of life, living in skin tents in summer and snow houses in winter, rapidly disappeared and was replaced by "urban" living in small wooden houses imported in prefabricated form from the south. A migration of "rural" people to "urban" places has taken place in the Canadian Arctic just as in other parts of Canada, but on a much smaller scale. For the Inuit, the past problems of adapting to a harsh natural environment (not unlike the adjustments which southern farming people made to their environments in the last century) are being replaced by new social problems similar to those of urban people in the rest of Canada.

In the 1960s, the Inuit began to organize themselves politically and socially. They have not come to agreement with the federal government concerning the ownership, or use, of land and sea in the Arctic, except on Banks Island. Their "rights" to land for hunting, trapping, fishing and sealing—as well as residential land—have to be negotiated with the federal government and agreed to by the Territorial government. The lack of such ownership agreements is of concern to some mining companies that wish to prospect in the Arctic. A new type of political unit with more self-government is being promoted by local Inuit leaders, but little is said about corresponding reductions of federal financial assistance. The Arctic region has a meagre tax base.

Older Inuit still do some hunting and trapping, but young people are not developing these skills. Although native people have exclusive rights to harvest the animal resources of the Arctic, they face increasing competition from tourists, with native guides, who seem willing to pay large sums to kill Arctic animals. Perhaps more wealth is brought into the region by a wealthy southern hunter who kills a polar bear compared with the bear's value as meat and fur to a local family? Alternative employment is not easily available in a land of few natural resources and with few processing or trade activities. As young Inuit attempt to work into a wage-based economy, they realize that such work is controlled by people and decisions from "outside" — a story familiar to many French-Canadians.

Because of improved health facilities, birth rates and infant survival are increasing rapidly. For example, almost half of the native population of the North is under 21 years of age. Many Inuit work for government social and administrative agencies, or receive welfare and transfer payments. The lifestyle of a whole society, although few in number, is in the process of rapid change. One will undoubtedly read about these changes, and conflicts, in the 1980s.

SETTLEMENTS IN THE NORTHWEST

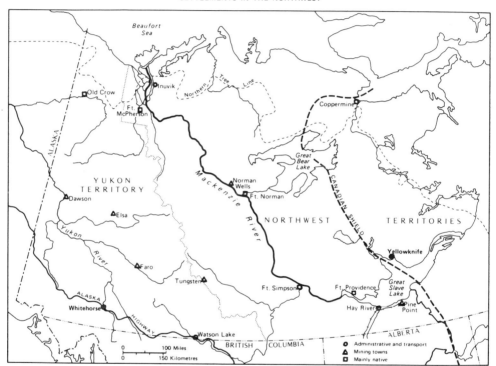

SUB-REGIONAL SETTLEMENT AND RESOURCE DEVELOPMENT

Yukon Territory

Transportation and Mining:
Mining has been the major primary occupation of people in the Yukon throughout this century; transportation was another principal source of employment. When the alluvial gold of the Klondike River and its tributaries brought the Yukon into the Canadian economy at the turn of the century, a water and rail transportation system was established which brought supplies

328

and equipment to the miners and to the service and commercial establishments at Dawson. A narrow-gauge railway from Skagway to Whitehorse connected with large, flat-bottomed, paddle-wheeled river steamers which carried freight and passengers downstream to Dawson, and later, also, to the lead-zinc-silver mines north of Mayo on the Stewart River. For about 40 years after 1900, the economy of the Yukon evolved around these three small towns—Dawson, Whitehorse and Mayo—and their water transportation links within the Yukon River basin.

The building of the Alaska Highway across unoccupied southern Yukon during World War II opened up a new transport route. Whitehorse, at the junction of the new east-west route and the old north-south route, became the gateway to the Yukon and the transport, commercial and service centre for the Territory. When the Territorial capital was moved in the mid-1950s from Dawson to Whitehorse, the latter city grew rapidly as an administrative centre. Because about 60 percent of the Yukon's population lives in Whitehorse, much of the rest of the Territory is sparsely populated. Large areas have no permanent residents.

The development of mineral resources has both caused, and been the result of, changes in transportation patterns and facilities. After 1950, the federal government built new roads in the Yukon, carrying traffic southward to Whitehorse and to the Alaska Highway, leading to Edmonton. The old, picturesque river steamers ceased operations on Yukon River when they could no longer compete with road and air traffic. Southern Yukon was closely tied by road and air to the hinterland of Edmonton, but traffic also moved by rail to Skagway and along the Inside Passage by ship to Vancouver.

Because there are no smelters in or near the Territory, all ore concentrates must be shipped out of the region. The ores from the lead-zinc-silver mines at Elsa and Faro and from a tungsten mine across the border in N.W.T. are all taken by truck to Whitehorse and then to external smelters. The mining of these metallic mineral resources resulted in the creation of new, single-industry, planned towns, such as Faro, which is similar in appearance and function to other mining towns on the resources frontier of the Canadian Shield.

The present economy of the Yukon, as in the past, is dependent on external markets for its development. Much of the economic "boom" of the 1970s in both the Yukon and Mackenzie Valley was based on exploration and survey for resources and *not* on increased production. This was a time of expected world shortages of resources when products with marginal, northern locations were worthy of consideration. Will conditions be different in the 1980s if world demands are less? For example, all mines in the Yukon were closed in early 1983.

The federal and territorial governments and mining companies have several questions to consider. Numerous sizeable mineral deposits have been delineated in the Yukon, particularly in the eastern mountains, but can these minerals compete with those less costly and more accessible to world markets? Should governments subsidize mineral development directly or indirectly in order to maintain and expand northern settlement? Are there any other natural resources in the Territory that can attract and keep new residents? Does the area have enough population, and a tax base from local resources, to permit it to achieve provincial status?

Other Resources:

The other natural resources of the Yukon are scanty and in little demand in Canada, or in the world. Although food was produced locally for the miners at the turn of the century, there is very little present agricultural production. The 1981 census listed only 24 farms in the Yukon with about 1,800 acres in total under cultivation. Soil surveys across southern Yukon reported about 60,000 hectares (150,000 acres) of class 3 and 4 soils dispersed along floodplains and terraces of several valleys. Some of these patches of arable land could produce more feed grains and pasture if there was a larger local market.

Statistics indicate the lack of forestry development in the Yukon. Only 40 percent of the Territory is mapped as having forest cover, but less than 15 percent of the area is classified as productive forest. Most of this forest grows on the lower slopes of valleys in the southern part; only five percent of the forest is classified as presently accessible. The largest area of commercial forest is in the Liard River valley of southeast Yukon, where local lumber production at Watson Lake is really part of the adjoining forestry use of the Interior Plains. The dispersed forests in the rest of the Yukon cannot compete with the larger and better located trees in B.C.

One of the promising resources of the Yukon is its "unspoiled" natural environment. As transportation facilities improve, thousands of visitors bring tourist income into the Territory and take back nothing more than the satisfaction of having enjoyed lakes, mountains, forests and historic sites (but also memories of having to contend with black flies, mosquitoes and the very dusty roads!). Unfortunately, most of these tourists arrive during a brief two months of the summer. Except for the activity in the few mining towns, and the commercial, transportation and government business in Whitehorse, the Yukon is almost dormant during the long winter.

Why does the enormous area of the Yukon support only 23,000 persons? Is there a lack of suitable physical environments to support a resource-based economy or is it a lack of "pioneering spirit" among southern Canadians who do not want to go to the Territory? Is the problem an environmental, cultural or economic one? Or, indeed, is it a problem at all? Perhaps one should be content that only a few people can inhabit and make a living in the vast area.

Mackenzie Valley, Northwest Territories

Although the dispersed, resource-based economy of the Mackenzie Valley is much like that of Yukon Territory, the physical character of the valley is much different. Whereas the Yukon River and its tributaries have cut down into the Yukon Plateau and flow in deep valleys with gentle upper slopes, the Mackenzie River is slightly entrenched into the glacial deposits of a broad, flat plain which is about 300 kilometres (200 miles) wide. Between these two main valleys of northwestern Canada lie about 500 kilometres (300 miles) of the rugged, inaccessible Mackenzie Mountains. Interaction between the two valley regions has been slight in the past; each sub-region still has more connections with adjoining regions southward than with each other.

For about 130 years after first exploration, the fur trade was the only resource-oriented activity in the Mackenzie Valley. Several trading posts were established along the river. Their linear spacing can be compared with the location and function of grain elevators and villages along a railway across the Interior Plains. In one sense, the fur-trading posts were service centres for the Indian population.

Mining:

Mineral resources brought the area into the Canadian economy, as they did for the Yukon, but not until the 1930s. The first pitchblende mine in Canada, on the east side of Great Bear Lake, a source of radium and later uranium, closed in 1961 when its reserves were depleted. The high quality of gold from Yellowknife, on Great Slave Lake, balanced the mine's high transport costs for supplies and equipment. An oil field and small refinery at Norman Wells supplied petroleum products to the two mines and other small fur-trading settlements in the Mackenzie Valley for more than 40 years. These three small mining settlements held most of the European population in N.W.T. prior to 1950.

Increased petroleum prices in the 1970s made it possible to consider building a pipeline south from the petroleum reserves near Norman Wells to connect with the pipeline network in Alberta. The reserves of petroleum, and particularly of natural gas in Beaufort Sea north of the Mackenzie River delta, may also be connected by pipeline to the south some day. Although the fuel resources are marginally located with respect to world demands, the Mackenzie Valley may yet have a smaller scale version of the Interior Plains non-metallic mineral economy.

The high quality lead-zinc deposits at Pine Point, on the south side of Great Slave Lake, added another single-industry mining town to the dispersed pattern of mining settlement across northern Canada. This mine brought the first railroad into the Northwest Territories in 1966 to transport the ore concentrates to distant refineries in Trail, B.C. The mine illustrated that northern ores must be of better quality than those in southern Canada to pay for higher transportation costs. The fact that individual mines are noted in this chapter, but not in the discussion of mining across southern Canada, is related to the *few* mines in the North compared with *many* in the south.

The mining economy of the Mackenzie Valley experienced few changes during the period 1935-1982 in comparison with the notable expansion of mining activity in the northern and central parts of the provinces. Although the media often discussed the "northern frontier"—primarily by persons writing in the comfort of southern Canadian cities—little of this "northern" resource development actually reached as far north as the Northwest Territories. The non-native population of the Mackenzie Valley increased from about 4,000 in 1941 to 25,000 in 1976. This modest increase was *not* a great "rush" to develop the resources of the North. Almost as many people came to the *one* town of Thompson, Manitoba, in fewer years in the 1960s.

Other Resources:

The other natural resources of the Mackenzie Valley are similar to those in the Yukon in their paucity, except for fish in Great Slave Lake. The cold and clear water of this large lake produces high quality trout and whitefish which are transported by refrigerated trucks or railway from Hay River to markets in the American Midwest.

Fur resources are harvested mainly by the Indians. The largest catches of muskrats are obtained from the innumerable lakes of the Mackenzie delta. Although fur resources are minor in the total Canadian economy, they are of local significance as a source of income for the native population—more so in the Mackenzie Valley than in the Yukon. Prices of furs, and therefore Indian incomes, fluctuate from year to year according to the natural cycles of abundance or scarcity of the fur-bearing animals, as well as due to market demands.

As in the Yukon, soils and climate permit the growing of hardy grain crops and vegetables, but local demand is minor; most food is imported. Only 15 farms were recorded in the 1981 census and, in total, they had 2,600 acres under cultivation. The level land across the southern Mackenzie Valley has a much larger area of class 3 and 4 soils than does land in the Yukon—estimated at one million hectares (2,500,000 acres). Few people want to use it. Although soil and drainage conditions are not good, some crops could be grown; climate conditions are similar to those in the Quebec Clay Belt. The problems of agriculture are more cultural and economic—an apparent lack of interest in farming as an occupation there and the lack of large local markets in one place. For example, the largest town, Yellowknife, is on the edge of the Canadian Shield and not near the areas with potential arable land.

Transportation and Settlements:

The transportation system of the Mackenzie Valley did not change as much after 1940 as that of the Yukon. A road network has not yet evolved. The first all-season road into the Northwest Territories was completed to Hay River in 1948, and reached Yellowknife in 1960, decreasing the cost of importing food and supplies. The single line of a road to beyond Fort Simpson, and one railway, penetrate northward into the Territory; they are similar to the scanty transportation pattern in the Canadian Shield and across the northern parts of the provinces. Otherwise, the small settlements along the Mackenzie River are still serviced during the summer by small diesel tugs pushing shallow-draft barges, or by aircraft. Why are the transportation systems different in the two northwestern sub-regions?

Yellowknife, the service-supply centre for nearby gold mines, and the Territorial capital after 1967, is slightly smaller than Whitehorse. Yellowknife, unlike Whitehorse, has a small percentage (20) of the population of the Northwest Territories. Population is more dispersed in N.W.T. than in the Yukon (refer back to p. 322 and Table 1, p. 323). Yellowknife does not have a crossroads position in the Mackenzie Valley, nor is it a supply centre for a wide mining hinterland. Will Hay River, on the south side of Great Slave Lake, grow as the main "gateway" settlement to the Mackenzie Valley? Would Hay River have been a better choice, geographically, as the capital of the Territory, even though its original site was subject to flooding in the spring break-up of ice? Hay River has a comparable geographical position to that of Whitehorse.

The Arctic Mainland and Arctic Islands

The northeastern part of the Northwest Territories does not have the resource potential nor even the small scale economic development of the Northwest. The treeless, Arctic land of the Inuit has few natural resources — either for the local population or for an external market. Normal agriculture is not possible — as much due to lack of soils as because of the cool summer climate. Most food desired by the non-natives in the administrative, military and scientific centres must be imported.

It is apparent that the scanty game resources on the land or sea cannot support a large native population. The introduction of guns resulted in the rapid depletion of caribou on the mainland, and these animals were never plentiful on the Arctic Islands. Caribou migrate north of the mainland treeline in summer and move south into the scrubby forest in winter where they are hunted by Indians. Because all Inuit living in the Arctic are now in coastal settlements, they are far from the inland caribou herds.

Walrus, almost exterminated in the eastern Arctic, are now legally protected, as are the few thousand remaining musk-ox in the central Arctic. Fish are few in the enormous water area of Hudson Bay, but a few thousand Arctic char are caught in some Arctic rivers and exported. The widespread killing of seals in international waters of the northwest Atlantic is an additional pressure upon this important food resource of the Inuit.

In summary, the renewable natural resources of the Arctic region seem barely sufficient for the present population. However, no Inuit now depends solely on local animal resources for food and clothing; in addition, young Inuit have less interest in a hunting economy. The imported food purchased in the local co-op store must be obtained by money earned by wage employment or government grants. The concept of an independent, self-reliant Eskimo "living off the land" is no longer correct.

As in the Northwest, mineral resources are the hope for the future economic development of the Arctic if the region is to become part of the southern Canadian economy. Ancient Precambrian rocks, well mineralized in the southern Canadian Shield, extend northward through Baffin Island. Scattered mineralization has been reported, notably a large iron deposit and a lead-zinc-silver mine on northern Baffin Island, and a rich lead-zinc mine on Little Cornwallis Island. The short ice-free season of only two to three months causes high transport costs for any future production in comparison with ore deposits elsewhere. The Arctic parts of the Canadian Shield west of Hudson Bay have been prospected and mineralized volcanic rocks, similar to those of the southern Shield, have been reported. The area has no interior land transportation and is therefore similar to the Labrador-Quebec area in 1950. Future development will be determined by world demand for metals outside of Canada.

The younger sedimentary rocks of the northwestern Arctic Islands contain natural gas in large quantities and some petroleum. Transportation to outside markets would seem to demand new techniques and ingenuity, such as carrying liquified gas in tankers. Constructing and operating pipelines under straits covered with sea ice seem unlikely in the near future. The open season for less expensive water transport is a very short one. Although modern technology could employ under-ice submarines, powerful ice-breakers, and even enclosed giant domes for workers, costs are high. The problems of ice and cold are just as real to modern northern pioneers, businessmen or adventurers as they were to the sea captains and explorers in their tiny ships of the 19th century.

Perhaps the increasing urban society in southern Canada will want to visit these empty areas in increasing numbers. Just as the lakes and forests of the physical environment of the Canadian Shield now attract people from the Great Lakes-St. Lawrence Lowlands, so the different environments of the North—no matter how harsh and unattractive for permanent settlement—may be a welcome change for southern Canadians and nearby Americans. Area in itself becomes a resource.

When one reads about the "unlimited" or "untapped" resources of the Canadian Arctic, consider the facts critically. Sometimes the problem is simply the misuse of the locative term, "Arctic," which may have been used loosely to include parts of Subarctic Canada. Also, people may use the word "resources" in an inclusive sense, when they are really referring only to *mineral* resources. As noted in the preceding sections, there are few agricultural, forestry, fish, wildlife or power resources in the Canadian Arctic. One can be pessimistic, and realistic, about the future "development" and settlement of the Canadian Arctic. Even if much of the area were to be officially "given" to the Inuit in settling land claims, one can wonder how many of them would remain in the Arctic once they learn more about the attractions of southern Canada. On the other hand, it should be a sobering thought to southern Canadians that many Inuit who have seen our southern "civilization" still prefer to live in the Arctic. These opinions are controversial.

Regional geography should study the natural environments of the region and compare them with other Canadian, and world, environments. What factual evidence do you have to form an opinion about the future of the Arctic and its people in the future of Canada? Would you have a different opinion of the purpose and future of the North if you were a northern resident? Most people across southern Canada probably think of the North as a possible source of future natural resources and raw materials to supply the people and industries of southern Canada—an example of the heartland-hinterland concept. Although few in number, some residents of the North think of the region as their *home*—an area *not* to be used or exploited to the advantage of "southerners." The implications of the term "northern homeland" are much different from the term "resources frontier." Are they different geographical concepts?

REFERENCES

Atlases:

"Ice Atlas: Canadian Arctic Waterways "edited by W.E. Markham, Dept. of Supplies and Services, Ottawa, 1981. 198 pages.
"Sea-Ice Atlas of Arctic Canada, 1975-1978" edited by Donald G. Lindsay, Dept. of Energy, Mines and Resources, Ottawa, 1982. 139 pages.

Periodicals:

The Musk-Ox, Institute for Northern Studies, Univ. of Saskatchewan, Saskatoon, Vol. 1, 1967 to Vol. 30, 1982. For example:
    No. 30, 1982. "The Rise and Decline of Agriculture in Mackenzie District and Yukon" by C.S. Mackinnon, pp. 48-63.
    No. 21, 1978. "Environmental Problems of Can. Arctic Oil and Gas Exploration" by Hugh French, pp. 11-17.
NorthNord, published by Dept. of Indian and Northern Affairs, Ottawa, Vol. 13, 1967 to Vol. 29, 1982.

Government:

Lands Directorate, Environment Canada, Ottawa.
    "Land Use Programs in Canada: Northwest Territories and Yukon Territory," 1979, 2 vols.
    Ecological Land Classification Series No. 6, "The Northern Yukon: An Ecological Land Survey," 1981. 197 pages.
Mackenzie River Basin Committee, Environment Canada, Ottawa.
    "Mackenzie River Basin Study Report," 1981. 231 pages.
Atmospheric Environment Service, Environment Canada, Toronto.
    "The Climate of the Mackenzie Valley-Beaufort Sea" by B.M. Burns, Vol. 1, 1973. 227 pages; Vol. 2, 1974. 224 pages.
Northern Science Research Group, Dept. of Indian Affairs and Northern Development, Ottawa. For example:
    "Fur Trade Posts in the Northwest Territories, 1870-1970" by Peter Usher, 1971. 180 pages.
    "A Cultural Geography of Northern Foxe Basin, NWT" by Keith Crowe, 1970. 130 pages.
    "Land Use and Public Policy in Northern Canada" by J.K. Naysmith, 1976.
Dept. of Indian and Northern Affairs and Govt. of NWT, Ottawa and Yellowknife.
    "Community Planning and Development in NWT" by H.J.F. Gerein, 1980.

Books:

"Northern Frontier, Northern Homeland: The Report of the Mackenzie Valley Pipeline Inquiry" by Thomas R. Berger, Dept. of Supply and Services, Ottawa, 1977. 214 pages.

"Permafrost in Canada—Its Influence on Northern Development" by Roger Brown, Univ. of Toronto Press, Toronto, 1970. 234 pages.

"A Choice of Futures: Politics in the Canadian North" by Gurston Dacks, Methuen, Toronto, 1981. 226 pages.

"Canadian Nordicity: It's Your North, Too" by Louis-Edmond Hamelin, Harvest House, Montreal, 1978. 373 pages.

"Contribution to the Northwest Territories Population Studies, 1961-85" by Louis-Edmond Hamelin, Science Advisory Board of NWT, Yellowknife, 1979. 54 pages.

"Northern Realities: The Future of Northern Development in Canada" by Jim Lotz, New Press, Toronto, 1970. 307 pages.

"Canada's North" by R.A.J. Phillips, Macmillan, Toronto, 1967. 306 pages.

"Northern Resource and Land Use Policy Study," Vol. 1, by E.B. Peterson and J.B. Wright, Can. Arctic Resources Committee, Ottawa, 1981.

"The Political Economy of Northern Development" by K.J. Rea, Science Council of Canada, Background Study No. 36, Ottawa, 1976.

"A Century of Canada's Arctic Islands, 1880-1980," Royal Society of Canada, Symposium at Yellowknife, NWT, 1980..

"Yukon Bibliography: Update to 1980" by I.G. Singh, Boreal Institute for Northern Studies, Occas. Publ. No. 8-7, Univ. of Alberta, Edmonton, 1982.

"The Mackenzie River: Yesterday's Fur Frontier, Tomorrow's Energy Battlegrounds" by James K. Smith, Gage Publishing, Agincourt, 1977. 259 pages.

"Eskimo of the Canadian Arctic" by Victor Valentine and Frank Vallee, Carleton Library Series No. 41, McClelland and Stewart, Toronto, 1968. 241 pages.

"Canada's Changing North" edited by Wm. Wonders, Carleton Library Series No. 55, McClelland and Stewart, Toronto, 1971. 364 pages.

"A Century of Canada's Arctic Islands" edited by M. Zaslow, Royal Society of Canada, Ottawa, 1981.

Some relevant articles in *The Canadian Geographer* between 1970-82, Can. Assoc. of Geog., Burnside Hall, McGill Univ., Montreal:

Vol. 26, No. 3, 1982.   "Unfinished Business on the Frontier" by Peter Usher, pp. 187-190.

Vol. 25, No. 2, 1981.   "Airports, Route Services and Remote Area Access: The Case of Northern Canada" by J.L. Courtenay, pp. 112-123.

Vol. 24, No. 4, 1980.   "Seasonal and Annual Variations in Ice Cover in

Baffin Bay and Northern Davis Strait" by B. Dey, pp. 368-384.

Vol. 19, No. 4, 1975.   "Trading and Trapping Frontiers in the Western Canadian Arctic" by Peter Usher, pp. 308-320.

Vol. 18, No. 3, 1974.   "Perception et Géographie: Le Cas du Nord" by Louis-Edmond Hamelin, pp. 185-200.

Vol. 15, No. 2, 1971.   "Large-Scale Annual Water Balance over Northern North America" by F. Kenneth Hare and John Hay, pp. 79-94.

CANADA: ONE COUNTRY, MANY REGIONS

Throughout this book, comments have been made about the need to divide Canada into regions in order to better understand the similarities and differences from place to place. The difficulties and problems of selecting criteria to define these regions and sub-regions were noted.

There are different ways to regionalize Canada, depending on one's purpose. Regions of Canada which may be suitable for study purposes may not be adequate for planning or administrative purposes. Regionalization of Canada for "understanding" purposes (a vague term!) depends on the amount of time and intensity available for consideration. This book has six main regions and several sub-regions. It would have had a different organization if 15 or 20 regions had been chosen. Factual detail has been kept to a minimum in order to bring out generalizations; but these generalizations, if valid, should be based on information available in the references or in official statistics and reports. Factual information about some small regions has been presented only as examples. It is certainly debatable as to how much, and what topics, Canadians should know about every part of Canada.

Criteria to define and characterize regions have to be considered carefully. Should these be physical, human, economic or political—or combinations of these? Should the *same* criteria be used consistently to define all regions across Canada? Is it possible to select certain criteria that bring out the similarities which characterize large regions? If so, since no large areas have complete uniformity, then a system of sub-regions is needed to show internal differences. Because every small part of Canada differs in some way from other parts of Canada, the country's complexity would be best illustrated by using many small regions or many sub-regions. But too much complexity may prevent one from seeing a comprehensive picture of the whole nation.

These decisions about regional characteristics and regional boundaries are subjective. Canadian geographers have not agreed upon them, nor is it expected that they will. Regions are not fixed, permanent entities; however, they exist in the minds of many people. Regional boundaries, or transition zones, cannot be determined, however, without an accurate knowledge of the main characteristics of each part of Canada. Regionalization is the *last* step in the study of Canada, not the first step. We know that the country has similarities and differences from place to place, but *how* similar and *how* different are they? Can one think better, and more deeply, about some of the economic, political and social problems of Canada if one understands a little, or a lot, about the geographical similarities and differences?

If your understanding and appreciation of Canada are better after reading this book, and studying other maps, articles and references, then it may be an appropriate time to discuss this, or another, regionalization of Canada. Read Chapter 1 again. Depending on your purpose and time available for study, what other regionalization would you prefer? For example, should Canada be thought of as *only* groups of political units? Regions are intellectual, academic devices; provinces and territories are real, legal entities. Canada is a uniform, political region only to people and other countries *outside* of Canada; Canadians know that there is little uniformity in most phenomena over large areas within Canada. Your opinion, at the end of a period of study about Canada, is worthy of discussion. Opinions will vary from place to place across Canada—like other geographical phenomena. People in each part of Canada probably perceive of the totality of Canada differently.

You may have the opportunity to travel to, visit the people in, and study other parts of Canada to confirm—or change—your opinions about the geography of Canada. It is my hope that your reading about the regional geography of Canada has helped to better understand this vast country—its similarities and differences from place to place, its problems and aspirations, its peoples and their environments. Canada is one country—and a union of regions.

J. Lewis Robinson
Vancouver, B.C.